TAXING THE STATE

Taxing the State: The Politics of Changing Taxes in the American States is a comparative analysis that explores the socioeconomic and political causes and effects of tax policy and budget spending at the state level.

The chapters analyze the level of taxation as political action undertaken by the state. Richard F. Winters makes a key contribution to the politics of taxation by examining the causes and electoral consequences of tax changes and compares the political strategies that governors employ in the face of tax changes.

This book will be of interest for students and scholars of American politics, state and local politics, comparative political economy, and public administration and policy.

Richard F. Winters taught for forty-three years and retired as the William Clinton Story Remsen Class of '43 Professor Emeritus of Government at Dartmouth College. He now lives in Oakton, VA, and Williamstown, Massachusetts, where he is also a research associate with the Department of Political Science at Williams College.

TAXING THE STATE

The Politics of Changing Taxes in the American States

Edited by Richard F. Winters

Routledge
Taylor & Francis Group
NEW YORK AND LONDON

Designed cover image: "Crossing the Divide" by Barry Blitt.
Originally published in *The New Yorker*, Nov 1, 2021. Image used with permission of the artist

First published 2026
by Routledge
605 Third Avenue, New York, NY 10158

and by Routledge
4 Park Square, Milton Park, Abingdon, Oxon, OX14 4RN

Routledge is an imprint of the Taylor & Francis Group, an informa business

ISBN: 9781032998473 (hbk)
ISBN: 9781032940441 (pbk)
ISBN: 9781003606291 (ebk)

DOI: 10.4324/9781003606291

Typeset in Sabon
by codeMantra

With love and thanks to:
Vicki and Cindy;
and to Megan, Chris, and Amanda; and A.J., Amy, and Ken;
and to my wonderful grandchildren;
Nate, Katie, Olivia, Grace, Sarah, Tyler, Roman, and Jaxon

CONTENTS

CONTRIBUTORS

Nicholas Dominguez is a graduate of the University of Texas School of Law and a Staff Attorney at the Texas Fourth Court of Appeals.

Tyler E. Frisbee is the Director of the Institute of Portland Metropolitan Studies in the School of Urban Studies and Planning at Portland State University.

Carlisle Rainey is an Associate Professor of Political Science at Florida State University.

Melissa Rich-Marroncelli is a graduate of the Quinnipiac Law School and a junior partner with the firm of Luks, Santaniello, Petrillo, Cohen & Peterfriend.

Daniel Rygorsky is part of the litigation practice group of the Los Angeles office of the Buchalter law firm. He is a graduate of the Columbia University Law School.

Kevin Stout received his Ph.D. from the University of Buffalo and is a data consultant at Blockwell Consulting, LLC.

Brian G. Stults was a chief product officer at YouGov and currently heads Stults Consulting. He holds an MBA from the Stanford Graduate School of Business.

Amanda Tomlinson is a honors graduate in Political Science at the University of Maryland.

Richard F. Winters taught for forty-three years and retired as the William Clinton Story Remsen Class of '43 Professor Emeritus of Government at Dartmouth College. He now lives in Oakton, VA, and Williamstown, Massachusetts, where he is also a research associate with the Department of Political Science at Williams College.

FOREWORD

While this book is dedicated to members of my family, it is also a tribute to the Dartmouth students who were my students, thesis advisees, and research assistants. Some of their work appears in Chapters 6, 7, 8, 9, and 10. These chapters reflect only a portion of work with honors students over my forty-three years at Dartmouth and only a handful of the very capable research assistants that I worked with are represented here.

After four decades in a department, one comes to appreciate the many colleagues who were formative for me – intellectually, collegially, and as friends and colleagues. From the outset, the late Denis G. Sullivan was the intellectual Godfather of our American politics program; he guided and shaped my and others' understandings of American politics. The introductory course is represented in print in *How America Is Ruled* (1980). The intro course, headed by Denis, was "team-taught" by a wonderful set of colleagues over the years. I learned much from teaching with Michael Smith, Ben Page, the late Jeff Pressman and Bob Nakamura, Lynn Mather, and Dianne Pinderhughes.

My years at Dartmouth were immeasurably helped by my Americanist colleague, Frank Smallwood. I learned much about small group politics and faculty collegiality from just observing the "Zinger," Professor Vincent Starzinger. Although we shared almost no common subfields nor approaches to political analysis, I was well-rewarded by my friendships with my now-departed colleagues, Dick Sterling, Roger Masters, Gene Lyons, and Larry Radway. I profited enormously from my friendship with co-teacher and co-author, Bob Nakamura. And I treasure to this day – and count each as a winning day – my continuing collegial friendships with

Don McNemar, Dave Baldwin, Nelson Kasfir, Lynn Mather, and Dianne Pinderhughes.

I thank my colleagues in the American state politics and policy subfield for their support, comments, and critiques over the past half century. I cannot imagine that there is another political science subfield with the personal vigor and contributions as ours. Thank you!

My first introduction to modern political analysis, with thanks, was with H. B. "Jack" Jacobini and William A. "Bill" Hardenbergh of Southern Illinois University at Carbondale. I owe thanks to Harry Friedman of the University of Hawaii, Manoa, who first spurred my interest in comparative political analysis as a body of formal knowledge; to Ray Wolfinger of UC Berkeley, then at Stanford, who pointed out, encouraged, and directed this comparative approach to the study of American state politics; and to Mike Haas also of the University of Hawaii, Manoa, who was instrumental in my continuing graduate instruction at Stanford.

I found teaching at Dartmouth to be a reciprocal process. Facing 15, 20, or 30 students two, three, or four times a week, to paraphrase Samuel Johnson, "clears the mind." But, in the aftermath of the "clearing" process, the "mind" is "re-ordered" and "reconfigured." While I hope that I have taught a lot, I have also learned much from my students. Oddly enough, the instructor-gets-educated process became more useful and vastly more enjoyable the longer that I taught. My last several years in courses on the introduction to American government, government and business, American state politics, and my seminar on the politics and law of the 2nd Amendment were a joy for being a common participant in venues of mutual learning and understanding.

I retired from Dartmouth and left a fabulous, first-rate *politics* department devoted entirely to undergraduate instruction and research collaboration with a graduate-school-quality faculty, albeit a department named to my continuing dismay as . . . "a department of government."

One final note as I finish this manuscript: I hope that this volume generates papers and articles confirming, elaborating, refuting, and possibly extending the chapters that follow.

--Richard F. Winters--

INTRODUCTION

Thinking about taxing and spending in the American States

Richard F. Winters

The politics of taxing? Aaron Wildavsky first published *The Politics of the Budgetary Process* in 1964; Richard Fenno published the even more noteworthy *The Power of the Purse: Appropriations Politics in Congress* in 1966. Both books were seminal for me and, importantly, shaped my thinking about budgeting. However, upon reflection, I was puzzled as to where the "tax-side" of the politics of budgeting was. Simply put, there is a myopic focus on *spending* that characterizes published works such as those by Wildavsky and Fenno and more generally in the field of the politics of the budgetary process and public policy in the American states. Why do analyses of appropriations politics dominate political and policy analyses of the politics of the national and 50 American states? And where is the politics of taxing? What follows is an attempt to argue for some balance in the field.

My purposes

- Personal interest in the links between taxing and spending originated in the mid-1970s in research on the two companion states of New Hampshire and Vermont, where I discovered that while overspending often led to increasing taxes, under-taxing also drove spending. My analysis of the two states diverging tax policies reinforced an *agency* explanation for taxing and spending; that is to say, *choosing to tax* and *choosing not to tax* are fundamental *political choices made by elected officials.*
- In pursuing, therefore, the question of "why, when, and how to tax," two colleagues and I exploited a dataset published by the National

DOI: 10.4324/9781003606291-1

Association of State Budget Officers that details over time gubernatorial recommendations for dollar-by-dollar changes in eight different types of revenues and, secondly, the figure finally agreed to for these eight revenue streams by the legislature.[1] Changes in the eight streams statistically cohere into three basic taxation dimensions: a *redistributional* one in the highly coordinated actions up or down on the personal and the corporate income taxes; changes in the *consumption-based* general sales taxes; and a separate factor of changes in several of the *quasi-priced public goods charges* of licenses, fees, tolls, and charges.

- Gubernatorial recommendations for change and legislative actions follow from expected causes, e.g. a looming deficit, falling personal income, but also from political causes such as unified partisan control or lack thereof in political institutions.
- We identify for a subset of governor-years the gubernatorial incumbent's ideological disposition and assess whether gubernatorial conservatism or liberalism profoundly shapes their recommendations. The answer is *yes* and *no*.
- Voters surely must assess tax increases as aversive and tax decreases as beneficial. If so, they likely punish or reward governors at the polls. If punishment/reward is observable, we test for whether the effects can be ascertained by assessing the impact at the *individual voter level*.
- Politicians, and in our case, governors, are not powerless in the face of the hypothesized negative electoral effects of tax increases; they employ strategies to attenuate voters' tax reactions. There appear to be no gubernatorial electoral gains in the face of tax cuts.
- Finally, can the above analyses bear at all on the quite different normative question of "are Americans in the American states undertaxed and/or poorly taxed?" I conclude the volume arguing that *both* characterize taxing in the states.

At the origin: My interest in the questions surrounding taxing and spending was spurred by my appointment to the faculty of Dartmouth College.[2] This small college sits alongside the Connecticut River athwart two of the most politically dissimilar of our fifty states in their taxing and spending policies. Indeed, while the Connecticut River separates the two states, but Robert Frost in 1923 wrote in *New Hampshire*:[3]

> She's one of the two best states in the Union.
> Vermont's the other. And the two have been
> Yoke-fellows in the sap-yoke from of old
> In many Marches.

While they were, indeed, historically, collared *yoke-fellows* in 1923, but the century that followed demonstrated the power of *agency* in politics as Vermont chose to veer away to become one of the most "liberal" spending and taxing states in the Union, while New Hampshire chose its own path by negation or avoidance as it drifted down to or near the bottom of the American states in many political economy policy indicators.[4] The most profound difference between the two states rested in their choices of quite different and developing tax policies. Vermont, under Democratic governor Phil Hoff in the 1960s, exploited a modest and already existing 1931 personal income tax in Vermont by ratcheting up its rates and scope.[5] The net effect was to generate revenue for a diverse set of programs sponsored by Hoff.[6] Hoff chose not to run for re-election in 1968 and was succeeded by Republican Deane Davis. Davis inherited a sizable budgetary deficit from Hoff and promptly called for and obtained a general sales tax to balance the budget. In the space of ten years, Vermont vastly broadened its personal income tax and adopted a general sales tax, now at 6%. In 1969, my first year at Dartmouth, New Hampshire had neither tax, and it still has neither.[7] I examine the political determinants of the growing divide of taxing choices between Vermont and New Hampshire in Chapter 2 of this volume.

Aggregates and composites vs. specifics: This was not my first encounter with the boundary conditions of the fifty states spending and taxing policies. In the late 1960s, my then-colleague, Brian R. Fry, and I wrote an American Political Science Association paper on "the politics of redistribution," which attempted to summarize the redistributive impact of the sum of each of the 50 states' taxing and spending policies (Fry and Winters, 1969, 1972). The paper, later published in the association's journal, was not entirely successful, but it did alert me to the possibilities of a comparative politico-economic policy analysis of the American states. That effort is furthered in this volume, but it takes a "micro-perspective" as opposed to the "macro-"approach of the highly aggregated "redistribution ratio." It is all well and good, as Fry and I did, to array the 50 states in some summary, composite, and highly aggregated measure of their "generosity" toward the not-wealthy, but the real question, as any New Englander would ask, is "how did a state get there from here?" In other words, we need a focus on the changes in the components of state taxing and expenditures, not on some global and highly summarized guesstimate of what was happening at some particular point in time. In addition to the well-deserved statistical criticisms of our paper and article,[8] our argument was short-sighted in its lack of attention as to *what*, precisely, caused states to change the redistributive qualities and of *which* of their taxing and spending policies were changed, and *when*, *how*, and *under what conditions*, and which could only be done by examining a causal assessment of actual and specific changes in spending and taxing that would lead to a change in the "redistribution ratio."

In a successful effort to get at precisely the actual and specific micro-level change in one redistributive *expenditure policy*, economist Robert Plotnick and I looked closely at a specific measure of welfare policy in "a politico-economic theory of income redistribution," centering on examining variations in the then-AFDC "legislative guarantee" adopted by the states' governors and legislatures (Plotnick and Winters, 1985, 1990). We contrasted a political understanding of generous welfare via competitive parties delivering on help for the needy because of the satisfaction of popular charitable preferences with an economic understanding that in a large, diverse society, welfare is provided by the state and nation so as "to ensure that the entire community contributes" in the face of free-rider problems (458). An innovation that we incorporated, and correctly so at Plotnick's insistence, was to focus on the *precise legislative act*; in that case, the *legislated changes* in the AFDC guarantee. As we noted, "[l]egislative decisions [on the guarantee], affirmed by the governor, directly establish redistributive policy" (bracketed added, 461). I follow that rule here in the chapters on taxing. I analyze and attempt to account for the specific dollar recommendations of the governor, as well as the final, dollar-by-dollar signed-into-law enactments of the legislature for changes in eight different taxes, fees, and charges.[9]

The "specifics" of tax policy changes: In analyzing the politics of the taxing policy process in this volume, I and my co-authors exploit several data sources that get at the "micro" level of taxation, but the most frequently employed and at the core of this volume (in Chapters 3–6) are the National Association of Budget Officials (referred to hereafter as NASBO) semi-annual publications, which list state-by-state and year-by-year from 1987 to the present for (1) the dollar amounts of tax increases or decreases recommended to the states' legislatures by their governors for eight different sets of taxes, fees, and charges, and (2) the fall edition details the amounts the legislature and governor finally settle on. In effect, the gubernatorial "ask" is a measure of the implied preference of the state's chief executive given coalitional constraints, while the final settlement, the "get," is the legislature's median preference for taxing, given the chief executive's own preferences.[10] My coauthors and I expect that the partisan and ideological preferences of the executive and the legislature shape the recommendations and actions of each.

Important for our analysis of the National Association of Budget Officers time-series dataset of the 50 states' tax actions as summarized into eight different revenue categories, it turns out that the eight taxes can be statistically and parsimoniously reduced to three general covariates: changes in the personal and corporate income taxes, the general sales tax, and the remaining general fees, charges, and levies all seem to hang together in both gubernatorial "asks" as well as legislative "gets." Put simply, governors and legislators tend to recommend or act on personal and corporate income taxes as coherent actions, while changes in the sales tax tend to occur independently of changes in the income taxes and fees and charges. The miscellaneous categories of fees, licenses, and charges tend to co-occur in recommendations and legislative actions.

Why a politics of "tax analysis?": One of the arguments in this volume is that the bulk of political science analyses of the budgetary process focuses on spending and neglects taxing.[11] Political scientists' views make sense. Politicians and the general public see taxes as assessed broadly across the population, e.g. a 0.25% increase in the sales tax or a cut of 2% in the income tax, but spending and appropriations are more often directed toward a particular activity (e.g. defense procurement[12] with specific providers and constituencies as beneficiaries) or a group (welfare recipients[13] as beneficiaries) or fixed infrastructure (rivers, dams, harbors, and bridges[14] and the construction company providers, motorists, truckers, and shippers as beneficiaries), and spending is often, if not typically, divisible and geographically focused so that members of Congress can, indeed, claim "credit" for the benefits.[15] Political scientists like Wildavsky and Fenno, as legislative scholars, focused on spending and appropriations because that's what politicians focus on. Politicians wanted credit for "good things," and spending is a good thing. No one gets credit for "takings." And taxing is taking. However, and puzzlingly so, if we are to believe the psychologists, voters will always be more sensitive to the immediate losses via their changing individual taxations as compared to the more remote, uncertain, shared, future-oriented benefits of spending.[16] If so, then politicians (and those who follow, observe, and write about them) will flood the populace with letters, articles, op-eds, news, and scholarly articles, and the airwaves touting (or examining) the benefits of government spending while busily fussing about obscuring or largely ignoring the extractions that enable spending.[17]

If in political science taxing is the less-well-examined variable in the politics of the budgetary process,[18] this is particularly puzzling because taxing is the near but not perfect nor precise complement to spending. To spend the state at some point, surely, must tax.[19] While political scientists have long been interested in the determinants and bureau- and agency-related consequences of spending (Wildavsky, 1964, 1974; Fenno, 1966; Fiorina, 1977), there appears to be much less comparable political science interest in the causes and consequences of taxing.[20] This is puzzling because when you fail to tax or exclude from a tax, you spend indirectly by not taxing via so-called "tax expenditures."[21] By exempting classes of entities or goods or services or some activities from a tax, the state basically indulges those beneficiaries as if by an indirect expenditure. Taxing activities thus can be both, in Lasswell and Kaplan's classic terminology ... *indulgences* and *deprivations* (1950). Further, and as examined in the following chapters, NASBO's quite broad time series of data extends for four decades and across the fifty American states covering changes by dollars in eight classes of taxes, fees, and charges. Such a dataset not only allows us to assess both the determinants of changes in these eight different types and classes of taxes but also some of the politico-electoral consequences of these tax changes.

Taxes, while generally broad in scope, also often have distributive components. Taxes on estate wealth target the wealthy; motor fuel taxes affect the trucking industry; state auto license fees are gradually changing to generate revenues from electric vehicles that are spared the gasoline tax, and so on. But my broader argument is that taxes are the less-seen, if not the underside, of the politics of the budgetary process. While taxes may be less seen, that does not mean that they should be less analyzed. The NASBO dataset, examined in Chapters 3 through 6, unpacks an array of changing taxes that is particularly appropriate for analysis.

Changing taxes: We ordinarily think of taxation as lagging spending. Taxes change when spending outruns revenues. To catch up with spending, the state must tax.[22] A variety of events might drive spending and the ensuing taxation. The state's lagging economic activities reflecting broader national economic trends may lead to a fall in a state's taxes and the necessity for seeking out new, more, or changed taxation. A more recent example: States are experiencing shortfalls in gasoline taxes as more electric vehicles are purchased. Some states, and I have in mind here New Hampshire, must continually appraise their revenue sources because the state has neither the general sales tax nor a general personal income tax, thereby foregoing large, generous tax programs by favoring an array of other taxes, fees, and charges. As I note later, states' governors and legislators vary widely in the number of times that they, in fact, change their taxes.[23]

Further, increased taxation may come about in a variety of flavors. The most widely examined tax changes are in the *rates* of taxation, e.g. increasing the general sales tax by 0.25% or increasing the income tax rate assessed against the wealthy. But the sales tax can also be increased by changing its *scope,* altering the coverage of a tax, e.g. levying or exempting the general sales tax on new goods or services. In the chapters that follow, we focus on rates and rate changes, but also on the direct dollars asked for or received in all changes of taxes, charges, and fees. A further note: We use "taxes" and "taxation" in the direct understanding, e.g. a "sales tax" or an "income tax," but also generically in referring to any increase or decrease in various revenue streams, e.g. sales and income taxes, but also changes in fees, licenses, or charges.

Party and preferences and taxation: We[24] want to infer causality about taxing and spending. And, frankly, I want to assert *agency* in the chapters that follow, examining some of the political determinants of taxation, focusing, for instance, on the differences that various forms of "party control" have on various taxing changes. The short story, and a fully expected one, is that taxation changes put into effect by Republicans differ from those made by Democrats. However, what has not been tested is the "symmetry of partisanship." Do Democratic governors ask to increase taxes that Republican governors desire to decrease, and are the parties' increases and decreases opposing and roughly proportional? Further, as a state moves from fully unified partisan control to divided or split chamber partisan control, in what ways are the tax effects elevated or attenuated? And, because we have data on the political control of each chamber in the states' legislatures, does control by a party in a state's House advantage that party, or does the Senate control appear to dominate? Or, maybe there is just no difference that can be attributed to institutional controls. If there is a difference, then by how much and symmetrically so? Additionally, an unanswered question is the story within each of the two parties: Does the personal political ideology of, in our case, the governor alter the array of taxes she recommends to the legislature? The most frequent conjecture suggests that a liberal Democratic governor typically recommends increases in the personal income tax, while the conservative Republican responds with a corresponding decrease. Wrong, it turns out.

An important component of the semi-annual material published by the National Association of Budget Officers, as examined in Chapters 3, 4, 5, and 6, is that the data captures all changes in the components of state revenue. Put directly, no selection bias here; the universe of changes in taxes is captured.[25] Big changes in broad-based taxes, new tax programs, small and incremental changes in fees ... whatever ... all fall into the dataset. If we, as political analysts, are interested in what shapes the imposition of trivial to severe deprivations, the quantitative analysis that unfolds here is relevant and important.

The political consequences of taxation: If taxing is generally thought of as acts of depriving citizens, the natural question is that there must be some electoral or political consequence of "depriving." Put simply, it must be the case that voters would punish "taxers." After all, as Kahneman and Tversky claim, we are more aware of expected *aversive deprivations* than we are of the prospect of future *beneficial indulgences.*[26] Susan Kone and I

(1993) examined aggregate gubernatorial election outcomes from 1957 to 1985 to assess the electoral consequences of new programs in or changes in rates of the general sales tax and income taxes in the states on the subsequent governors' races, and we discovered little if any electoral effects. There did appear to be a small electoral penalty for increasing the *rates* of the sales tax, but little else. Not even brand-new income or sales tax programs, albeit small in number over the time series, resulted in unambiguous electoral punishments.[27] In a new analysis of the issue, presented here in Chapter 9, Brian Stults and I pooled exit poll data of gubernatorial elections for eighteen years for forty-three states.[28] Pooling permits the addition of "fixed effects" for each state and for each election year, with the result that time-invariant, statewide, and electoral period effects are factored out. Further, our model contained a more comprehensive set of control variables and sets of "contextual conditions" that allow for answers to queries of when and under what conditions taxes directly impact voters. Pooling individual-level, cross-sectional data and adding key controls reduces the probability of omitted variable bias, thereby obtaining better estimates of the "true" effect of tax hikes on how voters react. Stults and I found that the direct net effect of increasing taxation on voter choices in gubernatorial races largely mirrored the aggregate effects noted by Kone and Winters. This is strong confirmation of – and perversely so – the lack of direct, unambiguous, and significant political effects of changing taxes on the personal vote.

Political responses to changing taxes: If there is little to no effect of changing taxes on the personal vote, does this mean that there are no electoral effects of taxation? I emphasize that this does *not* mean that tax changes don't affect elections. In Chapters 10 and 11, my coauthor and I examine the corollary and intervening variables here that governors in post-tax re-election or election campaigns are not defenseless in the face of attacks by the rival party. Governors employ strategies to overcome, or, at least, to attenuate the effects of their tax decisions on their re-election campaigns. I use "attenuate" advisedly: Governors are interested in winning big, but winning big is dominated by the corollary of greater interest in getting re-elected. Winning "small" is still winning … of a sort.

Examining taxing politics: I had an implicit model in mind of the politico-policy process embedded in the analysis. Represented causally, gubernatorial recommendations for changing taxes are shaped by a set of factors, some known and measured here, while others are unrecognized and omitted, such as the direct personal tax policy preferences of the chief executive, her beliefs about the tax preferences/aversions of her likely voter constituencies, and her understanding of the median tax policy preferences

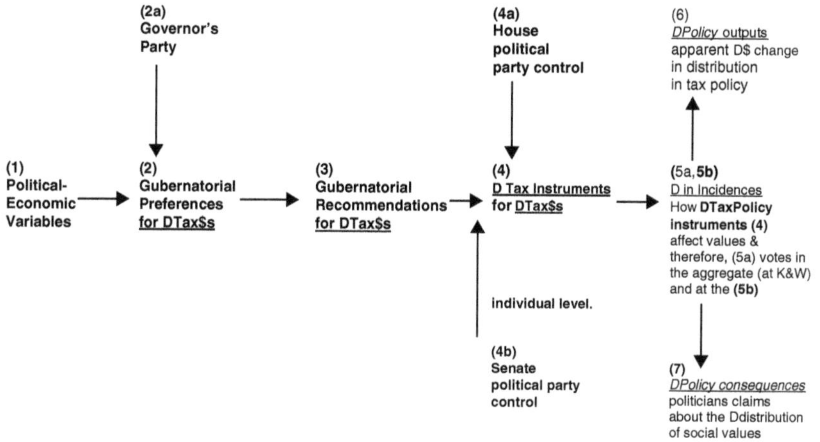

FIGURE 0.1 Sets out a Simple Model of Tax Changes as Further Elaborated in Chapters 3–6.

within the state's two legislative chambers.[29] What we[30] do have a handle on are the political and economic factors that prevail in her state, her partisan identity, and, for a subset of elections within our dataset, knowledgeable observers' best guesstimates as to personal ideology. The simplest hypothesis is, *ceteris paribus*, that Republican governors differ importantly from their Democratic counterparts, and as the two sets of governors become either more conservative or more liberal, then the tax effects become directionally elevated or cut.

Let me make the causal logic more specific in what is implicit in many of the chapters that follow. Given the data on changes of taxes asked for and/or granted as derived from the NASBO data, schematically, my argument appears as the following:

Entries that are *underlined* strike me as the relevant variables in a schema of the politico-policy taxing process. Variables that I believe are realistically and quantitatively measured in the analyses that follow are in **bold**. The D symbol indicates "change in…." The *italicized*-only variables, (6) and (7), are included here and in the chapter that follows (11 and 12) and rest on interview accounts and journalistic treatments of gubernatorial campaigns and are, therefore, more impressionistic and anecdotal and rest on my beliefs in their accuracy. Variables (6) and (7) are assessed in Chapter 11 by examining the various reactions exhibited and strategies employed by governors who tax (or their parties' successors) in attempts to mitigate the electoral consequences of their tax policies. Their inclusion recognizes the important role that these two classes of variables play in both political science and political activities. I develop this point of view in Chapter 3, but, in brief, legislated statutory changes in taxing and/or spending policy will have some sort of down-the-road apparent effects. Change the rate of the sales tax as applied to goods, and, sure enough, the state collects more the next year from its sales tax stream. A fraction of this increased tax collection was generated by the gubernatorial/legislative agreed-upon change in the sales tax but the *politically imposed change* is only some obscure part of the new money alongside the change in sales tax collection as affected by changing personal income in the state, changing inflation rates, changing consumer behavior independent of the tax changes, and so on. The direct and more proper focus of political analysis is *not* the change in policy outputs but step (4), which is the *instrumental change in the dollars of taxation.* However, the change in the *policy output* (6) is the easily obtainable figure and is therefore handy for analysis; however, it is wrong-headed in its conflation of several factors, including the *change in rate*. Variable (7) is equally affected and wrong-headed; it is what we observe on the campaign trail as politicians love to tout the consequences of their changing tax policies.[31] Alternatively, they engage in strategies to mislead, misrepresent, or redirect attention away from their punitive actions via heresthetic actions (see Chapter 11 in this volume and Riker, 1986; and Carsey, 2000).

Thus, my analyses of taxing argues:

1. In analyzing changes in the states' taxing and spending policies, we are mindful of the need for accounting for those politico-economic factors that *ought* to shape politicians' behavior. In the case of taxing, for example, the size of the existing *surplus* will obviously affect their calculations going forward, as would ordinary and usual factors such as *changes in population, personal income, and unemploy*ment. In the best of all worlds, I would have a standard repertory of such exogenous factors that I would employ from chapter to chapter, but, alas, that is not the case; the sets of politico-economic variables will vary across the following chapters.
2. The core chapters that follow most closely examine the NASBO data on taxing (Chapters 3–6), where for each state for each year, NASBO documents the gubernatorial recommendations to their legislatures for prospective *changes in eight different classes of taxes, fees, and charges*. Controlling for the effects of politico-economic variables, we expect that

Republican governors will differ significantly from their Democratic counterparts in their recommendations.

3 And, given the governors' "Republicanness" or "Democraticness," we further expect that how personally conservative or liberal the governor is will also affect her recommendations.

4 The legislature settles on *a final budgetary/tax document,* and it is signed into law by the governor. It must represent some point in the tax/spend continuum that represents the direct preference of the governor and the median preferences of the state's legislative bodies or body in the case of Nebraska.

(5a, 5b) Taxing is expected to have adverse effects on the vote for the incumbent or her party successor. We test for this using individual-level voter behaviors across the American states.

(6) and (7) In the face of taxing, governors employ strategies that focus on the spending benefits of the new revenue, the positive benefits of not running a deficit in the defense of existing programs, and touting the public's interest in satisfying important public goals and values, or, simply, leaving office (in Chapter 10).

A note on methods: The following chapters represent a long period of research and writing. The chapters also employ diverse approaches to analyzing the links between politics and taxing in laying out likely causes of changes in taxation and their possible political consequences. I was alerted to the values of diverse, multi-methodological approaches by some of my first readings in the social and policy sciences by social psychologist Donald T. Campbell and his colleagues, Donald Fiske and Julius Stanley. They set out their ideas in two path-breaking publications, the article "Convergent and discriminant validation by the multitrait-multimethod matrix" (1959) and the monograph *Experimental and Quasi-Experimental Designs for Research* (1966). The chapters that follow reflect *in spirit* the authors' arguments about the need for multiple measures of key concepts and multiple modes of explanation as ways of reinforcing causal arguments. To be specific:

A *A two-state, immersive analysis:* My first effort at "soaking and poking" political analysis[32] took me to Montpelier, VT, and Concord, NH, for extended stays during the 1973 and 1974 legislative sessions. There I shadowed and interviewed mostly appropriations committee members; the most important respondents were Ron Crisman, Vermont Representatives Emory Hebard, Madeleine Kunin, Dick Snelling, and Timothy O'Connor, and Senators John Boylan and Robert Gannett; and in

New Hampshire, Representatives Mary Chambers, Sharon Nordgren, Elizabeth Crory, Marion Copenhaver, Bob Guest, and Teddi Nardi, and Senator Rob Trowbridge. I set out my reflections on taxing and spending in these two states in Chapter 2.

B *Chapter 3 is my simple data analysis of changing taxes.* In Chapter 4, coauthored with Carlisle Rainey and Kevin Brown, we lay out the initial findings of the likely impact of party control and tax changes. These preliminary findings are elaborated in Chapters 5 and 6.

C *Conventional time series-cross-sectional analyses* comprise the bulk of the quantitative analyses in the book in Chapters 5–11.

D In Chapter 9, in a quantitative pooled analysis across time and across space, my co-author and I integrate states in the aggregate and states as individual voters. Co-author Brian Stults and I pool eighteen years of exit poll data on individual voters' electoral choices and their personal and political characteristics across forty-three states with their specific political traits so as to examine the impact of changing taxes on the political choices of individual voters.

E *Both quantitative data, journalistic treatments, and personal interviews* flesh out the difficult-to-quantify evidence regarding gubernatorial strategies attenuating the electoral consequences of imposing new or changing taxes in Chapter 11.

F *Measuring tax changes*: In Chapters 3–6, I and my coauthors set out the case for a focus on explaining executive and legislative changes in direct, dollar-denominated taxing. Our dollar-change argument is in contradistinction to the use of changes in the narrower rate of taxation. Nevertheless, in Chapter 9, Stults and I do employ a tax rate change variable in assessing the impact of raising taxes on the personal vote. A tax rate change is a gross and easily observable change in taxation; the NASBO data sweeps these and more subtle changes into dollar-denominated data.

In Conclusion, I make four main points in this volume. First, the political and policy sciences of the budgetary process need to turn directly to accounting for the direct, specific decisions that governors, legislators, and administrators make. It is all well and good to rank the states on some global summary statistic, but we should now focus on the specifics, the decisions, not the summations. Second, we need to spell out the direct causal influence on governors and legislators in explaining changes in, for example, taxation. In this volume, we focus on party and ideology. Third, taxing is a costly political decision in representative democracies and should have electoral consequences. But the absence of direct consequences – vote losses in the face of tax increases – only alters the dependent variables to the indirect strategies that politicians employ to dampen voter retribution. Finally, state politics and policy specialists need to wade into the issues of how we tax and how much we should tax. The NASBO data and our own analyses should further the debate on normative issues of taxation.

Notes

1 I extend my and my colleagues' thanks to the staff of the National Association of State Budget Officers for the data provided in their valuable publications. I hope that this volume will spur others to analyze the astonishing data resources that the semi-annual issues of the *Fiscal Survey of the States* provide our subfield. And, if so, my apologies to the NASBO staff for inflicting more bothersome academics on to your valuable work.

2 My New Hampshire and Vermont taxing and spending research, as discussed in Chapter 2, had its origin in a casual commitment made to Prof. Frank Smallwood at dinner when I was interviewing for the job at Dartmouth. He claimed, back in January of 1969 and rightly so, that the two states had embarked on wildly different public policy paths for reasons that he did not fully understand. He commented that this was a research opportunity that needed investigation. I quickly agreed.

3 Edward Connery Lathem, ed. *The Poetry of Robert Frost* (New York: Holt, Rinehart & Winston, 1969).

4 One could term New Hampshire's tax record as a series of "nondecisions," but what sets the New Hampshire record apart from the "nondecisionmaking" literature is that the state's politicians deliberately and publicly *chose not to act*; see Chapter 2 and, especially, its "addendum."

5 "Scope" is used to denote the change in coverage of a tax vs. a change in the rates applied to existing applications.

6 https://www.burlingtonfreepress.com/story/news/local/vermont/2018/04/27/governor-phil-hoff-democrat-transformed-vermont-died-93/557912002/.

7 "New Hampshire doesn't have an income tax. However, currently there's a 5% tax on dividends and interest in excess of $2,400 for individuals ($4,800 for joint filers). The tax on dividends and interest is being phased out. The rate will be 4% for 2023, 3% for 2024, 2% for 2025, and 1% for 2026. The tax will then be repealed on January 1, 2027" (Kiplinger).

8 See note 21 in Chapter 1 of this volume for references.

9 These figures are published in semi-annual publications of the National Association of State Budget Officers. See https://www.nasbo.org/mainsite/reports-data/fiscal-survey-of-states/fiscal-survey-archives.

10 A note on hypocrisy: In Chapter 1 of this volume, I directly criticize analysts who generate and analyze highly aggregated and composite measures of public policy in the American states, such as Fry and Winters. Readers who are familiar with the NASBO data will know that my dollar figures for gubernatorial recommendations as well as the dollared legislative agreements are themselves aggregates of any number of discrete changes in a state's taxes. A random example: In New York in 1990, the then-Governor, Mario Cuomo, recommended three different changes to the state's sales tax, yielding 77 million new dollars. The final legislative document produced four distinct changes in the sales tax, all changes different from the governor's to the sales, tax yielding 134 million dollars of new revenue. Our analyses in Chapters 3–6 examine these aggregated figures.

11 B. Guy Peters (1979) and Sven Steinmo (1998) made similar observations. Little has changed in this regard since.
12 Rundquist and Carsey (2002).
13 Plotnick and Winters (1985, 1990).
14 Ferejohn (1974); also see Rundquist (1980).
15 Mayhew (1974); also see Winters chapter in Rundquist (1980).
16 The careful reader will note throughout the volume, as well, the influence of Anthony Downs' arguments.
17 I must give credit where it is due to the finest single case study in America's taxing politics, Murray and Birnbaum's (1988) *Showdown at Gucci Gulch*.
18 This is not at all true in economics where revenue and tax analyses are routinely examined in issues of *Public Choice, National Tax Journal, Public Budgeting & Finance,* and *Public Finance Quarterly*.
19 This is especially true in the American states, the political domain examined here. It is less true of the U.S. federal government, which can deficit spend.
20 Excellent exceptions include Carsey (2000), Steinmo (1993, 1988), Levi (1988), Berry and Berry (1992, 1994), and Graetz and Shapiro (2010).
21 The classic and original analysis of "tax expenditures" is Surrey (1957).
22 I use the term "state" or "the states" throughout this volume in two ways: Most often and directly, it will refer to the American states, the objects of analysis here, but, as well, there are broader lessons at work here, so the reference might well be to the generic "state," that is to say, states within my nation as well as across nations.
23 In a dataset presented later, Alabama altered their dollar-arrayed revenue structure all of eight times over a thirty-year period, while Minnesota changed its taxes 114 times over the period. The "why" of the disparity remains an open question.
24 I use the plural "we" because a number of the chapters are co-authored, while I singly pen a number as well.
25 With an important caveat, we do not examine property taxes in the states.
26 Kahneman and Tversky (1979).
27 To be precise, the vote coefficients for new sales and income tax programs were negative, but the standard errors were so large that no reasonable conclusion could be drawn. The reasonable inference of the cause of the large standard errors is that some executives were able to overcome the electoral effects of imposing new taxes, thus the analysis in Chapter 9 on voters' electoral retribution.
28 Our three-way N was 228 elections and about 315,000 voters in forty-three states, as analyzed in Chapter 9. We excluded Hawaii and Alaska because Voter News Service did not canvas their exiting voters. We excluded the off-year elections in New Jersey, Virginia, Kentucky, Louisiana, and Mississippi, as well as the "independent" gubernatorial administrations of Weicker in CT and King in ME.
29 Nebraska's unitary legislature excepted.
30 "I" and "we" are used advisedly in this manuscript. Parts of the following manuscript are coauthored, while other parts are my own.
31 For example, "A triumphant President Donald Trump and jubilant fellow Republicans celebrated the passage of their $1.5 trillion tax overhaul Wednesday as a "historic victory for the American people," from https://apnews.com/article/north-america-donald-trump-us-news-business-laws-2d9e099660064f-2b8a8fc2237b4e7e4e.
32 The phrase originated with and admirably characterizes the analytic practices of the master Congressional analyst, Richard Fenno (1973).

PART I

Taxing politics

1

DECOMPOSING THE AGGREGATES AND DECONSTRUCTING THE COMPOSITES OF TAXING AND SPENDING IN THE AMERICAN STATES

Richard F. Winters

V. O. Key had it right: the value of studying the American states: While I was not present at the creation of the now-distinct subfield of "state politics and policy,"[1] which I date from V.O. Key's two seminal volumes (1949, 1956), I do have a five-decade retrospective on the field.[2] When I began my studies of American politics in the mid-1960s, the study of state politics was overwhelmingly the study of a single U.S. state (Epstein, 1958; Steiner and Gove, 1960; Anton, 1966; Litt, 1965), a handful of states (Key, 1949; Lockard, 1959; Fenton, 1966; Winters, 1976b), some institutional setting within a state (Steiner and Gove, 1960), or the study of one or two states' particular spending policy (Anton, 1966; Winters, 1976). These volumes, as well as more recent books (Smallwood, 1976; Loomis, 1994; Bryan, 2004; Milliken and Rozell 2024), were reflective of a focus on within-state politics and on traits and properties of one, a couple, or adjacent states that made it/them interesting or set them apart from others. For many of us in the field, this interest in and sensitivity to the political particularities or universals of a single or couple of states still resonate (see Chapter 2 in this volume). They also provide, as in Bryan's (2004), Smallwood's (1976), Loomis's (1994), and Milliken and Rozell's (2024) excellent studies, a demonstration for our subfield of the value of the authors' simple proximities to the scenes of political action – 246 Vermont towns for Bryan; one of 30 Vermont State Senate seats held by Smallwood; the nearby capital city of Topeka, Kansas, where Loomis assisted state-politics office-holders; and former office-holder and local Virginia political scientist Milliken and Rozell.

DOI: 10.4324/9781003606291-3

Numbers of states: Thinking more broadly of the subfield, one simple advantageous quality of the study of policy-making in the U.S. states is the sheer number as compared with, for example, smaller-unit federations such as Germany with its sixteen *Lander,* Canada with its ten provinces, and Australia with its six states.[3] Having the large "N" of fifty states generates much more powerful analytical tools for examining variations in politics and policies within and across states, and even more so with data for the states measured over time. Each of the fifty states has some unique – and sometimes enduring – qualities that make each ripe for particular analysis, while the simple fact that there are fifty of them also makes for powerful statistical analysis. And, given the fact that over my fifty years of study, the numbers and qualities of quantitative datasets about the states have greatly enlarged in number and formats, and now with datasets of overtime data, it makes for even more powerful forms of analysis (see the online data sources as described in Grossman, Jordan and McCrain, 2021; and at Klarner, n.d.). Further, as I write this, political leaders in the American states seem to be on a spree in establishing new and varied sets of public policies – from abortion to LGBTQ civil rights to gun control to local education (see references at https://myweb.uiowa.edu/fboehmke/methods.html), and for my purposes, taxing.

A corollary of the large N of states is the wide variability among them. Whether geographic footprint (Alaska vs. Rhode Island[4]), population (California vs. Wyoming), personal income (Massachusetts vs. Mississippi), personal wealth (Connecticut vs. Mississippi), education (Montana vs. California), and, for our purposes, state and local tax burden by state. Examples: Total state and local taxes in New York extract 12.75% of personal statewide income vs. Alaska at 5.1% and Tennessee with 5.74%. Each of these traits leads to speculative generalizations about spending and, therefore, taxing choices: "size" and highway spending; "population" and total taxing; "wealth" and types of taxation; "education" and differences between local and statewide funding for schools; and "state and local tax burden" and calls for tax reform and reductions.

In this volume, with its focus on taxation, I make no special claims as to the representativeness of taxing as a proxy for policy-making in other policy domains. Nevertheless, in this volume, I argue that taxes both lead and lag spending policy-making in the states. Put differently, new or changed taxes may follow from, i.e., "caused by," expenditure "run-ups" and the ensuing actuality or prospects of looming deficits, but enlarged and varied expenditures often follow from agencies, bureaus, and affected interest groups endeavoring to exploit the unexpected, windfall gains from existing taxes.[5] If so, the subfield's excessive focus on spending – which I note shortly – comes at the expense of a parallel and possibly antecedent examination of taxation ... that which enables spending.

Commonalities and differences: What distinguishes the study of the U.S. states and their public policies is the blessing of substantial commonalities among the states: We hold common citizenship, we elect one president, and we are protected by common federal political institutions. Our common qualities are reinforced by many common media sources. We identify as Americans, while we also consider ourselves to be Illinoisans, Hawaiians, or Vermonters. The federal political institutions that we have in common, the judicial and executive branches, are faced with the Congress that both promotes commonalities and differences across the states.[6] The state-based, thus, state orientation of representation in the Senate (see any recent press reference to Joe Manchin or the late Senator Robert Byrd of West Virginia) is further reinforced by cooperation and caucus behavior among state delegations in the House. The results are federal programs that reflect varying forces of the vertical politics of relationships between the state and nation. Some federal programs have strong unifying elements that promote common qualities, such as the interstate highway programs of the 1950s.[7] Other federal programs cater to the peculiarities of the states – varying wealth, varying bases of businesses and industries, etc. – and these differences generate varying federal programmatic effects on the states.[8 9]

Looking up and looking down: The continuing source of variation that within-state politics contributes to what is interesting in our analyses is complemented by vertical politics that has two faces: one looking upward to the federal government, the other downward to the states' local governments. Again, commonalities: While all states have some form of local governments, there is great variability; Hawaii has just 19 governments (state, counties, and cities), while Illinois is at the opposing limit with 6,900 governments. The amounts that state and local governments spend also vary dramatically. An interesting distinction is between New York, with its 3,420 governments, and Hawaii, again, with its 19 governments. All New York governments, state and local, spend nearly $13,000 per capita, with over one-half of this amount spent by its local cities, towns, counties, and district governments. The 19 governments in Hawaii spend about $7,600 per capita, with the State of Hawaii responsible for almost 80% of all spending. In other words, New York governments spend almost twice as much per citizen as Hawaiian governments; in fact, all local governments in New York spend almost as much as all Hawaiian governments combined. Which, of course, raises the interesting question of whether large numbers of local governments generate upwards pressure on total state and local spending. Or, alternatively, as you increase the number of local governments in a state, you multiply the opportunities for statewide politicians to "offload" part of their spending obligations onto local governments, thereby gaining self-credit for the programmatic benefits while not bearing the full tax costs of their actions. For example, in New York, for the now-historic Aid to Families with Dependent Children program, the federal government spent 50¢ of every welfare dollar supporting the poor in New York, while the state contributed 25¢, and by state mandate, the local – county – governments contributed the remaining 25¢.[10]

Looking sideways: Another source of both common and variable traits among the states comes from being embedded in a matrix of horizontal politics. Since the seminal work by economist Charles Tiebout (1956), economists and political scientists have been alerted to the impact that *both* competition and emulation among the fifty states shape variability among them. The early work by Jack Walker (1969), Virginia Gray (1973), and later work by Fred Boehmke and colleagues (2012) and Mooney (2020) alerted us to the diffusion of policy choices and policy innovations among the states, thereby promoting commonalities among the states. However, it is not only ideas, statutes, and policies that diffuse across state bounds and are emulated in the fifty state capitol buildings but also organizational and political practices across the American states that become commonly typified. Gray and Lowery (1996) outline emulation practices that generate similar political communities; in their example, lobbying communities in one state come to represent and appear like lobbying communities in similar states.

Charles Tiebout's essay,[11] which rapidly became a seminal one, although some had their doubts as to the author's purpose,[12] laid out a significant advantage of large-scale federal systems, such as that in the U.S. Tiebout, and echoed by a too-often-neglected classic essay by Gordon Tullock,[13] argues for the political value of an array of public policies represented across the fifty American state governments and their localities. Tullock termed the common, collective values embedded in the budgets and actions of the various states as the varied "menus" of public policies. He notes that states' governments provide collective goods for their citizens while funding these goods via taxations that cannot be avoided. But both the provision of goods and their financing vary across the states. If so, echoing Tiebout, then citizens can "vote" for their preferred bundle of services and preferred levels of taxation via the ballot box, shape public policies by their lobbying and "voices," or by migrating or "voting with their feet." This also reflects the argument by Albert Hirschman[14] of the varied political practices available to American citizens. They can express their opinions via "voice" – letters to politicians, to newspaper editors, to Facebook friends, to workplace colleagues, and their votes; or "loyalty," the complement to voice of expressing support and allegiance for the prevailing order; or "exit," leaving one locality for another, e.g. fleeing the high tax, welfare state liberalism of Vermont and moving across the Connecticut River to low tax, "Live Free or Die" New Hampshire.[15]

How best to represent our analytic efforts: Over the past half-century, the analyses of politics in the states have seen a dramatic increase in numbers and in the varieties of methodological approaches employed. At the outset in the 1950s and 1960s, our colleagues focused on the aggregate traits of the state, e.g. Key (1949, 1956). Analysts typically examined manifest characteristics of the state or states that could be plausibly argued to constitute the core of what was causally interesting, if not unique, about the state or a few states. These could be institutional traits, such as legislative reapportionment in Illinois, or the influence of progressive traditions within Wisconsin's political parties, or the nature of intra-partisan conflicts in the American Mid-South and South (see McDowell, 1967; Epstein, 1958; Key, 1949).

Complementing the aggregate focus from the 1950s into the 1980s was the development of a focus on individual-level behavior in state politics.[16] We now have many sources of information about how individuals politically vary across the states via biennial exit polls and surveys of states' populations that are typically supported by the states' various news media. Our analysts are also collecting comparable individual-level data on key state political decision-makers such as judges (Brace and Hall 1995).

The taxonomy of studies of the American states: For illustrative purposes, we can classify the empirical studies of American state politics since Key (1949, 1956) with a two-column distinction between studies that examine states as aggregate collectivities and those analyzing individual behavior within and/or across the states.[17] We can further array studies along five rows that distinguish among varying forms of the organization of information and the methodological analysis of the state-level data. I include some illustrative kinds of analyses. A cautionary note: In terms of scholarly output, the study of politics and policy in the states, has been overwhelmingly empirical. There is a re-emerging field of normative analysis of state politics and policy with the early examples of Riker (1964) and McConnell (1966). The more general field of political economy and public choice as applied to states in federal systems has re-awakened interest in normative analysis of those federal systems. Political economists such as Ferejohn and Weingast (1997), their students (e.g. Volden 2004), and others (Dougherty 2001) have produced impressive normative evaluations of the historic and current state of the American states. I also contribute via Chapter 12 of this volume (Table 1.1).

Where we appear to be currently: What I discuss below are representative writings on three of the most frequently encountered "paths of

TABLE 1.1 Studying the American States

	Studies of the States as Aggregates	*Studies of State Individual Behavior*
Within State Analysis	Epstein, 1958 Steiner and Gove, 1960 Anton, 1966 Winters, 1976 Bryan, 1974, 2004 Wright and Schaffner, 2002	Litt, 1965 Veblen, 1975 Carsey, 2000
Longitudinal, within-state analysis	Loomis, 1994 Milliken and Rozell, 2024	Lane, 1962
Longitudinal across-state and across-time analysis	Key, 1949, 1956 Tiebout, 1956 Walker, 1969 Lockard, 1959 Fenton, 1966 Truman, 1973	Weber et al., 1971–1972 Kovenock and Prothro, 1973
Quantitative across-state analysis	Dawson and Robinson, 1963. Plotnick and Winters, 1985 Gray and Lowery, 1996	Erikson, Wright & McIver, 1993
Quantitative pooled analysis, across states and across time	Chubb, 1985, 1988 Kone and Winters, 1993 Rainey, Brown, and Winters, 2019 Caughey and Warshaw, 2019	Delano and Winters, 2002 Stults and Winters, 2005 (Chapter 9) Frisbee and Winters, 2012

analysis" in the study of taxing and spending public policies in the states. I then set out the alternative presented most directly in this book in Chapters 3 through 6 and elaborated upon in following chapters. In brief, this chosen path is one of *tax analysis that is specific and not a composite measure; we examine gubernatorial tax proposals and legislative tax actions and not aggregated tax or spending levels or simple dollar-denominated budget overviews; and the essays analyze the appropriate level of political action, the combined state and local polities, and populations.*

There is a second broad purpose in this volume, and that is to *link changes in taxing to changes in electoral behavior of voters, candidates, and election outcomes* in Chapters 9, 10, and 11. My interest in this was originally prompted by an honors student at Dartmouth who wanted to write a thesis on the possible consequences of Lowell Weicker's income tax "flip-flop" in her home state of Connecticut. We settled on the broader and more interesting (in my opinion) question of whether there is a "vote cost" to governors responsible for adopting or changing the rates in the broad-based sales and income taxes. The revised results appeared in Kone and Winters (1993) and indicated little to no electoral outcome effects. In Chapters 10 and 11,[18] I analyze the ways and means that candidates and parties act to attenuate the consequences of new taxes or tax rate increases. Another purpose of the volume is to *demonstrate the benefits of integrating aggregate, contextual traits of the states with the individual-level results of across-state polls, in our case, exit polls of voters*. The quite small effects reflected in the Kone-Winters aggregate analysis raise the interesting question of whether these effects are, as well, reflected among the states' voters as individuals. The results in Chapter 9 astonishingly parallel the aggregate results:[19] Voters and electoral outcomes are barely moved by changes in taxes. Or voters are, per the later Chapters (10 and 11), convinced by candidates of the necessity and inevitability for the changes, and thus their tax concerns are allayed or attenuated.

One argument, decomposing the aggregate: One current general path focuses on highly *aggregated and summary measures* of public policies in the states. I was present at the creation of an original aggregate, composite "path" with the 1970 publication of "the politics of redistribution" with coauthor Brian R. Fry.[20] Fry and I devised a measure of the net redistributive impact of state spending relative to state tax burdens in reaction to the then-prevailing trait of across-state political analysis where the focus was on the highly summarized levels of measures of dollar spending of generalized programs such as in states' spending on welfare (Dawson and Robinson, 1963; Dye, 1966; Hofferbert 1966; Cnudde and McCrone, 1969). These early studies found that redistributive programs such as welfare outlays reacted quite strongly to measures of well-developed and wealthy economies among the fifty states. We – and they – were puzzled as to the weakness of "political variables." So as to reorient these analytic efforts, Fry and I generated a new composite measure of aggregate spending and taxing programs for the fifty states. We weighted the 1961 levels of thirteen expenditure programs, e.g. "Elem. & Sec. Education," "Higher and Other Education," etc., by an established assessment of the benefits of each dollar of such expenditure classes accruing to the benefit of the three lowest income classes.[21] We performed a similar calculation on the burdens of the states' twelve classes of revenue programs, e.g. "Alcoholic Beverages," "Individual Income," "General Sales," etc., on these three income classes. Then we simply took the expenditure benefits for the lowest income classes relative to their stipulated revenue burdens and calculated the "redistribution ratio." We performed a general politico-economic analysis to explain the across-state variations in the "redistribution ratio."[22]

Our expectation was that this "global" weighted measure of what states spend more for and extract less from the poorest among us would more strongly relate to a set of both economic and political variables.[23] Statewide wealth and levels of industrialization and education would lead to heightened ability to pay as well as more and better organized efforts to assist the poor. Similarly, closer levels of competition between the two parties should lead to greater redistributive efforts as the two parties compete to draw in less well-informed and less-active voters from among poorer voters, as would Democratic control in the states, then conventionally the party of the "working classes." Further, long-term measures of the nature and quality of political institutions – measures of civil service coverage, legislative professionalism, and heightened propensity to innovate – also should lead to greater redistributive efforts. In all, we found that "political variables" manifested themselves in the statistical analysis and likely at the expense of economic measures of wealth, industrialization, and unionization. What Fry and I did not quite come to grips with is if there is such a thing as the "redistributive state," then it should change slowly over time, and if redistribution manifested itself as an array of policy outcomes across the American states in 1961, then that was, in fact, the result of years, if not decades, of changing public policies, and not instantaneous or near-instantaneous reactions to the "politics of 1961." Measuring redistributive spending and taxing policies at time, one fails to appreciate adequately the prior years of policy-making. What was needed was a disaggregated measure or measures that presented themselves to the analyst over time. Furthermore, failing to analyze the redistribution ratio over time, we were unable to – or didn't think to – decompose our measure into its various redistributive components that might change over time – some slowly, others more rapidly – and therefore contribute to the changing rates of redistribution.

More recently, the scholarly path of aggregate composite measures grew more splendid with the publication of Erikson, Wright, and McIver's *Statehouse Democracy* in 1993.[24] This book (EWM) remains a model of theory, method, and analysis for the field. But their composite measure of "state policy liberalism" employed in the book incorporated eight disparate measures that included "public educational spending per pupil," the "'scope' of ... eligibility" for the then-Aid to Families with Dependent Children (AFDC), a scale of "state support for 'liberal' approaches to criminal justice," an "index of state legalization of 10 different kinds of legalized gambling," a measure of tax progressivity (pp. 75–76), and so on. The measures were well correlated with one another and resolved themselves into a single "factor" that indicated a "standardized index of composite policy liberalism" (77).[25] EWM's purpose in the book was to relate the liberal opinions of the states' electorates to the liberalism of their public policies, and in this regard, the book is a smashing success. But, again, it falls prey to the problems of the cross-sectional analysis of the – in their analysis – forty-eight states. What accounts for growth in "liberalism" in the states? Does public opinion lead elites, or is it that elites lay out a schedule of policy changes that voters buy into? The missing data are in the time series, and the plausible links that precede or follow specific changing measures of liberalism should be better explicitly spelled out.

Even more aggregated, composite measures appear in Devin Caughey and Christopher Warshaw's "Policy Preferences and Policy Change: Dynamic Responsiveness in the American States, 1936–2014."[26 27] This ambitious and persuasive article endeavors to present a single, unique "outcome of interest, the overall orientation of state policy." (899) Their 1936–2014 yearly measure of "policy liberalism [uses] a dynamic Bayesian latent-variable model designed for a mix of continuous, ordinal, and dichotomous policy indicators (p. 900)." And, in fact, they do employ a diverse set "of 148 distinct policies, and at least 43 policies are available in every year" for their seventy-eight-year longitudinal data set (902). Their measures range from many dichotomous variables, such as those over abortion policies in the states, to continuous variables, such as educational and social welfare spending, to the progressivity of tax rates (902–903). The graphic displays of their single measure of policy liberalism appear persuasive as they engage in convergent and construct validation tests (906–910).[28]

Caughey and Warshaw's data was utilized by Baumann and colleagues (2021) in assessing whether interparty competition might have divergent effects on "economic" vs. "social" "liberalism." They divide the Caughey and Warshaw data into its social and economic components and hypothesize that because lower income voters likely have liberal opinions on economic issues and conservative opinions on social issues, for which there is good evidence,[29] heightened interparty competition might lead the parties to adopt more conservative social policies and more liberal economic policies. Employing varying time frames and diverse tests, they do strongly reaffirm the economic liberalism and weaker but perhaps strengthening relationship between competition and social liberalism even in the face of a set of plausible controls. Still, their dependent variables, given the source and the general "stickiness" of public policies in the states, are a collection of disparate indicators of underlying policy change. What we don't know is how we got from here, step by step and policy by policy (conservatism), to there (liberalism), or vice versa. My hope for this volume is to set out some of the causal links in the chain of changes in taxing policies that give some indication of how we got from "here" to "there."

A second argument: deconstructing the composite: A second path is well illustrated by papers that Charles Barrilleaux and colleagues have published, a series of papers that also examine the determinants of redistributive spending.[30] In each of these well-thought-out and most interesting papers, they measure redistribution in a variety of intuitively plausible ways. In Barrilleaux and Berkman (2002), for four biennia in the 1990s, they classify redistributive programs as "...those that provide statewide benefits" and developmental programs as those where "... benefits are concentrated in specific geographic section of the states..." such as roads, parks, and so on. Their dependent variable is the ratio of "redistributive" program spending, e.g. "pensions, unemployment welfare, ... and education..." (413), to developmental" spending, such as transportation, police, corrections, and natural resources (413). In Barrilleaux, Holbrook, and Langer (2003, 421), their dependent variable is "welfare effort as per capita indigenous state expenditures for Aid to Families with Dependent Children (AFDC), general assistance, and income maintenance...." (421) And in Barrilleaux and Bernick, they measure redistributive programs by General Assistance spending as the percent of total statewide personal income (p. 8) and the Social Security Income Supplement, also as a percentage of state personal income. I find myself drawn to these three useful papers but anxious about, again, time as an omitted variable and, as well, about the sources and nature of changes in these programs and concerns about the measurements of the dependent variables. For example, in the Barrilleaux and Bernick paper, both GA and SSI-S are averaged over four biennia (1990–1996) and represent the effects of changing policy by state governors and lawmakers over a period of time with likely mixed legislative and executive political control as well as changing economic conditions that both attenuate spending in these two programs in economic good times but engorge them in poor times, added to the putative policy choices by decision-makers. The same causal anxiety can be assessed against the other two papers. What might constitute a cleaner measure of the efforts in these two programs rests in the specific *legislative* or *administrative decisions* that alter the amount and distribution of GA or SSI-S monies.

The use of a specific legislative decision appears in Plotnick and Winters, "A politico-economic theory of redistribution." As we noted, "...it becomes clear that the redistributive intent of a program is probably best reflected in its rules, not in the final distribution of benefits, the mean benefit, the number of recipients, or total outlays" (461).[31] We unpack this in the associated footnote:

> Almost every study of the determinants of redistribution or welfare focuses on other measures of spending, for example total welfare

> spending, total per capita, per $1,000 of personal income, or per recipient. These measures do not represent the direct political choice regarding the proper levels of statewide distribution. Rather they indicate outcomes [often] shaped by the factors separate from and often occurring after the political decision on the guarantee. For example, mobility into the state might be a response to the level of the guarantee and would then shape total spending, number of recipients, and aggregate per recipient.
>
> *(p. 461)*

The message here is that for the study of how, why, and under what conditions states' politics shape and change state public policy, we need to focus specifically on the politics of *proposed actions* and the specifics of *legislatively approved and enacted actions,* that is to say, *statutory actions.* And, in the best of all worlds, we might have authenticated recommendations of politicians from rivalrous political institutions – in the studies that follow, the governor' recommendations and the legislative branch's lawful actions.

A third argument: units of analysis: Another paper by William Jacoby and Saundra Schneider, "A New Measure of Policy Spending Priorities in the American States," generates a new measure of expenditure priorities by arraying "yearly state expenditures in nine policy areas: corrections, education, government administration, health, highways..." and so on, and constructs a measure of the "...states' relative priorities across the different policy areas (4)." In this new measure summarized over the 1982 to 2005 period (12), New Hampshire ranks as the seventh "most redistributive" state, while Vermont ranks thirty-first.[32] This ranking conflicts with Fry and Winters measure, where Vermont ranks twenty-first (for 1961 data) and New Hampshire thirty-ninth, and in the Erikson, Wright, and McIver measure, Vermont is thirteenth and New Hampshire twenty-sixth, and for the composite averaged measures in the Caughey and Warshaw measure, the two measures are wildly divergent. While I am unsure of the exact reasons why the Jacoby-Schneider index misplaces these two states, I suspect that it is probably because they relied on state-only measures of state expenditures. If you take a midpoint year in their measure, 1994, New Hampshire's state-only measure of spending comprised 52% of total state and local spending, while the comparable figure for Vermont state-only spending was 82% of total state and local spending. It's likely that the bulk of the New Hampshire local-only spending was on the K-12 local school systems across the state. It was for this period when it was almost entirely locally financed via the property tax system. New Hampshire's sharply greater decentralized financing is, of course, legislated in Concord, not in its multiple local governments. Decentralized financing is a choice that the center, in this case, those in the state capital of Concord, makes. It can change its decentralized rule; it can pile restrictions on local governments; and it can enforce rules about more, less, where, and when such local expenditures are made. Put simply, local government spending is properly the province, the actions, of its state government, per Dillon's Rule. As the Supreme Court opined in 1903, echoing Dillon:

> [Local governments] are the creatures—mere political subdivisions—of the state, for the purpose of exercising a part of its powers. They may exert only such powers as are expressly granted to them, or such as may be necessarily implied from those granted. What they lawfully do of a public character is done under the sanction of the state. They may be created, or, having been created, their powers may be restricted or enlarged, or altogether withdrawn at the will of the legislature; the authority of the legislature, when restricting or withdrawing such powers, being subject only to the fundamental condition that the collective and individual rights of the people of the municipality shall not thereby be destroyed.
>
> *(Richardson et al. 2003)*[33]

The remedy is to focus on those political recommendations and statutory actions that encompass the whole of the states' actions, precisely the actions analyzed in this volume.

Fitting taxes into this: The literature on the politics of taxation in political science is also prone to some of the tendencies outlined above – most analysts focus on quite broad measures and understandings of tax policy and tax policy change. Analysts typically focus on dollar measures of tax policy in the states; they examine taxes in summary dollar measures. Dennis, Moore, and Somerville (2007) examine the impact of party control on the dollar distribution of the aggregate tax burden by income class. Dilger (1998) examines total dollar aggregates as overall state taxes. Frederiksson, Wang, and Warren (2013) examine changes in tax levels, which are a mix of changes in the economy, personal incomes, changes in consumption of items/services taxed, and possibly changes in statutory enactments in the taxes that a state adopts. The latter, of course, is the proper object of political analysis attention, precisely that which we focus on here. Leigh (2008) examines income tax receipts, which, again, are a compound of many different causal influences. Finally, two widely cited articles in economics and political science also use aggregate measures. Alt and Lowry (2000, 1050) examine "revenue change, …the annual change in constant-dollar (1982–1984), per capita state general revenues from 1952 through 1995," and Poterba (1994b) focuses, as well, on dollar levels of taxation, expenditures, and deficits. A better focus is on what politicians authoritatively change by force of law, not on the aggregates that are shaped by a myriad of factors. The existing levels, amounts, or changes in taxes collected are a compound of many factors, where political choices are only one of many.

When analysts do focus on changes in specific taxes, they typically examine only the changes in rates of the taxes. But taxes can be changed via several routes other than rate changes. For example, conditions or coverages of the tax category might change. In 2013, Governor Rick Scott of Florida proposed eliminating the sales tax on industrial equipment, reducing revenue by about $50 million; Governor Peter Shumlin of Vermont proposed exempting cloud computing from sales tax, reducing revenue by about $1.5 million; and Governor John Kasich of Ohio proposed greatly expanding the sales tax base, increasing revenue by about $1.9 billion. None of these cases involved a change in the tax rate. Non-rate changes appear, in fact, to be the modal type of change in the data that we employ; we include the dollar amount of all changes in taxes irrespective of the modalities of the changes.

Mikesell (1978), replicated by Nelson (2000), looks at published sources that document changes in existing rates, usually of broad-based taxes such as the income and general sales taxes, and are typically derived from the Book of the States. However, the simple changes in the tax rates do not always capture changes in the amount of dollars collected. As an example, in the data source that I turn to in the next chapter, "The Fiscal Survey of the States," issued by the National Association of Budget Officers, the change-by-change details are, for example, unpacked in Table A-3 of the 2011 publication (p. 76). In fact, there were nineteen discrete statutory changes in sales taxes that year across the states. Only four of these changes might plausibly be caught up as a change of rates via the Book of the States. Our data sweeps up and aggregate all changes in taxes by the class of tax, not just changes in the tax rate. Changes in rates are certainly important, but the change in tax coverages remains the more politically relevant variable. In point of fact, it may be the case that elected political actors – executives and legislators – prefer non-rate changes in tax laws because these more subtle changes are less likely to gain public recognition and eventual voter opprobrium and thus more easily agreed upon. Mikesell's (1978) linkage of gubernatorial tax-rate-change aversion and the timing of the election year may be better thought of as an aversion to changes in tax rates in the year before the election, where rate changes will more likely catch the public eye and provide campaign fodder for an opponent. Nevertheless, an equal amount of new revenue can be enacted via non-rate changes in taxes and thus is more likely to be less visible to the typical voter.

Thus, I argue, what we need in the study of state politics and policy are unambiguous authoritative measures of changes in the public policies of taxing – or spending – made by elected state officials. I suggest that it is time to redirect and gain balance in our attention via:

1 away from a narrow focus on indulgent or benefit expenditures such as redistribution and welfare;
2 away from highly aggregated measures of "policy liberalism" (Fry and Winters; Erikson, Wright and McIver; Caughey and Warshaw; Baumann, Nelson, and Neumann);
3 use with care highly summarized measures of "state spending" that may not adequately represent actual state policies (Gamm and Kousser);
4 clarify when we use state-only measures or state-and-local measures (Jacoby and Schneider);
5 move from cross-sectional-only analysis (Fry and Winters; Erikson, Wright, and McIver) to longitudinal time series of policy changes;
6 focus specifically on specific decisions made in political institutions – governor and legislative chambers in bargaining models, as in Kousser and Phillips (2012);
7 render explicit the causal models that underlie our analyses (as in Erikson, Wright, and McIver);
8 balance our focus on policy outputs, such as expenditures, with an equal focus on what may be an equally relevant source ... and result ... of spending, that is to say, *taxation*; and
9 our focus, as well, should be on *changes in such policies*.

In somewhat more detail:

1 A focus on expenditures: In general, state politics and policy analysts have focused narrowly on expenditures and, in particular, on welfare and redistributive policies (Fry and Winters 1970; Plotnick and Winters, 1985; Barrilleaux et al. 2002, 2003a, b). The academic attractiveness of this focus is clear; welfare and redistributive policies take from the many and give to a select few. But, as well, political conflict should manifest itself when the deprivation of taxing the many must outweigh the prospect of welfare benefits for the few. Both "constituencies" are large enough to be disorganized (Olson, 1965), but simultaneously enough to be aggrieved or expectant and therefore capable of being organized by political parties.

2 State policy and politics analysts should begin focusing on hypothesizing when and what changes in specific legislated policies occur that alter the policy profiles of the states. We need to focus on specifics and not on highly summarized, aggregate, composite measures.
3 Cross-sectional vs. longitudinal: The proliferation of academic databases (Grossman, n.d.; Klarner, n.d.), the NASBO data, and the increasingly accessible useful data from the federal government (e.g. Bureau of Economic Analysis at https://www.bea.gov/data/by-place-states-territories) create opportunities for the analyst to more closely and better examine changes in discrete, albeit numerous, public policies, rules, and regulations that shape the benefits and burdens of state government actions.
4 Use the legislated action: Analysts need to focus on and utilize the precise authoritative actions undertaken by state government officials. Three distinctions: policy (I) *consequences* are the broad state-wide effects of changes in policy outputs (for an interesting example of the impact of outputs on consequences, see Gamm and Kousser (2021). Policy (II) *outputs* are those expenditure or tax items that politicians claim credit for – "In my administration, spending on K – 12 education increased by X hundreds of millions of dollars." Consequences ought to follow from changes in outputs, per Gamm and Kousser. If educational spending increased, then high school graduation rates should increase. If so, then a plausible link may occur between the output and the consequence. But neither output nor consequence can follow unless policy (III) *instruments* also change. And by *instruments*, I refer to the specifics of the legislative action, as examined in this volume. An excellent early example of "instrumental analysis" is Erikson (1971), and a more recent and also excellent example is Phillips and Lax (2009).
5 State vs. state and local actions: In every study, we need clarity as to the nature of the raw data employed. I can certainly imagine analyses that employ "state-only" data, but in the bulk of the cases, if using quantitative spending or taxing data, the state and local basis should be the likely source. In any case, clarity as to choice must be clear.
6 Legislative and gubernatorial decision-making: In the best of all worlds, state policy analysis would be advantaged if data were available on the preferences and/or actions of rivalrous institutional actors; in my case, governors and legislators.
7 Causal paths: Erikson, Wright and McIver (1993) offer a primer on thinking about causal paths in policy analysis. I divide the causal paths into six components: (1) secular origins, (2) secular changes, and (3) institutional determinants of (4) *tax policy instruments*, as well as (5) policy outputs

and (6) policy outcomes. This book focuses on the first three as determinants of *tax policy instruments*.

8 Tax Deprivations vs. Expenditure Indulgences: Harold Lasswell and Abraham Kaplan neatly categorized political actions into authoritative governmental *indulgences* and *deprivations*, which, conveniently so, map onto the budgetary axes of spending and taxing.[34] But, remarkably so, and I believe that my brief review of some of the relevant literature is representative, members of the subfield focus almost wholly on spending. That focus also corresponds, I believe, to a broader response by politicians, journalists, and activists who devote extraordinary attention to the "budget," both nationally in Washington, D.C., and in each of the state capitals, and by that they mean budgetary outlays, actions by appropriations committees, and local and constituency expenditure benefits. By contrast, the Senate Finance Committee, the House Ways and Means Committee and their fifty state counterparts, the annual as well as special revenue bills, and the change in tax assessments and burdens seem to fly far from the political, journalistic, and academic horizons.[35]

Compare the citation counts of the following classic book and that of a lesser-known, low-flying, and not-classic account: Richard Fenno, *The Power of the Purse* with 1,347 citation;

As compared with John Manley, *The Politics of Finance* ... with 423 citations.

The first – the classic text – is exclusively devoted to how the U.S. Congress spends and tries to control its House and Senate Appropriations committees and the federal agencies and (belatedly and maybe hopelessly so) its monies, while the Manley book, much less well known but still a standard text on how government taxes and raises monies, merits many fewer cites. So it is with the politics of spending vs. taxing in the American states. The subfield appears to be focused on the former and not particularly attentive to the latter. Oddly enough, Harold Lasswell falls prey to this myopic generalization in the title of his most quoted text, *Politics, Who Gets What, When, and How* (1936).[36] The central thesis of this volume is that politics is surely "who gets what when and how," but it is also ... *and extracted from whom, how, how much, why, and to what effect.*

The malattention of the public and academics to the deprivations of tax collections vs. the benefits of government spending, oddly enough, flies in the face of the well-known distinction that we are much more attentive to the negatives of deprivations in our day-to-day transactions than we are to the prospects of gains from future, indefinite, and not-well-calculated benefits of governmental spending.[37] What follows in this book is an effort, not necessarily to redirect our attention from expenditures to taxation, but to bring some balance into and widen our view of how governments operate in our nation's states.

9 And, finally, our focus should be on change; our scholarly focus should turn to analyses of change. In the best of all worlds, we need to generate propositions that relate "change" to "change." What does a change from a Democratic governor to a Republican governor entail in changing tax recommendations? Or, how does the change from a Democratic-controlled House to a Republican House alter gubernatorial recommendations and legislated tax actions in the face of continued Democratic control of the Senate and the "corner office?" The more useful analysis allows us to generate predictions about the consequences on policy outputs given a change in *tax policy instruments*. Changing *tax policy instruments*, in turn, must be a consequence of changing *social, economic, and political inputs*.

Notes

1 "Vibrancy" is denoted by the presence of an APSA section on "state politics and policy" founded in the early 1990s and by the section's journal, the *State Politics and Policy Quarterly*, now in its twenty-first year of publication, as well as an annual research conference. Credit is due to Chris Mooney, the *Quarterly's* founding editor and the original conference organizer.

2 Others might contest my characterization of Key's two volumes as "seminal," but the observation raises a linked issue: The 1950s dates (or thereabouts) are representative of seminal dates for similar developments in other American politics subfields. Wilson's seminal 1885 *Congressional Government* is, I suggest, an outlier along with Arthur Bentley's *The Process of Government* (1908), which was largely ignored until David Truman's *The Governmental Process* (1951) reinvigorated the study of interest groups. More relevant 1950s-era subfield books are Downs (1957), Berelson, Lazarsfeld, and McPhee (1963), and *The American Voter* (1964), and on the presidency, Neustadt (1960) and its canonical formulation by Peter Sperlich (1975), and for the Supreme Court, the pathbreaking article by Robert Dahl (1957). These cites are canonical for a discipline in transition to a disciplinary analysis that was becoming empirical, behavioral, and institutional. Bank of Sweden/Nobel Prize winner in economics Roger B. Myerson notes a similar impact of John Nash's contribution to economics in the 1950s (Myerson, 1999).

3 Canada does have three additional "territories." Note that there are other "large N" exceptions: Mexico has thirty-one states but with fewer and less reliable statistics, while data-rich Switzerland, with its twenty-six cantons, has generated many econometric studies frequently encountered in the journal *Public Choice*.

4 Rhode Island is scarcely wider than the normal marathon … 37 vs. 26.2 miles. Another New England comparison: Vermonters sometimes claim that if Vermont, the "Green Mountain State," were, by the grace of God, "flattened," its land area would be bigger than Maine.

5 There may well be soon a "coming to Jesus" moment for politicians in the American states. Transfers from the federal government to the fifty American

states in 2021 now total 1.2 trillion dollars, ranging from 169.2 billion dollars funneled to California to 3.2 billion dollars in Vermont. Obligations follow from these outlays; expectations rise for continuing programmatic support, which will be largely borne, in the intermediate-term future, by the states' taxpayers via new or increased taxes. Data source: https://usafacts.org/articles/which-states-rely-the-most-on-federal-aid/.

6 Lacy, Dean. 2002. "A Paradox of the Red States and Blue States: Federal Spending and Electoral Votes in the 2,000 U.S. Presidential Election," Ms. Dartmouth College, accessible at https://cpb-us-e1.wpmucdn.com/sites.dartmouth.edu/dist/9/280/files/2016/10/Paradox-of-Red-and-Blue-2002.pdf0

7 Albeit there might always be "coordinating issues" between and among states. I note the strange dogleg meetings of Interstates 35 and 44 between Oklahoma and Texas. Rumor has it that each state wanted its own distinctive highway path to the other's border, resulting in mile-long highway curves to join the two states' interstate highways.

8 An anecdote: Commonly accepted wisdom among some folks in Vermont and New Hampshire explains the interesting path that Interstate Highway 91 takes in Vermont. The chair of the committee that drew the initial maps of the interstate highway system was formed by the then-Bureau of Public Roads. The committee was made up of state highway superintendents and was chaired by New Hampshire's highway chief, Frank Merrill (for a succinct biography, see https://en.wikipedia.org/wiki/Frank_Merrill). Interstate 91 is described as travelling "along the eastern border of Vermont and serves as a major transportation corridor for eastern Vermont and western New Hampshire" (see https://en.wikipedia.org/wiki/Interstate_91). Many exits along Vermont's length of I-91 feature New Hampshire towns on the guide signs (for example, exit 3, which lists Brattleboro, VT and Keene, N.H. as the points of exit). If you sketch out the parallel towns in Vermont and New Hampshire that abut (in VT) or are nearby (in NH), the population figures are as follows:

Vermont	New Hampshire
Brattleboro (12,000)	Keene (23,000)
Springfield (9,000)	Claremont (12,000)
White River Jct. (2,000)	Lebanon and Hanover (21,500)

A simple rule of thumb might suggest that the I-91 highway would better serve the more densely populated areas on the New Hampshire side of the Connecticut River. But that would entail that New Hampshire would bear 10% of the initial cost of the highway now running in their state, as well as its ongoing maintenance costs. Instead, as Frank Merrill might have put it, "…let's put I-91 in Vermont, but no more than 1 to 10 miles from the New Hampshire border and towns at any one exit and let Vermont taxpayers bear the burden of financing the state's share of the new highway." Put simply, New Hampshire residents bear the fruits of the new interstate while not bearing any of the direct costs. I travel I-91 all of the time, and my informal license plate counts along the way bear out the point – New Hampshire plate-bearing cars and trucks comprise a large, and at commute times, the bulk share of I-91 traffic in Vermont.

9 I grew up in southern Illinois in a congressional district represented by Ken Gray, the so-called "prince of pork." It seemed to me that every hamlet, village,

town, and city in that part of the state gained a brand-new post office courtesy of Gray's efforts. Further, while the district lines barely changed during Gray's time in the House, its arable land area shrank dramatically due to his successful efforts at gaining federal dollars for "flood control" dams generating new lakes in southern Illinois. The lakes now are key sportsmen, boating, and tourism attractions in the state.

10 For this conjecture, analysis, and evidence on this, see Plotnick and Winters, 1985, pp. 464, 469, and 470.

11 Charles Tiebout, "A Pure Theory of Local Expenditures," *Journal of Political Economy,* Vol. 64, No. 5, (1956), pp. 416–424.

12 It might have been written partly as a joke, see https://taxjustice.net/2015/04/23/tax-competitiveness-was-charles-tiebout-joking/.

13 Gordon Tullock, "Federalism: Problems of Scale," *Public Choice,* Vol. 6, (1969) pp. 19–29.

14 Albert Hirschman, *Exit, Voice, and Loyalty: Responses to Decline in Firms, Organizations, and States* (Cambridge, MA: Harvard University Press, 1970).

15 In the 1970s and 1980s, New Hampshire citizens often referred to the neighboring state to their south as "Taxachusetts" and their neighbor to the west as "The People's Republic of Vermont." Maine, to their east, managed to escape local political opprobrium. New Hampshire is, of course, with Alaska, the only state with neither a general sales nor income tax.

16 For a very early, very interesting effort, see Weber, Hopkins, Mezey, and Munger (1971–1972); and for a seminal examination, see Erikson, Wright, and McIver (1993).

17 In a slightly different form, this table originally appeared in Lowery, Weber, and Winters (2008).

18 Also co-authored with Melissa Marroncelli.

19 As well, coauthored with Brian Stults.

20 The original paper was presented at the 1969 American Political Science Association meetings, where it subsequently won the 1970 Pi Sigma Alpha Award as the best paper presented at the 1969 APSA meetings. It was published in the *American Political Science Review*, Volume 64, Issue 2, June 1970, pp. 508–522. Credit for the original idea of a "redistribution ratio" rests with Brian Fry, now an emeritus professor at the University of South Carolina, via his research work at the Hoover Institution. The two of us worked out the ratio and established the likely causal links for assessing its political and economic determinants.

21 The allocation weights of benefits and burdens for the three lowest income classes were calculated using data from the Tax Foundation, Inc., *Tax Burdens and Benefits of Government Expenditures by income classes, 1961 and 1965* (New York: Tax Foundation, Inc. 1967).

22 There were some surprising anomalies in the forty-eight state rankings, e.g. the four states with the greatest "redistributive" budgets were Massachusetts (not a surprise), followed by Missouri, New York, and Oklahoma. The bottom four were Virginia, Wyoming, Arizona, and South Dakota.

23 In candor, this was one of the most criticized articles ever published in the *American Political Science Review*; see Deleon (1973); Booms and Halldorsen (1973); Sullivan (1973); and Uslaner and Weber (1975).

24 Erikson, Wright, and McIver, 1993, Statehouse Democracy. New York: Cambridge University Press.

25 The correlation between Fry and Winters 1961 index of redistribution and EWM's policy liberalism is .44.

26 Also see their related and equally interesting articles, Caughey, Warshaw, and Xu (2017); and Caughey and Warshaw (2018).
27 Caughey Devin, Warshaw Christopher. Policy Preferences and Policy Change: Dynamic Responsiveness in the American States, 1936–2014. *American Political Science Review*. May, 2018. Vol. 112, No. 2, pp. 249–266.
28 Parenthetically and pursuant to Chapter 2 of this volume, they note that "until the mid-1960s, Vermont's policies were a bit more conservative than the average state, but since then, Vermont's policies have become steadily more liberal relative to the nation. ... Vermont has been at the forefront of adopting gay marriage and other rights for homosexuals. Its welfare benefits and regulatory policies exhibit a similar evolution." (905) See Chapter 2 of this volume for an analysis of Vermont's changing public policies, driven by taxation as compared with its neighboring state of New Hampshire.
29 They note Rigby and Wright (2013); Flavin (2011); Ansolabehere, Rodden, and Snyder (2006); and Gilens (2009).
30 Barrilleaux, Holbrook, and Langer (2002); Barrilleaux and Berkman (2003); and Barrilleaux and Bernick (2003).
31 *American Political Science Review*, Vol. 79, No. 2 (1985), pp. 458–473. Again, to give proper credit, my co-author, economist Robert Plotnick, was insistent, and properly so, on using the precise legislated decision on the AFDC guarantee as the appropriate dependent variable in our analysis.
32 I was unable to obtain from the authors the raw data used in calculating the new measure of policy spending priorities.
33 As quoted in Richardson et al., 2003. Note that while all states are subject to "Dillon's Rule," some states via statutory or constitutional action have delegated powers to local governments via the so-called "Home Rule" provision.
34 Lasswell, Harold, and Abraham Kaplan, *Power and Society; A Framework for Political Inquiry* (New Haven: Yale University Press, 1950).
35 With the exception of the excellent articles by William and Francis Berry on taxation in the states (1992, 1994) and the book by Susan Hansen (1983).
36 Students of Lasswell might argue that taxation is bundled in the title by way of "getting"; that is to say, getting is also gained by avoiding taxation. Further, the idea of "getting" that bundles both indulgence and deprivation is wrapped up in the schoolyard taunt of "I'm gonna getcha!" The bully is threatening severe deprivation upon the wimp by simple assault, while the bully is also contemplating the indulgence of the satisfaction of delivering the punch. My preference for a revised, albeit cumbersome, title would be "*Politics, Who Gets or Forfeits What, When, How & by Whom.*"
37 Kahneman, Daniel, Paul Slovic, and Amos Tversky, *Judgement under Uncertainty: Heuristics and Biases* (New York: Cambridge University Press, 1982); also see Downs (1960).

2

POLITICAL CHOICE, TAXING, AND EXPENDITURE CHANGE

How, why, and when spending drives taxing ... and vice versa[1]

Richard F. Winters

Introduction

Midway through Robert Frost's *New Hampshire* (1923), he declares:

> She's one of the two best states in the Union.
> Vermont's the other. And the two have been
> Yoke-fellows in the sap-yoke from of old
> In many Marches. And they lie like wedges,
> Thick end to thin end and thin end to thick end,
> And are a figure of the way the strong
> Of mind and strong of arm should fit together, ...

To this literalist author, four of Frost's observations strike me: He declares the pair as one of the "two best states in the Union," which, of course, sums up my interest in these two states as well. Second, he terms them "yoke-fellows in the sap-yoke of old ... ." Teamed and paired together, they pull their way through history as if yoked at the neck, and nothing could budge them, with neither one ahead nor the other behind. While true when Frost published in 1923, and it was so for just about the next quarter century, but, in the last half of the 20th century, no two states diverged quite so dramatically in their public policies, a divergence that was driven largely, I argue, by their different tax policies.[2] Note that Frost does go on to compare them ... "they lie like wedges, Thick end to thin end and thin end to thick end ... ," as if they may not be quite so alike as the "yokefellows ... of old" image suggests. The one may be bigger or richer or more

DOI: 10.4324/9781003606291-4

populous than the other, but while alike, there are differences. Little did he suspect that fifty years after he wrote that, the two would begin a process that would lead to near-opposites in important public policy respects.[3]

His observation in the last two lines rings true for this reader: Both are New England states, small in geography and population, "whiter" than other states but with similar admixtures of ethnic immigrants; nevertheless, they are a "figure of the way the strong Of mind and strong of arm should fit together." Each state in Frost's time and in my and our time has exhibited strengths of mind and purpose. Originating as if yoked together in the late 1940s, over the next seven decades, each knowingly, purposefully, pointedly, and strongly so pursued quite different public policy paths.

Our understanding of the longitudinal development and the operation of different public policies in the American states is elementary.[4] Public policies in the American states have dramatically changed over the last seventy-five years, yet we lack secure understandings on such simple topics as the origins of present-day across-state public policy differences. In short, in this chapter, I want to know whether a present-day "progressive" state such as Vermont (and we can conjecture about other states with high spending levels) has always been so, or whether differences between states have appeared and possibly grown over time. If such variations exist, what appear to be the original determinants? What role does public opinion play in creating these differences, or that of the news media? What is the role of political parties? Of specific leaders? Of administrators and bureaucratic establishments? Of taxation?

The fifty states that make up the federal system are subject to common homogenizing influences, both national and regional, but they are also affected by important differentiating influences. The common forces function as quasi-experimental controls, while the differentiating forces establish patterns and correlates in the developments, operations, and effects of politics and public policies in the states.[5] Two or more states with many homogenizing and only a few differentiating forces would be most appropriate for political analysis, especially if they appeared similar at T – 1 but differed substantially in public policy by T + n.

For example, the question may be raised whether there are cases where similar determinants of public policy, such as size, population, region, and economy, coexist with the development of substantial differences in policy between states. If so, how can such variations be explained? For political analysis, the most interesting comparison would be one where two or more states at some point of origin with similar homogenizing forces and only a few differentiating forces reveal substantial developing differences in taxing and spending public policy. Are there states where:

- the size in land area and population are similar;
- where population and income differences are small;

- similar economies prevail;
- but where different public policies develop over time?

The following, I believe, is a causal tale of political agency. Decisions were made in Montpelier that fundamentally altered the path of public policies adopted in that state over a seventy-five-year period. Contrary decisions were made in Concord. In New Hampshire, these were decisions that were *not made*, but these are *not* cases of "non-decision-making."[6] Decisions made in Concord and by voters throughout New Hampshire were direct, conscious, and purposeful. New Hampshire politicians and citizens chose a path ... no "nondecisions" here ... they *chose* a path distinct from that of Vermont.

Vermont and New Hampshire[7]

Vermont and New Hampshire are appropriate subjects for such an analysis. Despite the similarity of region, ethnic composition, size, and economy, the differences in the public policies of the two states are striking:

1. In 1974, Vermont was the fourth highest and New Hampshire forty-fourth in total per capita state expenditures among the fifty states. In 2021, Vermont was 2nd and New Hampshire 47th.[8]
2. Vermont had the third most progressive tax system, while New Hampshire's ranks forty-second.[9] In 2019, in a similar, although not identical, ranking, the Tax Foundation rated Vermont's tax system as the fourth "most burdensome" of the fifty states, while New Hampshire was ranked twenty-sixth.[10]
3. Traditionally, in the 1960s and 1970s, Vermont had the second highest rate of increase in federal aid (Alaska was first), while New Hampshire has been among the bottom ten.[11]
4. In program after program, Vermont typically spends at a per capita rate of one-and-a-half to two times that of New Hampshire.[12]
5. And Vermont is a nationally recognized leader in environmental planning, pollution controls, land-use planning, bottle deposit laws, welfare rights and programs, social rehabilitation, and granting of LGBTQ rights, and in its correctional programs.[13]
6. Not much has changed between the two states over the past thirty years. A recent analysis by the libertarian-oriented Cato Institute ranked the fifty states along a number of "freedoms." In "state tax burden," New Hampshire is ranked second (least burdened) among the states and Vermont 49th (most). In a composite "overall fiscal policy score," New Hampshire is third and Vermont is 46th.[14]

7 Public opinion might drive state-by-state historic divergences. A 2014 survey by the Pew Center of "political ideology by state" sets out the array of ideological identities for the states, and I reproduce below the relevant data for the New England states ranked by "% Liberal."

While New Hampshire contains one of the "least liberal population" and is tied with Maine for "most conservative," I wonder if these public opinion differences between the two states are sufficient to account for the public policy differences. And, of course, per my later arguments, the greater New Hampshire conservatism exhibited in this 2014 report may follow from its different *prior* taxing and public policy "regimes," and not necessarily as causes for the origins of the distinct regimes. Vermont's liberalism and New Hampshire's conservatism scores in 2014 may follow from the divergent public policies that the two states employed over the prior half century. Put differently, Vermonters over time came to accept the greater taxation, spending, and programs entailed. Further, Vermont's public policies may have lured some to migrate to its progressive-friendly environs.[15]

Meanwhile, New Hampshire citizens came to accept and draw on the prevailing policy set of low taxation and low levels of state spending. There is some evidence for this; New Hampshire became the focus of energies nationwide of the "Free State Project" in an effort to lure libertarians and the like-minded to move to the state as the state most sympathetic to libertarian ideals.[16] Public affinities as well as spending levels may follow taxation.

TABLE 2.1 Political Ideology of New England Voters

	% Conservative	*% Liberal*	*Difference (– = more conservative) (%)*
MA	23	36	13
VT	30	35	5
RI	26	30	4
ME	34	30	–4
NH	34	28	–6
CT	33	25	–8

Ranked on % Liberal. Data as of 2014.
Obtained from the Pew Research Center as part of their 2014 Religious Landscape Study and accessed on 1/15/22 at https://www.pewforum.org/religious-landscape-study/compare/political-ideology/by/state/.

Many of the public policy differences between the two states are of relatively recent origin, dating back to about 1955. Before 1955, the public policies of the two states differed hardly at all. In 1950, New Hampshire ranked thirtieth and Vermont twenty-eighth in per capita general expenditures among the then forty-eight states. But in 1974, Vermont ranked second and New Hampshire forty-second, a gain of twenty-six ranks for Vermont and a loss of twelve for New Hampshire within the twenty-four-year period. In 2019, the two were ranked 4th and 39th, respectively, in general expenditure spending among the states.[17]

A specific longitudinal revenue comparison: The U.S. Census Bureau of the Department of Commerce published a comprehensive database for state and local revenues and spending for the period starting with 1942, then for 1953, and then yearly from 1957 to 2008.[18] The dataset is quite comprehensive in its array of disaggregated revenue figures. For my purposes, the category of "general revenue from own sources," stated as a percent of personal income of state and local revenues, is most appropriate. Figure 2.1 arrays for the two states the "own source general revenues" as a percent of statewide personal income. The value for each state in the time series that begins in 1942, mid-war, has Vermont at 8.9% and New Hampshire at 9.3%. I suspect, but do not know, that prior years

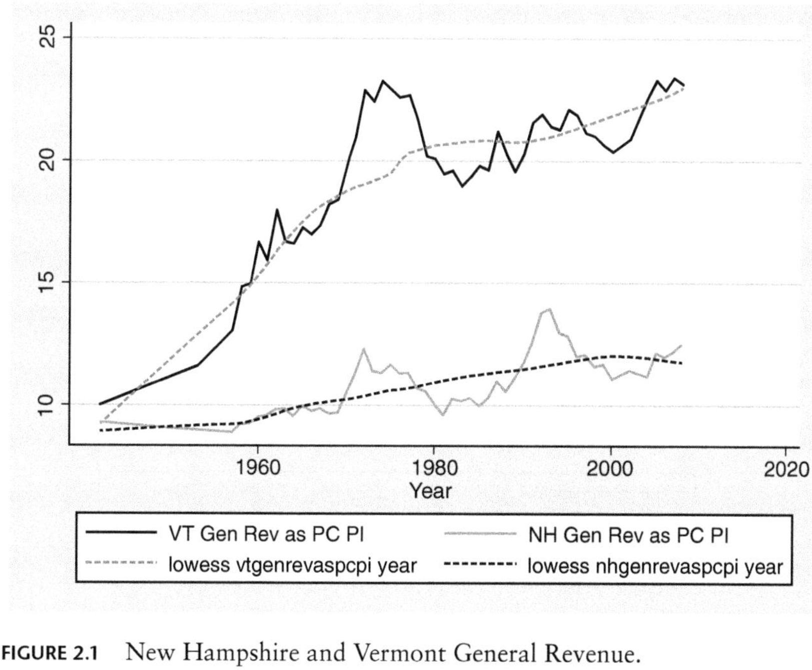

FIGURE 2.1 New Hampshire and Vermont General Revenue.

would demonstrate similar parallel and small percentage comparisons. But shortly thereafter, Vermont diverges from its "sister state," sharply rising in the mid-1950s and with even greater gains during the Great Society/Nixon years in the 1960s, slumping in the 1970s, and since the early 1980s, Vermont has shown consistent rising government taxing. Figure 2.3 adds the other four New England states while retaining the lowess smoothing function for the two states of interest. The case of Vermont becomes even more striking in a New England comparative contrast.

Statistical examination turns up equally dramatic figures. Let's assume that the simple indicator of state-by-state general expenditure spending as a percent of statewide personal income is an adequate measure of "fiscal scale."[19] General expenditure spending per '000 of personal income is a reasonable indicator of governments' overall impact, while a change in such an indicator measures the states' changing support for policy and programs.[20] As the dependent variable, I use the difference between the 1974 and 1950 general expenditure efforts by income of the then-forty-eight states.[21] Obvious predictors of such a variable include the expenditure per capita for the initial period (1950) and the present-day population (1974 population) and wealth (1974 total personal income) of the states. In a multiple regression equation, the combined power of the three variables accounts for about 10% of the variance of the 1974–1950 general expenditure difference. The regression yields a set of residuals showing differences between the actual budgetary change

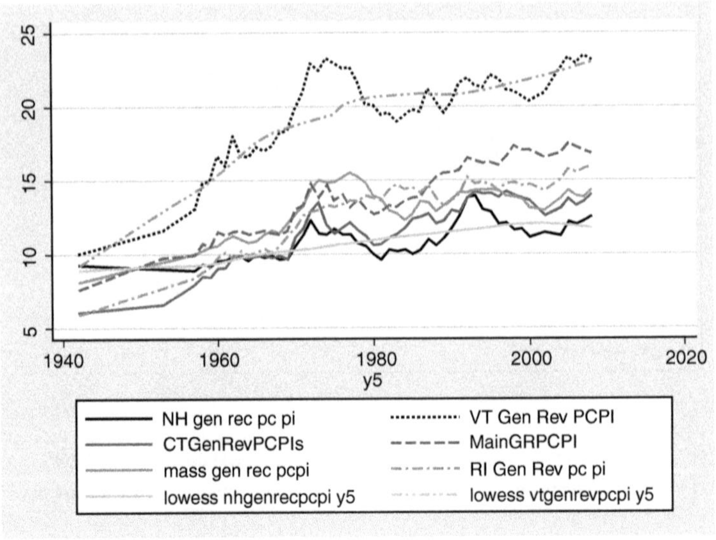

FIGURE 2.2 New Hampshire and Vermont in New England Perspective.

and the prediction based on the three variables of size, current wealth, and initial spending. Of the forty-eight states in 1950, Vermont's residual is the largest among the states, with a spending change of +5.42% greater than predicted over the twenty-four-year period. New Hampshire is forty-fourth with a negative residual of –1.71%, indicating less spending change than predicted.[22] Updating, the residuals for the 2010–1950 differences in general expenditures per '000 of personal income has Vermont, again with the largest of the 48 states with a residual of +6.41%, while New Hampshire's rank is 39th with a residual of –1.92% over the now sixty-year period.

Graphic displays over the 1950 to 2010 period[23] illustrate the diverging paths of the two states. Figure 2.3 displays the two states' spending as a percent of personal income over the sixty-year period and also folds in the New England sister states of Maine, Massachusetts, Connecticut, and Rhode Island. New Hampshire floors the figure while Vermont tops it. The spending origins of the six states range from 4.1% (CT), 5.5% (NH) to 6.6% (VT) and top out in 2010 at 22% (VT) vs. 12% (NH and Connecticut).

As I noted in Chapter 1, composite measures of state policymaking are useful in scorecarding the American states along any number of dimensions. Most recently, Chris Warshaw and Devin Caughey, in their articles (2016, 2017, 2018) and their book *Dynamic Democracy* (2022), generated a 1935–2020 time-series of some 200 state public policies along a conventional liberal-conservative dimension.[24] Figure 2.4 sets out over the eighty-five-year period from 1935 to 2020 the public policy conservatism to liberalism of New Hampshire and Vermont.[25] The zero point sets the average of the fifty states' liberalism/conservatism dimension for the year, thus putting states above the zero line indicating more conservative than the average state and below the line more liberal. In Figure 2.4, both states began the period with New Hampshire at or above the zero line, while Vermont began the period from 1935 to the mid-1960s, indicating marginally more conservative public policies than other states. New Hampshire's blue line cruised along the zero mark into the 1990s and then lurched a bit toward liberalism with the onset of Democratic governors Shaheen (1997–2003), Lynch (2005–2013), and Hassan (2013–2017).

For the first three decades of the Warshaw-Caughey study, Vermont was modestly to well above the typical state in policy conservatism. In the mid-1960s, there was a pronounced, vigorous, and consistent trend of increasing policy liberalism. The trend appeared to begin with the Hoff (D) administration and appears almost seamless over time.[26] Note that the post-1965 Lowess curves for each state are somewhat different. Vermont's

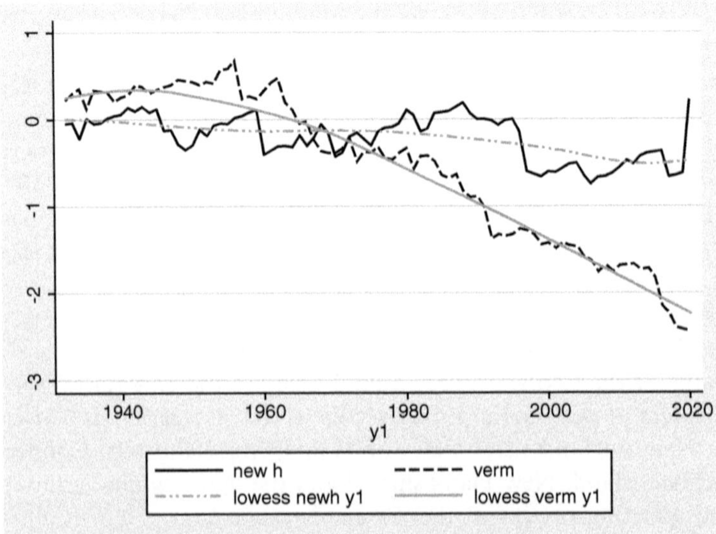

FIGURE 2.3 Caughey and Warshaw measures for Vermont and New Hampshire, 1935–2020.

slope of increasing policy liberalism quite finely fits the Lowess smoothing curve; deviations about the curve are small and the slope as it nears the terminal years suggests continuing liberalism gains. New Hampshire's Warshaw-Caughey measures deviate sometimes well above and below the slope, suggesting a more ragged and uncertain path. Secondly, as the slope nears the terminal year, it is flattening as if a near-term "limit" is approached. This may reflect a period of stasis with its Republican governor, Chris Sununu (elected 2017–2025), and its bicameral chambers almost evenly split between the two parties; in 2024, in the Senate, there were 14 Republican and 10 Democrats, and in the House, there were 200 Republicans, 195 Democrats, 3 Independents, and 2 vacancies. Meanwhile, in Vermont, with a fairly progressive Republican Governor, Phil Scott,[27] the Vermont Senate is composed of 23 Democrats, seven Republicans, and 1 Progressive, while its House is composed of 104 Democrats, 37 Republicans, and nine in other, minor parties.[28]

Figure 2.3 displays the Caughey and Warshaw measures of diverging policy liberalism/conservatism scores of New Hampshire and Vermont, 1935 to 2020.

Figure 2.4 puts the New Hampshire and Vermont experiences in comparative state contexts among the other New England states.[29] I array the Warshaw-Caughey time series over the eighty-five year period with the Lowess curves indicated for New Hampshire and Vermont public policy

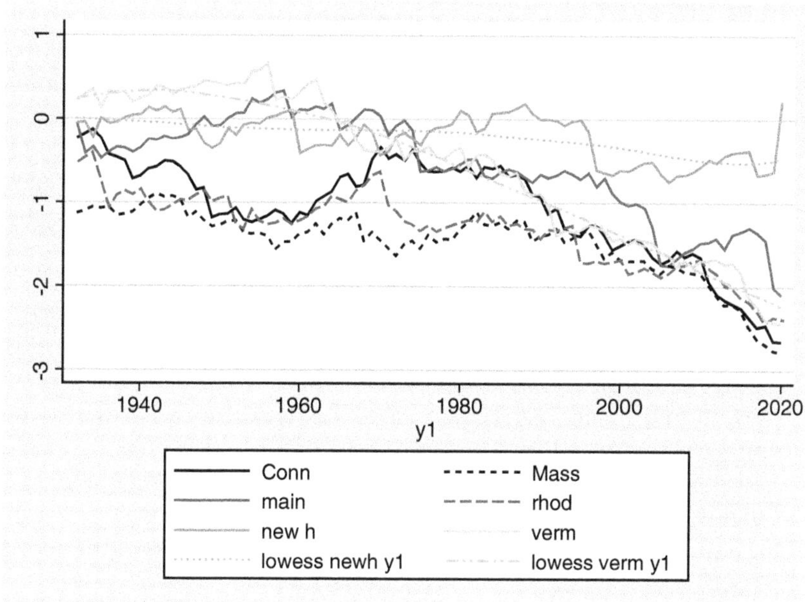

FIGURE 2.4 Caughey and Warshaw measures for the New England States.

paths. At the outset, from 1932 until the mid-1960s, the three northern New England states were much more conservative than their southern counterparts. After that point, Maine and Vermont began to converge with the southern states, leaving New Hampshire still hovering near the mean of the fifty states. Note that Vermont now aligns with Massachusetts, then Connecticut, and is tied with Rhode Island among the tight compact of the most liberal among the regional sister states.

The dynamic of these changes is the object of this study. Two states, similar in many respects and with similar spending policies seventy-five years ago, today exhibit distinctive, even contrary, spending policies. I shall attempt to explain this phenomenon by means of concrete evidence where possible and through interviews and impressionistic evidence where concrete evidence is difficult to obtain. I can lay no claim to methodological uniqueness; in fact, I have been consciously eclectic, drawing upon structured and semi-structured interviews,[30] newspaper accounts,[31] legislative observation,[32] two waves of questionnaires applied to state legislators in each state,[33] a multivariate statistical analysis of spending in the two states, and general political accounts. Nor can I claim theoretical closure for the model of expenditure change I am about to propose. Some of the links are better supported by the evidence than others.

I hope that I convey the appropriate degree of tentativeness.

It would be impossible to explain all policy differences between the two states. I shall therefore focus only on the differences in taxing and spending, partly out of personal interest, but mainly because of the influence of the dollar on other aspects of public policy. Since the budget is the primary instrument of public policy, general differences in policy are reflected in budgetary differences, as Aaron Wildavsky has pointed out:

> Perhaps the "study of budgeting" is just another expression for the "study of politics"; yet one cannot study everything at once, and the vantage point offered by concentration on budgetary decisions offers a useful and much-neglected perspective from which to analyze the making of public policy. The opportunities for comparison are ample, the outcomes are specific and quantifiable and, a dynamic quality is assured by virtue of the comparative ease with which one can study the development of budgetary items and programs over a period of years.[34]

It is the dynamic quality of spending differences in the two states which focuses me here.

The Common Hypotheses

The five folklore hypotheses in the late 20th century, listed below, were commonly used to account for the differences between Vermont and New Hampshire. While the last three are usually stated in such general terms as to be misleading, the first just cannot be correct. They can be summarized as follows:

- Severe malapportionment of the state legislatures affected politics in these states.
- The size of the New Hampshire House of Representatives (400 members strong!) precludes any truly liberal or innovative legislation.
- Public opinion in New Hampshire is more "conservative" than in Vermont.
- The very conservative *Manchester Union Leader,* through its publisher, William Loeb, distorts the New Hampshire political process.
- Geography and geology: It's not just the bird's-eye geographic view, but it's their differing geologies. Steve Taylor, a noted New Hampshire

political analyst, explains the difference between the two states this way; he begins with a quote from Emerson and concludes with Robert Frost:

> "Emerson said,
> 'The God who made New Hampshire
> Taunted the lofty land with little men.'"

Taylor then writes:

> As to the explanation of why Vermont and New Hampshire differ so sharply on public policy matters--My favorite theory is that it traces to the geology of the two. Vermont has sweet, limestone, sedimentary rock, while New Hampshire is underlain by barren, unforgiving, granitic, igneous rock. Vermont attracted settlers wanting to farm, they were peaceful and looked to the capital in Montpelier for political leadership.
>
> New Hampshire drew people wanting to make a buck, and those many waterfalls brought the mill towns with their mix of ethnic rivalries and top-down industrial managers. Acidic soils discouraged much agriculture, and people came to distrust Concord and to define themselves by the view from their back step, not as 'New Hampshiremen.'

And, as Frost wrote:

> "Anything I can say about New Hampshire
> Will serve almost as well about Vermont,
> Excepting that they differ in their mountains.
> The Vermont mountains stretch extended straight;
> New Hampshire mountains Curl up in a coil."[35]

There is much to like about Taylor's view, and I have come around to accept one of its basic perspectives: The strong, well-dispersed Vermont agricultural community played a key, albeit unknowing, role in the development of the emerging states' differences.[36] But like many genetic stories of political traits, Taylor's story neglects the role of human agency in manifesting the unfolding process. The alternative explanation rests on the efforts and activities of individuals like Vermont governors Phil Hoff and Deane Davis, but also on the efforts, decisions, and decisions-not-made of New Hampshire governors Sherman Adams, Walter Peterson, Meldrim Thomson, and Hugh Gallen.

Malapportionment

Since both states were severely malapportioned before the middle of the 1960s, malapportionment cannot explain the difference. Moreover, public policies were similar in the two states before 1955, a period when both had badly apportioned legislatures. Substantive changes in policy began in Vermont in 1955, some ten years before reapportionment. Finally, since reapportionment (following the Baker v. Carr and Reynolds v. Sims decisions) in the 1960s, the differences in spending and policy between the two states have changed less relative to one another, indicating that reapportionment cannot have had a substantial effect on state policy.[37]

Size

The size of the New Hampshire House is often cited as the reason for the conservatism of the state's public policy. Until 1966, however, the size of the Vermont House was constitutionally set at 250, one representative per town, but effectively 246 – four "towns" had no population sufficient to represent. Many of the differences between the two states were established in the 1955–1966 era, when the Vermont House had a lower legislature-constituent ratio than the New Hampshire House (1:1642 vs. 1:1682). In 1966, Vermont, unlike New Hampshire, reduced the size of the House from 250 to 150.[38] Thus, unless it can be shown that organizational or institutional differences exist between a House of 250 and one of 400, it is hard to accept the explanation based[39] on size. Thus, neither the malapportionment nor the House-size hypothesis seems to me to be a convincing explanation of why Vermont, from 1955 to 1975, accelerated its spending and reached its present position as one of the leading progressive states in the union.

Public opinion is often said to be more conservative in New Hampshire. The evidence is not strong, as Table 2.1 indicates. The national voting record for presidential races is a comparable voting statistic. As the record of postwar voting for the president indicates, the difference between the two electorates amounts to no more than a few percentage points in their support for the Republican nominee over the last several presidential elections leading up to 1974. Even when the choices are more varied, as in the presidential primary, the New Hampshire electorate accurately mirrors the preferences of the nation as a whole. To take one case, Gerald Ford and Jimmy Carter did just about as well in New Hampshire (50% and 29%, respectively) as they did in the rest of the popular primaries. Even in 1964, when faced with the Republican primary choices of Goldwater and Rockefeller, New Hampshire decisively rejected both in favor of the write-in candidacy of Henry Cabot Lodge – hardly the image of rock-ribbed New Hampshire conservatism.[40]

More specific data on the attitudes and opinions of legislators in the two states toward taxing and spending programs are available.[41] Three budgetary dimensions seem to be the main concerns of the legislators: human services/welfare spending, business taxes/economic development programs, and a sin tax/tax displacement. Interestingly, the two states differ significantly on these dimensions: Vermont stresses a progressive set of welfare and human services programs, while New Hampshire has an aggressive and successful business development program and a revenue system relying on sin taxes, business levies, and the property tax. Yet, it was impossible to distinguish statistically between the attitudes of New Hampshire and Vermont legislators toward the three budgetary issues. This may indicate that other, more general factors are responsible for the differences in policies and that the political opinions of the people and their representatives are more similar than thought of in both states, thus a continuing search for a more general explanation of the two states developing differences.[42]

Union Leader

New Hampshire's alleged conservatism receives the widest attention in the pages of the *Manchester Union Leader.* William Loeb's editorials in the era analyzed here achieved a kind of national "fame" in this period.[43] In fact, the influence of the *Leader* is often cited as one of the causes of differences in policy between New Hampshire and Vermont. The public opinion and *Union Leader* hypotheses are closely related and actually do, I argue, affect the policy differences between the two states. I argue that the influence of the *Leader* is specific and operates under certain conditions, as I explain below.

Agriculture vs. Industry

Steve Taylor's quote above on page 47 about the sweet soil in Vermont's largely dairy agriculture vs. granitic, rapid-water, mill-oriented New Hampshire resonates with many residents that I have spoken with. It is, however, difficult to confirm, or, even if confirmed, difficult to establish the bounds of it as an "explanation." Farming and dairy farming in the rolling hillsides and hilltop farms have always been part of Vermont's "Beckoning Country" attraction, as has been the contrasting and astonishing mile-long row of industrial mill buildings abutting the Merrimack River alongside Interstate 293 in Manchester, NH. But New Hampshire has long had successful farming in its southeast and in the Connecticut River valley, while Vermont has had successful mill industries in St. Johnsbury (Fairbanks Co.), Winooski (textiles), Barre and Proctor (marble and granite), and Windsor and Springfield (machine tools). My conclusion, as I draw out below, is that it is not the "sweet soil agriculture" in Vermont vs. the industrial base in New Hampshire, but that the political efforts of Vermont dairy farmers after a disastrous 1927 flood that destroyed the many "farm to market" roads and bridges that helped to pass a personal income tax in a malapportioned Vermont House that elevated the power of the state to tax and to elaborate that tax over time. The rest is, as they say, history.

An Alternative Model

Let me sketch an alternative, more complex and more realistic explanation. Despite the lack of conclusive evidence, sufficiently concrete data are available to serve as a basis for plausible constructions of the set and sequence of causes and events. The overarching model is

Figure 2.5: A causal model of emerging policy differences between Vermont vs. New Hampshire represented

Let's stipulate the causal model, basing it on the experience of the state of Vermont:

1 Vermont's revenue system at the outset – the 1950s – had a *higher and developed an even greater income elasticity of revenue*. The post-WWII economic boom resulted in greater revenues flowing into state coffers.
2 In my "soaking and poking" observing and interviews in the early 1970s, I was surprised to discover a fundamentally different *entrepreneurial style of administration/bureaucracy* in Vermont. Vermont in

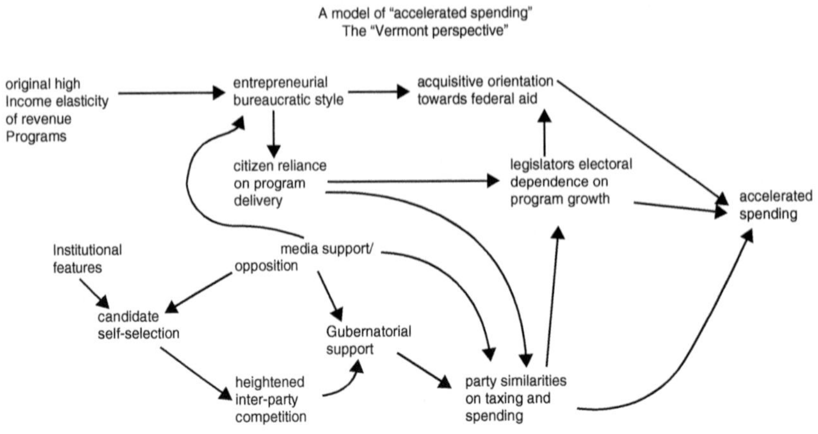

FIGURE 2.5 A Model of "Accelerated Spending": The "Vermont Perspective."

the 1970s attracted policy entrepreneurs. I was struck by their relative youth and their commitment to the professional delivery of programmatic services. Administrators wedded to the delivery of their agencies' services → more money by aggrandizing administrators and their legislative supporters.

3 Institutional features in Vermont enhanced the *within-party competitiveness of gubernatorial candidates* and the *professionalization of its gubernatorial candidates*. Statewide, Vermont elects a governor, a separately elected lieutenant governor, the secretary of state, a state treasurer, an attorney general, and an auditor of accounts. Statewide, New Hampshire elects only a governor (and, of course, its two U.S. Senators). It has no lieutenant governor. In Republican and Democratic primary elections, Vermont's governors tend to be drawn from the pool of experienced candidates already holding or previously holding statewide offices. Over the past seventy-five years, New Hampshire governors have been disproportionately those with little or no electoral or office-holding experience. Governors Meldrim Thomson and Hugh Gallen – a Republican and a Democrat, respectively – of the 1970s are prime examples in each party: Thomson having only served on the Orford, New Hampshire, school board and Gallen having served one term in the 400-member-strong N.H. House.

4 The succession of experienced statewide candidates and strong within-party competition in both parties in Vermont shaped *gubernatorial support for existing spending programs*, which led to *interparty agreement and similarities* on taxing and spending programs.

5 Party agreement was reinforced by media support for an expansionary budget in Vermont, which, in turn, promoted citizen/clientele program support, in part leading legislators and administrators to focus on and depend on growing spending programs. High elasticity of revenue is attractive to highly professional, bureaucratic entrepreneurs who are mainly interested in the application of programs to clients and/or citizens. Two other conditions for an entrepreneurial bureaucratic style are active media support by the news media or at least the absence of active opposition, which New Hampshire has consistently experienced with the Manchester Union Leader, as well as vocal and articulate support from the citizenry at large or the beneficiaries of programs. The press in New Hampshire during this period was dominated by the Union Leader. The Union Leader was notorious for its direct attacks on legislators and office-holders, but also for attacking administrators and bureaucrats. Other newspapers in the state, such as the Concord Monitor and the Nashua Telegraph, paled in influence and were, in any case, more moderate than liberal. Contrasting in Vermont were the yoked pair of

jointly owned capital city Montpelier Times Argus and the Rutland Herald, the state's largest daily newspaper, the latter edited and led by a supportive liberal editor in Robert Mitchell, who in editorials continuously weighed in on the benefits of state government policies. The only conservative media counterweights in Vermont were the moderate-to-conservative Burlington Free Press and the news staff of Vermont's only TV station, WCAX in Burlington. Then in place, free speech balance rules at the time attenuated WCAX's news staff conservatism.

6 During the 1960s and 1970s, this led to an acquisitive orientation toward federal aid programs by Vermont's executive and legislative officials in an already heavily taxed state, in turn accelerating state spending. Rapidly rising state revenue was often used by governors for electoral reward and punishment. At the same time, rapidly rising program expenditures cause greater public involvement in statewide programs, such as special education programs; these lead in turn to increased legislative involvement and electoral dependence on them.[44] The final stage, reached in the mid-1960s, is a positive inclination in Vermont toward federal aid programs on the part of the governor, legislature, and administrators. This is partially the result of the increased availability of federal aid, but also of the entrepreneurial abilities of bureaucrats, the special interest of the clientele in expanded program funding, and growing legislative and executive realization of the high tax load existing at the time.

While all of the factors are operative in Vermont, they are either absent or tend to dampen changes in spending in New Hampshire. New Hampshire has neither an income nor a sales tax and relies on less-sensitive, less-elastic revenue sources. Taxes on alcohol and liquor, rooms and meals, cigarettes, and horse racing-often referred to locally as the "Five Bs" – on "beer, bets, belly, butts, and booze" taxes are stable sources of revenue and relatively insensitive to changes in personal income. Less elastic taxes lead to low expectations of program funding, making New Hampshire unattractive to entrepreneurial bureaucrats. Gubernatorial candidates exaggerate the influence of the *Manchester Union Leader,* which in turn leads to shared gubernatorial hostility to new tax programs. Lack of program funding dampens both legislative and citizen demands for new programs and support for old programs thus, obviating reliance on federal aid programs.

The two states are similar in many of the ways that aggregate, fifty-state analyses suggest are important in determining interstate differences – they literally bound one another geographically, socially, economically, and culturally. However, in spending and revenue policy, they are at opposite ends. In Vermont, the factors affecting such policies as those indicated in 2.5 are present and positively reinforcing, while they are either absent or negatively reinforcing in New Hampshire. The situation is remarkably asymmetrical – a multitude of forces suggests spending convergence, while the behavioral politics of the two states have promoted divergence.

The Initial Divergence

My hypothesis to account for the differences between the two states looks to initial differences in the income elasticity of their respective revenue systems. Vermont's revenue system is more closely related to changes in the total personal income. Income in the two states increased rapidly between 1955 and 1965, and income growth and revenue elasticity may explain the greater rate of change in growth of Vermont's revenues and expenditures. However, revenue differences cannot arise from differences in income change, because both states are susceptible to similar national trends. In fact, the 1945–1974 time series of personal incomes in the two states are almost perfectly correlated. The correlation of the across-time, first differences of income in the two states is a positive .93, indicating an almost perfect lockstep motion of income changes across the two states. And when Vermont's income rises, New Hampshire's does as well by a roughly equal amount. But because of the adoption by Vermont of an income tax in 1931, which has accounted for a postwar low of 6% of revenue (in 1946) progressing to a high of 34% (in 1968), the Vermont revenue system is more sensitive to income change than the New Hampshire tax system.[45] This is a straightforward and easily testable hypothesis. If the income elasticity of Vermont's revenue system is greater than New Hampshire's, the correlation of the first differences of total personal income and total tax collection ought to be higher in Vermont. However, if the whole 1946–1974 time series is used, the correlations are practically the same: .75 in Vermont and .76 in New Hampshire. If, however, the period is broken up into tenyear segments, then the correlations become highly variable. For my purpose, the 1955–1965 decade is crucial. In these last years of Republican rule and the first years of the Hoff administration, the correlations between income changes and tax changes are as hypothesized: .53 in Vermont and .11 in New Hampshire. In addition, Vermont was generally prosperous during this period, with personal income increasing by an average of over 30 million per year as against an average of 18 million per year during the preceding decade. And because of the progressive nature of the income tax in Vermont, as incomes grew, ever-larger increments of money flowed into the state treasury. The progressive income tax is more sensitive to fluctuations in incomes than any other tax program.[46]

The effects of revenue elasticity are varied and important. In the cases of Vermont and New Hampshire, the greater the elasticity of revenues, the faster the revenue growth and the greater the bureaucratic expectation of rapid program funding and expansion. My hypothesis is that the expectation and realization of more rapid program funding are responsible for a significant difference between the two states and between their governments. In Montpelier and Concord, the difference in "style" between the administrators is striking.

Although they provide mainly impressionistic evidence, interviews with many key administrative officials in both states lead to the following generalizations: New Hampshire bureaucrats tend to be promoted from within, have longer in-house service, and are more agency-oriented and less professional minded. They conform to the model of the "local" or "bureaucratic" orientation as proposed by Merton (1957). They tend to be natives and are less likely to be from out of state. In contrast, to use Merton's terms, Vermont bureaucrats are more likely to have a "professional" orientation. Vermont administrators appeared in their testimonies before the appropriations committees to be receptive to new program initiatives, willing to innovate, imitative of other states' practices (typically looking westward to New York), "cosmopolitan," "national," and "professional" in orientation in contrast to the tendency of New Hampshire administrators to be wary of federal programs, cautious in adopting new programs, less imitative, and more state- and agency-oriented. Vermonters tend to be younger and more aggressive, change jobs more frequently, include more "out-of-staters," and act more like bureaucratic entrepreneurs than their New Hampshire counterparts.[47]

In a recent (2024) discussion with a faculty colleague, I elaborated on this point. Looking back now on my two years spent traveling to Montpelier and Concord, I became more and more aware of a quite vague feeling that I had of my impressions of the two "places." The following is a brief discussion either (a) of my inherent bias in my analyses of the politics of the two states or (b) of a hard-to-document, much less "provable," sense of the political culture in the two state capitols. In brief, I was fascinated and impressed by my meetings, encounters, and observations of politics in Montpelier. I was not similarly impressed with Concord. Two anecdotes and a tax-related observation. In 1975–1976, the Vermont House was composed of 78 Republicans, 68 Democrats, and four Independents. Nevertheless, they elected Tim O'Connor, a Democrat from Brattleboro, as Speaker of the House. In turn, he appointed Emory Hebard, a Republican from Glover, Vermont, as Chairman of the Appropriations Committee. His counterpart in the Vermont Senate was Republican John Boylan from Island Pond, Vermont, and they shared backgrounds – both were small-town storekeepers. Hebard was the owner of a general store in Glover, and Boylan was a longtime storekeeper for the Canadian National Railway, which ran through his hometown. Both brought green eyeshade perspectives to their appropriations work. Each was personally impressive to me. Joining Hebard on House Appropriations in 1975 was a young Democratic woman from Burlington, Madeleine Kunin. She quickly became the leading Democratic spokesperson on Appropriations and rightly so. She was bright, quick, and eager to learn. And in the Committee's chair, she had a masterful teacher in Hebard. Joining in the often three-way discussion between Hebard and Kunin was another former storekeeper, Ronald Crisman, the budget advisor to Democratic Governor Thomas Salmon. The exchanges in Committees meetings were vivid. Kunin pushing Hebard for changes; Hebard arguing for constraints in the short term and laying out paths for Kunin for the intermediate and long-haul changes in spending that she wanted, but clearly appreciating her views and contributions. Crisman would chime in with the executive office perspective and with an encyclopedic understanding of past budget(s) and the Governor's proposed budget. It was an illuminating seminar on budgeting.

My counterpart's experience in Concord was not so impressive. My most vivid memory was an angry exchange in the New Hampshire House Appropriations Committee, where the item under discussion was the line-item budget for the public health programs of the Department of Health and Human Services. The discussion was "where to cut," and one set of line items centered on diagnosing and controlling sexually transmitted diseases. The chair had proposed cutting back appropriations for mobile transports that were in use in STD diagnoses and treatments. The discussion quickly became inflamed, and when it became clear that the motion would pass, one of the leading Committee Democrats, Terri Nardi of Manchester, stood up, shoved her chair to the table, and announced as she left the room, "you can't find and cure syphilis by phone!"

Two "takeaways": (a) I'm biased favoring liberal spenders and taxers as in Vermont; or (b) Vermont, with its multiple and multi-faceted statewide taxing programs, politically practiced positive-sum politics of trying to fit in as many partners as it could in its budget bill, versus just-noticeably-above-constant-sum fiscal politics in New Hampshire, where highly constrained revenue programs severely limited the arts of the possible. Much was possible in Vermont; in New Hampshire, much was "on the table" every two years for cuts or elimination. It was like a roundup of the herd of oxen every two years in Concord; a few were gored, some were lamed, many were put out to forage for sustenance in the arid "back 40 acres," and a few were relatively well fed in the large committee room of the Appropriations Committee.

An important causal path links income elasticity to bureaucratic entrepreneurialism. The greater the income elasticity of Vermont's revenues, with its frequent periods of high income growth, the greater revenue increases in the state available for programmatic consolidation and expansion. But second, the greater the revenue volatility, the less predictable revenue projections become. Both causal paths lead to increased demands for state spending. The link between increasing revenue growth makes Vermont attractive to entrepreneurial program administrators with expansive and expensive professional aspirations. The second forces appropriators in Vermont to search for new or expanded revenue sources so as to cushion downward pressures on spending in times of revenue shortfalls.

The Manchester Union Leader reinforces administrative and budgetary conservatism in New Hampshire. It carries out – and often with astonishing success – vendettas against administrators who show the slightest inclination toward personal and/or agency aggrandizement. The most notable examples in the 1960s and 1970s were Thomas Bonner, who was driven from his new appointment as president of the University of New Hampshire, and Dr. James Dykens, the commissioner of mental health, who collapsed in my presence during a confrontation with a hostile New Hampshire Governor Meldrim Thomson and the Executive Council. The most conspicuous failure of the *Leader's* vendetta strategy in this period was its attack on Major Wheelock, the superintendent of the New Hampshire Hospital, a polished and articulate exception to the general administrative rule of conservatism in New Hampshire.

The Influence of News Media

While income elasticity of the two revenue systems may account for Vermont's acceleration of expenditures in the 1950s and 1960s, the actions of the *Manchester Union Leader,* purchased in 1946 by the conservative William Loeb, dampened efforts to change and reform New Hampshire's expenditure and tax programs, and therefore the rate of revenue rise. But it is important to examine in detail how the *Union Leader's* editorial policy can affect budgetary policy.

During the period of this study, probably no other state had the combination of a dominant, vigorously conservative statewide daily newspaper with the lack of competing news media. Political observers agree that the *Leader's* political influence is substantial but disagree on *what* it influences and *how.* It is my view that the *Leader* influences, in descending order of importance, (1) the selection of gubernatorial candidates; (2) the determination of prominent issues and campaign style; and (3) finally, voters' behavior. As stated previously, voting data from New Hampshire and

Vermont presidential primary and general elections from 1945 through the 1970s show the two states to be similar to each other and, though somewhat more Republican, to the nation as a whole. The electorates of the two states do not greatly differ on issues of national concern. However, New Hampshire has had some of the most unusual governors and would-be governors of any state in the Union. One governor of the 1970s, Meldrim Thomson, is no exception. A transplanted Georgian, Thomson ran for governor five times, each time with the support of the *Leader*, winning three terms by successively wider margins. Before his gubernatorial campaigns, he had publicly served only as chairman of the Orford, New Hampshire (pop. 793), school board and was once defeated in a bid for election to the New Hampshire House. Another recent governor, John King, the only Democratic governor since 1945 (1962–68), was rather conservative by national standards.[48] As Veblen notes, when King was running for governor, he pledged to veto a sales tax, supported sweepstakes, opposed milk price controls, and supported a bill banning "communist speakers from state colleges."[49] One of King's campaign aides stated, in describing campaign strategy:

> the *Manchester Union Leader* is a major factor in New Hampshire politics. No other newspaper, or radio station, or anything else comes anywhere close to being as important as the *Union Leader*. I don't think anybody runs for statewide office without one eye on what Bill Loeb is going to do or what he's going to say; and they do this in a positive or negative way. And they try to avoid getting him attacking you. This has been the Governor's general strategy, to try to stay out of his way.[50]

As for the selection of gubernatorial candidates, the influence of the *Leader* has deterred some likely candidates from running. Others, who would be implausible candidates in any other state, make a "run" for Loeb's approval. The effect of the *Leader* is to shift the ideological continuum of the governorship of New Hampshire to the right. And since this is the *only* statewide public office, it makes sense for the *Leader* to focus its energies on that office. It exerts its influence on candidate selection in several ways.

First, the *Union Leader* reinforces a unique feature of New Hampshire gubernatorial politics, both Democratic and Republican – the remarkable success of insurgent candidates. The evident weakness of the political establishment is probably attributable to the *Leader's* ability to discover candidates who are virtually unknown to the establishment and promote them into viable, if not always successful, contenders. While it took two campaigns to promote Meldrim Thomson to the governorship, only one campaign was needed for Gordon Humphrey, the Republican candidate, to succeed Thomas McIntyre in the United States Senate. In effect, insurgency whipsaws both parties: in both parties, insurgents on the right spring from nowhere seeking Loeb's blessing, while insurgents on the left (and center) hope to ride an antiLoeb campaign to victory.

Second, the *Leader* affects the selection of key issues and the style of campaigns. In New Hampshire, gubernatorial campaigns usually revolve around taxes. But unlike other states where the urgency of the need for additional revenue and the most appropriate way to generate it are at issue, in New Hampshire the issue invariably revolves around a candidate's promise for suppressing new taxes. As the *Union Leader* put it in an editorial:

> Gov. Walter Peterson said yesterday that he 'will not propose' either a sales or personal income tax to the 1971 Legislature. He also told a State House press conference yesterday morning he 'will not advocate' either of these broad base taxes. However, the governor once again avoided saying he would veto either of the taxes if the Legislature should pass one.[51]

And, while Democratic Governor John King "took the veto pledge" in New Hampshire in 1966, a Republican, Richard Snelling, running for governor in Vermont, proposed a sales tax increase in part to alleviate rising local property taxes and to finance local educational expenditures.

The issue that is of greatest interest is the *Leader's* effect on individual voting behavior. Veblen's book is the most complete study of the subject. His conclusions concerning the role of the *Leader* for the period preceding 1968 are mixed. But for the years after 1968, his data show a strong correlation between the *Leader's* approval or disapproval and the vote obtained by candidates in the *Leader's* circulation area. This is especially true in primary and off-year gubernatorial elections, since primaries are not heated up by party competition, while gubernatorial elections do not involve major national issues. Among the six pre-1968 senatorial and gubernatorial primaries studied by Veblen, the average correlation between countywide *Leader* circulation and support for *Leader-backed* candidates was a positive .25. In the six post-1969 primaries, the correlation was a positive .56. The *Leader's* influence in general elections, both before and after 1968, was markedly less, according to the correlations reported by Veblen. Note that the circulation area for the *Union Leader* encompasses the largest "metro area" in New Hampshire – its home city as well as the large southeast New Hampshire towns.

Veblen's findings are not surprising; they imply that the influence of the *Leader* may well be incremental and growing stronger with time.

Constant repetition over three decades of a few central themes has its effect on the people. The gradual conversion of voters explains the *Leader's* greater success in the present than in the past. Foolish consistency may be the hobgoblin of small minds, as Emerson notes, but it may also be the means of great influence. However, the consistency of the *Leader* has had more profound effects than simple conversion. The longer certain themes are presented, and the less they change over time, the more likely the committed ideologue will queue up behind the *Leader* and look to it for guidance on appropriate political issues. In fact, the *Leader* prides itself on publishing more letters to the editor (amounting to several full pages in small type per week) and having more thematic partisans than any other newspaper in the country. The interaction of readers and the paper's influence is not accidental. Followership is generated by a system of rewards in printing letters and through editorial support. In his editorials, Loeb often refers approvingly (and sometimes disapprovingly) to letters he has received and prints and frequently builds editorials around readers' letters. This unusual interaction between a newspaper and its readers comes about when the newspaper has a consistent, simple, and longstanding political ideology.[52] There has been very little change in the editorial policy of the Loeb press over the last thirty years. A few catchwords summarize a very conservative, fiscally oriented political ideology. Unlike other newspapers, with frequent turnovers of editorial staff and consequent changes in political leanings, the editorial staff and sentiments of the *Leader* have been virtually unchanged over the last three decades.

What has developed is a responsive and ideologically sophisticated claque at the public, legislative, and executive levels. Familiar names appear continually in the letters to the editor. Favored bureaucrats are praised for their actions, while disliked ones are criticized. The process is reciprocal. There was a well-known group of legislators who espoused the *Leader's* line in their public pronouncements and speeches on the floor. In a sense they are *Leader* vigilantes, ever watchful for possible transgressions on taxing, spending, education, equal rights, and human rights. In turn, they regularly deliver the *Leader's* messages in floor speeches. House and Senate floor action, even over a few days, clearly showed the steady clarification, elaboration, and hardening of the line advocated by the *Leader* in the speeches of members. This consolidation of views had its parallel in the pages of the *Leader*. A reciprocal reinforcing process seemed to be at work. A common stand on current political issues was worked out in tandem – on the legislative floors and in the pages of the *Leader*.[53]

The *Manchester Union Leader* influences the New Hampshire political process in three ways. It affects leadership selection by supporting ideologically supportive insurgents and by substantially shifting the position of the average, and especially of the successful gubernatorial candidate, to the fiscal right. Second and third, through its single-minded and highly ideological style, it has generated public and legislative partisans who are highly sensitive to and willing to act in line with that ideology.[54]

Institutional Features

Particular institutional features of the New Hampshire and Vermont systems complicate the gubernatorial selection process. New Hampshire has only one statewide elected officer, the governor. All other officers, such as the treasurer, secretary of state, and attorney general, are either selected by the legislature alone or by the governor in concert with the Executive Council (a relic of colonial days) and/or the legislature. By contrast, Vermont separately elects six statewide officers – the governor, lieutenant governor, secretary of state, treasurer, attorney general, and auditor. In most states, the lesser elective offices form a sort of natural pathway to the governorship.[55] The typical state governor has been an attorney general, a lieutenant governor, or has been among legislative leaders. New Hampshire has no elective offices that could regularly serve as steppingstones to executive office. The attorney general, who holds a non-partisan post, is appointed for a four-year term that is longer than the governor's term, which means that his term overlaps that of the next governor. The secretary of state is appointed by the state legislature, which often chooses a senior legislator or party elder as a reward for past service. But the main point is that there are no intermediate offices, which are natural training grounds or provide a public platform for gubernatorial races.

The New Hampshire state legislature does not and, in the case of the lower house, cannot fill the gap. The lower house, because of its size (400 members) and low pay ($100 per annum), does not attract persons with long-term political ambitions.[56] Either they cannot afford a term in the legislature, or they are intimidated by the sheer size of the chamber. Consequently, the House consists of part-time legislators, women (averaging about 33%, the then-highest in the nation[57]), the retired, the elderly, or the wealthy. The unattractiveness of legislative service in New Hampshire is illustrated by the fact that only two of twenty-four members of the Senate are lawyers, and, according to one lawyer in the House, only three of his colleagues are practicing lawyers. That amounts to 8% and 1% for the Senate and House, respectively.[58]

These institutional features lead to an "off-the-wall" selection of primary candidates for the state's executive. For example, in 1976, the Democrats included: (1) Hugh Gallen, auto dealer, one-term former state legislator, and former state Democratic Party chairman; (2) Harry Spanos, lawyer and two-term former state senator; and (3) James Connor, ex-district attorney of Hillsborough County. Republicans included: (1) incumbent Meldrim Thomson, law book publisher, former member of the Orford School Board, and unsuccessful candidate for the state legislature; and (2) Gerald Zeiller, former state administrator in the New Hampshire welfare department.

The *Manchester Union Leader* clearly intensifies this situation through its influence on the primary process. If cultivating the Loeb press is the pathway to the governor's office, candidates are sure to exploit it. And the Loeb press, freed from the normal constraints of candidate progression and recruitment, exploits the situation for its own ends by promoting the lesser-known or unknown candidates who align with its political views for the governor's chair, as was the case of the Thomson candidacy.

The New Hampshire State Senate plays a peculiar role in the selection of gubernatorial candidates. It is widely recognized as the largest pool of potential candidates, but like the House, it too is saddled with low pay and therefore unattractive to many gubernatorial aspirants, as reflected in the occupational backgrounds of the senators. Unlike the Vermont Senate (30 strong with biennial compensation of $5,500), where college professors, lawyers, and farmers are the most widely represented occupations, the New Hampshire Senate largely consists of owners of trucking companies, insurance agents, and self-employed land and property investors in this order. All are occupations directly affected by state laws and regulations. Service in the Senate guarantees a direct hand in regulating one's own occupation. Although most people would agree with one senator who commented, "You're talking about twenty-four little governors, in effect," the political motives of senators are obviously mixed but appear to this observer to be keenly focused on state rules, regulations, and spending that directly or indirectly affect their income. But the Senate does remain a pathway to the governor's office in New Hampshire.

By contrast, Vermont has few of these peculiarities. With a 150-member House and a 30-member Senate, and with biennial pay scales of $5,500 plus expenses (in 1976; this equals $32,000 in 2024 dollars),[59] the legislature does *provide* candidates for the governor's chair. The independent election of five lower state officials also furnishes a pool of available candidates. In the 1976 gubernatorial election, the candidates in the two-party primaries were, for the Democrats: (1) Brian Burns, insurance agent, former multi-term state legislator, and then-lieutenant governor at the time of the primary; (2) Stella Hackel, former employment security commissioner and elected state treasurer at that time; and (3) Robert O'Brien, "gentleman" farmer and long-time state senator at the time of the primary. The Republicans were (1) Richard Snelling, a wealthy industrialist, multi-term state legislator, previous gubernatorial candidate, and majority leader of the House at the time; and (2) William Craig, former president of the Vermont State College system. Except for Craig, each candidate held elective office at the time of the election. Snelling, the eventual victor, by common agreement is the most experienced political leader in the state.

The role of the governors: In Vermont, the revenue and expenditure trends of Republican governors from 1955 to 1962 were accelerated by the administration of Philip Hoff. Hoff is as unique to Vermont as Meldrim Thomson is to New Hampshire politics. The first Democrat in modern times elected to the governor's chair, he surrounded himself with a young, aggressive, liberal set of associates who reinforced an already existing entrepreneurial administration. As Frank Bryan notes:

> ... his early and unequivocal support of Robert Kennedy in 1968, his connection with the Hyannisport syndrome generally, indicating that he might be up for a vice-presidential bid, his dealings with John Lindsay in New York and his treatment of the Humphrey forces in the state all served to set him apart from the typical American governor, and especially from the typical Vermont governor.[60]

His impact on Vermont politics was profound, probably as a result of his links to Democratic administrations in Washington. Vermont increased its reliance on Washington by a factor of two during the six Hoff years, increasing its per capita total federal aid from $80 in 1963 to over $160 in 1969. The comparable per capita figures for New Hampshire are $40 and $71, and for the median state, $46 and $90. The familiar pattern appears again. At the beginning of the sixties, Vermont's lead over New Hampshire had already asserted itself, and the gap widened during the Hoff administration. While the typical state increased its per capita federal aid by 95% between 1963 and 1969, Vermont's aid grew by 103%, while New Hampshire fell further behind, with an increase of only 77%. The atypical growth of federal aid to Vermont during this era is captured in a comparison of the fifty states' rates of absolute increase. While Alaska, at the top of the list, increased its aid by $169 per capita during these six years, Vermont was second with $83; New Hampshire ranked among the bottom ten.

The full measure of Hoff's extraordinary achievements becomes apparent if contrasted with the experience of John King, New Hampshire's Democratic governor who served during the same period. Hopes were high in New Hampshire as well but were frustrated by the strong influence of the *Leader*, which locked King into a narrow fiscal path. As a result, King was unable to attract bureaucratic entrepreneurs into his administration (which reinforces a previously discussed hypothesis). Thus, while partisan change occurred at the highest levels of the state's leadership, the middle and lower levels of the administration remained essentially unchanged. No new programs were developed because there were few new ideas as to how to secure funding. Thus, no new clientele groups emerged because no new administrators came to the state with new programs. As a result, even with a Democratic governor actively supported by the federal government under Kennedy and Johnson, New Hampshire fell farther behind in mean per capita federal aid.

The adaptation of Vermont's and New Hampshire's expenditures to changes in federal aid is easy to test. If my generalization is correct, Vermont should be more sensitive to aggregate measures of change in federal aid than New Hampshire. Statistically, the correlation between the first difference of Vermont spending by program and the first difference of the total *fifty-state federal aid* supporting that program should be higher than the comparable correlation in New Hampshire. In other words, as federal support changes, Vermont's expenditures are much more likely to change dollar for dollar than New Hampshire's, and the correlations ought to be higher for all programs. Because the plot of state and federal spending is sharply curvilinear over time, both the simple linear correlations and the correlations of the log-transformed data are included in Table 1, which shows the simple correlations for highway, agricultural, educational, and public welfare spending in the two states. The generalization is sustained in both linear and log estimates for all programs. Vermont is consistently more responsive to changes in federal aid than New Hampshire, especially in the large public welfare programs. There is no doubt that as the federal government changes, Vermont changes in turn. It would seem reasonable to attribute Vermont's growth to its entrepreneurial bureaucracy and the support of governors such as Hoff and his successor, Republican Deane Davis. However, the causal links may be circular. As the program becomes ever more dependent on federal aid, circumstances force the administrator to rely increasingly on existing or growing federal aid.[61] Clients depend upon services generated by present programs, which are substantially funded by federal aid, and the states, especially Vermont with its tax load, may be reluctant to expand the state share of the program funding. Vermont's programs are dependent on federal funding to ensure the continued fiscal well-being of Vermont state services.

Clientelism: The final factors in the model are the progressive reliance of both individuals and groups of citizens and their legislators on

TABLE 2.2 Correlations Between the First Differences of Total, Fifty-state, and Federal Aid and the First Differences of New Hampshire and Vermont Program Expenditures

	Linear Regressions		*Log-transformed Regressions*	
	VT	NH	VT	NH
Total highway spending	.31	.29	.99	.97
Total agriculture spending	.45	.17	.97	.88
Total education spending	.50	.43	.98	.97
Total Pub. welfare spending	.90	.69	.99	.97

rapid growth in funding. Citizen participation in the budgetary process is naturally constrained by factors common to all the states. The budget's complexity and arcane language impose a formidable barrier to informed and effective influence by citizens; its tortuous executive, legislative, and finally administrative implementation contribute to a general helplessness among the citizenry toward this most important legislative measure. Yet, while I have no conclusive evidence concerning the extent of public participation in the budgetary process, my interviews with legislators and administrators, as well as my observation of many appropriation committee sessions, lead me to conclude that New Hampshire and Vermont differ dramatically. Citizen and group involvement is substantially higher, more forceful, intense, and articulate in Vermont. Involvement seems to depend largely on the prior level of government activity and where budgetary volatility and benefit uncertainty during periods of economic downturn generate activism and where administrators profit from citizen stimulation.

Special educational programs are an interesting case of citizen participation. While citizens – usually the parents of the enrolled students – are active in both states, the intensity of their commitments to such programs and their personnel is extraordinarily strong in Vermont. Program administrators can and did rouse parents to instant action when budgetary problems appeared to threaten the program. The special education personnel apparently manufactured a demonstration of support for the program in 1976, largely to impress the Senate Appropriations Committee with the strength of its constituency's commitments.[62]

Legislators, in turn, are becoming increasingly aware of the effect spending and taxing programs may have on their own political futures. There is a subtle difference, though, between New Hampshire and Vermont legislators. Individual taxing and spending issues exist for those in Vermont, but not so much for the New Hampshire legislator. As the budget increases, constituencies take a greater interest in the future of funding, which in turn leads to legislative involvement in taxing and spending issues. Vermont legislators are, or perceive themselves to be, electorally shaped by program spending decisions and, therefore, appear to be less tax-averse.

Conclusion

When Frost wrote in his classic poem "New Hampshire,"

> Anything I can say about New Hampshire Will
> serve almost as well about Vermont,

little did he know what was to happen some thirty years later. But perhaps he was more prescient than it seems, for he closes the work with these lines:

> Well, if I have to choose one or the other,
> I choose to be a plain New Hampshire farmer With
> an income in cash of, say, a thousand (From, say, a
> publisher in New York City). It's restful to arrive
> at a decision,
> And restful just to think about New Hampshire. At
> present I am living in Vermont.[63]

I have traced out a theory of budgetary change using two states as the basis for generalization. Many of the generalizations are amenable to broader tests, while others are more idiosyncratic and limiting cases, such as the role of the *Union Leader*. Yet even the media variable points to the more fundamental kinds of organizational, media, and personal supports that draw out and reinforce political leadership in a state. My major point is to show that useful generalizations about the budgetary process can be drawn from the study of unusual and important emerging and changing budgetary differences between a few states.

For many states, such as Vermont, current policies were shaped decades ago with the adoption of state income and sales taxes. No one could possibly have imagined at that time that an era of prosperity, commencing in 1955, would literally pour money into the state treasury. By contrast, New Hampshire has opposing combinations of attributes, including the dominance of a vigorous, anti-tax, conservative newspaper; peculiarities of the gubernatorial candidate pool; and a narrow revenue base. The comparison of the two states reveals the need to see the spending pattern as the result of a historical process of genesis, development, maintenance, and change.

Considered in this fashion, the inherent political qualities of spending emerge as a series of choices – some purposeful and informed, others serendipitous or unknowing, but often-times dependent on revenue availability. Have I proved that taxes inexorably lead to expenditures, as well as vice versa? No, but my major purpose is to realign the academic interests of those studying public policy changes in the states so as to balance the interest in expenditures with an interest in tax and revenue change.

The opening and closing stanzas of Frost's "The Road Not Taken" capture this relationship between uncertainty, choice, and consequence in Vermont and New Hampshire fiscal politics:

> Two roads diverged in a yellow wood, And
> sorry I could not travel both And be one
> traveler, long I stood
> And looked down one as far as I could To
> where it bent in the undergrowth;
> I shall be telling this with a sigh
> Somewhere ages and ages hence: Two
> roads diverged in a wood, and I took the
> one less traveled by,
> And that has made all the difference.[64]

A counterfactual addendum on choice and consequence ... 1949 style

Political opportunities foregone quickly vanish from memory. Well, after the original version of this manuscript was published, I happened to chat with a former Republican gubernatorial candidate, John Pillsbury, who was also a former N.H. House member and former House speaker.[65] We chatted about politics in the Granite State, and I mentioned my research. He then relayed a New Hampshire taxing tale that I had never heard before. He commented, while chuckling, "Well, you should check out Sherman Adams' inaugural address, his tax proposals, and his first year as governor."

Pillsbury was correct. It is a story about the failed origins of legislation enacting broad-based taxes – plural on purpose – in a state where the Governor (Adams), the Speaker of the House (Richard Upton), the President of Senate (Perkins Bass), and the House and Senate chairs, vice-chairs, and members of both the Appropriations, Finance, and Ways and Means Committees – Republicans and Democrats alike – overwhelmingly favored the passage of one, or the other, or both a general sales tax and personal and corporate income taxes. According to Pillsbury, Senate President Perkins

Bass guaranteed that whatever the House sent over would get approved by the Senate. All the proposals failed in the House with the last alternative, for a 1% sales tax, failing by nine votes in a 400-member chamber.[66] It is, in a way, a counterfactual episode. After all, given the above conditions, what does it take to get a bill passed? It was the only time in modern New Hampshire history where all of the political stars were aligned to get a broad-based tax ... or two ... in place in the state.[67] If failing is the story here, how does this story square with what went before in this chapter?

The backstory: Adams was born in Vermont, and after briefly serving in the Marine Corps in World War I, he was a 1920 graduate of Dartmouth College.[68] Post-college, Adams first entered the timber business in Vermont and shortly thereafter moved to Lincoln. New Hampshire, abutting the White Mountain National Forest, and was active in the timber and lumber business and in local banking in the Lincoln-North Woodstock, NH area. He entered politics via the New Hampshire House in 1941 and was, for a short time, speaker of the House and then an elected Member of the U.S. Congress. He ran for and was elected Governor in 1948.[69]

Adams succeeded Charles Dale, a Portsmouth, NH lawyer who had served in the New Hampshire Senate, had been president of the Senate, and was, as well, elected to New Hampshire's Executive Council.[70] In 1944, Dale challenged the then-two-term Republican incumbent, Robert Blood, in the gubernatorial primary, won with 59% of the vote, and then was handily elected governor. He, in turn, was challenged in the 1946 Republican primary by then-New Hampshire Congressman Sherman Adams, and Dale won the primary by 185 votes out of 45,000 cast. Dale chose not to run in 1948, and Adams won the Republican primary with about 85% of the vote. There appeared to be few hard feelings between Dale and Adams, as Dale endorsed Adams and served in his campaign. In the December 1948 preparatory hearings for the 1949/1950 biennial budget hearings chaired by Dale, Adams noted his full cooperation with his successor, unlike the complete lack of cooperation Dale experienced in his 1944 succession with Robert Blood.[71]

Concurrently, in the Adams' 1948 elections, New Hampshire voters rejected three technical tax amendments to the state's Constitution. The most significant rejection vote was banning in the state's Constitution the concept of "graduated" taxes; not general or broad-based, simply the concept of tax gradations as for income graduations. The state capital's newspaper of record, *The Concord Monitor,* statehouse reporter, Allen Parker, wrote a several-times-a-week column, "Candid Politics," and in the November 6, 1948, post-election column, Parker notes that the 20th-century New Hampshire Republican party has been more liberal than the national party and noted the pivotal nature of the John Winant governorship.[72] Parker goes on to claim that while the electorate may have rejected the tax amendments, this does not conflict with a heightened "conception of public responsibilities" for the governor and legislature.

Importantly, Dale and Adams, facing a projected deficit of from 10% to 30% of the current state budget, appeared to take Parker's "Candid Politics" advice to heart. Dale, then still New Hampshire's governor, scheduled early December budget hearings with agency heads to discuss their priorities, tax constraints, and possible budgetary resolutions. It was clear at that time in 1948 that "unprecedented taxes" would likely be needed. In another unexpected move, incoming Governor Adams chose to join the budget hearings of his predecessor scheduled for December 6th to the 9th of 1948.[73] The evidence of the budget hearings made public the unusual cooperation between Adams and Dale. Adams took a particularly active role. Interestingly, two weeks before the hearings, the influential N.H. Farm Bureau came out with a resolution favoring a general sales tax. A week after the hearings, the also-influential farm membership organization, the Grange, came out in support of both an income and sales tax.[74]

The appearance of the before-and-after tax endorsements is consistent with the well-orchestrated spending and taxing observations of both Dale and Adams at the budget hearings. Adams, in particular, embraced the goals of greater efficiency and rooting out administrative waste, fraud, and abuse "through examinations and reappraisal of the expenditures of New Hampshire government," but he also noted the need for new taxes.[75] Meanwhile, in Parker's "Candid Politics" column, there was a drumbeat of analyses of poor spending comparisons between New Hampshire and sister states.[76]

The performative aspect of the hearings was widely perceived but puzzled over by the administrative agency officials involved. In an extended "Candid Politics" column, Parker notes the officials were "perplexed" by three questions that were posed by soon-to-be governor Adams to each of those testifying: (1) what spending changes could be involved in their agency? (2) what was the sum of taxes collected in New Hampshire? and (3) from whence do these taxes come?[77] What puzzled the agency officials pleading on behalf of their agencies was that only the first question was directly relevant to their knowledge and experience. On the other hand, looking back seventy-five years from my present perch, one could also conjecture that this was a fishing expedition by the incoming governor to gain agency officials' support for the substantial changes needed for publicizing the need for increasing taxation.

At the end of the Dale administration and at the outset of Adams', all agreed that a deficit of several million – in a 30 million dollar annual budget – would occur.[78] Dale, Adams, and the incoming legislative leadership agreed that new taxes were necessary. Right before Christmas, an interim tax commission appointed by Dale issued a report and concluded that a 1% sales tax combined with a 1% personal and corporate income tax should both be adopted during the next, 1949, legislative session. Two traits stood out in assessing Dale's tax proposals – traits that endured and became sticking points over the next six months of debate, deliberation, and action. First, the sales tax at 1% was levied on all purchased goods, including food and medicine. Second, the income tax was a flat tax, and as a "flat tax," its burden was regressive, falling most burdensome on the lower income classes. Further, even those falling below the taxable threshold would, nevertheless, be liable for a $5 filing fee. Thus, even if a worker was untaxed, to all intents and purposes, this income tax was also a poll tax levied on all wage earners – again a regressive levy.

By early January, the deficit estimates appear to equilibrate at about a $6 million figure. In mid-March, the conventional Concord wisdom was that a sales tax was unavoidable, and by late March, Adams had fully endorsed its passage. Meanwhile, the Democratic Party contingent in the legislature came out against such a levy.[79] The party division in 1949 was 254 Republicans and 145 Democrats, a not-quite 2/3rd majority Republican. By late April, doubts began to creep into both Adams' office and the legislative leadership regarding passing the sales tax. On April 23, Adams came out favoring a 2% income tax and dropping the sales tax, but for unknown reasons, three days later, he reaffirmed the two-tax strategy.[80] Adams' vacillation, vague signaling, and in-and-out-of-the-issue behavior characterized the next two months of crucial action – the Legislature adjourns and the fiscal year ends, in principle, on June 30. Meanwhile, the House Appropriations Committee, with only two dissenters, at least one of whom was a Republican, Dan Healy, had approved and reported out a budget bill with a built-in deficit of $6 million. David Barry, leader of the House Democrats and member of the Committee, voted in favor of the appropriation bill. Meanwhile, the well-respected chair of Appropriations, Bradley Atherton, came out in support of the sales tax as the solution to bridging the budget gap.[81] The budget bill passed the House in early June by a vote of 228 to 68, the losers made up of a mix of Republicans and Democrats. In the floor vote, House minority leader, Democrat David Barry, voted in favor of the spending bill.

Before the end of the fiscal year and the date of legislated adjournment, a sales tax bill was reported out on June 14 by the House Ways and Means Committee by a vote of 16 to 2. The sales tax bill was taken up by the House the next day after Speaker Richard Upton banned lobbyists from the House lobbies. That day, the House rejected the sales tax by a vote of 206-147. The Democrats in the House actively opposed the bill, including Minority Leader, David Barry, as did merchants from all over the state.[82]

By that time, the merchant and commercial community had organized to oppose the tax. Particularly active were merchants from the VT/NH border area from Claremont, Lebanon, and Keene, NH. Neither Vermont nor Maine at that point had a sales tax in place.

By late June, Adams had turned his support to a 1.5% income tax on persons and corporations. Barry, the Democratic leader and supporter of a budget bill with a $6 million budget deficit, came out against the income tax as well as having voted against the sales tax. On June 22, Speaker Upton brought up a proposed broad-based income tax and lost the vote 178-161.

Consequences followed: (1) After House members by vote asked the Senate Appropriations Committee to return the bill to the House for its reconsideration, the Senate rejected the vote and proceeded to report out a nearly balanced budget in large part by cutting school aid by 80%, returning aid to its WWII level, and thereby saving 2 million dollars, and tinkering with other spending line items. (2) In a retrospective after the Senate action, Senator Eugene Daniell asked on the Senate floor why the House failed to consider (a) a sales tax that excluded food and medicine, thereby obviating the two main voiced objections to the sales tax, and (b) reconsidering that sales tax combined with an income tax that dropped the $5 filing fee on all income earners, thereby mooting that prime objection to a personal income tax.[83] No one appeared to answer him, according to news reports.

Lessons Learned

There are traits of this counterfactual, "what if" addendum that conflict with or embellish the earlier 1950–1970 story above.

First of all, there is the matter of *reconsidering the effects of malapportionment,* especially as they relate to Vermont, about which I have changed my mind ... and perversely so. It is a case of malapportionment leading to a liberal, redistributive outcome. I lack at hand a good historical analysis of the passage of Vermont's 1931 income tax act; however, the conventional story is that the Great Vermont Flood of 1927 was the proximate cause for its passage.[84] Autumn rainfall totals for Vermont towns varied across the state, but many towns received two to three times the normal amounts. The most severely affected was the sparsely populated town of Somerset, which received nearly ten inches of rain in early November.[85] The net effect across the state was that 1285 bridges were destroyed, 84 people died, and state, county, and local roads were destroyed over a wide area. The 1931 income tax was passed in order to finance the costs of bonds to rebuild roads and bridges, restoring the "farm to market" road and highway map of Vermont. The bill was also passed, I surmise because each of Vermont's towns was represented by a House member. Burlington had one House member (population in 1930, 24,789), and Stratton had one House member with a population of 38. The Vermont House was malapportioned to vastly overrepresent the agricultural interests of the small towns, villages, and hamlets. An income tax bill would draw resources from the wealthy of Burlington and the manufacturing towns of St. Johnsbury, Springfield, Windsor, Bellows Falls, and Brattleboro and redirect them to assist the agricultural community ... a case of spatial, income, and economic sectoral public redistribution. It is a case of conventional, modern political liberalism: the poor *successfully* taxing the rich so as to redress grievances of the poor. It was redistribution from the wealthy to the large number of spatially distributed, not-wealthy, farm-based Vermonters.

I have also changed my mind regarding *institutional size and bill passage*. Large legislative chamber size – in this case, New Hampshire's 400-member House – hampers decisive outcomes. As I noted earlier, the sales tax lost in the New Hampshire House 208 to 147 (a total of 355 voters). The income tax vote lost in the House by 178 to 161 (a total of 339 voters). Had eight votes been changed or 18 new voters cast "aye," the outcome would have been reversed. The issue, in the latter income tax vote, is not just the closeness of the vote but also the total votes cast. The House consists of 400 members, but ten seats were vacant in June of 1949. Nevertheless, fifty members of the House were either present and not voting or not present at all in Concord, one-eighth of the House not voting. This is a failure of executive leadership and/or of legislative whipping operations. When is whipping likely to fail, and when will executive leadership be most crucial to winning or losing? As the numbers of legislators increase, it becomes more and more difficult to track votes and to enforce attendance, especially in what was then a legislature made up of many "amateur" politicians, many living far away and from places hard to get to, such as North Country towns and hamlets. Further, large numbers promote incentives to shirk, either because members believe that their "one" vote cannot affect the outcome; or that they believe that their absence will not be noticed; or that their absence simply reflects that the vote outcome is already "known" and that they would have voted in the majority had they been present, so why show up; or they just did not want to go on the record with their vote. But it's the jobs of the executive and the legislative leadership to turn these rationales on their heads and enforce discipline. The *size* variable interacts with an *amateur politician* variable in the N.H. House. Legislative pay is $100 per year. Biennial sessions run from January to June in year one and typically for a briefer session in year two. Legislators in the 1940s and on into the present day tend to be older, often retired, yet with many legislative veterans, but still they are amateurs in the sense of not being closely and *politically* beholden to their constituents. In 1948, legislators, on average, represented about 1300 people. Their home constituency support is likely to be as much personal as electoral/political. If personal, there is less likely to be electoral competition, and if little competition, then little interest in party fealty and cohesion. Legislative life among political amateurs is more fluid than contained; if fluid, then difficult to control and unpredictable, creating a not-easily-uncontrollable flow of votes on the floor.

Further Revisions

There are confounding, omitted variables in my analysis, namely that of *generational changes in governors, political expectations, and "timing."* Republican Sherman Adams of New Hampshire preceded Republican Deane Davis of Vermont by one generation, yet Adams was unable to obtain either one or both of a modest income tax and/or a modest sales tax in 1949, while Davis was able to pass a sizable sales tax in an already heavily taxed state. What's going on here? It turns out that the two of them had similar backgrounds – very successful businessmen, each was in finance, each was a previous office-holders, and both were well-regarded by each state's public. Yet Adams failed in each of a couple of modest "tax tests," while Davis proposed a 4% sales tax and succeeded in installing a 3% sales tax. Davis was widely credited for both proposing the new sales tax and also pushing it through the legislature to his desk, while Adams was criticized during the June 1949 battles as well as after the fact as being missing in action. In June, Adams was reported to have remarked that it was the legislature's duty now, "it's up to the legislature ...." He has done "all he could do," as if his job was complete.[86] On June 26, at the height of the tax battle in Concord, for reasons no one could quite figure out, Adams attacks state workers for not working hard enough.[87] After the fact, both Albert Baker of the *Monitor* and Eugene Daniell, a freshman senator from Franklin, N.H., questioned where the governor was during the tax battle. My surmise is that Adams was a classic New England Republican executive of his time: an ex-military officer where duties were laid out clearly, lines were drawn, and those involved were expected to do their duties.

There is a second omitted variable in this portrayal of Adams and Davis. Adams' two terms in office preceded the *massive increase in federal programs and aid* enacted during the Eisenhower/Kennedy/Johnson administrations. In my newspaper reviews of the Adams tax proposals and the subsequent legislative action, there was no mention of any implications of federal assistance or aid being jeopardized by the budget deficit or prospective cuts. Davis in Vermont, on the other hand, heir to Democrat Phil Hoff's 1963–1969 expansionary actions, inherited programs and federal aid commitments across the board. Davis faced pleas from program administrators, program beneficiaries, and legislator stakeholders to sustain the budgetary outlays. Further, given the analysis in subsequent chapters of the broad-based taxes among Republicans, a novel sales tax innovation may be their least worst preference.

Finally, Adams efforts may have been at the *tail end of broad-based tax innovations in the states* and well before a burst of tax activity in the 1950s to 1970s. States adopted a variety of taxing schemes during and after the Great Depression in the 1930s. Nearly half the states adopted a sales tax, and nineteen states adopted an income tax in the 1930s. In the 1940s, only the District of Columbia and Alaska adopted an income tax, and five states and the District adopted a sales tax, half adopted in 1947 and the other half in 1949.[88]

I conclude with two predictions – hunches, really – regarding the sales and income tax in New Hampshire. New Hampshire is one of five states without a sales tax. It is surrounded by Massachusetts with a sales tax of 6.25%, Vermont at 6%, and Maine with 5.5%. The tax-free benefits to the commercial and business community in New Hampshire are significant. No sales tax will be passed in my grandchildren's lifetime in New Hampshire absent a federal "value-added tax" with a "state add-on" provision. Further, if a broad-based tax is to be adopted by the state, it will be the income tax, but I am certain that that will not happen in my lifetime. It may not even happen in my children's lifetime … at present, their ages are 53 and 49.

Notes

1 This chapter originated in a 1980 article that appeared in the journal *Polity* [Vol. 12 (No. 4)]. That 23-page article was an abridgment of an original 69-page manuscript. The 69-page manuscript was fully printed in two nearly complete pages in the July 3 and July 10, 1980 Sunday editions of the *Rutland Daily Herald.* My appreciation to the publisher of the *Herald*, the late Robert W. Mitchell, who saw value in its public presentation. This version has been revised, and some new material has been added. Nothing that I have read or observed since 1980 vitiates the basic analysis here as represented in Figure 2.1 regarding causes of the emergence of the dramatic and continuing taxing and spending differences between New Hampshire and Vermont. Most of the original 1980 article is reproduced below with some revisions, updates, and elaborations, with an added counterfactual addendum.

2 For evidence of this divergence, see Figures 2.1–2.4.

3 Note that in the Caughey-Warshaw volume (2023), the authors compare the diverging public policy choices of Idaho and Vermont as almost limiting cases in public policy innovation and policy change in the American states.

4 For a review of our "understandings" from the period consistent with the timing of the original analysis of this study, see Richard Hofferbert, "State and Community Policy Studies: A Review of Comparative Input-Output Analysis," in James Robinson, ed., *Political Science Annual*, 1972 (Indianapolis: Bobbs-Merrill, 1972), pp. 3–72; and Herbert Jacob and Michael Lipsky, "Outputs, Structure and Power: An Assessment of Changes in the Study of State and Local Politics," *Journal of Politics* (1968), pp. 510–538.

5 The diversity and experimentation arguments are classic justifications of federalism; see the articles by Tiebout (1956) and Tulloch (1960). For the quasi-experimental methodology, see Donald Campbell and J. C. Stanley, "Experimental and QuasiExperimental Designs for Research on Teaching," in N. L. Gage, ed., *Handbook of Research on Teaching* (New York: Rand McNally, 1963).

6 Irrespective of the notion of "non-decision-making" above, decisions about taxing and spending in the two states do not satisfy the ordinary conditions for the "second face of power," per Bachrach and Baratz (1962). In the case of New Hampshire, political leaders and voters deliberatively chose not to act; see the addendum for a case study. On the other hand, it is not entirely clear what the "conditions" are that would satisfy an empirical search in the "Two Faces of Power." As Ray Wolfinger notes (1971), in order to ascertain that a "non-decision" occurred, a theory of decisions is required. Non-decisions occur when the "empirical theory of decision-making" predicts an occurrence and no decision is made. In our case, a theory of decisions is about when and where **not** to tax.

7 The literature as of 1980 on politics in New England is relevant, though not voluminous. Some of the early stirrings of political change in Vermont are reported in the basic regional politics text by Duane Lockard, *New England State Politics* (Princeton, NJ: Princeton University Press, I959). A collection of works on Vermont politics is Frank Bryan's *Yankee Politics in Rural Vermont* (Hanover, NH: University Press of New England, 1974). Some of the problems of modern Vermont state government were wonderfully analyzed in Frank Smallwood's *Free and Independent* (Brattleboro, VT: Stephen Greene Press, 1976). There are no comparable books on New Hampshire politics. A broader political analysis is Neal Peirce, 1976, *The New England States of America* (New York: Norton, 1976). Also, on New Hampshire and the effects of the *Manchester Union Leader*, see Veblen (1975).

8 See https://taxfoundation.org/2022-state-tax-data/.

9 Stephen Lile, "Family Tax Burden Differences Among the States," in *State Government* (Chicago: Council of State Governments, 1976), pp. 9–17.

10 See https://taxfoundation.org/publications/state-local-tax-burden-rankings/.

11 Federal aid differences were calculated by the author from the 1964 and 1974 editions of the *Compendium of State Government Finances* (Washington, DC: Department of Commerce).

12 More detailed and graphic evidence is presented in Richard Winters, "Legislators' Budgetary Attitudes and State Spending," mimeographed (Hanover, New Hampshire: Dartmouth College, 1977); and Colin and Rosemary Campbell, "A Comparative Study of the Fiscal Systems of New Hampshire and Vermont, 1940–1974," (Hampton, NH: Wheelabrator Foundation, Inc., 1976). The Campbells and I draw quite different inferences from the data.

13 This is a difficult point to document. Interviews with political leaders, legislators, and administrators in both states suggest that these images of national leadership – and followership – are appropriate self-images. The introductory comments in Michael Barone et al., *The Almanac of American Politics, 1976* (New York: Dutton, 1975), pp. 507–509 and 865–866, illustrate the point. An interesting example is Vermont's active program of support for the arts. It is one of the few states placing abstract sculptures at the rest stops on the interstate highways and carrying out the program with little debate and discussion. Compare this to the debate over the issue of modern sculptures at rest stops in Nebraska, as reported by the *New York Times*, 18 March 1975, p. 40.
14 See the complete analysis at https://cdn.freedominthe50states.org/download/2021/print-edition-2021.pdf.
15 Several of my Dartmouth College faculty colleagues chose to live in Vermont for flat-out political reasons. Another smaller group chose New Hampshire residencies for opposing reasons. Personal "nondecision-making:" Most of us simply chose to live close to campus, rationalizing our residential choices while enjoying "tax-free" living.
16 See https://www.fsp.org/move-to-nh.
17 The 2019 data was accessed here: https://www.taxpolicycenter.org/statistics/state-and-local-direct-general-expenditures-capita.
18 Data is from the REX-DAC time series data set.
19 I adopt "fiscal scale" as the term for the scope of government size per Alt and Lowry (1994). "Fiscal footprint" is my measure of overall government revenue burden.
20 A measure of general expenditure as a percent of statewide per capita results in similar findings.
21 The 1974 terminal figure here represents my findings for the original 1980 *Polity* article.
22 The ranks and the regression were calculated by using data from the Michigan State University public policy files on the American states. Bottoming out the 1974–1950 prediction of spending change are North Dakota (–2.38), Oklahoma (–2.07), Kansas (–2.05), Colorado (–1.77), and, close behind, New Hampshire (–1.75).
23 Again, to note: the U.S. REX-DAC highly disaggregated time-series ends here.
24 While I criticized the "composite" score-carding per Caughey & Warshaw, but as Ecclesiastises notes in Chapter 3, vs. 1:

> "To every thing there is a season, and a time to every purpose under the heaven."

25 I thank Chris Warshaw for sharing the Caughey-Warshaw policy data set.
26 Caughey and Warshaw (2022) also take note of Vermont's divergence in their data set with a close comparison between its and Idaho's path, see pp. 51–59.
27 Republican Scott publicly supported Kamala Harris in the 2024 presidential race.
28 Wikipedia entries for New Hampshire and Vermont House and Senate, accessed January 31, 2024.
29 Forty-eight state contexts for the first couple of decades of the time series.
30 Both structured and semi-structured interviews were carried out during 1975 and 1976 with members of the appropriations committees, legislative leaders, and a sampling of legislators in both chambers in both states. Interviews were also carried out with a sample of administrators.

31 I followed newspaper accounts over a period of years in the *Manchester Union Leader* (N.H.), the *Concord Monitor* (N.H.), and the *Rutland Herald* (Vt.).

32 Over fifty day-long observations of the operations of the appropriations committees and floor sessions in the states were carried out during 1975–1976.

33 A four-page questionnaire seeking opinions in 1975 on a variety of taxing and spending issues was returned by over 50% of the members of each of the chambers except for the New Hampshire Senate. A briefer 1976 version had similar return rates.

34 Aaron Wildavsky, "Political Implications of Budgetary Reform," *Public Administration Review* (Autumn 1961), p. 190.

35 via email communication, June 17, 2023.

36 For a delightful, ground-level view that supports Taylor's point of view (sort of), see this story about traversing the Appalachian Trail in the two states in 2024: https://www.washingtonpost.com/opinions/2024/10/11/new-hampshire-vermont-appalachian-trail/?utm_medium=email&utm_source=newsletter&wpisrc=nl_popns&utm_campaign=wp_opinions_pm.

37 Perversely, during the early decades of the period under study, Vermont, by several measures, had the worst apportioned lower house among the fifty state legislatures. Robert Dixon in *Democratic Representation* (New York: Oxford University Press, 1968), p. 625, claims that 11.9% of Vermont's population elected a majority of the lower house. The actual maximum and minimum figures were 35,531 voters and one legislator for Burlington and 38 voters and one legislator for Stratton. (These figures are from *Buckley* v. *Hoff,* 234 Fed. Supp., p. 194, D. Ct. 1964.) These malapportioned Vermont legislatures passed an early income tax in 1931, changed it to a graduated income tax in 1947, and increased the graduated or "progressive" quality of the tax three more times in the next ten years. Meanwhile, New Hampshire with a marginally fairer apportionment (see Dixon, p. 613) failed to pass any progressive tax levies during this period. This may simply demonstrate, as most of the cross-sectional studies do, that there were few predictable policy correlates of malapportionment. For a critical review of the literature, see William Bicker, 'The Effects of Malapportionment in the States-A Mistrial," in Nelson Polsby, ed., *Reapportionment in the 1970's* (Berkeley: University of California Press, 1971), pp. 151–200.

38 A sorely missing political science analysis is the history of and explanation of why, when, and under what conditions do legislatures reduce their size. Reducing a legislative chamber from 250 to 150 members suggests massive collegial defenestration. The reduction in House size was done *at the same time* as the House and Senate were reapportioned following Baker v. Carr.

39 Later in this chapter and in an addendum, I do conclude that the absolute sizes of the two states lower chambers did have an appreciable impact on tax policy – expansionary taxation in Vermont with its 246 members and a tax-aversive outcome in New Hampshire with its 400-member chamber. Two large chambers assumed opposing stances for plausible political reasons.

40 For the period 1948–1960, both states were more Republican than the nation: Vermont about 10–15 percent and New Hampshire about 5–10% more. In 1964, they supported Johnson more heavily than the national electorate. In subsequent elections into the 1970s, they reverted to an equal and about 5% more Republican presidential vote than the nation as a whole.

41 See my "Legislators' Budgetary Attitudes and State Spending" available from the author.

42 Two other general sets of budget questions failed to generate differences between the two sets of legislators. These were questions seeking attitudes toward specific

federal aid programs and questions about attitudes in general toward federal aid. Detailed analysis is in Winters, "Legislators' Budgetary Attitudes… ."

43 The most scholarly treatment is Eric Veblen, *The Manchester Union Leader in New Hampshire Elections* (Hanover, NH: University Press of New England, 1975); also see Kevin Cash, *Who the Hell is William Loeb* (Manchester, NH: Amoskeag Press, 1975).

44 In one of my soaking and poking forays, I experienced a bit of this. The *Rutland Herald* of March 12, 1976 carried the full story. An experienced Vermont State Senator, Robert Gannett of Brattleboro proposed a shift for funding part of special education support by the state. Gannett's proposed shift to already scheduled Federal funding was on a Wednesday of the legislative session. He immediately contacted Jean Garvin, director of special education for the state as well as Robert Whitney, Vermont's education commissioner. Both signed on to the proposed shift. On Thursday, Sister Janice Ryan, chairman of the interest group, "…the Vermont Committee for the Handicapped, held a press conference during which they released a statement threatening legal action if the state money was not allocated" (Rutland Herald, March 12, 1976). That day and Friday, Vermont Senators were inundated by telegram and telephone by "[F]rantic parents … saying they has been told their children would be cut from special education programs because of the Senate action…." This was not true, but the anecdote does suggest how program clients can be energized to defend their benefits and to target the relevant actors in Montpelier.

45 A different test of the elasticity hypothesis also yields the expected differences between the two states. The figures in the following table are coefficients of elasticity, defined as the increase in percent of total revenue of each state when total state personal income is increased by 1%.

Coefficients of Revenue Elasticity by Time Periods:

A 1% increase in total statewide personal income is associated with revenue changes in the following time periods:

Years	1945–1975	1945–1955	1955–1965	1965–1975
Vermont	1.5%	2.4%	2.2%	1.4%
New Hampshire	1.3	2.0	1.4	1.3

46 The relationship would be even stronger if I had used subclasses of taxes as the dependent variable. Because of the disparate quality of the two states' revenue systems, total tax collection are the only meaningful level of interstate comparison. Obviously, the difference in the revenue bases in the two states – an income and sales tax base in Vermont vs. a fragmented and selective tax system in New Hampshire – is the driving, exogenous variable in the model. I strongly resist the interpretation which would attribute a fundamental and enduring difference between the two states to the adoption of an income tax by Vermont and its absence in New Hampshire. Vermont legislators could hardly foresee when they adopted the income tax in 1931 the time when it would raise over one-third of the state's revenues. Further, the current place of the income tax driving spending in Vermont is the result of a series of incremental change in the tax that has enhanced its income elasticity. I suggest that it is preferable to treat the income tax, and the final adoption of the sales tax, as exogenous variables rather than as a dependent variable to be explained. The history of the income tax is discussed in Gillies, (1997) "History of the Vermont…."

47 The distinction is similar to Merton's distinction between "professional" and "local" and Gouldner's characterization of "cosmopolitan" and "local." See Robert Merton, *Social Theory and Social Structure* (Glencoe: Free Press, 1957), pp. 387–420; and Alvin Gouldner, "Cosmopolitans and Locals," *Administrative Science Quarterly* (1957), pp. 281–306.
48 Since Thomson, four of the nine governors elected since 1978 have been Democrats: Hugh Gallen, John Lynch, Jeanne Shaheen, and Maggie Hassan. Only Gallen indicated that he would not oppose enacting a broad-based sales or income tax. He was subsequently defeated in the 1982 election by John Sununu.
49 Veblen, *The Manchester Union Leader in New Hampshire Elections*, p. 60.
50 Veblen, *The Manchester Union Leader in New Hampshire Elections*, p. 60.
51 Veblen, *The Manchester Union Leader in New Hampshire Elections*, p. 102.
52 The most complete review of the ideology is contained in Kevin Cash, *Who the Hell is William Loeb?* Loeb also owned two newspapers in Vermont: the *St. Alban's Messenger,* with an estimated (unaudited) circulation of 3,000; and a weekly, the *Vermont Sunday News,* with an estimated circulation (unaudited) at its peak of 10–15,000. Once the Burlington *Free Press* and the Rutland and Montpelier *Herald-Times Argus* started Sunday editions, the circulation of Loeb's *Sunday News* went into steep decline. Thus, while Loeb did have a toehold in the Vermont press, the circulation figures did not compare with those of the *New Hampshire Sunday News* and the *Manchester Union-Leader* with over 60,000 each. Loeb's *Vermont Sunday News* stopped publication in the spring of 1976.
53 Rod Paul, a correspondent for the *Concord Monitor,* reports that, according to the telephone company records, Governor Meldrim Thomson frequently consults by phone with (I and Paul assume) William Loeb at the *Union Leader* headquarters and at Loeb's home in Pride's Crossing, Massachusetts. See Paul's article, *Concord Monitor*, 9 October 1974, p. 1.
54 The political leanings of the two major papers in Vermont have undergone the kinds of changes one would normally expect. As the state seemed to move in more progressive directions over the last thirty years, the *Burlington Free Press* and the *Rutland Herald* have moved along with it. The change was culminated a few years ago in the *Herald* with a shift to the left. It now is the leading paper in the state.
55 For the classic analysis of the backgrounds of governors and pathways to the governor's office, see Schlesinger (1957).
56 In a chamber of 400 members in a state as small as New Hampshire, peculiar coincidences arise. What other legislative chamber, in the case of the 1975–1976 session, can claim two brothers as legislators, or a father and son duo, and a mother and son pair
57 This is not quite the "sexist" statement it appears. By the mid-1970s, except for service in the House, women played a small part in New Hampshire politics. No woman has run for a statewide office with the exception of the widow of United State Senator Styles Bridges, who unsuccessfully sought the Republican nomination for her husband's Senate seat. The lack of statewide women leaders probably flows from the same set of causes outlined above: the lack of opportunity to progress naturally upwards in state politics. Compare this to Vermont which had the country's first elected woman lieutenant governor (Consuelo Northrop Bailey) and whose Democratic nominee for governor in the 1976 general election was the then-elected State Treasurer, Stella Hackel.
58 My 1975 survey found four lawyers, for a sample rate of about 1%, well below the percentage of lawyers in the typical state legislature; see Table 5.1 in W. J.

Keefe and Morris Ogul, *The American Legislative Process* (Englewood Cliffs, NJ: Prentice-Hall, 1973), p. 117.
59 The precise pay for Vermont Senators varies by the session. It is $811 per week as long as the legislature is in session and an added $134 per night for lodging during the session and a $69 per day for meals which yields about $1,400 per week which, in turn, yields about $30,000 for a typical twenty-two week biennial session.
60 Frank Bryan, *Yankee Politics in Rural Vermont* (Hanover, NH: University Press of New England, 1974), p. 114.
61 This is the kind of process described by Martha Derthick in *The Influence of Federal Grants* (Cambridge, MA: Harvard University Press, 1970).
62 *The Rutland Herald*, 12 March 1976.
63 Robert Frost, "New Hampshire" in Edward Connery Lathem, ed., *The Poetry of Robert Frost* (New York: Holt, Rinehart and Winston, 1969), pp. 164, 165, 172.
64 Lathem, *The Poetry of Robert Frost*, p. 105.
65 Pillsbury came from a prominent and well-known local New Hampshire family. The founder of the Pillsbury Company had its family origin in New Hampshire. John P. Pillsbury was a prominent politician and business executive in New Hampshire.
66 Actually 390 members, ten seats were vacant. But, as I note later fifty representatives, a seventh of the House, failed to vote or were not present for the vote on the last measure.
67 Post-the-Adams-administration, there were a few efforts to obtain a broad-based tax in the state, generally advanced by incumbent governors. The weakest was by Republican Walter Peterson who refused to say that he would veto such a tax. One such effort at reform with a New Hampshire income tax originated in the legislature in the 1980s, co-sponsored by Senator C. Robertson Trowbridge and Representative Jack Menge, was a fruitless endeavor facing the vigorous "ax the tax" message of then-Governor Meldrim Thomson.
68 Unlike the present, in the 1940s and 1950s when Adams was politically active in New Hampshire, graduation from Dartmouth was seen as a net electoral "positive."
69 https://en.wikipedia.org/wiki/Sherman_Adams.
70 The New Hampshire Executive Council is a unique state institution. Its roots can be traced back to the Royal Charter of King Charles II separating the state from Massachusetts. It has lasted through various iterations, e.g. a founding American state and its 1784 Constitution. It consists of five district-elected Members plus the governor. It is called into session by the governor and the majority assent of the Council is necessary for gubernatorial appointments and significant New Hampshire administrative contracts. It is, to coin a term, a "3.5th branch of government."
71 Concord Monitor, November 17, 1948, p. 12.
72 Winant served three, two-year terms as Governor of New Hampshire, the latter two terms from 1931 to 1935. During that period, he actively supported New Deal efforts in the state. In 1941, he was appointed Ambassador to the Court of St. James where he served until 1946. Winant's Wikipedia entry (at https://en.wikipedia.org/wiki/John_Gilbert_Winant) emphasizes his personal commitments to the positive role of government.
73 Concord Monitor, November 17, 1948, p. 12.
74 Concord Monitor, November 18, 1948, p. 22; December 13, p. 1.
75 Concord Monitor, December 7, 1948, p. 4.
76 For an example on education, see Concord Monitor, December 12, 1948, p.4.

77 Concord Monitor, November 18, 1948, p. 22; December 13, p. 1; and December 17, p. 4.
78 Concord Monitor, November 10, p. 4.
79 Concord Monitor, March 25, p. 1; March 28, p. 1; and March 19, p. 4.
80 Concord Monitor, April 23, p. 1; and April 26, p. 1.
81 Concord Monitor, May 2, p. 4.
82 Estimates of the number of Democrats supporting the bill ranged from 5 to 10 members, Concord Monitor, June 18, 1949.
83 Concord Monitor, June 29, p. 1.
84 Data and Information is drawn from https://en.wikipedia.org/wiki/Great_Vermont_Flood_of_1927.
85 In 1930 Somerset has a population of 20; in 1940 its population was 5 (https://en.wikipedia.org/wiki/Somerset,_Vermont). Its population has since varied in the single digits from 2 in 1980 and 1990 to 6 in 2020.
86 Concord Monitor, May 25, p. 1.
87 Concord Monitor, June 26, p. 1.
88 https://taxfoundation.org/data/all/state/when-did-your-state-adopt-its-sales-tax/; https://taxfoundation.org/data/all/state/when-did-your-state-adopt-its-income-tax/.

PART II

How party and ideology shape taxation

3

TAXING OR NOT-TAXING AS VARIABLES

Richard F. Winters

taxes, Taxes, TAXES ...

A *New Yorker* cartoon has two vultures perched on a desert cactus. One vulture remarks to the other, "Only two things are certain – death and food." This is a wonderful riff on Benjamin Franklin's aphorism directed to Revolutionary War Americans that "nothing can be said to be certain, except death and taxes."[1] And the classic explanation for the inevitability of taxation is the associated public goods benefits, as stated by Justice Oliver Wendell Holmes, "Taxes are what we pay for civilized society...."[2] By a "civilized society," Holmes implies a society with non-excludable, non-rivalrous, government-provided public goods such as national defense, law, order, justice, personal and public rights, and democratic order.

Why we tax: The many quotes on taxation in the Oxford Dictionary of Political Quotations[3] can be lumped into three categories of the "positives," the "negatives," and the "strategic behaviors of taxers." One suggestion in the last category and one that leapt out to me given the nature of this set of essays is Sir Robert Peel, who lamented that "[t]here are those who seem to have nothing else to do but to suggest modes of taxation to men in office." But is there any wonder that many would gather by the wayside advising governors and legislators as to how and who they should tax? Indeed, the tax advocates' rule of thumb is that if taxes are inevitable and government needs resources, how can we strategically generate taxes, per Jean-Baptiste Colbert, Minister to Louis VI, as "so plucking the goose as to obtain the largest possible amount of feathers with the smallest possible amount of hissing." I cannot, in good conscience, lay claim to any

DOI: 10.4324/9781003606291-6

strategic advice to those who tax; my claim is that I am interested in the determinants of increasing and/or decreasing taxing and some of those consequences. By laying out those paths, I may better inform those who wish to tax and those who wish not to tax.

Oliver Wendell Holmes put the positive case for taxing in straightforward terms: "I pay my tax bills more readily than any others – for whether the money is well or ill spent, I get civilized society for it." And Holmes would claim his choice would be liberty, as in the Montesquieu distinction: "In moderate states, there is a compensation for heavy taxes; it is liberty. In despotic states, there is an equivalent for liberty; it is the modest taxes." The lament in "moderate states" as to the increasingly heavy burden of taxation was echoed by the English physicist Michael Faraday when asked about the value of electricity: "Why sir, there is every possibility that you will soon be able to tax it."[4]

If, as Chief Justice John Marshall in *McCulloch v. Maryland* (1819) asserts, "The power to tax involves the power to destroy," then an obvious strategy is to avoid taxation, or, as the wildly successful heir to a hotel fortune, Leona Helmsley, was famed for noting (and famed only for this), "Only the little people pay taxes." Or, alternatively, David Lloyd George remarked, "Death is the most convenient time to tax rich people." But we now discover that even then it is not so easy to tax the dead.[5]

Edmund Burke observes that while "to tax and to please, no more than to love and to be wise, is not given to men," then strategically a taxer must calculate when and under what conditions she can tax. Obversely, it is far easier not to tax, but one must still behave strategically. There is no better example of Thomas Schelling's "commitment strategy" than George H. W. Bush literally tying his hands with the invocation of "Read my lips: no new taxes."[6] He, of course, broke his commitment two years later, and while he subsequently lost reelection, there is some question as to the impact of his broken commitment.[7]

Figure 3.1 lays out for this last sixty-year period taxes levied against U.S. citizens by the federal government and the state governments and their instrumentalities, our local town, city, district, and county governments, as well as the "all government totals" as expressed in billions of dollars. The figure portrayed at the top line is the total tax burden – federal, state, and local – stated as the amount all governments collected as a percentage of the gross domestic product. Below that are the two lines for total revenues collected by the federal government and those collected by state and local governments. I also include the "lowess smoothing routine" to indicate the "best guesstimate" of the ongoing path of revenues collected. The simple regression estimates for the

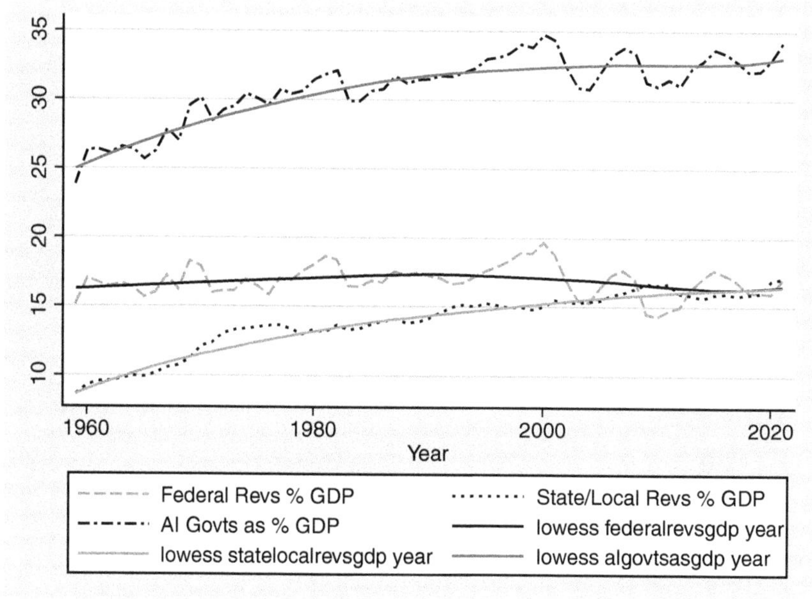

FIGURE 3.1 All Government, Federal, and State and Local Governments Revenues stated as Percent of national GDP, 1959–2021.

year-over-time suggest (indicated by the b = regression coefficient for "year") an ever-so-gently rising of total all-government revenues as a % of GNP, but falling federal revenues and increasing revenue collections for state and local governments. What is missing from the data about falling total and federal revenues is the debt financing by the federal government. Tax receipts may be slowly falling while federal spending may be increasing; the difference is deficit spending. What is, of course, striking about the graph is the convergence of federal revenue collections with those of state and local governments. When it comes to the burden of taxation on current American citizens – setting aside the burden on future citizens affected by federal borrowing – the current burden is just about evenly divided.

Figure 3.2 sets out some simple basics of government spending. The top line in blue beginning in 1958 is total federal spending, and the red line is total state and local spending. I have, however, added a second line. The green line at the 1958 mark represents federal spending *minus* defense spending, *minus* spending on international affairs, *minus* interest on the national debt, which results in a figure, which sums up to a *very rough estimate* of total *domestic* current federal, direct, programmatic spending –

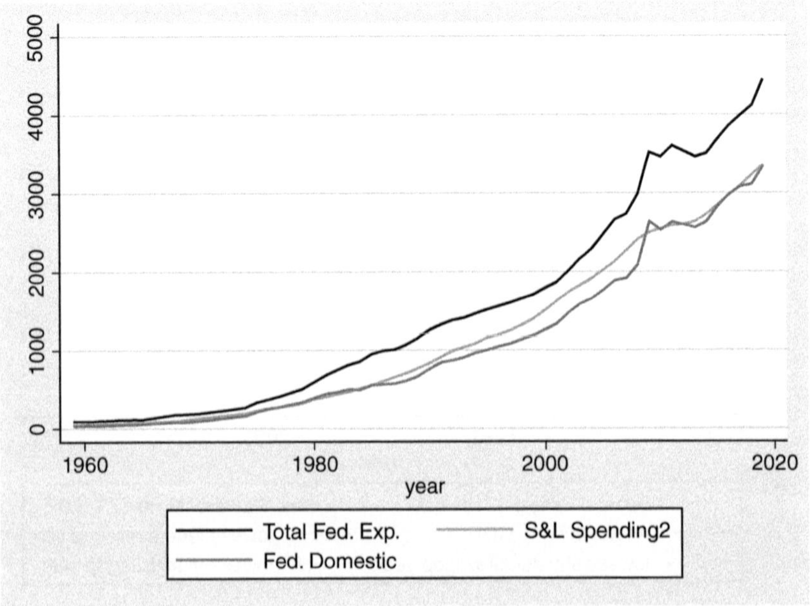

FIGURE 3.2 Total Federal, Total Federal "Domestic," and Total State and Local Spending.

a counterpart figure for state and local spending that is overwhelmingly domestic in nature.[8] By excluding federal defense, international affairs, and the costs of financing past spending, I have attempted a sort of "apples to apples" comparison by excluding from the federal figures spending on non-domestic collective goods that benefit us all.

Figure 3.2 compares total federal spending and total federal spending less defense, international affairs, and interest to yield an estimate of total federal "domestic spending" as compared with state and local spending, which is entirely "domestic." The focus on comparing the bottom two lines is a debatable one, but I want to point out how important state and local spending is to the ordinary day-to-day life of the American citizen. The beating heart of our political life, of conflict over who gets what, when, how, and who pays, is domestic politics, and that is importantly politics in the American states and their localities. The essays that follow explore various facets of the choices that we make at the state level, or the choices that are made for us by others, as to how to finance these important domestic governmental decisions.

Taxation in the American states

Each of us is aware, albeit with lesser-to-greater degrees of uncertainty,[9] of the raw dollar numbers of our state's taxes, fees, and charges; after all, each of us is subject to one, many, or all of them. A most convenient source for diving into the state-by-state particulars is the semi-annual publications of the National Association of State Budget Officers (hereafter NASBO). The spring issue of NASBO's *Fiscal Survey of the States* (FSS) records specifically what each of the governors of the fifty states requests in their annual budget messages to the legislatures for *proposed changes in taxes*, a state-by-state assessment of recommended statutory changes in rates, coverages, or extensions for eight classes of revenues, taxes, charges, and fees for that legislative year, plus the sum of all such recommended assessments. The fall issue of *Fiscal Survey of the* States displays the counterpart table of what the s*tate legislatures have, in fact, done to the governors' recommendations which she "signs on to."* Three traits make the spring and fall enumerated data sets particularly interesting: The revenue changes are arrayed into politically relevant categories of general sales, personal income, corporate income, cigarette/tobacco, motor fuel, alcohol taxes, other taxes, fees, and total, and the data are presented in terms of the nominal amounts of *new* dollars expected, given the statutory changes. Put simply, this array of tax and revenue changes represents the tax-related actions for that year's regular and special legislative sessions on new revenue dollars put into place.[10] It is the state-by-state politicians' plans for extracting greater – or, possibly, lesser – shares of income or wealth from their citizens so as to finance existing, new, or a stable, or shrinking arrays of public goods. Finally, NASBO divides in the spring and fall issues the data on what the governors request – the "ask" – and what is the final agreed-upon figure between the governor and legislature – the "get."

An example: In the Spring 2011 issue of *The Fiscal Survey of States* (hereafter FSS), for example, NASBO's Table 21 reports on the *Recommended Fiscal 2012 Revenue Actions by Type of Revenue and Net Increase or Decrease (Millions)* – reproduced below – where, for example, California's then-Governor, Democrat Jerry Brown, *recommended* \$4.549 billion in new sales taxes, \$3.595 billion in new personal income taxes, \$1.253 billion in corporate income increases, and \$1.382 billion in new fees and charges for a total of nearly \$11 billion in total revenue increases. In Table 21, figures for tax and revenue increases as recommended by the states' governors were reported for all fifty states (plus Puerto Rico). Half of the states reported no recommended increases, while Connecticut Governor Daniel Malloy recommended a total of \$1.924 billion in increases across each of the eight reported categories – the general sales tax, personal income, corporate income, cigarettes & tobacco, motor fuels, alcohol, other taxes, fees, and totals. Gubernatorially recommended taxes ranged from California's increase of $10.8 billion to the lows of a $695 million cut by Florida Governor Rick Scott and a $417 million cut in Ohio by Governor John Kasich.

The 2011 Fall issue of *The Fiscal Survey of States* (in NASBO's Table 20 below) reports on the finally *enacted* tax and revenue increases, those written into law by the legislature and agreed to by the governor. In California, there was *not* an $11 billion set of tax increases, but a cut of $38 million in personal income taxes. But Connecticut Governor Malloy got his increases in all eight revenue categories, but for $1.85 billion, a small cut from the $1.924 billion that he recommended. No increases were reported by nineteen states, down from the twenty-five states with gubernatorial recommendations. In 2012, the fifty state totals of *recommendations* summed to $13.33 billion in increases, while *enacted* taxes and revenues were down by a little over $1 billion. North Carolina saw especially large cuts of $1.45 billion enacted by a Republican House and Senate and signed into law by Democratic Governor Bev Perdue.

Twenty-nine states took some sort of final revenue action, ranging from Missouri's seemingly trivial and possibly fine-tuning $400,000 aggregate decrease in taxes, which was a compound of a $1.9 million decrease in the state's sales tax and a counterpart $1.5 million increase in fees, to California's nearly $1.2 billion total dollar increase that included a $2.5 billion decrease in the sales tax and a counterpart $2.5 billion increase in motor fuel taxes.[11] In all, as the lower right figure suggests, tax and revenue legislated changes in twenty-nine of the fifty states increased by $6.2 billion in 2011. The raw counts suggest that the states enacted 75 increases in various tax categories that year while putting into place 23 tax decreases. Note that these totals are derived from the 2011 array of fifty states by eight revenue classes for a total N of 400 possible "revenue change events."

Changes in "other taxes" were most frequently observed, as were changes in the personal income tax. Oddly enough, changes in the "sin taxes" of tobacco and alcohol were not that frequently observed. In the bottom row of panel (A), we note counterintuitively that the "number" of tax decreases exceeded increases in all three "broad-based" tax categories, with, for example, the number of income tax increases barely one-half that of income tax decreases.

Table 3.3 (A), (B), and (C) rearranges and summarizes this data array for the twenty-five-year period. For the set of eight revenue programs for the fifty states over the 1987–2011 period, there are 10,000 possible "revenue events" in a data array of "50-states-by-twenty-five-years-by-eight-revenue-sources." In 24% of these state-year-tax data points, some kind of change occurred, either a tax increase and/or decrease.[12] Note that there are many years in the states where some taxes were increased and others were

TABLE 3.1 Gubernatorial Tax Recommendations, 2012

State	*Sales*	*Person Income*	*Corp. Income*	*Cig/ Tobacco*	*Motor/ Fuel*	*Alcohol*	*Other Taxes*	*Fees*	*Total*
Alabama									0
Alaska									0
Arizona									0
Arkansas	–15.5								–15.5
California	4549	3595	1253					1328	10725
Colorado									0
Connecticut	464.3	877.8	36	54.3	51.6	9.2	409.9	21.3	1924.4
Delaware									0
Florida			–458.8					–235.7	–694.5
Georgia									0
Hawaii		50.2	21.3				23.4		94.9
Idaho									0
Illinois									0
Indiana									0
Iowa		–11.9	–136.2				190		41.9
Kansas									0
Kentucky									0
Louisiana									0

(*Continued*)

TABLE 3.1 (Continued)

State	*Sales*	*Person Income*	*Corp. Income*	*Cig/ Tobacco*	*Motor/ Fuel*	*Alcohol*	*Other Taxes*	*Fees*	*Total*
Maine	49.9	13.9	–25.1				19		57.7
Maryland	17.8					84.8	1.9		104.5
Massachusetts									0
Michigan		804.4	–1075				0	13.5	–257.1
Minnesota	15.4	1089.9	182.9				450.3	10.8	1749.3
Mississippi									0
Missouri									0
Montana			3.9				–1.5		2.4
Nebraska		–2							–2
Nevada									0
New Hampshire									0
New Jersey	–2.5	–23	–100.2				–73.5		–199.2
New Mexico									0
New York									0
North Carolina	826.6	–65	–115				–2		644.6
North Dakota		–25							–25
Ohio		–400					–17		–417
Oklahoma									0
Oregon							–78.4	27.9	–50.5

(*Continued*)

TABLE 3.1 (Continued)

State	*Sales*	*Person Income*	*Corp. Income*	*Cig/ Tobacco*	*Motor/ Fuel*	*Alcohol*	*Other Taxes*	*Fees*	*Total*
Pennsylvania							–66.6		–66.6
Rhode Island	164.9		–5.8				–0.7	4.9	163.3
South Carolina									0
South Dakota									0
Tennessee							100.4		100.4
Texas			–75						–75
Utah									0
Vermont								30.9	30.9
Virginia									0
Washington									0
West Virginia	–11								–11
Wisconsin		–36.8	–43.2						–80
Wyoming									0

TABLE 3.2 Gubernatorial Tax Recommendations, 2011

State	*Sales*	*Person Income*	*Corp. Income*	*Cig/ Tobacco*	*Motor/ Fuel*	*Alcohol*	*Other Taxes*	*Fees*	*Total*
Alabama									0
Alaska									0
Arizona									0
Arkansas	–28.6							4.6	–24
California	–38							–38	–38
Colorado									
Connecticut	326.9	875.1	39	50.5	8.7	9.8	521.8	19.9	1851.7
Delaware		–6.8					–19.1		–25.9
Florida	–25.5		–17.7				–1.6		–44.8
Georgia									0
Hawaii	50	45.3					60.6		155.9
Idaho									0
Illinois									0
Indiana			–2.9						–2.9
Iowa		–29.1	–5.6		2.5				–32.2
Kansas	8.8	–1.5	–5						2.3
Kentucky									0
Louisiana									0

(Continued)

TABLE 3.2 (Continued)

State	*Sales*	*Person Income*	*Corp. Income*	*Cig/ Tobacco*	*Motor/ Fuel*	*Alcohol*	*Other Taxes*	*Fees*	*Total*
Maine	–1.4	–36.4	–17.1						–54.9
Maryland	18.8	–7.5	–1.3			84.8	1.9	8.1	104.8
Massachusetts								45.9	45.9
Michigan		559.1	–1094.3				0	1.9	–533.3
Minnesota	2.2	–44.8	8.6				35.7	2.3	4
Mississippi									0
Missouri		–15	–24.3						–39.3
Montana							–1.3		–1.3
Nebraska		–2							–2
Nevada	1.1						158.8		159.9
New Hampshire									0
New Jersey		–23	–100				–62		–185
New Mexico									0
New York				3					3
North Carolina	–1061	–177	–26				–189		–1453
North Dakota		–60	–12.5				–4.5		–77

(Continued)

TABLE 3.2 (Continued)

State	*Sales*	*Person Income*	*Corp. Income*	*Cig/ Tobacco*	*Motor/ Fuel*	*Alcohol*	*Other Taxes*	*Fees*	*Total*
Ohio		–446							–446
Oklahoma									0
Oregon							–10.3	31.2	20.9
Pennsylvania							–66.6	-	–66.6
Rhode Island	17.2		0.8					3.7	21.7
South Carolina									0
South Dakota									0
Tennessee	4						101.8	1.8	107.6
Texas									0
Utah									0
Vermont			4.6					8.4	13
Virginia			7.4						7.4
Washington									0
West Virginia	–10.8		–5				–15		–30.8
Wisconsin		–16.1	–9.2						–25.3
Wyoming									0

TABLE 3.3 Exploratory Data of Tax Changes

Panel (A) The numbers of positive, negative, and no changes in taxes, 1987–2012:

	Sales	*Inc Tax*	*Corp Income*	*Cig/Tobacco*	*Motor/Fuel*	*Alcohol*	*Other Taxes*	*Fees*	*Total*
N of increases	189	162	171	193	106	41	238	255	1355
No Change	815	789	890	1051	1125	1195	800	965	7630
N of decreases	246	299	189	8	19	14	212	30	101
Inc/decr	0.77	0.54	0.90	32.17	5.58	2.93	1.12	8.50	1.34

Panel (B) The sum of amounts of tax increases and tax decreases, 1987–2012:

	Sales	*Inc. Tax*	*Corp Income*	*Cig/ Tobacco*	*Motor/Fuel*	*Alcohol*	*Other Taxes*	*Fees*	*Total*
pos. sum $s	35024.2	33848.7	12852.8	12280.9	8798.2	1025.5	14932.4	15067.1	133829.8
neg sum $s	−12906.9	−30201.9	−9043.6	−14.9	−547.1	−169.9	−13570.5	−1377.4	−67832.2
ratio abs +/-	2.71	1.17	1.42	824.22	16.08	6.04	1.10	10.94	1.97

(*Continued*)

TABLE 3.3 (Continued)

(C) Largest positive and negative changes in two leading taxes, 1987–2012:					
Positive Increases					
Year	*State*	*Sales Tax*	*Year*	*State*	*Income Tax*
2010	California	4411.0	2010	California	4261.0
1992	California	2538.0	2010	New York	4145.0
1995	Michigan	1629.3	2011	Illinois	2884.0
2007	New Jersey	1587.2	1992	California	1773.0
2004	Ohio	1309.1	1992	Pennsylvania	1506.0
Negative/Decreases					
Year	*State*		*Year*	*State*	*Income Tax*
1993	New Jersey	−608.0	2008	New York	−995.0
2007	New York	−632.0	1988	California	−1100.0
2001	Minnesota	−640.5	2007	Ohio	−1136.6
2012	California	−1061.0	1998	New York	−1658.0
2011	California	−2525.0	1997	New York	−1871.0

decreased. As panel (A) of Table 3.3 notes in the last column, across all states for all years, 1,355 tax increases surpassed the 1,014 tax decreases. Each column in panel (A) reports on the frequency of each tax change relative to 1250 possible "state-by-year-by-one-revenue-class" events.

Changes in "other taxes" were most frequently observed, as were changes in the personal income tax. Oddly enough, changes in the "sin taxes" on tobacco and alcohol were not that frequently observed. In the bottom row of panel (A), we note counterintuitively that the "number" of tax decreases exceeded increases in all three "broad-based" tax categories, with, for example, the number of income tax increases barely one-half that of income tax decreases.

Symbolism is partly at work here. Panel (B) of Table 3.3 gives the complementary nominal dollar values of these tax changes. No surprise, then, that the dollar figures show a quite different picture of tax changes. The sum of all tax increases over the states by years equals $133.8 billion, while the sum of tax decreases equals 67.8 billion dollars.[13] Not surprisingly, the simple sizes of these positive and negative changes are driven by state economic size and years.[14] While there were many more sales tax decreases than increases, dollar-denominated increases from the sales tax changes were almost triple the size of sales tax decreases. Again, the number of decreases outnumbered increases in the income tax by an almost two-to-one ratio; however, as panel (B) shows, the real dollar effects of income tax changes were almost evenly balanced, which implies that, on average, the dollar size of income tax increases was much greater than decreases.

In the revenue categories of cigarettes, tobacco, motor fuel, alcohol, and fees, the "Five Bs,"[15] truth flies from the numbers: the simple number of increases in these sin taxes, hidden taxes, and user charges outstripped decreases by anywhere from 32 to 1 (cigarettes/tobacco[16]) to 9 to 1 (fees), 5.5 to 1 (motor fuel) and to 3 to 1 (alcohol). These numbers obscure an even more striking disparity: the dollar ratios of tax increases to tax decreases in these sin/hidden/user revenue streams are, at the extreme, 824 times larger than dollar decreases for cigarette and tobacco revenues and 3 to 1 for alcohol. Both of these are classic sin taxes where the needs for revenue align with health concerns and are applied to "inelastic" taxes; an increase in alcohol taxes translates into an increase in retail liquor costs for consumers but with a small-to-negligible impact on changes in consumption. And, finally, as the lower right-hand cell of panel (B) notes, the sums of all dollar-denominated revenue increases were about twice the size of decreases over this twenty-five-year period.

Panel C of Table 3.3 presents the largest such tax changes occurring in the two largest taxes examined here, the "broad-based" taxes of the general sales and personal income taxes. California alone accounted for four of the 10 largest such increases and two of the 10 greatest decreases. Large increases and decreases appear for other large, wealthy states and for the most recent years, indicating the impact of state economic size, inflation, budget growth, and the fiscal impact of "The Great Recession of 2008-2011" on truly large statewide enactment of large revenue changes.

A note about the raw data for those whose interests are piqued by non-obvious "state rankings." Table 3.4, vertical panel (A), ranks the states by the simple number of all tax change events to the states' revenue codes recorded here. These vary elevenfold with Alabama, Alaska, and Mississippi having the fewest number of tax changes by class of tax at nine for the twenty-five-year period, with Minnesota, Connecticut, and Rhode Island topping the list ... or should that be "bottoming" the list ... with 109, 91, and 89, respectively.[17] There also appears to be no natural order to the rankings of the absolute value of tax changes in panel (B) over this time period, with the two largest states, New York and California, anchoring the ranks at the top and bottom. A simple regression of the values for the 2000 population and disposable personal income on each of these two

TABLE 3.4 State Rankings in the Number & Size of Legislated Tax Changes: 1987–2011

State	*Number of Tax Changes*	*State*	*Sum of Tax Changes*
Alabama	9.0	New York	-3747.3
Alaska	9.0	Michigan	-523.7
Mississippi	9.0	Minnesota	-364.3
South Dakota	16.0	Nebraska	-124.8
New Hampshire	20.0	North Dakota	-109.2
Arizona	21.0	Hawaii	-92.8
Nevada	25.0	Idaho	-79.3
Colorado	27.0	South Carolina	-53.8
Idaho	29.0	Ohio	-36.0
Georgia	30.0	Georgia	-19.4
Texas	32.0	Wisconsin	0.0
Oklahoma	34.0	Missouri	47.3
Tennessee	36.0	Utah	51.7
Delaware	37.0	Iowa	83.1
Iowa	37.0	Montana	106.7
South Carolina	37.0	Maine	112.2

(Continued)

TABLE 3.4 (Continued)

State	*Number of Tax Changes*	*State*	*Sum of Tax Changes*
Illinois	38.0	South Dakota	180.8
Utah	40.0	Wyoming	214.8
Indiana	41.0	Florida	232.4
Nebraska	41.0	Mississippi	264.2
North Dakota	41.0	Kansas	285.6
Wyoming	41.0	Alaska	286.2
New Mexico	43.0	Arkansas	290.7
Arkansas	44.0	West Virginia	294.4
Kentucky	44.0	Alabama	333.1
Montana	44.0	Vermont	352.3
Oregon	45.0	New Mexico	372.4
Virginia	45.0	Oklahoma	458.9
Louisiana	46.0	Delaware	518.2
Maine	46.0	Louisiana	552.2
Missouri	49.0	Colorado	553.3
Vermont	50.0	Virginia	600.6
Hawaii	51.0	Pennsylvania	696.3
Pennsylvania	51.0	Arizona	697.4
Michigan	52.0	Indiana	856.3
Kansas	53.0	Oregon	922.8
West Virginia	53.0	Rhode Island	928.2
Wisconsin	54.0	Kentucky	934.2
Massachusetts	55.0	Maryland	1057.3
New Jersey	56.0	North Carolina	1087.8
New York	56.0	Texas	1097.3
Maryland	57.0	New Hampshire	1212.9
Washington	57.0	Nevada	1457.3
California	61.0	Massachusetts	1759.7
Ohio	70.0	Washington	1980.1
North Carolina	80.0	Tennessee	2489.5
Florida	84.0	Connecticut	4437.3
Rhode Island	89.0	Illinois	5473.0
Connecticut	91.0	New Jersey	7068.1
Minnesota	109.0	California	19518.5

variables confirms, at best, a modest relationship between population and total statewide income and the sum of all new taxes paid[18]

Table 3.4 ranks the 50 American states by the number of their tax changes and the sum dollar totals of their changes over the 1987–2012 period.

Let me emphasize four more important traits of the NASBO data set. In the literature relating political variables to taxation in the American states, most analysts focus on tax sums or aggregates, that is to say, the amounts of general or specific taxes or general revenues *collected* by the states. None, to our knowledge, focuses on when and by how much the governor and legislative chambers request a change or actually change existing tax policy and by means of which tax or revenue class. For example, Dennis, Moore, and Somerville (2007) examine the impact of party control on the simple dollar distribution of the aggregate tax burden by income class. Dilger (1998) examines total dollar aggregates as "overall state taxes." Frederiksson, Wang, and Warren (2013) examine "changes in tax levels," which are determined by a mix of changes in the economy, personal incomes, changes in consumption of items/services taxed, and (possibly) changes in statutory enactments in the taxes that a state adopts. The latter, of course, is the proper object of political analysis attention, precisely that which we focus on here. Leigh (2008) examines "income tax receipts," again, a compound of many different causal influences. Finally, two of the most widely cited articles in political science and economics also use aggregate measures. Alt and Lowry (2000, 1050) examine "revenue change, ... the annual change in constant-dollar (1982–1984), per capita state general revenues from 1952 through 1995," and Poterba (1994b) focuses, as well, on dollar levels of taxation, expenditures, and deficits. It strikes me that political scientists ought to focus on what politicians authoritatively request or change by force of law, not on the aggregates that are shaped by a myriad of factors. The existing levels or amounts of taxes are a compound of many factors, political choices only being one of many. It is political choice that I examine here.

Second, when analysts do focus on changes in specific taxes, they typically examine "changes in rates" of the taxes. Taxes can be increased or decreased without rates being changed – that appears, in fact, to be the modal type of change – and the NASBO data captures the dollar amount of all change in taxes irrespective of the modalities of the changes. Obvious relevant examples of rate change analysis are Mikesell (1978), a replication by Nelson (2000), Kone and Winters (1993), and Chapter 9 in this volume, and as well, each looks at published sources that document changes in existing rates, usually of broad-based taxes such as the income and general sales taxes. By contrast, note an example of a data page that represents our dependent variables in Table 3.1, a reproduction from the 2011 *Fiscal Survey of the States*. The "sales" tax column appears to have thirteen changes in the tax. The change-by-change details are unpacked in Table A-3 of the publication (p. 76), and it notes that, in fact, there were nineteen discrete changes in the sales tax statutes that year, of which only four might plausibly be caught up as a "change of rates" via the *Book of the States* or by data from the Tax Administrators Association. Our data sweep up all changes in taxes by the class of tax, not just changes in the "rates" of the taxes.[19]

Third, both NASBO and I ignore (or avoid!) the property tax in the American system of state and local revenue politics. In 1956, property taxes accounted for about one-third of state and local revenues, 30% greater than the sales tax and 700% greater than the personal income tax. By 2017, state and local property taxes roughly equaled sales and personal income taxes in size, but the bulk of these taxes were locally assessed and collected. I suspect that NASBO, in its two publications, as I do here, ignores the property tax because it is difficult to assess the balance between the state-level tax and the local property taxes.

Fourth, one central concern of this book is the determination of the effects of party control and political liberalism/conservatism on tax policy changes as presented in Chapters 3, 4, 5, and 6. In those analyses we focus on the determinants of changes in different taxes – sales, income, corporate income, etc. What we *do not* analyze is "tax-swapping." Some sets of governors and legislators engage in reducing their favored tax collections while increasing taxes on their disfavored, e.g. decreasing the personal income tax while increasing the sales tax. We can hypothesize when this might occur … under unified party control and in politically liberal or conservative states, but we leave this analysis to others utilizing the NASBO data set.

The figures in Tables 3.3 and 3.4 raise further interesting questions and issues. First, there surely is a link, a correlation, between what a governor recommends and what is finally signed into law. The correlation between governors' "asks" and legislatures' "gets" ought to be positive across all categories, but not necessarily equally so. If unequal, what explanations seem plausible for the distributional array of coefficients? Second, there appears to be, even given the illustrations in Table 3.3 drawn from 2011 NASBO's FSS reports, some kind of a partisan effect at work here. The partisan effect set out below appears to me to satisfy the simple I.O.T. test.[20] Third, even with a modest number of eight different revenue categories, there must be a simpler way of arraying revenue increases and decreases that is statistically satisfactory but that also makes sense … even in the fashion of the simple-minded I.O.T. test.

TABLE 3.5 The Linkage, by Tax, between the Governors' "Asks" and Legislatures' "Gives."

(A) ALL years, all states; pooled correlations	
Enacted. Actions (N = 1299)	
Proposed sales tax changes:	0.32
Proposed income tax changes	0.16
Proposed corp. income tax changes:	0.32
Proposed tobacco tax changes	0.38
Proposed motor fuels tax changes	0.31
Proposed alcohol tax changes	0.23
Proposed other taxes tax changes	0.44
Proposed fee changes:	0.45
Proposed TOTAL tax changes	0.38

Table 3.5 arrays the correlations between all gubernatorial "asks" and all legislative "gets." Note that this conflates all partisan configurations into one table. I lump all governors and legislatures together – gubernatorial Democrats, Republicans, and Independents. All correlations are, as expected, positive, but the correlations range in size. The income tax coefficient is the lowest, suggesting that there may well be greater conflict between the "asker" and the "getter," e.g. a conflict between a tax-cutting Republican governor and a Democratic House and Senate. The correlations between ask and get are the two highest in the cases of "other taxes and charges" and "fees." I suspect that this reflects agreement on these more obscure and often minor charges as the simplest of all ways to balance budgets, especially so where the difference between needed revenues and required expenditures is small. "Other" and "fees" may simply act as bipartisan "band-aids."

The three leading coefficients – general sales, personal income, and corporate income – vary with "income tax asks" and what the legislature and governor finally decide upon in this tax class being the lowest. It likely reflects over this time period of the increasing partisan political conflict over the personal income tax. Comparatively so, the higher coefficients on sales and corporate income may reflect lessened conflict on raises or declines in these taxes, asks, gives. Note also that the correlation between the "totals" asked for and the "totals" enacted is quite modest. Again, I suspect partisan conflicts over taxation.

There is no surprise that all of the correlations are positive. Positivity reflects both demands and expectations. All governors with wildly varying specificities campaigned on the budgetary issues of taxing and spending.

Campaigns generate public commitments to deliver, and executives will spend "political capital"[21] to ensure that some or most of her promises are met. As well, however, governors forecast the tax raises/cuts that can be passed and therefore propose a revenue and tax program that will be met with some level of legislative approval. Sales tax proposals are met more favorably by the legislature than income tax proposals. Tax changes that appear to meet with higher general legislative approval are the "minor," non-obvious ones of "other," "user," and "fees." Nevertheless, overall there appear to be modest links between "asks" and "gets." Part of that will surely be clarified by a more partisan analysis. Partisanship reaches its limits in the states with the RRR and DDD configuration – united gubernatorial and legislative control by one of the parties.

TABLE 3.6 At the Limit, Linkages, by Tax, by Party of Governor, and Party in the Legislature

(A) Under United Republican Control	*(RRR = 1; N = 306)*
Enacted. Actions (N = 306)-->	
Proposed sales tax changes:	0.38
Proposed income tax changes	0.62
Proposed corp. income tax changes:	0.90
Proposed tobacco tax changes	0.26
Proposed motor fuels tax changes	0.09
Proposed alcohol tax changes	0.08
Proposed other taxes tax changes	0.39
Proposed fee changes:	0.63
Proposed TOTAL tax changes	0.42

(B) Under United Democratic Control	*(DDD = 1; N = 312)*
Enacted. Actions (N = 312)-->	
Proposed sales tax changes:	0.43
Proposed income tax changes	0.47
Proposed corp. income tax changes:	0.39
Proposed tobacco tax changes	0.71
Proposed motor fuels tax changes	0.27
Proposed alcohol tax changes	0.31
Proposed other taxes tax changes	0.53
Proposed fee changes:	0.49
Proposed TOTAL tax changes	0.67

Table 3.6 reflects the initial slice into partisanship and taxation, partisanship, and the linkages between asks and gives. I present only the coefficients when there is unified partisan control – when the governor and legislative houses are controlled by each of the two parties.

Vastly greater differences occur between the correlations of gubernatorial asks and legislative gets, both within each control and across the two conditions of unified control. Under unified Republican Party control, extraordinary agreement occurs between the legislative chambers and the governor with respect to the treatment of the corporation income tax and strong agreement regarding the personal income tax. No surprise here, as these two taxes have been targets of Republican action for several years. What is quite surprising are the small to near-zero coefficients between Republican "asks" and legislative "gets" in the more marginal tax categories of tobacco, fuels, and alcohol. When the Democrats fully control the state governments, all the coefficients are both positive and typically modest in size. Of the two sizable coefficients, that between the gubernatorial request and the final legislative action for total revenue requests is strikingly greater for the Democrats (+.67) as compared with the same coefficient under unified Republican control (+.42). This may simply indicate that the Republican legislative chambers, even with a Republican governor, may play a more active role in shaping tax policy as compared with the unified Democrats.

Third, what is the simplest way of capturing an *elementary* partisan effect? Table 3.7 arrays the increase in tax revenue changes recommended by Republican and Democratic governors as a percentage of that tax's previous size, as well as the partisan "difference" in "asks." Note that these are simply the proposed tax changes offered by the respective parties' governors. Confirming the obvious of the last half century, Republican governors are more penurious than their Democratic counterparts, but they vary in their asks across the eight revenue categories.

The expected partisan differences occur, especially so in the two income taxes, as well as in the sales tax "ask." The gross difference in the personal income tax "asks" almost equals a ½% difference. Republican governors, on average, request a cut of a quarter percent in the income tax, while Democratic governors ask for the near-obverse of a 0.19% increase. Similar negative vs. positive asks in the corporate income tax also appear, but of a smaller size. And, contrary to what might be expected, both sets of partisans request increases in the sales tax, especially Democratic governors. This flies in the face of, at least, my conventionally derived belief about Democratic governors likely

TABLE 3.7 Partisan Differences in Gubernatorial "Asks"

	Sales	*Inc Tax*	*Corp Income*	*Cig/ Tobacco*	*Motor/ Fuel*	*Alcohol*	*Other Taxes*	*Fees*	*Total*
A: If Governor is Republican (N = 683), her/his average proposed tax "asks" in % change are:	0.09	-0.24	-0.04	0.09	0.05	0.01	0.03	0.06.	0.04%
B: If Governor is Democrat (N = 616), her/his average proposed tax "asks" in % change are:	0.27	0.19	0.09	0.18	0.10	0.01	0.27	0.09	1.21%
C: Partisan difference in percent: between Democratic and Republican governors (= Dem - Rep)	0.18	0.43	0.13	0.09	0.05	0.01	0.24	0.03	1.17%

proposals, given the regressive quality of the sales tax and the putative representation of lower-income classes in the Democratic party coalition. On the other hand, there is, I suspect, among the broad voting public a simple rationale that might favor increasing the sales tax. Everyone consumes and thus is taxed, while everyone also benefits from the collective nature of government services provided. While it is the case that the tax is "regressive," the rich "consume" more than the poor and thus pay more in sales taxes; nevertheless, the sales tax for the poor accounts for a much larger share of their personal income. And while the rich may pay more in sales taxes as they consume more, as the rich get richer and richer, their sales-taxed consumption falls as a percentage of their income. Further, unless we unpacked the precise nature of the Democratic governors' proposals for increasing the "sales tax," we might discover that the bulk of the proposed Democratic changes *might* focus on changes in taxes on high-end luxury goods.[22]

The last column in the table notes the average sizes of the "asks" across the two sets of partisan governors. Note that this is the average of the averages, so it does not account for the size of the increases, where, for example, a 1% increase in the sales tax would be vastly larger than a 1% increase in the tobacco tax. Republican governors manage to scrape by with a small set of typical asks, while Democratic governors seem to shoot for the moon. Panel (C) of Table 3.7 sums the differences across the eight categories between Democratic gubernatorial "asks" from their Republican counterparts under the condition of unified partisan control. All the differences are positive, as the difference between the "totals" indicates – Democrats are, indeed, the taxing party in the American states.

We are still dealing with eight different and disparate revenue categories that range from income taxes to a variety of simple user fees. While the categories may be different and disparate, politicians, whether gubernatorial or legislative, may well treat them as more common categories. If that is the case, then there should be systematic correlations among the "asks" as well as the "gets." Table 3.8 and panels (A) and (B) display the simple correlations between the gubernatorial asks of the legislature (in (A)) and the enacted response (in (B)).

Table 3.8 indicates that the gubernatorial "asks" and legislative "gets" are correlated.

I have **bolded** all correlations greater than .10. Some commonalities do appear. Among proposals, increases (or decreases) in the personal and corporate income taxes are linked. More general consumption taxes – sales, cigarette and tobacco, motor fuel, and other taxes – also appear bunched together in gubernatorial presentations. Commodity and sin related taxes on tobacco, motor fuels, and alcohol appear to be linked. In the enacted figures, the two income taxes are strongly related, as are the minor consumption taxes. In pursuing commonalities of tax proposals and tax actions, a factor analysis was performed on the correlation matrix of Table 3.8, panels A and B, presented in Table 3.9, A and B.

Table 3.9 indicates that both "asks" and "gets" across the eight revenue categories tend to "hang together" into redistributional, user/fees/and consumption taxes.

In both gubernatorial proposals and in legislative actions, the personal and corporate income taxes are bound together. Note that this likely indicates that increases in the two taxes are bundled, but decreases are as well. They are perceived and acted on as if yoked. Second, factors in both "asks" and "gets" of "fees, charges, and others" are promoted or diminished in tandem. There are two wrinkles here. Changes in motor fuel taxes appear linked to changes in the sales tax in gubernatorial proposals, while

TABLE 3.8 Correlations among Categories of "Asks" and "Gets"

Panel (A) Correlation among the tax changes as proposed by the governor

	Sales	*Inc Tax*	*Corp Income*	*Cig/Tobacco*	*Motor/ Fuel*	*Alcohol*	*Other Taxes*	*Fees*
prop sales	1.0000							
prop inctax	−0.2214	1.0000						
prop corpinc	0.0494	**0.2508**	1.0000					
prop cigtob	**0.1260**	0.0242	0.0780	1.0000				
prop motofuel	**0.2504**	0.0189	0.0562	0.0192	1.0000			
prop alkie	0.0825	0.0257	0.0572	0.3084	0.0981	1.0000		
prop others	0.1327	0.0725	0.2358	0.3280	0.1349	0.2183	1.0000	
prop fees	0.0420	−0.0257	0.0633	**0.1085**	0.0702	0.0684	**0.1224**	1.000

Panel (B) Correlation among the tax changes as enacted by the legislature

	Sales	*Inc Tax*	*Corp Income*	*Cig/Tobacco*	*Motor/Fuel*	*Alcohol*	*Other Taxes*	*Fees*
enact sale	1.0000							
enact inctax	0.0743	1.0000						
enact corpinc	0.0229	**0.8132**	1.0000					
enact cigtob	0.0022	0.0223	0.0734	1.0000				
enact motof	0.0522	0.0543	0.0247	0.0103	1.0000			
enact alkie	0.0798	0.0246	0.0471	**0.3525**	**0.1123**	1.0000		
enact others	**0.1407**	0.0709	0.0555	0.0873	0.0667	**0.1569**	1.0000	
enact fees	0.0259	0.0323	0.0115	0.0848	0.0598	0.0729	0.0923	1.000

TABLE 3.9 Rotated Factor Analysis of "Asks" and "Gives"

(A) Governors Proposed Actions on Tax Changes; Highlighted Loadings in Bold The Rotated Factor Matrix:			
Variable	*Factor 1 User/Fees*	*Factor 2 Redistribiton*	*Factor 3 Consumption*
prop sales	0.1562	−0.1287	**0.4524**
prop inctax	0.0359	**0.4397**	-0.1809
prop corpinc	0.1616	**0.4188**	0.0764
prop cigtob	**0.5353**	0.0205	0.0510
prop motfuel	0.0885	0.0800	**0.3791**
prop alcohol	**0.4357**	0.0168	0.0647
prop others	**0.4648**	0.213	0.1737
prop fees	0.1766	0.0331	0.0988

(B) Legislative Actions on Tax Changes; Highlighted Loadings in Bold. The Rotated Factor Matrix:			
Variable	*Factor 1 Redistribution*	*Factor 2 User/Fees*	*Factor 3 Consumption*
enactsales	0.0295	-0.0949	**0.7962**
enactinctax	**0.9337**	-0.0028	-0.1010
enactcorpinc	**0.9301**	-0.0165	0.1040
enactcigtob	-0.0250	0.1013	**0.8096**
enactmotofuel	-0.0120	**0.6339**	-0.0954
enact alkie	-0.0340	**0.7116**	0.0661
enactothers	0.0876	**0.4793**	-0.0281
enactfees	0.0093	**0.4347**	0.0909

changes in sales taxes and cigarette and tobacco taxes march, positively or negatively, in tandem in the final revenue bill.[23]

Conclusions

We tax, as Holmes claims, to obtain a civilized society. A civilized society necessitates the provision of collective goods such as the policing of the society, judging, law and order, and other generally beneficial goods and services within and across the society. The implication of providing such goods is that all members of society benefit and none can be excluded. But if these goods are equally distributed and non-excludable, then why pay via taxes to provide them? Tax aversion is a rational response to financing collective goods; thus, the need for coercion. If all benefit, all must pay. To ensure all will pay, penalties are assessed for evasion.

The states have devised an array of taxes, fees, and charges to fine-tune assessments on citizens for providing collective goods. The array of revenue-raising choices provides politicians multiple opportunities to distribute the burdens of financing the states. Nevertheless, we believe and establish in this chapter that their choices can be presented in the most summary and convincing way as redistributive, consumption, and user & fees. Redistributive taxes are corporate and personal income taxes, and, in principle, their burdens fall on those best in a position to "pay." What is the logic of "position to pay?" Part of the "position" is that corporations and the wealthy have the ability to pay. Part of the logic is that the wealthy are usually in positions where their wealth is well recorded and documented and therefore accessible. And part is the biblical prescription "to whom much is given, much will be required" (Luke 14:28). Put differently, the wealthy are the best beneficiaries of the current scheme of law and order; a greater burden should be placed on those who are best benefitted.

There is a logic to consumption taxes such as the general sales tax. All consume, and all will bear the burden of financing the state. The wealthy consume more and will bear a heavier burden, but the not-wealthy will pay a greater share of their income via consumption taxes. There is an inherent logic to fees and charges as well. Gasoline and diesel fuel taxes are levied on those who drive a lot ... big "users." Auto and driver licenses tax those who use public roads, and so on.

It turns out that both in gubernatorial recommendations and in the legislative final enactments, the eight different revenue sources analyzed in future chapters do tend to cohere, more or less, according to the above schema. By combining the several taxes, fees, and charges analyzed in this volume in this threefold way, we are better able to assess both the political determinants of these forms of taxations and the politico-electoral consequences of changes in these taxes.

Notes

1 The complete quote from Franklin: "Our new Constitution is now established, and has an appearance that promises permanency; but in this world nothing can be said to be certain, except death and taxes." {https://constitutioncenter.org/blog/benjamin-franklins-last-great-quote-and-the-constitution].

2 The full quote in his dissenting opinion from the case of *Compania General de Tabacos de Filipinas v. Collector of Internal Revenue:* "It is true, as indicated in the last cited case, that every exaction of money for an act is a discouragement to the extent of the payment required, but that which in its immediacy is a discouragement may be part of an encouragement when seen in its organic connection with the whole. Taxes are what we pay for civilized society, including the chance to insure."

3 Robert Jay, ed. *Oxford Dictionary of Political Quotations* (New York: Oxford University Press, 2012).

4 Monthly assessed consumer electricity bills in Virginia and Massachusetts set out 9 and 8 tax charges, respectively, added on to homeowners' electricity bills. These taxes and charges are allowed by the state or directed to the company to be assessed by the state and are only the tip of the tax spear – hidden away are multiple state and local taxes assessed on the local facilities and operations of the electricity-providing companies.

5 See Michael Graetz and Ian Shapiro, Death by a Thousand Cuts: The Fight Over Taxing Inherited Wealth.

6 Proclaimed at the 1988 Republican National convention. For a discussion of commitment strategies, see Thomas Schelling, *The Strategy of Conflict* (Cambridge, MA: Harvard University Press, 1960), and his *Strategies of Commitment and Other Essays* (Harvard University Press, 2006).

7 For an interesting review of the politics of the pledge, see https://en.wikipedia.org/wiki/Read_my_lips:_no_new_taxes.

8 There is more than a bit of my "sleight of hand" here. The largest fraction, somewhere around 90%, of all defense spending is spent domestically. Thus, a federal "defense dollar" is seen by politicians as just as locally valuable as a "national park dollar" or an increasing "Federal welfare match."

9 As in Downs (1960).

10 We note that some of the enacted changes occur in years that some states' legislatures were not even in session. This happens because of the tax-smoothing nature of some legislative acts. A change may be adopted in year 1 of a session, and part of it is put into place in that year and the remaining in year 2, a year when the legislature may not even be in session.

11 Note that a "$1,900,000" decrease in Missouri's sales tax itself is a compound of changes in several different classes of the state's sales tax program. The NASBO reports detail each specific change in appendices to the semi-annual reports, but, of course and alas, we have no political theory that can encompass that level of detail.

12 The sheer number of tax changes is, of course, much larger. Many states will fine-tune their revenue bases by decreasing one part of a tax stream, say, the sales tax, while increasing, marginally, another part of the sales tax.

13 All NASBO tax data are in nominal dollars, as are all of our other monetary variables.

14 When examining revenue aggregates, change in total statewide aggregate nominal personal income will be one of our ordinary and usual "control variables."

15 State legislators in New Hampshire typically referred to these fees and charges as "the Five Bs," that is to say, taxes on "beer, booze, butts (cigarettes), beds & bellies (rooms and meals taxes)."

16 Note that the data employed in this analysis generally brackets the changes in cigarette taxation that followed from the Tobacco Settlement Agreement. For more sources on the settlement, see https://www.publichealthlawcenter.

org/topics/commercial-tobacco-control/commercial-tobacco-control-litigation/master-settlement-agreement.

17 This is a simple count by year using the "Table 1" data by year. It does not account for each and every change within a tax class. For example, when California "changes" its sales tax in a year, it may change dozens of classes of items within the broad class of "sales taxes," yet it is counted here as "one change."

18 Sum of N of tax changes = −189 + .036* PersIncinMillions$ – .0008* Annual Popul. (Adj R^2 = .39) (479) (.014) (.0004)
Sum of $ Tax Changes = 42.92* +.0002* PI Millions $s – .000005 Annual Pop. (Adj R^2 = .07) (3.95) (.0001) (.000004).

19 This raises an issue in the analysis of state tax policy change enactments that relate to "electoral timing." Politicians may be averse to "changes in rates" during an election year, but if faced with the need for revenue, they may enact non-rate changes that are not published in a table or text of a tabulation of "changes in tax *rates,* e.g. in the section on "trends in state taxation ..." in the chapter on "State Finances" in the *Book of the States.* Changing tax *rates* may be a much more difficult electoral task as compared with changing tax components.

20 I first heard of the "Inter-Ocular Traumatic test" (I.O.T. test) from Ray Wolfinger in the 1960s, which is to say, these partisan effects strike me, so to speak, as if a "blow between the eyes."

21 "Political capital" is a now-common politics term that gained prominence from our nation's chief executive in 2004; see https://www.theguardian.com/world/2004/nov/05/uselections2004.usa5.

22 This is, in fact, a doable project. In the Appendices to each issue of FSS, NASBO decomposes proposed changes into discrete or semi-discrete components.

23 The labels for the factors appear appropriate. These behavioral results mirror the results of a questionnaire that I distributed in the mid-1970s to legislators in New Hampshire and Vermont. When asked which revenue source they would choose in the face of a deficit, the legislators in both states cleaved neatly into those favoring the charges/user fees vs. changes in corporate and personal income taxes and those favoring increasing sales taxes ... in Vermont. New Hampshire has no sales tax. New Hampshire does have several business income taxes, but no direct, general personal income tax.

4

TAX POLICY CHANGES IN THE AMERICAN STATES

Carlisle Rainey, Kevin Stout and Richard F. Winters

Introduction

The zero, weak negative, or weak positive relationship between measures of political party control and measures of policy change is one of the puzzling findings of analyses of American state politics (e.g., Caughey, Warshaw, and Xu 2017). In spite of these results, political party control ought to have some predictable consequences for public policy across the states and across time, especially in Democratic and Republican responses to budgetary difficulties, such as an unexpected imbalance in revenues. After all, Republican and Democratic politicians campaign differently—Republicans on the basis of lower taxes and Democrats on the basis of greater services. If these campaign promises predict policy at all, then predictable changes in public policies should occur under Democratic leadership and different changes under Republican leadership (Alt and Lowry 1994). For example, income taxes might decrease when Republicans are in power, and Democrats will respond to budget shortfalls by increasing taxes, especially corporate and personal income taxes.

In this paper, we focus on the 1987–2011 period in the American states and examine the effects of several economic and political variables on changes in several classes of taxes. We develop several intuitions about when and how certain classes should change. Our empirical analysis is largely exploratory, and we identify several regularities in tax policy changes that demand further empirical and theoretical investigation.

Barrilleaux, Holbrook, and Langer (2002) note that a good portion of the literature on partisan control in the American states appears contradictory.

DOI: 10.4324/9781003606291-7

On the one hand, some research adopts the naïve view (e.g., Winters 1976b) that partisans have sincere preferences and, once elected, seek to implement policies upon which they campaigned. Other research, though, adopts the Downsian perspective (Downs 1957)—a more strategic view of politicians' behavior—where "parties formulate policies in order to win elections, rather than win elections in order to formulate policies" (1957, p. 28). As Barrilleaux and colleagues note, under some conditions partisan sincerity may well emerge, while under opposing conditions, the more strategic view likely dominates. Barrilleaux and colleagues examined the effects of the just-completed gubernatorial campaign and argued that as the incumbents' margins of victory increase, governors are more likely to engage in sincere programmatic behavior. We examine the institutional equivalent of this condition and argue that under unified party control, we expect greater sincere behavior from the two parties—more taxation and personal and corporate tax increases advocated and passed by Democrats and less taxation and cuts in the income tax by Republicans.

Our analysis can also respond to three other issues in the partisan control-policy change literature. First, most analysts focus on quite broad understandings of policy and policy change. Many of the analyses employ highly aggregated measures of public policy. Most recently, Caughey, Warshaw, and Xu (2017) rely on a time series of the summation of 150 different public policies over the 1936 to 2014 period.[1] Erikson, Wright, and McIver (1989, 1993) employ a similar composite measure of public policy liberalism in assessing the impacts of public partisanship and ideology.[2] These global views of the policy process are attractive summations of what, on balance, governments do state-by-state. However, an important focus of political science, if not the dominant focus, ought to be the explanation of changes in *particular*, deeply sanctioned public policies (e.g., Erikson 1971). We can think of no set of policies where the authoritative allocations of indulgences and deprivations are more keenly distributed and felt than in the dollar-by-dollar changes in taxes actually altered by state actions. In contrast to a broad view of policy, we focus on a *particular tax* being changed at a *particular moment* by *particular politicians* and by a *particular amount.*

Secondly, even when analysts focus on dollar measures of tax policy in the states, they typically examine summary dollar measures. Dennis, Moore, and Somerville (2007) examine the impact of party control on the dollar distribution of the aggregate tax burden by income class. Dilger (1998) examines total dollar aggregates as overall state taxes. Frederiksson, Wang, and Warren (2013) examine changes in tax levels, which are a mix of changes in the economy, personal incomes, changes in consumption of items/services taxed, and possibly changes in statutory enactments in the taxes that a state adopts. The latter, of course, is the proper object of political analysis attention, precisely that which we focus on here. Leigh (2008) examines income tax receipts, which, again, are a compound of many different causal influences. Finally, two widely cited articles in economics and political science also use aggregate measures. Alt and Lowry (2000, p. 1050) examine "revenue change, …the annual change in constant-dollar (1982–1984), per capita state general revenues from 1952 through 1995," and Poterba (1994b) focuses, as well, on dollar levels of taxation, expenditures, and deficits. A better, or at least a sharper, focus is on what politicians authoritatively change by force of law, not on the aggregates that are shaped by a myriad of factors. The existing levels, amounts, or changes in taxes collected are a compound of many factors, where political choices are only one of many. In our analysis, we focus on the actual dollar-by-dollar proposals by the states' governors as well as the final statutory actions of the governors and legislatures.

Finally, when analysts do focus on changes in specific taxes, they typically examine the changes in rates of the taxes. But taxes can be changed via several routes other than rate changes. For example, conditions or coverages of the tax category might change. In 2013, Governor Rick Scott of Florida proposed eliminating the sales tax on industrial equipment, reducing revenue by about $50 million; Governor Peter Shumlin of Vermont proposed exempting cloud computing from sales tax, reducing revenue by about $1.5 million; and Governor John Kasich of Ohio proposed greatly expanding the sales tax base, increasing revenue by about $1.9 billion. None of these cases involved a change in the tax *rate*. This appears from the year-by-year NASBO data to be the modal type of change, and the data that we employ captures the dollar amount of all change in taxes irrespective of the modalities of the changes. Mikesell (1978), replicated by Nelson (2000), looks at published sources that document changes in existing rates, usually of broad-based taxes such as the income and general sales taxes, and are typically derived from the *Book of the States*. However, the simple changes in the tax rates do not always capture changes in the amount of dollars collected. For example, the change-by-change details are unpacked in Table A-3 of the 2011 publication (p. 76), and, in fact, there were nineteen discrete statutory changes in sales taxes that year across the states. Only four of these changes might plausibly be caught up as a change of rates via the *Book of the States*. Our data sweeps up and aggregates all changes in taxes by the class of tax, not just changes in the tax rate. Changes in rates are certainly important, but the change in dollar-change in taxes remains the more politically relevant variable. In point of fact, it may be the case that elected political actors—executives and legislators—prefer *non-rate changes in tax laws* because these more subtle changes are less likely to gain public recognition (and eventual voter opprobrium) and thus more easily agreed upon. Mikesell's (1978) well-known linkage of gubernatorial tax-rate-change aversion and the timing of the election year may be better thought of as an aversion to changes in the tax *rates* in the year before the election, where rate changes will more likely catch the public eye and provide campaign fodder for an opponent.

The NASBO Data: Annually since 1986, the National Association of State Budget Officers (NASBO) has published a record of the tax policy change recommendations of the governors of the states in their budget and revenue messages to the states' legislators. In a like-and-later table, they also publish the legislated changes in taxes, a state-by-state assessment of the enacted statutory changes in rates, coverages, or extensions for eight classes of revenues, taxes, charges, and fees for that legislative year, and the sum of all such legislated assessments. Two traits make this data particularly interesting: as noted above, the revenue changes are arrayed into politically relevant categories (sales, income, corporate, cigarette and tobacco, fuel, alcohol taxes, other taxes, and fees), and they are presented in terms of the nominal amounts of *new* dollars expected, given the statutory changes. We have collected these data into a usable table. Figure 4.1 plots the total enacted changes for each year.

This figure plots the total enacted revenue changes in each state-year from 1987 to 2011. The year of the smallest and largest tax change is labeled on the plot.

Notice that there is a lot of variation to explain. Some states, such as Ohio and Florida, tend to change taxes quite often, while other states, such as Vermont and New Hampshire, change taxes less often. These data raise three interesting and important questions about tax policy changes:

- Under what political and economic conditions do states change particular tax policies?
- Under what political and economic conditions do governors propose changes to particular tax policies?
- What is the impact of the governor's proposal on the actual changes in particular tax policies?
- As part of our larger project, we are examining each of these three questions in detail. In this chapter, though, we examine the first question—the political and economic conditions under which states change particular tax policies.

Figure 4.2 plots the direction (i.e., increase, no change, decrease) of the tax changes in the forty-nine states (we exclude Nebraska from our analysis) across the twenty-five years from 1987 to 2011 for each of the eight tax

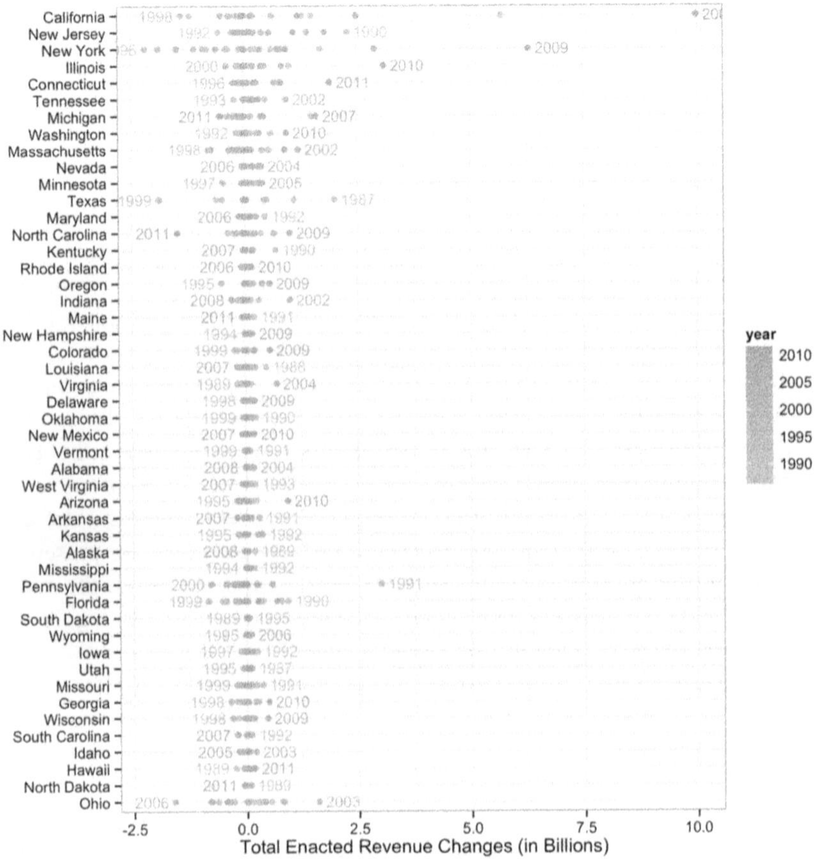

FIGURE 4.1 Tax Changes in State by Year.

classes and the total change. In sum, this presents 9,800 possible revenue changes—forty-nine states for twenty-five years in eight tax classes. The status quo prevailed in 71% (7,706) of these state-year-tax class observations, an increase occurred in 16% (1,780), and a decrease occurred in 12% (1,350).

This figure shows the distribution of the direction of enacted revenue changes across the eight tax categories and the total taxes.

But the distribution of the direction of changes varies across the categories. Figure 4.2 plots the distribution of the direction of the changes for each tax class. The total enacted revenue changed in 71% of the observations, with about 1.2 times more increases than decreases. Interestingly, sales taxes were 1.3 times more likely to be *decreased* than increased. Income taxes were 1.7 times more likely to be decreased. Corporate

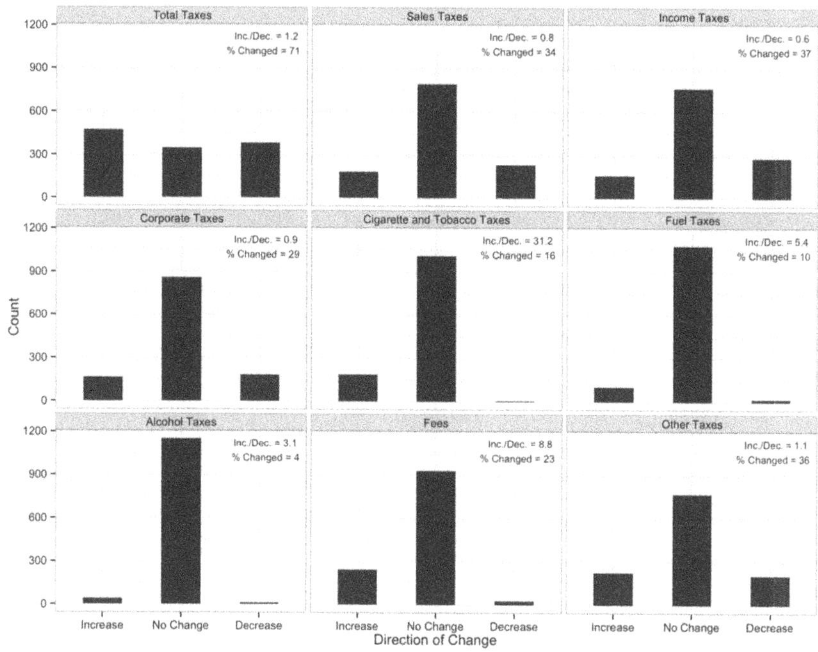

FIGURE 4.2 Direction of Enacted Revenue Changes.

taxes were slightly more likely to be decreased, and other taxes were slightly more likely to increase. However, states were much more likely to increase rather than decrease the remaining tax classes. Cigarette and tobacco taxes were 31.2 times more likely to be increased,[3] fuel taxes were 5.4 times more likely to be increased, alcohol taxes were 3.1 times more likely to be increased, and fees were 8.8 times more likely to be increased.

Incentives for changing taxes

John Mikesell (1978) begins his analysis of electoral cycles in taxation with observing the homily that "an old tax is a good tax" (as quoted in Goetz, 1977, p. 182). An old tax has three positive attributes: (1) it is an existing tax, and citizens have incorporated its burden into their personal income and outlay calculations; (2) voters accept existing taxes as the ordinary and usual charge for the current array of public goods and services that they know and may well appreciate; and (3) most taxes grow more or less as fast as statewide income (and sometimes faster) even with no legislative action at all. Thus, an old tax is a reliable source of revenue that normally keeps up, though often with lags and leads, with the political demand for spending that an existing budget requires for financing current services.

However, changes in existing taxes come about, and we argue that they do so at some political risk to elected leaders (Niemi, Stanley, and Vogel 1995, though see Kone and Winters 1993, and Chapter 9 in this volume). The greatest change, and therefore the most politically damaging, is the adoption of a brand-new and especially broad-based tax—a new income or general sales tax. In principle, tax changes are likely to be negatively assessed by voters, depending on their level of political information. While information in general may be costly, voters can rely on opposition party leaders to inform them of choices made by the party in power, and enacting a brand new tax, especially a broadly based one, or raising significant tax monies will catch the voters' attention. This would be especially telling if the opposition party was in control of none of the state's political institutions. That is to say, we expect policy sincerity under unified party control, but that is the condition that not only heightens the incentives for policy change but also heightens the telling effects on voters by opposition party appeals.

There is a counterpart positive attraction to voters for the policy benefit changes of the new-revenue-financed increased array of governmental goods and services. Changes in taxes might well accrue counterpart expenditure benefits. If so, then as Downs puts it, political leaders need to balance the risks and rewards of both tax and expenditure change: "expenditures with a higher vote-gain potential than the marginal one are included in the budget, which is financed by revenue collection methods with lower vote-loss potentials than the marginal one" (Downs 1960, 542).

Voters may weigh the increased tax costs variously relative to the expenditure gains, and different voter-types may weigh these gains and losses differently. Increases in the broad-based taxes, such as the personal income and the sales tax, might well be seen as the least popular of all tax changes—all are taxed, while government likely targets or selectively indulges constituencies via expenditure gains. That is to say, most if not all voters will be affected by an increase in these two broad-based taxes, but not all voters will gain from a new or enlarged set of governmental benefits. Sin taxes may be less aversive (tobacco and alcohol in this data set). Subjects of this tax choose to indulge with well-known and manifestly public costs (e.g., public health and drunk driving); thus, the rationale for an extraordinary tax burden on users. Fees and charges are typically assessed on those who also choose to gain from or indulge in some activity (e.g., highways, driving, and occupational licensing) and also with associated public costs (e.g., road maintenance, policing, and public health).

However, even in the absence of new actions by politicians to change the level of current services, if Baumol and Bowen (1965) are correct, financing even an unchanging array of governmental goods and services—the current services budget—may well come at ever-increasing costs and therefore the possible need for greater revenue; it is in the nature of government providing public goods.[4] Labor involved in providing government goods and services is not typically associated with significant gains in productivity. Nevertheless, government must compete with the private sector for workers; thus, their labor costs increase while productivity providing government goods and services remains roughly the same. The cost of government ineluctably rises even though there may be no changes in what governments do.

Further, government goods and services are characterized by the absence of a measurable output or product (Olson 1973, 362). The bulk of governmental goods and services typically provides public goods or goods and services with pronounced externalities, and:

> ...the very characteristics of a collective good that make it a kind from which nonpurchasers cannot be excluded, also make it a kind of which the output is not in the form of divisible units that can be readily counted.
>
> *(p. 362)*

If the output cannot be "counted," then productivity cannot be measured; and if productivity cannot be genuinely measured, then efficiency calculations are notoriously difficult to calculate, and absent such calculations, then cost-savings strategies are inherently unpersuasive to politicians and to voters.[5]

Thus, even in a state with a revenue system that has positive income elasticity, the state may require new or increased revenues simply in order to finance even the existing array of governmental goods and services, the current services budget. And, of course, financing new programs and services likely requires new sources or added sources of funds. But politicians face electoral constraints. Voters are thought to be notoriously averse to increased or new taxes. As Downs (1960) notes, every voter is in constant disequilibrium with government actions. Many governmental actions may well benefit every voter, e.g., law and order and public health, but government also accretes agencies, programs, goods, and services that largely benefit others, or at least so in the minds of most voters. As Downs notes:

> ...there is always some change in government policy that would benefit him. Furthermore, the government is always spending money on

> projects that he dislikes; hence his welfare would be improved if these projects were eliminated and his taxes reduced. *Therefore, every citizen believes that the actual government budget is too large in relation to the benefits he himself is deriving from it.*
>
> (1960, p. 550, italics in the original)

Strategic targeting of taxation by a partisan and ideological political coalition might attenuate these calculations by voters. Not all tax changes are created equally for the two parties' coalition. There should be some redistributive choices among taxes by the respective political parties: Taxes are inherently redistributive, and Democratic governors are likely to ask for personal and corporate income tax increases, and Republican governors ask for tax decreases and/or increases in consumption taxes. Under the condition of unified Democratic and Republican institutional control, we expect to see heightened effects of the partisan central tendencies.

The empirical approach

Rather than set up a structural statistical model based on strong and perhaps unreasonable assumptions about the conditional distribution of the outcome (i.e., normality) and the relationship among the explanatory variables and the conditional mean of the outcome (i.e., linearity), in this chapter we adopt a more flexible approach using Random Forests (Breiman 2001, Jones and Linder 2015). Especially with these data, we expect highly nonlinear and interactive relationships, such as a kink in the relationship between the estimated imbalance and the expected changes in tax policy. We also expect many interactions, such as Democratic and Republican politicians dealing with an estimated imbalance in different ways. Standard statistical methods require prespecifying a precise functional form that can capture these interactions and nonlinearity. However, rather than *prespecify* this functional form, our approach is to *estimate* it with a Random Forest. We expect a complex relationship between our explanatory variables and changes in tax policy. Random Forests allow us to capture that complexity.

This approach has two distinct advantages: First, using a highly flexible approach based on theoretical intuitions rather than a precise theory, we are free to *explore* the relationships in our rich data and discover substantively interesting and relevant regularities. We hope our work can then motivate scholars to investigate these regularities more carefully using detailed case studies, formal models, and clever research designs. We are not interested in testing specific hypotheses using a specific statistical model implied by a precise theory but in exploring the data using our theoretical intuition. In light of these goals, the flexibility of Random Forests offers an enormous benefit.

Second, these data have a highly unusual distribution. Figure 4.3 shows a scatterplot of the enacted revenue changes and the estimated imbalance. Notice that the outcome variable has an unusual distribution. There is an unusually large number of exact zeros. Also, there are a large number of highly deviant cases. This suggests that a standard parametric model (e.g., a normal-linear model or a linear random-effects model) might offer misleading inferences. Random Forests make no assumptions about the distribution of the outcome variable, so they offer an especially useful tool for these data. To aid interpretation, we standardize each of the enacted changes in revenue (in dollars) by the total taxes collected last year. This allows making the changes across large and small states comparable. Second, we scale the change by the standard deviation of changes in each tax class. This makes the changes comparable across tax classes.

This figure shows the relationship between the estimated imbalance and the standardized tax change. To aid interpretation, we standardize enacted revenue changes to have a mean of zero and a standard deviation of one.

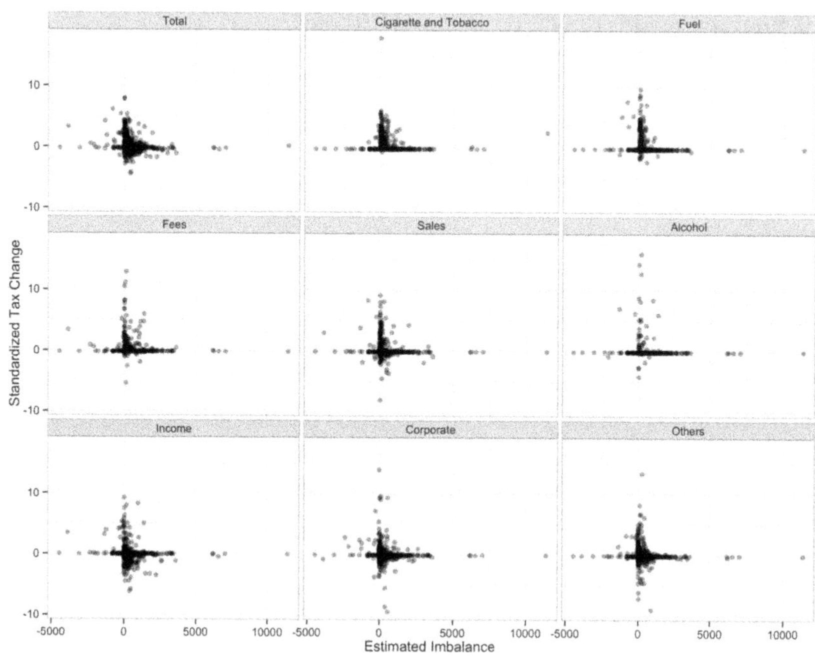

FIGURE 4.3 Standardized Enacted Revenue Changes by Estimated Imbalance and Citizen Ideology.

Notice the unusual distribution of the outcome variable—many zeros and many highly unusual changes (e.g., 10 standard deviations or more).

Explanatory variables

In our analysis, we include a range of explanatory variables intended to capture the political and economic context suggested by the previous literature. Note that all dollar values in this paper are in nominal values, normalized to have a reasonable scale (e.g., in billions of dollars).

1. the governor's partisanship (derived from Klarner 2013a);
2. whether there was a change in the governor's partisanship from the last year to the current year;
3. the Democrat's two-party seat-share in the state house (Klarner 2013b);
4. the change in the Democrat's two-party seat-share in the state house;
5. the Democrat's two-party seat-share in the state senate (Klarner 2013b);
6. the change in the Democrat's two-party seat-share in the state senate;
7. statewide citizen ideology (Berry et al. 1998);
8. total statewide personal income (Klarner 2013a);
9. percentage change in the total statewide personal income;
10. total statewide population (Klarner 2013a);
11. percentage change in total statewide population;
12. total state taxes in the previous fiscal year (NASBO, various volumes);
13. gubernatorial January budget balance estimate (NASBO, various volumes).

Random forests

Random Forests are simply a large collection of decision trees—conditional inference trees (Hothorn, Hornik, and Zeileis (2006), in our case—used to predict the enacted revenue change. This approach allows a variety of interactions and non-linearities to enter the model *without prespecification* (Biau, Devroye, and Lugosi 2008) and offers an effective method to assess variable importance (Strobl et al. 2007). Intuitively, Random Forests are simply a collection of decision trees that predict enacted revenue changes for each state-year. The forest contains many trees, and each tree is built as follows:

1. Select 63% of the cases from the data set without replacement to train the model. Set the remaining 37% of cases aside as a test set (for use when calculating variable importance, for example). Use training cases to build a decision tree to predict enacted revenue changes.

2 Select four predictors at random from the set of thirteen predictors mentioned above. From these four predictors, choose the variable and, if continuous, the split that best classifies the observations in the training data. Continue drawing four predictors at random and optimally partitioning the data using these predictors until the splits are no longer statistically significant.

There are two features of each tree that make it random. First, each tree is fit to a random 63% of the data. Second, at each node of the tree, only a subset of the explanatory variables are considered for the split. We consider four explanatory variables at each split. When repeated many times, the resulting trees can be combined into a forest. We used 2,500 trees in our forests. Predictions for a particular scenario are calculated by averaging across the predictions from each tree. We use the party package in R (Hothorn et al. 2006, Strobl et al. 2007, and Strobl et al. 2008) to build our forests.

Out-of-sample comparison to least squares

To further justify our approach, we randomly split the data into categories. We randomly placed 70% of the data into a training set and 30% of the data into a test set. We use the training set to (1) build a Random Forest and (2) estimate a least squares regression. We then use these models to predict the observations in the training set (i.e., in-sample prediction) and the test set (i.e., out-of-sample predictions). The results illustrate the inadequacy of the normal-linear model for these data.

This figure compares the observed revenue changes to the predictions from a Random Forest and least squares regression. The top row shows the predictions for the training set (i.e., in-sample prediction), and the bottom row shows the predictions for the test set (i.e., out-of-sample prediction). Notice that the predictions from the Random Forests follow the actual values noticeably better than the least squares estimates.

Figure 4.4 compares the predictions for the training and test sets using both a Random Forest and least squares. The Random Forest predictions map noticeably more closely to the actual values than the least squares predictions. This pattern holds in both the training and test sets.

To quantify the differences in explanatory power between the two models, we computed the mean squared error of the predictions in the test and training sets. Figure 4.5 shows the results. In both the training and test sets, the Random Forest reduces the mean squared error by about 25% compared to least squares. This evidence suggests non-linearity and/or interaction that least squares cannot capture, at least without a strong

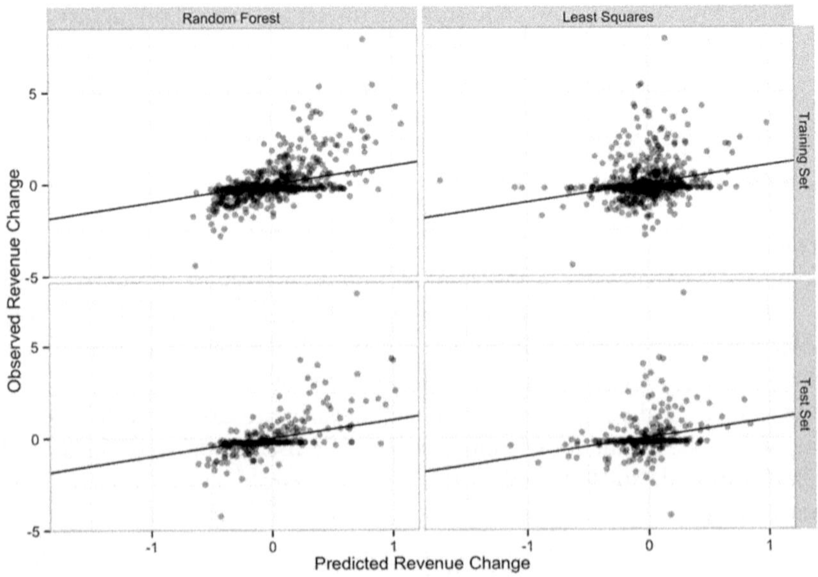

FIGURE 4.4 Comparing In-Sample and Out-of-Sample Predictions for Random Forest and Least Squares.

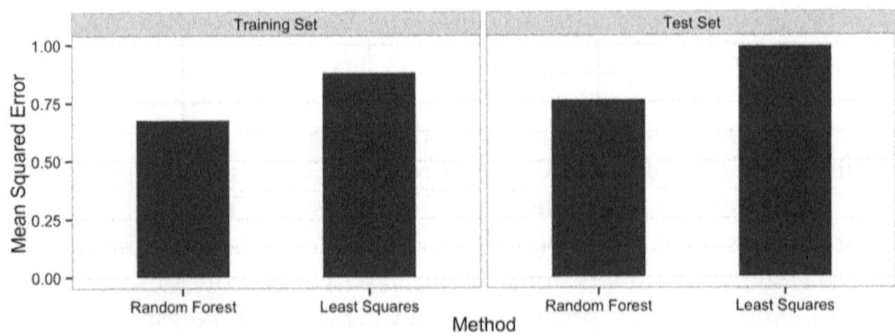

FIGURE 4.5 Comparing In-Sample and Out-of-Sample Performance for Random Forest and Least Squares.

theory allowing the researcher to pre-specify particular forms of each into the model.

This figures present the mean squared error for the predictions in both the training and test sets for both a Random Forest and least squares. Notice that the Random Forest produces considerably smaller errors than least squares in both the training and test sets.

Results—what variables matter most?

The first question we address is variable importance. Of the variables we consider, which are most important in predicting enacted revenue changes? We quantify "importance" in a specific way. If we permuted (i.e., randomly switched values) an explanatory variable and used those permuted values to predict the outcome, how much worse would the predictions be? In particular, we calculate the difference between the mean squared error (i.e., predictive power) of the model on the test set (i.e., the "out-of-bag" sample—the 27% of data set aside as a test set when building each tree) using the actual and permuted explanatory variables for each tree. We then average these differences in mean squared error across the forest to obtain an overall measure of importance.

Note that more positive values indicate greater importance, and negative values can occur by chance for unimportant variables. Note that this measure of importance reveals nothing about the *direction* of an effect, simply its importance as a predictor of changes in tax classes.

Figure 4.6 shows the importance of each explanatory variable. For the total taxes, the most important variable is the estimated imbalance in the budget. This is intuitive, since states should respond to budget surpluses and shortfalls with changes in tax policy. (Note though, that the measures of variable importance do not indicate the *direction* of the relationship between the explanatory variable and the outcome.) Perhaps surprisingly, given the literature suggesting that partisanship does *not* have a large effect, we find that the Democrats' share of the state house and senate is among the most important predictors in our model. Alt and Lowry (2000) "find *limited* but explicable party differences in state-level taxing and spending" (p. 811). Caughey, Warshaw, and Xu (2017) find that "legislative and gubernatorial elections have small but statistically significant impact on policy outcomes" (p. 30).

This figure shows the variable importance for each explanatory variable and each tax class. We standardized the outcome variables to have a standard deviation equal to one prior to the analysis.

While the results suggest that the party of the governor is relatively less important, these results suggest that party control might shape tax policy more than previously thought. However, note that the variable importance measure does not indicate the nature of the relationship between partisan control and the tax policy changes. It could be, for example, that partisanship matters because it conditions the effect of other variables (i.e., interaction), not because it has a large effect on its own.

Other relatively good predictors of total enacted changes in revenues are the percent change in personal income, taxes collected in the previous

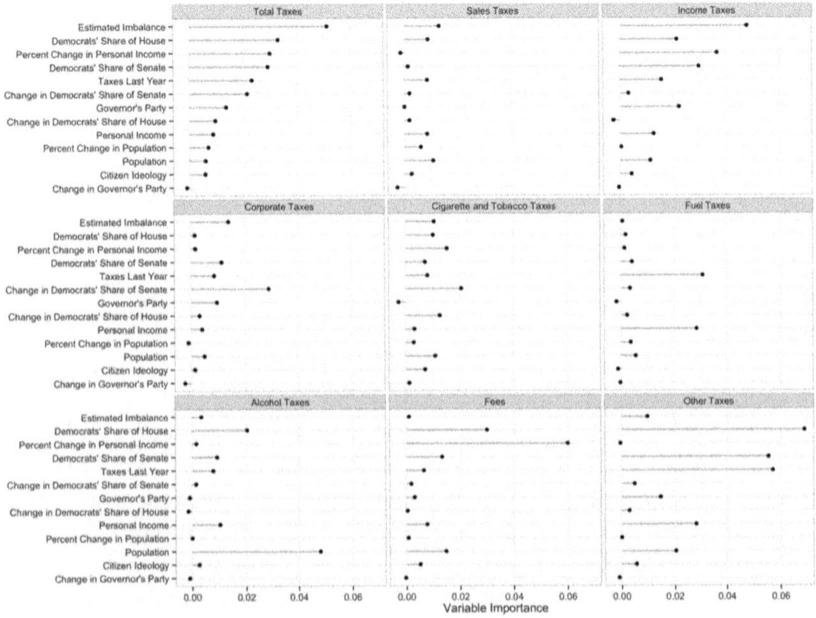

FIGURE 4.6 Variable Importance of Potential Explanatory Values Across the Nine Outcomes.

year, and the change in the Democrats' share of the state senate. Predictors that perform relatively less well include the governor's party, the change in the Democrats' share of the state house, the personal income, the percent change in the population, the population, the citizen ideology, and whether there was a change in the governor's party. The pattern of importance for sales taxes is quite different, and no variable we consider seems to exert much explanatory power. However, the pattern for income taxes closely mirrors the patterns for the total taxes.

Estimated imbalance[6]

We now turn to the relationship between the explanatory variables and the predicted changes in tax policy. However, while interpreting a single tree is straightforward, interpreting an entire forest of 2,500 trees is difficult. Jones and Linder recommend partial dependence plots, in which the researcher plots the prediction from the forest as the key explanatory variable varies from a high value to a low value, averaging across the other variables combinations of variables that occur in the data set. This is our basic approach, but we also include the predicted values for each combination of variables in the data set. Thus, for each value of the explanatory variable, we have many predictions—one prediction for each state-year-class. This additional information reveals the subtle nonlinearities and interactions that might go into the mean. In the plots below, the mean prediction for each value of the relevant explanatory variable is indicated by the heavy black line. The predictions for each observed combination of the other explanatory variables are indicated by the light line and shaded by the citizen ideology for that observation. Blue lines indicate liberal states, yellow lines indicate moderate states, and red lines indicate conservative states.

This figure shows the predicted tax change for each tax class as the estimated imbalance varies. Each colored line corresponds to a particular state-year. We fix the other explanatory variables to the values observed for that particular state-year and allow the estimated imbalance to vary from a high value to a low value. We repeat this for each state-year. The lines are colored by the ideology of the state's citizens. The heavy black line shows the mean prediction at each value of estimated imbalance. The first differences reported in the upper-right corner report the difference between the maximum average prediction and the minimum average prediction.

Figure 4.7 shows the predicted outcome for each state-year-class if we varied the estimated imbalance from the lowest observed value in the

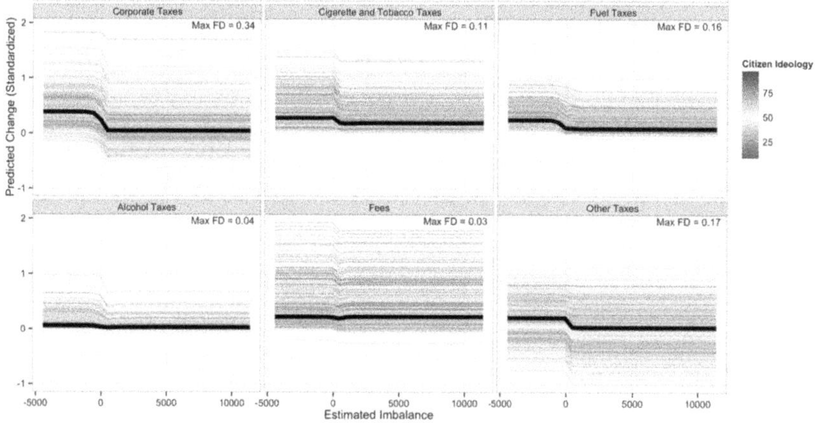

FIGURE 4.7 Predicting Changes in Taxes with Estimated Imbalances.

data set to the highest. These results point to an interesting, intuitive, and encouraging result. States respond to budget imbalances by changing tax policy. Conservative states are less likely to decrease taxes when facing a budget shortfall and more likely to decrease taxes when facing a budget surplus. Liberal states are always predicted to increase taxes, but even more so when facing a budget shortfall. Further, these effects are quite large. The enacted changes are standardized to have a standard deviation of one in each category. An average decrease of about one-half of a standard deviation is quite a large effect. Further, the effect of a budget imbalance is found across most tax classes and is particularly large for sales taxes, income taxes, and corporate income taxes—exactly where we would expect states to look for extra revenue.

Observation 1: Estimated imbalances in the budget have a large effect on a state's predicted tax policy changes. On average, states facing a budget shortfall increase taxes substantially. On average, states facing a budget surplus increase taxes only slightly. A similar pattern emerges for most tax classes, but most prominently for sales, income, and corporate taxes.

We investigate this further by plotting the predicted changes by the partisan control of each institution. Figure 4.8 groups the cases by control of

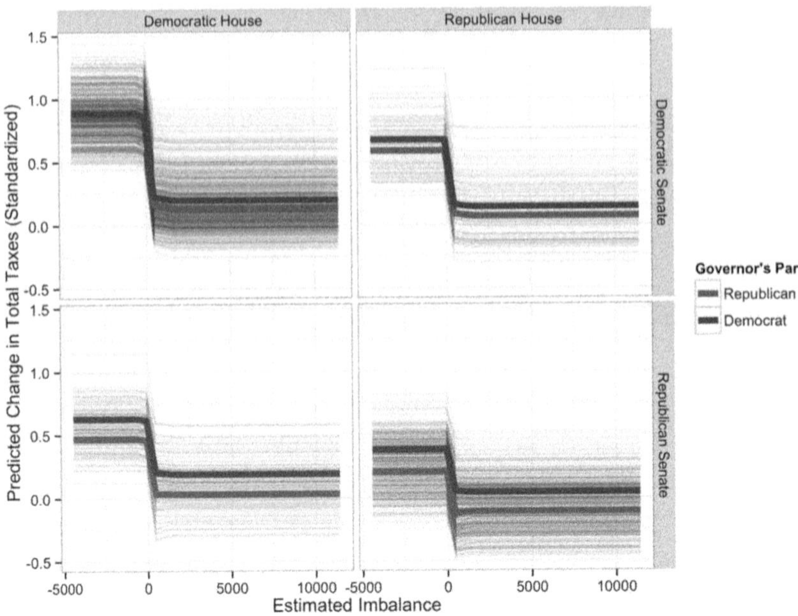

FIGURE 4.8 Partisan Control and Response to Imbalances with Total Taxes.

the house and senate in the columns and rows, respectively, with the color indicating the partisanship of the governor. Of particular interest here are the differences in the responses of a unified Democratic state government and a unified Republican state government.

This figure shows the predicted tax change for total taxes as the estimated imbalance varies by party control of the house, senate, and governor. Each light line corresponds to a particular state-year. We fix the other explanatory variables to the values observed for that particular state-year and allow the estimated imbalance to vary from a high value to a low value. We repeat this for each state-year. The left-hand column contains those observations with a Democrat-controlled house, and the right-hand column contains those observations with a Republican-controlled house. The top row contains those observations with a Democrat-controlled senate, and the bottom row contains those observations with a Republican-controlled senate. The heavy red and blue lines indicate the average across the predictions for Democratic and Republican governors, respectively.

The predictions for a unified Democratic state government are given by the blue line in the upper-left panel. The predictions for a unified Republican government are given by the red line in the lower-right panel. Notice that when facing a budget shortfall, the model predicts that Democratic governments respond with about a 0.9 standard deviation increase in the total taxes. When facing a surplus, the model still predicts that Democratic governments will respond with an increase, but smaller—about 0.2 standard deviations. On the other hand, the model predicts that unified Republicans will respond to a shortfall with about a 0.2 standard deviation increase in total taxes and respond to a surplus with about a 0.1 standard deviation *decrease* in total taxes. That is, the model predicts that Democratic governments will increase taxes, regardless of the direction of the imbalance, but the direction of the imbalance has a large effect on the magnitude of the increase. The model predicts that Republicans, on the other hand, will increase taxes slightly when facing a shortfall and decrease taxes slightly when facing a surplus. Figure 4.9, Figure 4.10, and Figure 4.11 reproduce this figure for the sales, income, and corporate taxes. They show that much of the difference in overall response is due to differential action on income taxes—little difference emerges between the parties in adjustment of sales and corporate taxes in response to imbalances.

This figure shows the predicted tax change for sales taxes as the estimated imbalance varies by party control of the house, senate, and governor. Each light line corresponds to a particular state-year. We fix the other explanatory variables to the values observed for that particular state-year and allow the estimated imbalance to vary from a high value to a low value. We repeat this for each state-year. The left-hand column

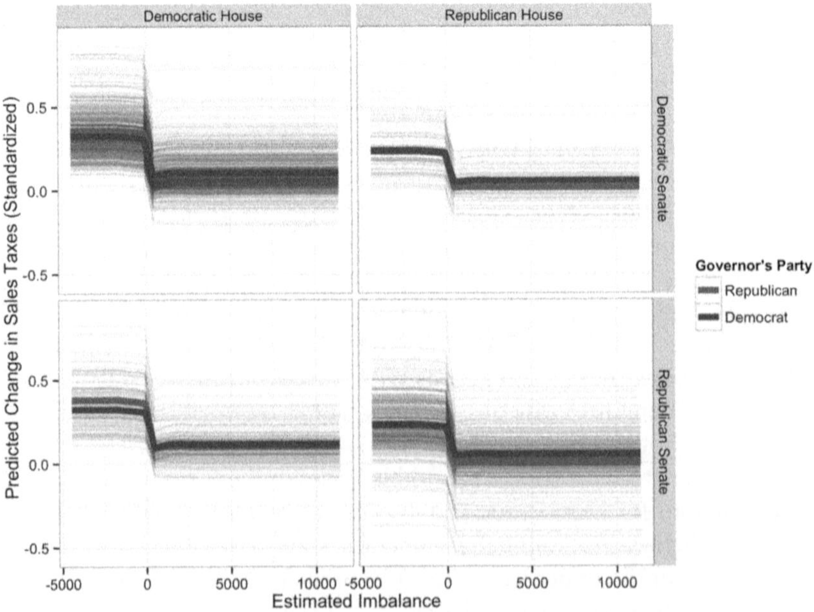

FIGURE 4.9 Partisan Control and Response to Imbalances with Sales Taxes.

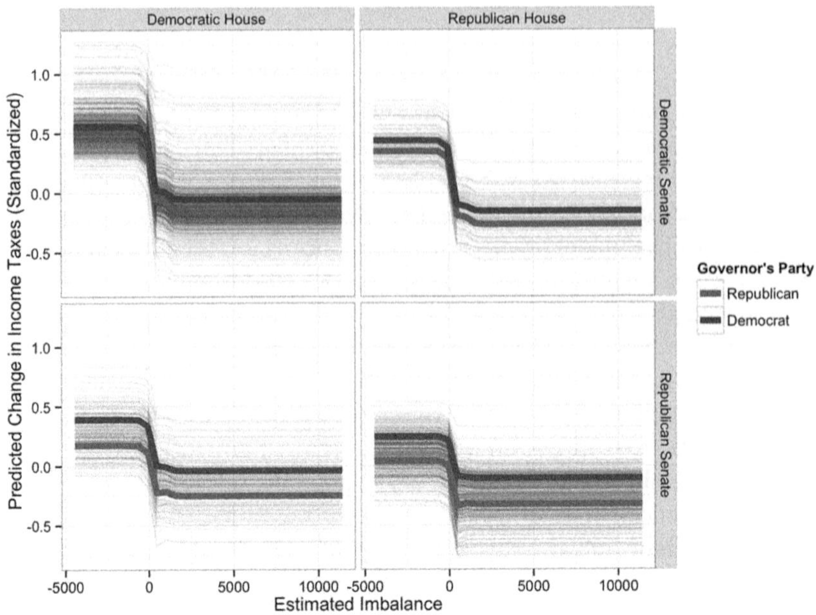

FIGURE 4.10 Partisan Control and Response to Imbalances with Income Taxes.

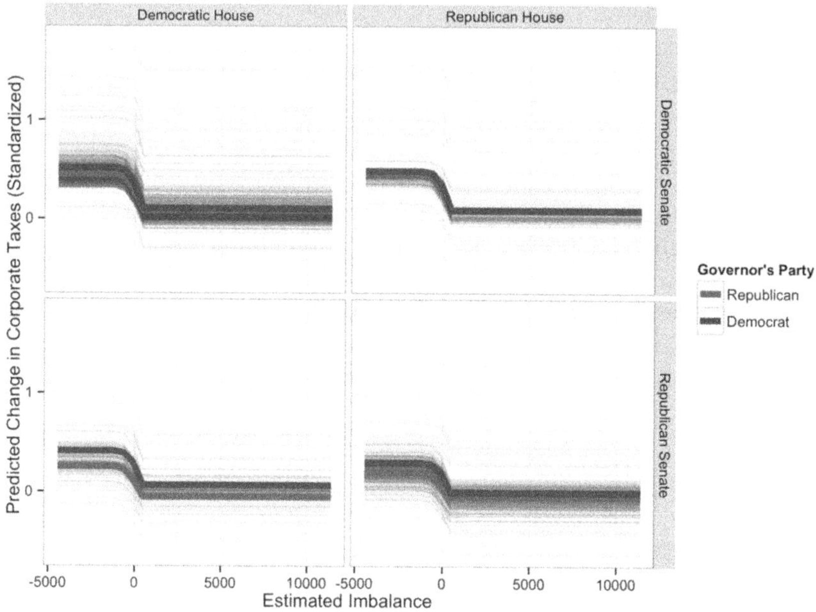

FIGURE 4.11 Partisan Control and Response to Imbalances with Corporate Taxes.

contains those observations with a Democrat-controlled house, and the right-hand column contains those observations with a Republican-controlled house. The top row contains those observations with a Democrat-controlled senate, and the bottom row contains those observations with a Republican-controlled senate. The heavy red and blue lines indicate the average across the predictions for Democratic and Republican governors, respectively.

This figure shows the predicted tax change for income taxes as the estimated imbalance varies by party control of the house, senate, and governor. Each light line corresponds to a particular state-year. We fix the other explanatory variables to the values observed for that particular state-year and allow the estimated imbalance to vary from a high value to a low value. We repeat this for each state-year. The left-hand column contains those observations with a Democrat-controlled house, and the right-hand column contains those observations with a Republican-controlled house. The top row contains those observations with a Democrat-controlled senate, and the bottom row contains those observations with a Republican-controlled senate. The heavy red and blue lines indicate the average across the predictions for Democratic and Republican governors, respectively.

This figure shows the predicted tax change for corporate taxes as the estimated imbalance varies by party control of the house, senate, and governor. Each light line corresponds to a particular state-year. We fix the other explanatory variables to the values observed for that particular state-year and allow the estimated imbalance to vary from a high value to a low value. We repeat this for each state-year. The left-hand column contains those observations with a Democrat-controlled house, and the right-hand column contains those observations with a Republican-controlled house. The top row contains those observations with a Democrat-controlled senate, and the bottom row contains those observations with a Republican-controlled senate. The heavy red and blue lines indicate the average across the predictions for Democratic and Republican governors, respectively.

Observation 2: Unified Democratic and unified Republican governments respond to budget imbalances differently. On average, unified Democratic governments increase taxes overall regardless of whether they face a shortfall or surplus, but they increase taxes much more when facing a shortfall. Unified Republican governments, on the other hand, increase taxes slightly when facing a shortfall and decrease taxes slightly when facing a surplus, on average. Most of these differences are due to differential changes to income taxes. Unified Democratic and Republican governments tend to change the sales and corporate taxes similarly in response to budget imbalances.

Personal income

A second important variable in the random forest is the percent change in personal income. The pattern here is intuitive as well. Figure 4.12 shows that, on average, states that see shrinking personal income increase taxes overall, and much of this increase comes from the income tax. As income shrinks, states need to increase taxes to raise additional revenue. The relationship between personal income and sales and corporate taxes is weak, as we might expect. Interestingly, states with large decreases in personal income are those most likely to raise fees.

This figure shows the predicted tax change for each tax class as the percentage change in personal income varies. Each colored line corresponds to a particular state-year. We fix the other explanatory variables to the values observed for that particular state-year and allow the percentage change in personal income to vary from a high value to a low value. We repeat this for each state-year. The lines are colored by the ideology of the state's citizens. The heavy black line shows the mean prediction at each value of estimated imbalance. The first differences reported in the upper-right

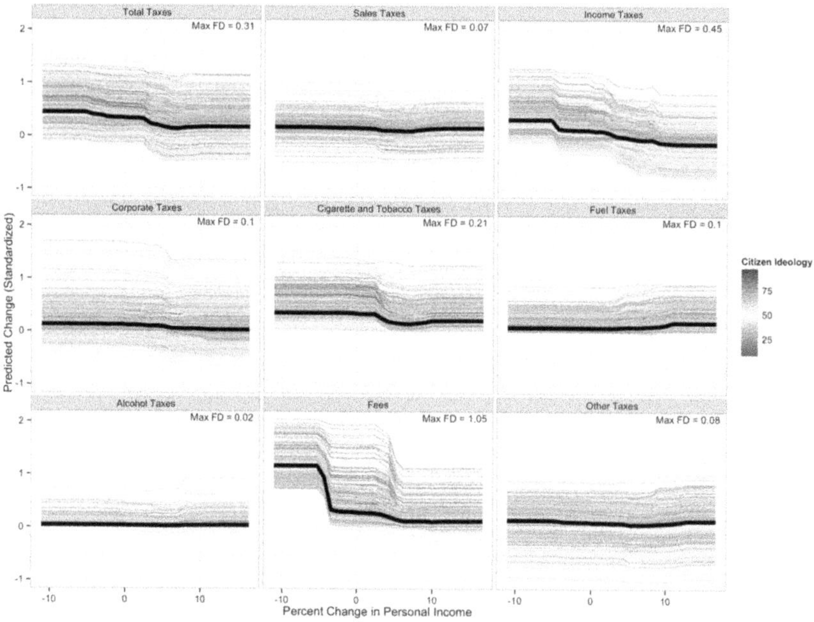

FIGURE 4.12 Predicting Changes in Taxes with Percent Change in Personal Income.

corner report the difference between the maximum average prediction and the minimum average prediction.

Observation 3: On average, states with shrinking personal income increase income taxes.

Observation 4: On average, states with shrinking personal income substantially increase fees.

Changes in partisan control

While some studies suggest little to no effect of government control on policy (e.g., Hofferbert 1966, Winters 1976, Hansen 1983, Plotnick and Winters 1985, Alt and Lowry 2000), we find a substantial effect of changes in the partisan composition of the legislature on changes in tax policy. Figures 4.13 and 4.14 show the predicted changes in tax policy as the change in the Democrats' share of the state house and state senate varies, respectively.

This figure shows the predicted tax change for each tax class as the change in Democrats' share of the state house varies. Each colored line corresponds to a particular state-year. We fix the other explanatory variables

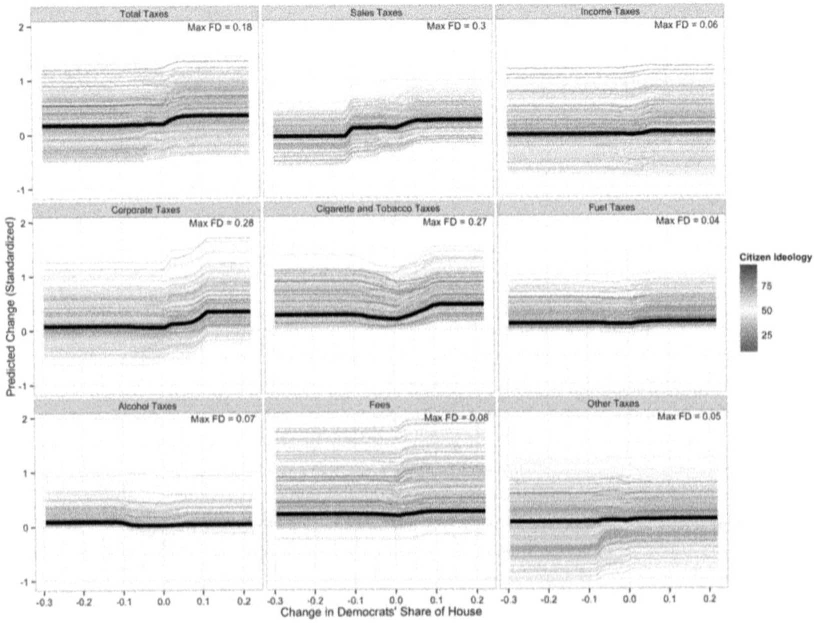

FIGURE 4.13 Predicting Changes in Taxes with Change in Democrats' Share of House.

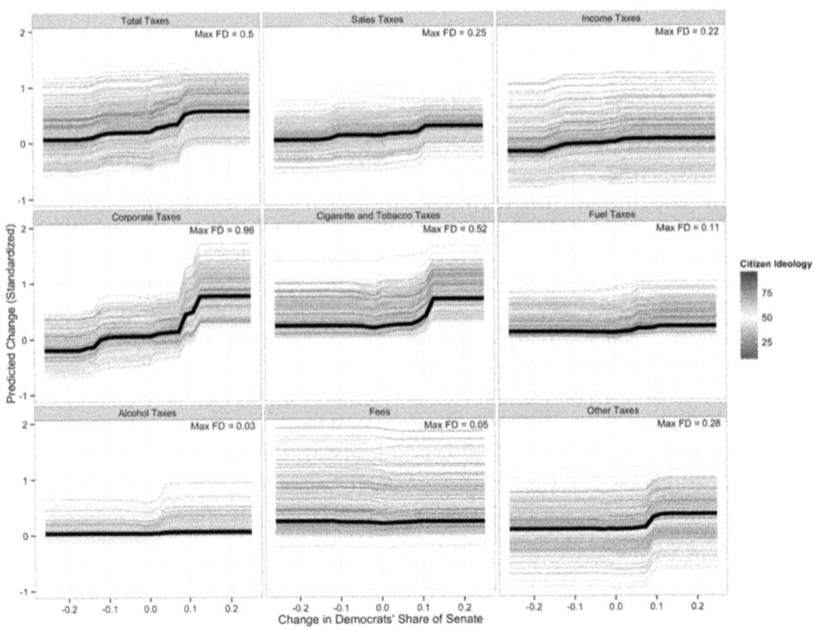

FIGURE 4.14 Predicting Changes in Taxes with Change in Democrats' Share of Senate.

to the values observed for that particular state-year and allow the change in Democrats' share of the state house to vary from a high value to a low value. We repeat this for each state-year. The lines are colored by the ideology of the state's citizens. The heavy black line shows the mean prediction at each value of estimated imbalance. The first differences reported in the upper-right corner report the difference between the maximum average prediction and the minimum average prediction.

This figure shows the predicted tax change for each tax class as the change in Democrats' share of the state senate varies. Each colored line corresponds to a particular state-year. We fix the other explanatory variables to the values observed for that particular state-year and allow the change in Democrats' share of the state senate to vary from a high value to a low value. We repeat this for each state-year. The lines are colored by the ideology of the state's citizens. The heavy black line shows the mean prediction at each value of estimated imbalance. The first differences reported in the upper-right corner report the difference between the maximum average prediction and the minimum average prediction.

Changes in the Democrat's share of the state house have a relatively weaker relationship with tax changes. The difference in predictions for a ten percentage point loss in seat share compared to a ten percentage point gain is about 0.2 standard deviations for total taxes. The predictions seem to change little in income taxes. The relationship is stronger for sales taxes and corporate taxes. For sales taxes, the model predicts a difference of about 0.3 between states in which Democrats have suffered a 15 percentage point loss and states in which Democrats have suffered a 10% gain. This runs counter to the conventional wisdom that Republicans should prefer sales taxes. For corporate taxes, the model predicts a difference of about 0.3 standard deviations when Democrats increase their seat share by ten percentage points or more compared to losing seats. The model predictions change little for the remaining taxes.

The model predictions vary much more strongly with changes in the Democrat's share of the state senate. For example, moving from a small loss to a ten percentage point gain suggests about a 0.4 standard deviation increase in taxes overall. A similar change suggests about a 0.2 standard deviation increase in the sales tax. As before, this is somewhat unexpected; there is not a large change in the prediction for income taxes, though the model does predict a small decrease in income taxes when Democrats suffer a major loss of 18 percentage points or more. The prediction for changes in corporate taxes depends *heavily* on changes in the Democrats' share of the senate—even more so than the Democrats share of the house. When Democrats gain 10 percentage points or more in the senate, the model predicts about a 0.8 standard deviation increase in corporate taxes. This is an enormous difference. We also see a similar, though not quite as strong, pattern for cigarette and tobacco taxes—when Democrats make large gains in the state senate, the model predicts a 0.5 standard deviation increase in these taxes. A similar, but even weaker pattern emerges for other taxes. The predictions for the remaining tax classes do not depend heavily on the change in the Democrats vote share.

As Figure 4.6 suggests, the relationship between the party of the governor and the enacted revenue changes is much weaker. This is consistent with Kousser's (2002) finding that control of the legislature is "important" but the party of the governor "appears irrelevant" (p. 667).

Observation 5: On average, Democratic gains in the state legislature are associated with a moderate increase in the sales tax and a large increase in the corporate income tax, but little to no relationship with the income taxes.

Conclusion

Politics is sometimes characterized as "who gets what, when, and how" (Lasswell 1936). Fundamental to the distribution and redistribution of goods and services is taxation. Yet political scientists have a relatively poor understanding of how politics and economics affect taxation. Indeed, many studies find little to no relationship between public policy, including taxation, and partisan control. This presents a fundamental problem for the functioning of a democracy. Parties compete and win or lose based on a series of policy proposals put forth to voters. The usual assumption is that parties will, at least to some extent, govern based on these platforms. The 1950 APSA report "Toward a More Responsible Two-Party System" observes that:

> An effective party system requires, first, that the parties are able to bring forth programs to which they committed themselves and, second, that the parties possess sufficient internal cohesion to carry out these programs.
> *(p. 305)*

If parties, through institutional constraints or some other reason, are unable to follow through on their campaign promises and party platforms, this suggests that the people have little control over the government.

While previous results find little to no impact of party control on policy outcomes, we find that party matters. Not for all policy areas, but for important ones. We find that a Democratic gain in the legislature predicts greater taxes, on average, especially corporate taxes. Most importantly, we find that state governments respond to the changing economic climate, and these changes are consistent with the general party positions. When facing a budget surplus, Democrats enact small tax increases on average, and Republicans enact small tax cuts on average. When facing a budget shortfall, Democrats enact large tax increases on average, and Republicans enact small tax increases on average. This suggests two basic points that paint quite an optimistic view of state government. First, parties are able to change policy. Second, parties are able to present platforms and carry out those platforms in office.

Notes

1 Caughey, Warshaw, and Xu (2017), p. 1 and pp. 6–11.
2 The highly aggregated, compositional approach in state policy analysis can be traced back many decades, and surely an outlier in this regard was an analysis of the determinants of the ratio between the sum of income-class-weighted classes of state expenditures over the sum of income-class-weighted tax categories, the so-called "redistribution ratio" (Fry and Winters 1972).
3 This is almost certainly due to associated tax increases associated with the completion and actions associated with the Tobacco Master Settlement Agreement of 1998; see https://en.wikipedia.org/wiki/Tobacco_Master_Settlement_Agreement.
4 The original analysis was of the costs of the performing arts in Baumol and Bowen (1965).
5 This is belied by the frequency of political campaign appeals of the need for and promises of greater efficiency in the provision of government goods and services. How to ascertain the inefficient among government programs and bureaus remains unclear.
6 The multi-colored versions of Figures 4.7 to 4.13 can be obtained from the author at rfw@dartmouth.edu.

5

VARYING POLITICAL PARTY CONTROL AND TAX CHANGES

Richard F. Winters

Introduction

Two relatively recent articles are intriguing. Caughey, Warshaw, and Xu (2017) undertake a sophisticated reanalysis of the effects of partisan control on public policy in the American states. They confirm the expected but generally elusive effects of Democratic vs. Republican control on changes in state public policies. However, their new measure of policy liberalism aggregates an enormous number of liberal vs. conservative policy choices in the states along a single dimension, thereby obscuring which policies get changed, when, and under what partisan conditions so as to boost or dampen "conservatism."[1] In this chapter, I annually decompose tax and revenue programs into eight components and pose the questions of what kinds of tax/revenue programs are Democrats likely to favor and Republicans oppose, and when will such partisan effects manifest themselves under different conditions of "partisan control."

Kousser and Philips (2012) propose, test for, and establish the non-obvious hypothesis that American state governors may be more successful in their "budgetary" requests than in their "policy" initiatives with state legislatures. The theoretical distinction that they adopt is that the annual or biennial budgetary game is a finite game time-wise and entails necessary agreement, while policy proposals typically are not time-wise urgent, so they do not require agreement between the executive and legislative branches within a set period. The legislature is free to accept or reject the executive policy proposals, while the budget requires agreement between the two branches by some date, or the government shuts

DOI: 10.4324/9781003606291-8

down – an outcome that neither wants. But Kousser and Philips's powerful analysis, by focusing on the highly aggregated variables of total gubernatorial budget request and final legislative action, obscures the more interesting political questions of exactly what and which of the spending policies get changed within the total amount and between executive "asking" and legislative "getting." Governors may request a spending amount of $X size and get revenue financing of $Y or near-$X via changes in revenue and tax programs with which she might profoundly disagree. In the cases of financing the state, it is most certainly the case that "the devil is in the details."[2] *How* the state is financed, by *what* revenue programs, and with what *kind of tax incidences* are *crucial* political questions answered quite differently by partisans in the American states.

Two dimensions of this financing strike me as important. First, states vary in the size and distributional burden, that is to say, the state's "taxing footprint" that they place on their citizens and businesses, the revenue corollary of the spending concept of "fiscal scale" per Alt and Lowry (2000).[3] Further, over the postwar era, the distributional burdens of these taxes have changed across the states, both cross-sectionally and temporally. Some state taxes that burden the poor have increased or decreased over time, and other taxes that burden individual or business incomes have increased or decreased over time. If the population burdens of financing the states have shifted over time, then some individuals and families are harder hit by tax bills, and in some states more than others, and at some time, periods more so than at other times. The fundamental interests, then, are changes in "footprint," "burdens," and "distributions."

For this analysis, I have data on changes in the total dollar amounts proposed by the state's governor (the "asks") for each fiscal year and the amounts actually legislated for eight statewide revenue programs by state by year for the 1989 to 2014 period among forty-nine American states (the "gets").[4] Because of the coercive nature of final passage, I am particularly interested in how enactments are affected by variations in party control of state political institutions after controlling for plausible covariates. I ask: Do parties systematically favor increases or decreases in taxes and some taxes as compared with others? Finally, what is even meant by "partisan control?" A Republican (or Democratic governor) with a Republican (or Democratic) senate and house – I "shorthand" it as RRR and DDD – are understandably "united partisan control." But how do the awkward "split chamber control" (RDR, RRD, DRD, DDR) and "split institutional control" (DRR, RDD) fit into the understanding of predictions regarding tax policy change with distributional consequences? I venture answers to each and assess evidence for the answers.

Given the serial and decomposed nature of the data, the analytic postures begin somewhat differently from others. Alt and Lowry (1994, 2000, 2003) and Poterba (1994b) are the archetype of politico-economy analyses. They – and others – examine the results of what states end up with by analyzing "revenues collected," i.e., the final "stage" in the revenue process, well after the "proposal" and "enacted" stages.[5] I approach the issue more from the perspective of "the politics of the budgetary process" (Wildavsky (a) 1964, 1974; Wildavsky (b) 1988, 1992, 2001). Governors propose, legislatures dispose and come to agreement with the governor, while revenue administrators collect, and citizens and businesses pay up, obfuscate, shelter, dodge, evade, or move to another state.[6] Legislatures may "dispose" by ignoring the governor's proposals and simply not changing revenue programs, choosing instead to cut expenditures to balance the budget.[7] Alternatively, legislators may enact new and quite different revenue changes from that which the governor proposed. But the governor's proposal is the initial stage; it's the stage that I turn to first in this analysis and pose the question of whether and what kinds of footprint and distributional differences manifest themselves in "first actions," the set of gubernatorial proposals for changing taxes.

The NASBO data and the dependent variables

Traditionally, at the beginning of the legislative session, each state's governor delivers his/her state of the state and/or budget addresses, which contain spending and taxing recommendations. NASBO collates reports from each state's budget office on the revenue changes proposed by each state's governor for eight different tax and revenue programs. These recommendations – published in the spring issue of *Fiscal Survey of States* (hereafter FSS-S) – are embedded in the beginning-of-the-year gubernatorial budget proposals and are published in the form of "dollars of revenue change recommended" for each of the eight revenue classes. [8] Forty-five of the forty-nine states under review here have "fiscal years" (FY) that end on June 30. The fiscal years in Alabama and Michigan end on September 30; New York's year ends March 31; and the Texas FY ends on August 31. Nevertheless, all states operate under the same constraints of beginning-of-the-year gubernatorial revenue proposals and late winter to spring to early summer legislative consideration and agreement-making with the governor. The final agreement between the governor and legislature is recorded in the fall issue of *Fiscal Survey of States* (FSS-F) and reflects the final stage of bargaining between the governor and legislature.

The tax policy schema that I propose is outlined in Figure 5.1.

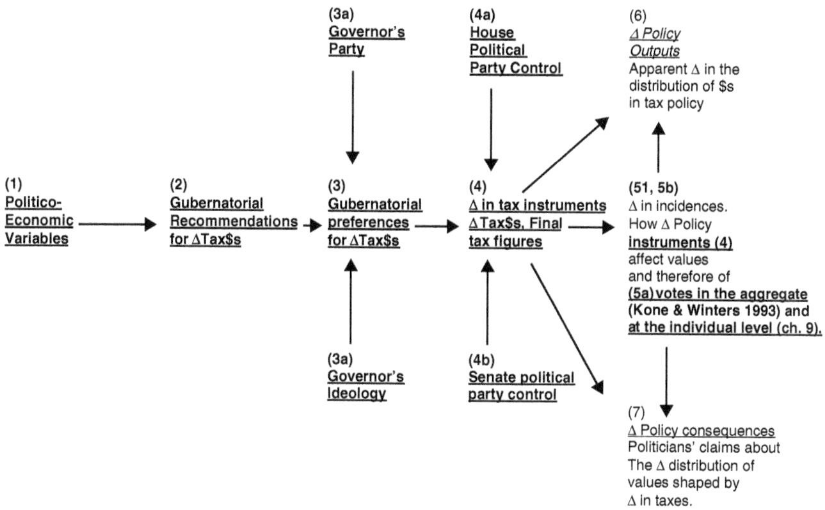

FIGURE 5.1 Sets Out the Proposed Causal Sequence and Chain in the Tax Policy Schema.

To aid interpretation, for each of the measures, I standardize the proposed and enacted dollar changes in each tax and revenue program by the previous year's revenue data. That is to say, I measure these tax changes as the recommended change in taxes as a percentage of the prior year's "revenue resources." This makes the changes across large and small states comparable.[9] Thus, the dependent variables are:

1 *Gubernatorially (1) proposed and finally (2) legislatively enacted changes in the totals of taxes, fees, licenses, and charges as a percentage of past total revenue resources.*
2 *Gubernatorially (3) proposed and finally (4) legislatively enacted changes dollar changes in the "personal income tax," the "corporation income tax," and the "general consumer sales tax," each stated as a percentage of past revenue resources.*

In the multivariate analyses that follow in Sections "Modeling tax proposals and tax enactments" and "Analysis: party control, size of state, and gubernatorial tax proposals and legislative tax enactments," I report fixed effects, time-series/cross-sectional (TSCS) regression estimates via the stata command xtreg, fe vce(cluster stateno), that is to say, with fixed effects and standard errors clustered by state.

Arraying taxes in the American states

In the best of all worlds, the gubernatorial recommendations regarding changes in the eight tax programs as well as the final eight enacted products might show some patterning across the revenue program choices. Put succinctly, tax proposals and tax enactments ought to cohere sensibly.

I hypothesize that there exists among elected political leaders an implicit politico-cognitive map of the revenue terrain that "fit" the understandings of where the burdens of taxation should fall. Some taxes loom large on a governor's horizon – large in size and in political attractiveness. The "political attractiveness" of a tax among politicians is that the "vote loss" (gain) associated with an "increase" (decrease) in a tax is "minimized" (maximized) (Downs 1957). I postulate that increases in the personal and corporate income taxes have greater positive value for Democrats and lesser, if not opposing, value for Republicans, and the opposite is the case for the sales tax. Further, the obverse is true for cuts in these taxes, i.e., personal income tax cuts are attractive targets for Republican governors. I test for the coherence of tax changes across tax terrains by hypothesizing that when a governor advocates increasing (or decreasing) the personal income tax, she may also advance changes to the corporate income tax or avoid increasing the sales tax. Or, if she suggests changes to fees and licenses, she also sends along a package of "other" minor tax changes. The first-order argument in this paper, then, is that the eight varieties of proposed and enacted tax changes, stated as a percent of prior year's revenues, can be usefully arrayed along three dimensions: as (1) "income redistributive" for the personal income tax and corporation income tax; (2) the sales tax characterized as "income regressive/consumption" taxes; and (3) charges, licenses, fees, and other taxes as "individualist/user-levied."[10]

As I showed in Chapter 3, arraying the data on the eight programs by state (49) by year (28),[11] a simple correlation analysis (in Table 3.8 (A) and (B)), and a factor analysis (in Table 3.9, (A) and (B)) generally support the threefold characterization of taxing in the American states. Table 3.10 sets out the simple correlations among the eight programs *as proposed by the governor*, assessing if when there is a proposed change in X, Y is also proposed to be changed. I **bolded** the interesting coefficients – those of +/–0.10.

The first column links proposed changes in "dollars as percentage of last year's resources," as announced by the governor in the general sales tax, to the other seven programs, and there appears to be little in the way of common positive changes, suggesting that governors proposing consumption-related taxation limit their recommendations to this one tax with one possible link to another consumption-related tax, that on motor fuels. Note that when changes to the sales tax are proposed, this is negatively associated with recommended changes in the personal income tax.

The second column, assessing how changes in gubernatorial proposals for the personal income taxes might be related to changes in other programs, indicates a positive linkage with changes in the corporation income tax but no linkages to other programs. Thus, if a governor proposes changes to its personal income tax, up or down, she is most likely to also propose comparable changes to the corporation income tax as well. There appear, as well in columns four through eight, to be some not-entirely-consistent links among proposals to change minor, individualist/user taxes on alcohol, fees, and other taxes.

In Table 3.8, panel (B), I present the cross-program correlations, the corollary data, on changes in the *final legislative – or enacted – actions* for all eight tax programs as percentage change from the prior year's total revenue figure. The correlations are more robust. Again, the sales tax appears to be a solo choice – when a change is enacted in the sales tax, no other taxes appear to be proposed for change. The personal and corporate income taxes show a closer relationship, indicating commonalities of legislative perception of the terrain of tax burdens. There also appear to be a number of modest correlations among the minor taxes.

The linkages become clearer in factor analyses of the proposed and enacted eight tax changes. The rotated factor loadings by revenue programs are presented in Table 3.9 (A) and (B) (on p. yyy). The understandings of the first three principal factors, as rotated, are highlighted in bold and underlined. Looking first at the analysis for gubernatorially proposed tax changes in panel (A), there do appear to be three factors of interest. Factor (1), with its high loadings on tobacco, alcohol, and "other" taxes, seems most closely associated with our understanding of "user" taxes and is so labeled. Factor (2), with its high loadings on the personal and corporate income taxes, is a redistributive factor, and factor (3) has high loadings on two "sales" taxes – the general sales tax and motor fuel taxes.

In Table 3.9 (B) for the analysis of "enacted programs," Factor (1), with its high loadings on the personal and corporation income taxes, is clearly a redistributional factor, while Factor (2) is the "individualist-user" set of changes loading on license and user fees, and Factor (3), with its unique loading on the general sales tax, is the consumption taxation factor.

There are two ambiguities in the factor analyses. Governors appear to advance changes in motor fuels in concert with changes in sales taxes, treating each as consumption goods. Legislators, turn around, however, and treat in like fashion changes in the sales tax and changes in cigarette and tobacco taxes. These unlike treatments of motor fuels and cigarette and tobacco taxes render the "consumption" and "user fees" as somewhat ambiguous if I insist on examining changes in all eight programs. Note, however, that the massive Master Tobacco Settlement between the four large tobacco companies and fifty states was completed in 1998, about one-third of the way through the time series of revenue programs. I suspect that the net effect of the settlement was to inject large and random revenue shocks into the tax calculations of political leaders, thus rendering this part of the data set somewhat suspect. The odd role of motor fuel taxes may be tied to its ordinary direct linkage and, often by statute, limited to highway spending. Changes in this tax may be driven by a complex of spending-side beneficiaries that range from ready-mix contractors to the state Farm Bureau associations.

There is greater clarity, per our expectations, regarding the personal and corporate income taxes and the general sales tax. Thus, in an interest in analytic parsimony as well as clarity of choices, I focus on changes in these three taxes: (1) consumption: change in sales taxes as a percentage of prior year's revenue; (2) redistributive: the change in the personal income tax; and, also redistributive, (3) the change in the corporation income taxes as a percentage of prior year's revenue.

Party and proposing and enacting changes in taxes

Table 3.7 sets out the set of simple average changes as proposed by the states' Republican and Democratic governors in the 1989–2014 time period. For Republican governors (in panel (A)), the personal and corporate income tax recommendations were, on average, negative and small, while the proposals for the remaining six are positive but quite small. This reinforces the widely held popular view of the laser-like – and negative – focus of Republicans on the personal and corporate income tax programs. The last column gives the "average" of the percentage changes in all tax programs in panel (A) for Republican governors, panel (B) for Democratic governors, and the net differences in panel (C). Republican governors, on average by state by year, propose a near-zero set of changes in the array of tax programs before them. Democratic governors (in panel (B)), however, on average, propose a 1.21% average increase. Republican governors typically advance positive tax changes for non-redistributive tax programs, but miniscule ones. And for each of the eight tax programs, Democratic governors invariably proposed greater tax changes than did Republican governors. Contrary to our redistributive expectations regarding Democratic governors, their largest proposed increases are in the general sales taxes, although, on average, they also propose increases in the personal and corporate income taxes.

Table 5.1 (panels (A), (B), and (C)), reproduced from Chapter 3, links what governors propose to what legislators and governors finally agree on – the "enacted budget," or "the get." What is especially striking about this table is the modesty of these relationships. In panel (A), the correlations, when all observations are pooled, are all positive, indicating some modest levels of shared cooperation – proposed changes do tend to get enacted. Alternatively, and likely as a complement, the positive relationships may simply indicate strategic behavior by the governor forecasting what kind of tax changes might be "politically saleable." But all are small in size, as I would expect when I pool all situations of partisan control (or lack thereof) in state governments where the executive and legislatures are separate institutions but share the powers of raising the money to finance the state. Among this pooled set of all observations, I find that the two smallest correlations between proposal and action are in the two large, broad-based programs of sales (.23) and personal income taxes (.15). These two taxes sit at the poles of the redistribution vs. individualist/consumption, and in a pooled situation reflected here, there should be little surprise that conflict and disagreement would be particularly acute between the governor and the two legislative bodies, and, as well, I suspect, in conflict within each of the parties. The two highest correlations are in user taxes of "other taxes" and "fees." I conjecture that these tax programs likely get employed to tide over and patch up small budget imbalances – they are the low-conflict, easy-to-bargain-about, "go to" alternatives for modest budget balancing. Plus, there is always the persuasive argument that the proposed and/or final actions on user fees and charges simply levy assessments on those who enjoy the states' public goods.

When I divide the pool of observation into the partisan cases of unified Republican control (panel (B)) and unified Democratic control (panel (C)) – note the diminished Ns – where I would expect the most "sincere" behavior or action, I find quite disparate relationships.[12] My expectations in this panel are that all simple correlations should increase in size when each of the political parties controls all three branches of government, indicating heightened partisan coordination across institutions, and that these increases should be particularly noticeable among the sales and income taxes – the "high" points of the taxation terrain. A fascinating mix of findings occurs when the pooled sample is parceled out by unified partisan control. First, on balance, most correlations do increase in size, indicating greater shared agreement among co-partisans about proposed and enacted tax changes. However, Republican gubernatorial proposals tend to fare worse, on average, with their partisan counterparts in the legislature than their Democratic peers. In the cases of links between gubernatorial proposals to change the personal income tax and the corporate income tax, quite

TABLE 5.1 Correlation of Gubernatorial Proposals and Legislative Actions

(A) ALL, Pooled Correlations Enacted. Actions (N = 1299)–>	
Proposed sales tax changes	0.32
Proposed income tax changes:	0.16
Proposed corp. income tax changes:	0.32
Proposed tobacco tax changes:	0.38
Proposed motor fuels tax changes	0.31
Proposed alcohol tax changes:	0.23
Proposed other taxes tax changes	0.44
Proposed fee changes:	0.45
Proposed TOTAL tax changes:	**0.38**

(B) Under United Republican Control (RRR = 1; N = 308 Enacted. Actions (N = 306)–>	
Proposed sales tax changes	0.38
Proposed income tax changes:	**0.62**
Proposed corp. income tax changes:	**0.90**
Proposed tobacco tax changes:	0.26
Proposed motor fuels tax changes	0.09
Proposed alcohol tax changes:	0.08
Proposed other taxes tax changes	0.39
Proposed fee changes:	**0.63**
Proposed TOTAL tax changes:	**0.42**

(C) Under United Democratic Control (DDD = 1; N = 315) Enacted. Actions (N = 312)–>	
Proposed sales tax changes	**0.43**
Proposed income tax changes:	**0.47**
Proposed corp. income tax changes:	0.39
Proposed tobacco tax changes:	0.71
Proposed motor fuels tax changes	0.27
Proposed alcohol tax changes:	0.31
Proposed other taxes tax changes	**0.53**
Proposed fee changes:	0.49
Proposed TOTAL tax changes:	**0.67**

large simple correlations occur under unified Republican control.[13] There appear to be high levels of agreement for minor taxes and fees as well. The across-institutional coordination correlations for Democrats appear on balance to be stronger, especially for sales, personal income tax, tobacco, and "other" taxes.

Modeling tax proposals and tax enactments

I argue that diverse partisan control effects on tax proposals and enactments should hold after controlling for (1) relevant socio-economic and (2) relevant institutional controls; then "footprint" and distributional changes will be related to (3) varying gubernatorial partisan identities, (4) unified party control of state political institutions, and (5) differently to varying mixed compositions of party control of the states' political institutions – split institutional or split chamber conditions. In these last cases of divided partisan controls, I expect substantial attenuations in the relationships that exist for the cases of unified partisan control in the case of split institutions, but greater deference to the partisan tax tilt toward the party in control of both the governor's office and one of the two legislative chambers.

Socio-economic controls

In the last chapter, my coauthors and I noted that wealthier states are better positioned to finance arrays of public goods. When states' populations are wealthier, voters may well come to prefer a broader array of public goods, services, and amenities, but high personal incomes also suggest easier governmental financing without increasing taxes. Similarly, well-populated states may affect the demand for changes in revenue because of a growing "base" for assessing taxes. Further, revenue and tax proposals and enactments may reflect contemporaneous changes in these two covariates. Our predictions, then, for our dependent variables measured as change in taxes as a percent of revenue, first for "footprint" or total revenue change (+ or –), and, second, for "redistributive" taxation (+ or –) are:

1 *total statewide population* (+ for footprint, + for redistribution);
2 *total statewide income* (+, +);
3 *year-to-year changes in population* (+, +);
4 *year-to-year changes in total statewide income* (+, +).

The greater the increase in the state unemployment rate, the greater the need for extra revenue to meet population need.[14] Further, existing tax collections suffer in periods of increasing unemployment, furthering the need for greater tax support; thus, I expect the fiscal footprint of the state to increase with increases in unemployment. I also hypothesize that reliance on redistributive taxes will increase.

5 *January to January changes in the state's unemployment rate* (+ for footprint, + for redistribution).

Institutional variables

The spring and fall issues of FSS contain a variety of plausible institutional covariates. In the last chapter, however, we found that there appeared to be little to no systematic effects of factors such as the state's existing revenue burden in dollars stated as a percentage of personal income, or the percentages of total state revenues collected by the income and sales taxes and, respectively, the tax shares of the income or sales tax as a percentage of total resources, or the growth or shrinkage in the state's budget stabilization fund. The one systematic effect was with

(7) the *expected surplus as a percentage of total resources* (+ for footprint, – for redistribution).

NASBO publishes the "balance" estimate in the spring issue. The "balance" ranges in nominal dollar terms from a -$5.855 billion in 2009 in CA to a surplus of $10.8 billion in CA in 2007. Stated as a percentage of "resources," Oregon in 2003 led the way with a projected deficit of –28%, while Texas once had a 42% surplus forecasted. I expect that increases in resource footprint are likely the greater the deficit, and shrinking the size of the state taxes is likely as the surplus swells.

Political determinants

For governors as elected officials, the political factors of the party of the governors mediate changes in size and direction in taxing. Governors' revealed preferences in taxing – both in footprint and distribution – would be shaped by:

(8) *Governor is a Republican = 1, Democrat = 0;* (- for footprint, - for redistribution).

Alt and Lowry (1994) stipulate that the Republican Party is the "low demand" party for public goods and the Democrats are the "high demand" party. Further, I argue that the political parties differ on tax distributional issues, with the Democrats favoring redistributional taxation (the personal and corporation income taxes) and the Republicans favoring greater distributional equity among persons via consumption taxation (the sales tax). Given that, Republican governors are more likely to propose decreases in footprint in taxation and less redistributive taxation (– and –), while I expect the opposite from Democratic governors (+, +).

Further, greater footprint changes in taxes and greater redistributive taxation will be proposed and enacted with

(9(a)) *unified Democratic Party control of the states' legislative chambers* (DDD: + and +).

(9(b)) The opposite will be true of *unified Republican control* (RRR: – and –).

In the cases of unified control, I expect preference-opposing revenue changes. Growth in the government "footprint" will be positive in DDD and diminished in RRR. Further, changes in our fundamental measures of revenue programs will be highest for DDD in redistributive taxation and lowest in sales tax programs.

Clearly so, but murkier in predictions, the interesting cases are the mixed cases of divided government – that of split institutional control where one party controls the governorship and the other party controls both houses (DRR, RDD), and split chamber control where one party controls only one chamber (DDR, DRD, RDR, RRD).[15] Note that these conflicting control situations comprise roughly half of the collected data.

For "split institutional control," where the configurations are DRR and RDD, I expect that the configuration of changes for our three measures of revenue changes will more closely reflect that of the legislative branches. Contemporary examples abound from each of the two parties – Republican Charlie Baker facing unified Democratic legislative chambers in Democratic Massachusetts, Larry Hogan the same in Democratic Maryland, and their counterparts such as Steve Bullock, a Republican in Montana, and Democrat Roy Cooper in the now-Republican legislature of North Carolina. Our logic here is twofold. First, with split institutional control, governors are more likely to represent insurgent candidacies that reflect minority party alternatives to the preponderant party in control of the legislature, but these governors, e.g., Baker, Hogan, etc., also represent more "centrist" positions. And, while the minority party governor may "propose," it truly is the legislature that will "dispose." Final legislative action on revenue bills comes late in the session – May or June in most states, thereby verging on a "take it or leave it" bid to the governor. If the governor "leaves it," any shut down will likely reflect on the executive who had the "last clear chance" to affect the outcome, that is to say, "sign the damn bill."[16] Finally, many of these DRR and RDD governors face term limits while confronting legislators with no such limits. State legislators evince long-term views and likely maintain their partisan/taxation commitments in the face of the short-term governor of the opposing party. Thus, I expect a mixed outcome in the DRR/RDD situations, but one that favors the majority legislative party; the final disposition will reflect the majority/legislative party preferences. Further, with both legislative chambers in the hands of the other party, the greater the difficulty any minority party governor might have – or conjecture having – in mobilizing any winning legislative coalition that includes his/her minority party along with some fraction of disaffected majority party legislators willing to defect in each chamber – witness the lack of success of Republican Bruce Rauner in Democratic Illinois.[17] Opposing party gubernatorial proposals, on average, will reflect their party's modal proposal but be attenuated in the face of the strength of the opposing legislative party.

Therefore, (10(c)) the *split institutional control of DRR* will more closely reflect legislators' and Republican party preferences of smaller revenue "footprint" and lower income/corporate taxes (- and -).

(10(d)) the *split control of RDD* will reflect Democratic preferences of greater footprint, more redistributive taxation, and lessened consumption taxation (+ and +). Either of the split institutional situations will display final outcomes that are less partisan than the full controls of DDD or RRR.

The tax footprint and tax choices under the split chamber conditions of RDR, RRD, DRD, and DDR are more difficult to predict. On balance, I expect that the institutional majorities contained within the "split chamber" conditions will prevail, but weakly so. Proposals by Democratic governors will likely favor a positive but small fiscal footprint and redistributive choices. The opposite will be true of Republican governors. The final enactments should favor the party that controls two of three institutions, but bargaining will reduce the effects substantially toward zero. Thus, (10(a)) The DRD and DDR gubernatorial proposals will favor greater taxation and more redistributive taxation, but less in comparison with unified party and split institutional conditions (weakly + and +). The legislative enactments of DRD and DDR will more likely favor the "majority institutional" preferences, that is to say, positive on fiscal footprint and on redistributive taxation, but weakly so (weakly + and +).

(10(b)) Similarly, Republican gubernatorial proposals under the RDR and RRD conditions will show preferences for smaller footprints and diminished interest in redistributive taxation but at attenuated rates (weakly – and –).

Analysis: party control, size of state, and gubernatorial tax proposals and legislative tax enactments

Unified party control

Table 5.2 reports on the results of our full model for the total of taxes, fees, and charges, the total "taxing footprint," for gubernatorial proposals

TABLE 5.2 Party Control: All Taxes Proposed and All Taxes Enacted with Unified Party Control – the Tests for Revenue "Footprint"

(A) Gubernatorial Proposals				
	Unified Democratic Control		*Unified Republican Control*	
	Coeff	*St. err.*	*Coeff*	*St. err.*
Pers. Inc. (millions) (+)	.000006*	(0.000003)	0.000008**	(0.000003)
Population (+)	−0.0000007	(0.0000004)	−0.0000007*	(0.000003)
% change in Pers. Inc. (+)	−0.05	(0.04)	−0.05	(0.04)
Population growth (+)	0.000	(0.000)	0.000	(0.000)
Change unemployment(+)	0.34**	(0.11)	0.31**	(0.11)
Governors end balance (−)	−0.0004#	(0.0003)	−0.0004#	(0.0003)
Unified control	**1.14****	**(0.25)**	**−1.67****	**(0.33)**
Constant	3.48*	(1.54)	3.79**	(1.48)
N =	312		306	
F (7,48) =	6.1**		6.3**	

(B) Enacted Taxes				
	Unified Democratic Control		*Unified Republican Control*	
	Coeff	*St. err.*	*Coeff*	*St. err.*
Pers. Inc. (millions) (+)	0.000	(0.000)	0.000	(0.000)
Population (+)	-0.000	(0.000)	-0.000	(0.000)
% change in Pers. Inc. (+)	-0.05	(0.04)	-0.05	(0.04)
Population growth (+)	0.000	(0.000)	0.000	(0.000)
Change unemployment(+)	0.72**	(0.20)	0.71**	(0.21)
Governors end balance (-)	-0.0004*	(0.0002)	-0.0004*	(0.0002)
Unified control	**1.06****	**(0.37)**	**−1.12****	**(0.26)**
Constant	1.76	(1.34)	2.11#	(1.28)
N =	312		306	
F(7,48) =	4.7**		8.2**	

The sum of all taxes proposed and enacted is stated as a percentage of NASBO's past year's "total revenue resources."
significance of #=.10, *=.05, **=.01

and legislative actions under the condition of unified partisan control. First, looking at gubernatorial proposals for increasing (or decreasing) taxes and examining the covariates, there is consistency across the sets of equations. High levels of personal income lead to greater proposals for taxation. Perversely, as population rises, albeit after controlling for state wealth, proposed taxation falters. The variables of changes in these two are each small and insignificant. As unemployment rises, taxation proposals increase, and when the state is in an end-balance surplus condition, there is, not surprisingly, diminished taxation. These covariates hold across both conditions of unified partisan control and across "tax proposals" and "tax enactments." The effects of unified partisan control, as I hypothesized, are sizeable and in opposing directions. Republican governors, *ceteris paribus*, typically request cuts in taxes, and Democratic governors call for increases. These symmetrical findings in signs are reflected in both proposals (Panel (A)) and enactments (B). Note that while symmetrical, the proposals from Democratic governors and Republican governors are greater in size – and probably scope – as compared with legislative enactments, which may well reflect the sincere preferences of the opposing partisan executives, but it may also be consistent with a gaming strategy of asking for more than you expect to receive ... and settling for less. Further, an alternative explanation is that legislative enactments occur later in the "budgetary political year" and may simply reflect updated and improved current revenue information available to legislators. Note that under both Democratic and Republican unified control, the taxes changed by the legislature are, on average and *ceteris paribus*, less than what the governors propose. Governors appear to stake out either a more extreme position of increases or decreases, per the party predictions, or, and a likely effect, better understandings of the precise revenue needs as the legislative session proceeds – what appeared to be the need/opportunity in January for the governor may not be reflected in the May/June legislative information, knowledge, and actions. Note also that Republican governors appear to be more entrepreneurial than their Democratic counterparts in asking for greater tax cuts. They are also marginally less successful in gaining their ends.

Split institutional control

Table 5.3 (a) and (b) contains the results of our analysis of the total tax footprint with "split institutional control," where the governor is of one party and both legislative chambers are held by the opposing party. I present results for both gubernatorial proposals as well as final legislative

TABLE 5.3 Party Control: Total Taxes Proposed and Total Taxes Enacted with Split Institutional Control – the Tests for Revenue "Footprint"

(A) Gubernatorial Proposals

	Democratic Governor Rep House & Senate		*Republican Governor Dem House & Senate*	
	Coeff.	*St. err.*	*Coeff.*	*St. err.*
Pers. Inc. (millions) (+)	0.000007*	(0.000003)	0.000007*	(0.000003)
Population (+)	−0.00000008*	(0.00000004)	−0.00000008*	(0.00000004)
% change in Pers. Inc. (+)	−0.05	(0.04)	−0.05	(0.04)
Population growth (+)	−0.0000008*	(0.0000004)	−0.0000008*	(0.0000004)
Change unemployment(+)	0.0005#	(0.0003)	−0.0005#	(0.0003)
Governors end balance (-)	−0.37**	(0.11)	−0.37**	(0.11)
Split prty.cntrl.	**+0.69#**	**(0.38)**	**−0.52#**	**(0.327)**
Constant	4.1**	(1.6)	4.4**	(1.6)
N =	138		256	
F(7,48) -	3.3**		3.8**	

(B) Enacted Taxes

	Democratic Governor Rep House & Senate		*Republican Governor Dem House & Senate*	
	Coeff.	*St. err.*	*Coeff.*	*St. err.*
Pers. Inc. (millions) (+)	0.000	(0.000)	0.000	(0.000)
Population (+)	−0.000	(0.000)	−0.000	(0.000)
% change in Pers. Inc. (+)	−0.05	(0.04)	−0.05	(0.04)
Population growth (+)	0.000	(0.000)	0.000	(0.000)
Change unemployment(+)	−0.0005*	(0.0002)	−0.0005*	(0.0002)
Governors end balance (-)	−0.74**	(0.21)	−0.74**	(0.21)
Split prty.cntrl.	**−1.08**	**(0.97)**	**0.24**	**(0.33)**
Constant	2.67*	(1.30)	2.34#	(1.26)
N =	138		256	
F(7,48) -	6.6**		4.7**	

The sum of all taxes proposed and enacted is stated as a percentage of the past year's NASBO's "total revenue resources."
significance of #=.10, *=.05, **=.01

enactments. Gubernatorial proposals hold the expected size and sign – positive for Democrats and negative for Republican governors – but on average are much reduced compared to "unified party control." The resulting legislative enactments also confirm our expectations. Even in the face of positive tax proposals by the Democratic executives, the Republican control of both chambers results in lowered taxes. The large standard errors suggest that the tax records of Democratic governors facing two hostile chambers are quite mixed. Democratic legislatures react similarly to their Republican governors but enact much smaller tax increases in the face of the calls for larger tax decreases by their Republican executives, but, again, with large standard errors. It's as if both Democratic and Republican governors facing both houses in the other party's control attenuate their demands for, respectively, tax increases and decreases. And, true to expectations, the opposing party in the legislatures reacts with cuts if controlled by the Republicans and comparatively modest increases when controlled by the Democrats. Note the differences between the larger Republican legislative cuts relative to the smaller Democratic legislative increases. The coefficient for enacted tax cuts in the DRR situation, albeit with large standard errors, is almost as large as the tax cuts in the RRR unified control context.

Split chamber control

The mixed four cases of partisan governors with one co-partisan house and the second in the opposing party's control present a more complicated picture. Table 5.4 holds panels displaying the results for the analysis of the four conditions of "split chamber control" (DRD, DDR, RDR, RRD). I drop the information on the covariates; they are much the same as in Tables 5.2 and 5.3.[18] As expected, the estimates of both the proposals for increasing or decreasing taxes by Democrats and examining total taxes collected as a percent of the past year's revenue resources. Part A-1 of Table 5.4 examines proposals and enactments under the two split conditions of DRD and DDR. Only one of the four coefficients is marginally significant – positive tax increases proposed by Democratic governors under the DRD condition. None are significant for the Republican governors facing the RRD or RDR conditions. The case of split chamber government appears clearly to be one of little change in the way of tax actions, either proposed or enacted, and either increases or decreases. I note that of the eight coefficients, while only one is marginally significant, the most sizeable coefficients appear, and are appropriately signed, when the partisanship of the governor and of the House are signed.

TABLE 5.4 Governmental Size and Split Chamber Control: Taxes Proposed and Taxes Enacted with Split Chamber Government

A-1: Gubernatorial Proposals of Democratic governors				
	Democratic Governor Rep House & Dem Senate		*Democratic Governor Dem House & Rep Senate*	
	Coeff.	*St. err.*	*Coeff.*	*St. err.*
Split chamber	1.45#	(0.85)	–0.32	(0.60)
N =	139		49	
F(7,48) =	2.89*		2.74*	

A-2: Enacted Taxes				
	Democratic Governor Rep House & Dem Senate		*Democratic Governor Dem House & Rep Senate*	
	Coeff.	*St. err.*	*Coeff.*	*St. err.*
Split chamber	0.27	(0.46)	1.17	(1.24)
N =	139		49	
F(7,48) =	4.83**		4.95**	

The sum of all taxes proposed and enacted are stated as a percentage of the past year's "total revenue resources."

B-1: Gubernatorial Proposals of Republican governors				
	Republican Governor Rep House & Dem Senate		*Republican Governor Dem House & Rep Senate*	
	Coeff.	*St. err.*	*Coeff.*	*St. err.*
Split chamber	–1.25	(0.98)	0.24	(0.72)
N =	60		47	
F(7,48) =	2.83*		2.79*	

B-2: Enacted Taxes				
	Republican Governor Rep House & Dem Senate		*Republican Governor Dem House & Rep Senate*	
	coeff.	*st. err.*	*coeff.*	*st. err.*
Split chamber	–0.89	(0.72)	0.48	(0.38)
N =	60		47	
F(7,48) =	6.71**		4.91**	

The sum of all taxes proposed and enacted is stated as a percentage of the past year's NADBO's "total revenue resources."
significance levels of #=.10, *=.05, **=.01, ***=.001.

Analysis of changes in redistributive vs. regressive tax burdens: party control

Our tests for partisan effects on the *changing distributional burden* of the personal income and corporate income taxes, as well as the sales tax, are presented in Table 5.5. I further truncate the presentation for brevity and clarity. Each entry is the regression coefficient for the stated partisan condition with all of the controls (unreported) present per the earlier tables. The unreported coefficients largely mirror those present in Tables 5.2 and 5.3. The effects of *unified partisan control* are in **bold**, while those for *split chamber control* are underlined, and those for *split institutions* are in *italics*. Of the nine significant coefficients – with significance generously assessed at the +/–.10 mark – across the forty-eight different regression equations, seven appear in the gubernatorial proposal stage. Consistent partisan positions pro and con taxation are easier to state and propose than to enact. Talk is cheaper than action. And, again, of the nine significant coefficients, five reflect income tax talk or actions ... that appears to be where the "tax ducks" are nesting. Across the three taxes, Democratic governors will more likely not only propose increasing the personal income and corporate income taxes but also, contrary to our simple expectations, call for increases in the consumption/regressive sales tax. Republican governors consistently call for cuts to each of the taxes. All coefficients for gubernatorial proposals in the "unified party control" conditions are significant, and each pair of partisan coefficients across the taxes is rivalrously signed. Six appear in the two rivalrous cases of a Democratic governorship and each house and its Republican unified counterpart. Democrats call for increases; Republicans for decreases.

TABLE 5.5 Party Control and Tax Burdens: Proposals and Enactments of Changes in the Personal and Corporate Income Taxes and the General Sales Tax

A) Changes in the personal income tax:				
Gov./Senate/House	*Proposals*		*Enactments*	
	Coeff.	*St. err.*	*Coeff.*	*St. err.*
Dem/Dem/Dem (ddd)	**0.35****	**(0.13)**	**0.43#**	**(0.21)**
Dem/Dem/Rep (ddr)	0.10	(0.23)	0.70	(0.75)
Dem/Rep/Dem (drd)	0.47	(0.62)	0.21	(0.19)
Dem/Rep/Rep (drr)	*0.29#*	*(0.16)*	*–0.51*	*(0.62)*
Rep/Rep/Rep (rrr)	**–0.60****	**(0.14)**	**–0.49****	**(0.14)**
Rep/Dem/Rep (rdr)	–0.89	(0.69)	–0.95	(0.61)
Rep/Rep/Dem (rrd)	–0.02	(0.20)	0.05	(0.14)
Rep/Dem/Dem (rdd)	–0.02	*(0.16)*	*0.30*	*(0.22)*

(*Continued*)

TABLE 5.5 (Continued)

B) Changes in the corporate income tax:				
Gov./Senate/House	*Proposals*		*Enactments*	
	Coeff.	*St. err.*	*Coeff.*	*St. err.*
Dem/Dem/Dem (ddd)	0.10#	(0.05)	0.15	(0.11)
Dem/Dem/Rep (ddr)	-0.06	(0.09)	0.53	(0.44)
Dem/Rep/Dem (drd)	0.28	(0.20)	0.16	(0.11)
Dem/Rep/Rep (drr)	*0.05*	*(0.06)*	*-0.38*	*(0.33)*
Rep/Rep/Rep (rrr)	-0.23#	(0.12)	-0.11	(0.08)
Rep/Dem/Rep (rdr)	-0.20	(0.14)	-0.00	(0.11)
Rep/Rep/Dem (rrd)	-0.11	(0.07)	-0.00	(0.04)
Rep/Dem/Dem (rdd)	*0.03*	*(0.09)*	*-0.01*	*(0.02)*

C) Changes in the general sales tax:				
Gov./Senate/House	*Proposals*		*Enactments*	
	Coeff.	*St. err.*	*Coeff.*	*St. err.*
Dem/Dem/Dem (ddd)	0.23#	(0.13)	0.17	(0.14)
Dem/Dem/Rep (ddr)	-0.21	(0.27)	0.05	(0.20)
Dem/Rep/Dem (drd)	0.26	(0.33)	-0.05	(0.22)
Dem/Rep/Rep (drr)	*0.12*	*(0.14)*	*-0.08*	*(0.18)*
Rep/Rep/Rep (rrr)	-0.31*	(0.15)	-0.17	(0.14)
Rep/Dem/Rep (rdr)	0.07	(0.14)	0.15	(0.30)
Rep/Rep/Dem (rrd)	0.26	(0.41)	-0.07	(0.08)
Rep/Dem/Dem (rdd)	*0.03*	*(0.09)*	*-0.01*	*(0.02)*

Each coefficient represents the regression coefficient for the dummy variable of each "party condition" in an equation with fixed effects with state-clustered standard errors and with the (unreported) six covariates per the equations in Table 5.5. Unified party control effects are in **bold**. The complete set of results can be obtained from the third-named author.
= 0.10. * = 0.05, ** = 0.01.

Oddly enough, there even appears to be a consistency in proportionality – Republican governors' calls for cuts across the three taxes typically exceed Democratic calls for increases by about 2 to 1. In the gubernatorial proposal stage, Republican governors can stake out tougher positions than legislatures can or are willing to enact. Note that the proportionality does not apply to enactments. In enactments, the paralleling of Republican "cuts" and Democratic "adds" are roughly equal in size. In enactments, action is more meaningful where talk (and votes) on the floor is not cheap.

Democratic governors propose a 0.35% increase in the personal income tax, on average, but then get handed a 0.43% increase by their co-legislators. This Democratic gubernatorial positive "serve" and even more positive legislative "return" is also weakly present in the analysis of the corporation income tax. Republican governors with Republican legislative chambers tend to commit to a tax-cut position more dramatic than their legislators accept.

Once again, the partisan effects in distributing the burden of financing the states appear most clear-cut in the cases of unified partisan institutional controls. Our expectations are that unified Democrats will favor increases in the redistributive taxation of personal and corporate income and unified Republicans will more likely favor changes in the consumption tax on consumer sales. While it is the case that Democratic regimes are more likely to favor increases in the personal and corporate income taxes, they also favor positive, albeit smaller, changes in the general sales tax. By favoring increases in the regressive general sales tax, the message here seems clear for Democrats – "fiscal footprint" trumps "distributive burden." I suspect that in the quest for resources on the spending side, Democrats are – weakly – likely to favor increases in the sales tax. This is more consistently true for gubernatorial proposals as compared with legislative enactments. Further, I cannot claim that full Republican control (RRR) generates much difference across the three taxes. Here, tax-cutting trumps considerations of distributive burden. Republicans, when in full control, are as eager to cut sales taxes as they are the personal and corporate income taxes.

The partisan effects are most pronounced in the case of changes in the personal income tax. Democratic governors propose increases, and their co-partisans in the legislature concur, albeit with variable responses. Republican governors strongly push for cuts to the income tax, and Republican legislators strongly agree. In terms of proposals, the RRR condition leads to strong gubernatorial proposals and gain, by and large, weaker legislative responses. In the case of DDD, there are modestly strong pro-tax proposals by governors and much weaker legislative responses in increases for the corporate and general sales tax. For the personal income tax, unified Democratic legislatures strongly endorse increases in the personal income tax.

The parallel cases of split institutional control (DRR, RDD) provide some contrasting effects. The cases of Democratic governors facing Republican legislatures promoting increases in the personal income tax as recommendations to their legislative Republican counterparts, only to be rebuffed by the legislative chambers. Republican governors facing Democratic chambers appear to pursue a different path. Little in the way of tax increases of any kind is proposed by these minority party Republican executives. In turn, little gets changed by their Democratic legislative counterparts. It's as if all are stuck in the *status quo* of inter-institutional conflict.

The cases of split chamber control (DDR, DRD, RDR, RRD; in red or in fainter text) present mixed and quite attenuated results. Democratic governors tend to (signs of four of six coefficients) promote tax increases to the legislators, one chamber of which is other-party controlled. Similar results appear for Republican governors. Note that while Republican governors in the split chamber situations recommend increases (signs only, not significant), only in the regressive general sales tax situation does the split chamber also respond with increases. Split chamber control, where Republicans hold only one chamber, by and large, reacts with tax increases. Split chamber with Democrats holding one chamber react – with one exception also with tax increases. The one exception – the RDR configuration – the Republican governor asks for an income tax cut, and the DR legislature responds with a tax cut of roughly equal size. However, none of the coefficients in the split chamber regressions is significant.

Conclusions

What can I conclude about the links between party and tax changes? I do believe that taxes in the American states "cohere." When one kind of tax change is proposed and/or enacted, another corresponding tax is also likely to be proposed or enacted. This correspondence, I argue, fits onto a politico-cognitive mapping of the taxing terrain basically defined, I would now argue, by "fiscal footprint" and redistributive taxation, and weakly so by consumption/regressive taxation.

Second, whatever ambiguities there might be on the impact of Democratic control vs. Republican control in America's capitals, the taxing differences are profound in both the aggregate and at the level of particular taxes.[19] Democrats prefer and more often enact tax increases, while the opposite is true of Republicans. Further, Democrats appear to be more broadly "taxers." They propose increases in the Big Three taxes and in the minor taxes as well. Further, when they are in a position to enact them (DDD), these taxes do get increased. The fiscal footprint is large and positive for Democrats and small, if not negative, in the case of Republican control.

The necessary conditions for assertion of both footprint and distributive effects depend strongly on unified party control. As one moves from unified control to, say, split institutional control, both proposal effects and enactment effects, both in footprint and distributive burdens, become attenuated. That is even more so the case in the split chamber condition, where the one institution under majority party control appears to effectively stymie the other two institutional counterparts.

Notes

1 For the earliest time period in their study, 1936, there were a total of forty-six policy measures. They employed 148 measures in the last period of their study, which ended in 2014.

2 The phrase appears most often as "God is in the details," and, appropriately so, is most often attributed to the architect, Mies van der Rohe. For financing the state, the "devil" phrasing may be more appropriate.

3 Alt and Lowery's "fiscal scale" concept points to their manifest interest in the *size* of state-by-state governmental outlays. The concept of the *taxing footprint* points in two directions: both the depth of the tax extractions from those affected as well as the fineness or the differences across the variety of tax extractions. In backpacking, you can judge the nature of the previous hiker's shoes via her *footprints*: deep and finely articulated impressions (per new Vibram™ boot soles) or less distinct and well-rounded impressions (old, well-used boots, sneakers, or – believe it or not in the Sierra Nevada mountains – Crocs or flip-flops).

4 I drop Nebraska with its nonpartisan, single-chamber legislature from the analysis.

5 Revenues collected are only fractionally affected by contemporaneous political actions by the governors and legislators. Collections are largely a function of past actions and economic performance. I have labeled these in an earlier chapter as "policy outputs."

6 A personal footnote from the author: Upon retirement, many of my fellow Hanover, New Hampshire residents move to Florida homes or condominiums for the required six months plus one day a year – no surprise during the winter months – thereby gaining legal residence in Florida and benefitting from living in a sunny, warm, and *income-tax-free* state. In late spring, they flock back to their condominiums in Wilder, Vermont, where they, as non-residents, escape the Vermont income tax (as now-Florida residents), but they also continue to do their shopping in nearby Hanover and West Lebanon, NH – and thus their *consumption outlays are sales-tax-free.* Put simply, they have devised a tri-state retirement strategy of living free of broad-based taxes – the winter half of the year in the "Sunshine State" and the summer half of the year in Vermont, the "Beckoning Country," while shopping in sales-tax-free "Live Free or Die," New Hampshire.

7 Note that I have no data on gubernatorial proposals for expenditures nor final legislative action on expenditures. A full fiscal model would, of course, include both.

8 Our data on gubernatorial proposals for changes in state taxes are drawn from the spring issues of *Fiscal Survey of the States* (hereafter, FSS) published by the National Association of State Budget Officers (hereafter NASBO) and accessible here: http://www.nasbo.org/mainsite/reports-data/fiscal-survey-of-states/fiscal-survey-archives. The final agreements between the governor and legislature are recorded in the fall issue of FSS-F.

9 Note that the figure for "revenue resources" includes expected federal aid, expected revenue given current program estimates, and other sources of revenue.

10 Our "individualist/user" set of taxes, fees, and licenses is known among New Hampshire legislators as the "Five Bs" – taxes and charges on "beer, booze, bellies, beds, and butts," taxes, respectively, on beer, alcohol, meals, hotel/motel rooms, and cigarettes. In a survey of NH and VT legislators, Winters (Winters 1976) discovered strong linkages among precisely these programs when asked, given a hypothetical state budget deficit, what kinds of revenue changes legislators would prefer to resolve the state deficit.

11 As noted, for institutional reasons, Nebraska was dropped from the analysis, a conventional decision in studies of the American states.

12 In all analyses of "party control," the "mixed" cases where either the governor is an "independent" (e.g. Ventura in MN, Chafee in RI, King in ME) or when either of the chambers is split 50/50 (N=41) are dropped from the sample.

13 In bivariate regressions with fixed effects and clustered by state – of the two simple links in Table 5.1 panel (B) – the simple regression coefficients indicate that for every 1 percent increase/decrease in the personal income tax proposed by the Republican governor, the Republican House and Senate respond, on average, with a .65% increase/decrease. The comparable coefficient for the 1% recommendations for the corporation income tax is .94%.

14 The state-by-state unemployment rates were obtained here: https://www.bls.gov/web/laus/ststdsadata.txt. The changes in unemployment rates by state reflect the January-to-January changes and were calculated by the author.

15 The Ns for the various configurations of party control are:

DDD = 312 DDR = 49 DRD = 90	DDD + RRR = 618 = unified party control
DRR = 138 RRR = 306 RDR = 47	DRR + RDD = 394 = split institutional control
RRD = 60 RDD = 256	DDR + DRD + RDR + RRD = 246 = split branch control

16 See the discussion by Thomas Schelling on the "last clear chance" and conditional commitment strategies in *Strategies of Commitment and Other Essays* (2006) and *The Strategy of Conflict* (1980).

17 Albeit, there was another simpler explanation for Rauner's failure ... he was a terrible politician.

18 The complete results are available from the author, who can be reached at rfw@dartmouth.edu. The covariate results largely replicate what I present in Tables 5.5 and 5.6.

19 Caughey, Xu, and Warshaw (2017) review the very mixed literature on the impacts of party control on policy change in the American states.

6

PARTY AND IDEOLOGY IN GOVERNORS IN SHAPING TAX CHANGES

Richard F. Winters, Nicholas Dominguez and Tyler E. Frisbee

Introduction

In his first inaugural address (January 20, 1981), Ronald Reagan remarked: "In this present crisis, government is not the solution to our problem; government is the problem." What followed was a stream of tax-cutting proposals by Reagan and Republican presidential successors as an effort to "starve the beast." While the tax-cutting strategy, well-articulated by Reagan and with intellectual origins in the writings of James Buchanan and colleagues,[1] the Republican tax-cutting strategy may have had, as well, an attractive electoral and political appeal as a dramatic equilibrium point in a Republican reverse electoral "coalition of minorities" strategy.[2]

By cutting taxes, Republicans argued, "we will force politicians to make choices and we, the Republicans, will not allow self-indulgent, undeserving minorities to continue feeding at the government trough." At the national level, Republicans failed to identify who, precisely, constituted these aggrandizing minorities, nor how the party would amass a winning legislative coalition of binding constraints on spending. It appears that the party leaders were attempting to persuade diverse minorities that only government beneficiaries such as "welfare queens" would be trimmed,[3] or, alternatively, groups other than the listening minority voter would be deprived. The result was Republican cuts in taxes, but few, if any, cuts in spending, which resulted in ballooning deficits. At some point, Washington Republicans would claim that "government-as-Leviathan" would choke on its own debt. But the situation in Washington is quite different from that

DOI: 10.4324/9781003606291-9

of the American states, where debt as a consequence of budgetary deficits either does not exist or is a short term – two years at most – phenomenon.

All the states but one state have some sort of binding rule, and, if not a rule, then the appearance of a binding norm that results, year after year, in budget balancing over a one- or two-year period.[4] If a state's leaders cut taxes and revenues fail to meet budgetary needs, either spending cuts must be made or new taxes, fees, or charges must be imposed to balance the budget. The most telling recent drama of Republican tax-cutting strategy at the state level must be Sam Brownback's eight-year, two-term governorship in Kansas.[5] Brownback's eight years and the very sizeable post-Reagan Republican gubernatorial cohort pose the question: Whether, in fact, Republican governors in the American states have followed a tax-cutting strategy. Further, is there a Democratic counterpart strategy of increasing taxes? If so, we ask: How would we know it? Further, which taxes were proposed to be changed, and which governors, when, and under what political conditions?

While in Washington, both tax cutting and tax increasing focus on the personal income tax, but the states possess a wide array of taxes, fees, and charges. Both in cutting and increasing, do Republican/Democratic governors systematically favor one tax over the other? In this paper, via examining gubernatorial proposals to change the general sales tax and/or the personal income tax, we can assess whether Republican governors differ systematically from their Democratic counterparts when they propose increasing or cutting taxes. And for the 1990–2006+ period, and as the added value of this chapter, we have informed judgments regarding the liberalism or conservatism of individual governors, which will allow us to assess whether moderate governors differ from their more extreme – left and right – colleagues in their tax proposals.

Put simply, do very conservative Republican governors ask for greater tax cuts than their more moderate Republican colleagues? Further, if they ask, are the more conservative Republican governors more successful in gaining the assent of their legislative partisans? And is there a complement present for Democrats? Are more liberal Democratic governors greater "taxers," are their requests more "redistributional," and are they more successful in legislative passage?

Empirical assessments of tax changes

Utilizing Random Forest techniques, Rainey, Stout, and Winters (Chapter 4 in this volume) assessed plausible factors associated with 1990–2014 enacted revenue changes in eight classes of taxes, fees, and charges in the fifty American states. Our largely exploratory findings were a compound of the expected, e.g. budget shortfalls lead to increased taxes, but also complementary and unexpected ones – even states facing surpluses were likely to "increase taxes ... slightly."[6] Embedded in assessing tax change differences, however, were questions of "causal origin." While unified Democratic governments differed from unified Republican governments, did these differences have their origin in the "corner office" of the governor and reflect the governor's party, her sincere preferences, or foresightful strategic choices; or, were tax change differences a product of partisan legislative control? Plausibly, Democratic governors might propose a quite different "schedule" of revenue changes – increasing the income tax or slashing the sales tax – reflecting either personal choice or the "second best" strategy of recommending that which can pass.[7]

Further, Democratic governors or more "liberal" ones might propose different schedules of taxes as compared with their more "moderate" peers. A similar observable difference might appear for the proposals of "very conservative" vs. "moderate" Republican governors. In this paper, we characterize the present effort as assessing what governors reveal regarding their preferences in changing three measures of taxation:

> (1) the totals of taxes, fees, and charges – changes in "fiscal footprint,"[8] and (2 and 3) the gubernatorial recommendations in the two most important statewide, "broad-based" taxes, changes in the personal income and the general sales tax, and changes in "distributional direction."

Our prior work points to partisan differences that might have legislative origins (Chapter 5). Puzzling "leads" were in our findings: While the impact on tax changes of the Democratic share of the House exceeded the variable of the Democratic share of the Senate, in and of itself not entirely understandable, both legislative variables dwarfed the effects of the governor's party in effecting enacted changes in existing taxes, fees, and charges (see Fig. 5:6). But these findings do not shed much light, one way or the other, on what goes on earlier in the "causal funnel," whether governors as a function of party, ideology, or personal views may propose quite different schedules of tax changes.[9] Our earlier paper examined enacted changes; this paper pushes backward causally to the first stage – what does the governor propose regarding tax and revenue changes? And, as stated above for our purposes, the relevant measures of "tax changes" are twofold: (1) the scale of the proposed change in taxes (the total size or footprint of the enlarging or shrinking taxes, fees, and charges), and (2) are the proposed tax changes redistributive (progressive via changing the personal income taxes) or (3) distributive (regressive via changes in the sales tax)?[10]

Our current data set allows us to decompose the "budgetary process" into three "stages" of revenue actions: (1) gubernatorial "proposals" for changing taxes, fees, and charges; (2) final legislative agreement with the governor as "enacted"; and (3) the final revenues actually "collected." Given the serial nature of our data, our analytic postures, we believe, begin from a pose somewhat different from others. Alt and Lowry (1994, 2000, 2003) and Poterba (1994a, b) are the archetype of political economy analyses. They – and others – examine the results of what states end up with by analyzing "revenues collected," i.e. the final "stage" in the revenue process. We approach the issue more from the perspective of "the politics of the budgetary process" (Wildavsky (a) 1964, 1974; Wildavsky (b) 1988, 1992, 2001). Governors propose, legislatures dispose and force agreement with the governor, while revenue administrators collect, and citizens and businesses pay up, shelter, dodge, evade, move to another state, and so on. Legislatures may "dispose" by ignoring the governor's proposals and simply not changing revenue programs, choosing instead to cut expenditures in order to balance the budget. Alternatively, legislators may enact new and different revenue changes from that which the governor proposed. But the governor's proposal is the initial stage; it's the stage that we turn to in this analysis and pose the question of whether and what kinds of scale and distributional differences manifest themselves in "first actions," the set of gubernatorial proposals for changing taxes. We expect that tax cutting is not indiscriminate, much the opposite: Tax cutting should discriminate among taxes as a function of their distributional impact.

There is another telling factor in assessing gubernatorial "first moves." Barrilleaux, Holbrook, and Langer (2002) note, under some conditions, partisan sincerity may well emerge, while under opposing conditions, a more strategic view likely dominates. They examined the effects of just-completed gubernatorial campaigns and argued that as incumbents' margins of victory increase, governors are more likely to engage in sincere programmatic behavior. We suggest a proxy and institutional equivalent of this condition and argue that under unified party control, we expect greater sincere behavior from the two parties – more taxation and personal and sales tax increases forwarded by Democratic governors and/or less taxation and/or decreases in the income and sales taxes by Republican governors.

Analytic considerations for tax policy analyses in the American states

Several considerations condition our analysis. First, many analysts of state politics and policy focus on broad understandings of policy and policy change (Caughey, Warshaw, and Xu 2017; Erikson, Wright, and McIver

1989, 1993; Jacoby and Schneider, 2009). These sometimes breathtakingly broad views of the policy process sum up what, on balance, governments do state by state and what might be termed the states' broadly thought-of public policy "dispositions" and their measures as state-by-state scorecards.[11] An alternative focus of political science is the explanation of changes in particular, deeply sanctioned public policies. We can think of no set of policies where the authoritative allocations of indulgences vs. deprivations are more keenly and widely distributed than in the dollar-by-dollar changes in taxes actually altered by state actions. In contrast to broad macro-views of policy, we focus on particular taxes being changed by particular amounts at particular moments in time by particular individuals and partisans.

Second, when analysts focus on more narrowly precise dollar measures of tax policy in the states, they typically examine summary dollar measures of revenue collected, which are very much "after the fact" of policy change and only partially reflect the politics of actual changes in tax policy (Besley and Case 1995b; Dennis, Moore, and Somerville 2007; Dilger 1998; Fredriksson, Wang, and Warren 2013; Leigh 2008; Alt and Lowry 1994, 2000, 2003; Poterba 1994b). Revenue dollars collected are a mix of changes in personal incomes, changes in consumption of items/services taxed, and possibly changes in statutory enactments that a state adopts. The latter is the proper object of political analytic attention, precisely that which we focus on here. The existing levels, amounts, or changes in taxes collected are a compound of many factors, where political choices are only one of many. We focus on the discrete tax choices that politicians, in our case governors, make in promoting revenue change.

Third, even when analysts focus on other-than-dollar changes in specific taxes, they typically examine the changes in rates of the taxes (Kone and Winters (1980); Mikesell, 1978; Nelson, 2000; Case, 1994). But taxes are changed via routes other than rate changes. Put directly, changes in tax rates do not always capture changes in the amount of dollars collected. Non-rate changes appear, in fact, to be the modal type of change, and the NASBO data that we employ capture the dollar amount of all changes in taxes – in the totals and in specific classes of taxes, irrespective of the modalities of the changes.[12] An example: NASBO's data on state-by-state, change-by-change details are unpacked in Table A-3 of – as an example, on p. 76 of the Fall 2011 publication – and, in that year, there were nineteen discrete statutory changes in sales taxes across the states, but only four of these changes might plausibly be caught up as a change of rates via the Book of the States. Our data sweeps up and aggregates all changes in taxes by the class of tax, not just changes in the tax rate. Changes in rates are important, but the dollar change in taxes remains the more politically relevant variable.

In point of fact, it may be the case that in any electoral timing of tax changes by politicians, our elected political actors – governors and legislators – may well prefer non-rate changes in tax laws in the electoral year because these more subtle changes are less likely to gain public recognition (and eventual voter opprobrium) and thus more easily agreed upon. If so, there may be an election year aversion to rate changes in taxes, per Mikesell and Nelson, but there may be absolutely no relationship at all between dollar changes and electoral timing. Budget making and balancing have strict timings. How the budget is balanced – the modalities of budget balancing via different revenue strategies may be electorally timed; rate changes may be "okay" for year 1 of a gubernatorial and legislative terms but not at all "okay" for the year before an election. We suspect that how taxes and revenues might be changed is electorally sensitive; the actual revenue dollar amounts changed might be quite smooth over a two- or four-year electoral cycle.

Fourth, most political analyses of public policy changes in the American states are outlay or expenditure based; the studies focus on spending such as AFDC/TANF welfare or on summary spending aggregates (Chapter 8 of this volume; Plotnick and Winters 1985; Barrilleaux, Holbrook, and Langer 2002; Jacoby and Schneider 2001, 2009). As aggregates, these can be faulted as conflating the supply of budget monies (how much is budgeted) with the actual demand for spending. Or, in the case of Jacoby and Schneider, spending aggregates of many different programs are folded together in an effort to make sense, politically, of what a state "does" (2009).[13] In contrast, our dependent variables are specific changes in specific tax programs in specific years and expressed in dollar terms. There is no ambiguity about the breadth of dollars authorized or conflating like and unlike spending programs at work in our data. When a governor proposes an increase of $4.77 billion in the state's income tax (Governor Arnold Schwarzenegger (R-CA) 2009) or a $2.92 billion increase in the state sales tax (Governor Pat Quinn (D-IL) 2009), there is no confusion as to who advanced what nor by how much.

An analytic advantage of focusing on the American states is to begin resolving the question of what choices politicians make about taxes when "deficits do matter." For the fifty governors and for their states' legislators, deficits matter.[14] Many have noted that there are state constitutional or statutory limits on debt financing in forty-nine of the fifty states, and in the 50th, Vermont, there appears to be a budgetary norm that precludes debt carried over past a two-year budget cycle. So, if budget balancing is the controlling practice in the states, the regimen for gaining equilibrium has to be either spending cuts or tax increases. Our focus is on the latter, and this research will, we hope, throw light on the determinants of who uses what taxes to gain budget balance. Who favors what kinds of taxes and why motivates our analysis, and answering for American governors may well indicate what the answer might be for American presidents if faced with a similar enforceable "rule" for budget balancing.

Given gubernatorial recommendations for change, we suggest that two dimensions of these 1990–2016 changes are questions of initial importance: first, whether to expand or contract the taxing "footprint" via greater or lesser taxes, the question of tax scale; and, second, whether the choice to expand/contract is redistributive – in our case, the more progressive personal income tax[15] or the corporate income tax – or individualist and consumption – the general sales tax. Put simply, we ask whether (1) the governor's recommendation is to increase or cut taxes; that is to say, whether to expand or contract the tax base of his/her state; and (2) are the gubernatorial recommendations to expand/contract progressive – in our case, the personal/corporate income taxes – or regressive – the general sales tax? We focus on these revenue programs in part because of size – they comprise about 75% of all taxes collected by the states.[16] Further, these programs span the perceived, if not the actual, redistributive tax choices made by governors and legislators.[17] For our purposes, we characterize a proposed positive change in a state's personal or corporate income tax as positive redistributive change and an increase in the general sales tax as its opposite – diminished redistribution. Of course, a decrease in the personal income tax is a negative redistributive change, as would a decrease in the general consumption sales tax be represented as, and seen as, positively redistributive.

The NASBO data and our dependent variables

Annual data are available from fiscal year (FY) 1988 to 2014 on the recommended revenue dollar changes in taxes, fees, and charges that governors advance in messages to their states' legislators.[18] What is striking about the data is their breadth and concreteness. Traditionally, at the beginning of the legislative session, each state's governor delivers his/her state of the state and/or budget addresses, which contain spending and taxing recommendations. The National Association of State Budget Officers (hereafter NASBO) collates reports from each state's budget office on the revenue changes proposed by each state's governor for eight different tax and revenue programs. These recommendations – published in the spring issue of Fiscal Survey of States (hereafter FSS) – are embedded in the beginning-of-the-year gubernatorial budget proposals and are published in the form of "dollars of revenue change recommended" for each of the eight revenue classes.[19] To aid interpretation, we standardize each of the enacted changes in revenue (in dollars) by the previous year's revenue data. We measure these tax changes as the recommended change in taxes as a percentage of the prior year's "revenue resources." This makes the changes across large and small states comparable. Thus, our dependent variables of interest are:

1 Gubernatorially proposed total changes in all taxes, fees, licenses, and charges as a (1a) in nominal dollar terms and (1b) as a percentage of past total revenue;
2 gubernatorially proposed total dollar changes in the "personal income tax" (2c) in nominal dollars and (2d) as a percentage of past total revenue; and
3 (3e) gubernatorially proposed total nominal dollar changes in the "general consumer sales tax"; and (3f) changes in the sales tax as a percentage of past total revenue.

Plausible determinants

We believe that gubernatorial tax proposal differences will emerge after controlling for (1) relevant socio-economic and (2) relevant institutional controls. Relevant "footprint" and distributional changes will be related to (3) varying gubernatorial partisan identities, (4) personal ideological differences – more or less liberal or conservative – between and among Democratic and Republican governors, and (5) unified party control of state political institutions.

Socio-economic controls

(1) In our earlier work (Chapter 6), we noted that wealthier states are better positioned to finance arrays of public goods. Further, as the states' populations grow in wealth, they may well prefer a broader array of public goods, services, and amenities. As the states grow in population, this may also affect the demand for changes in revenue. Changes in these two socio-economic measures may well indicate changes in the demand for public goods and the available supply of income for assessing revenues; therefore, we add, with expected causal direction in parentheses for nominal and percentage change dependent variables:

1 total statewide population (+, +);
2 total statewide income (+, +);
3 change in population numbers (+, +); and
4 change in statewide income in nominal dollars (+, +).

Fiscal institutional variables

(5) The higher the existing revenue burdens in dollars and as a percentage of personal income in the state, the smaller the likelihood of a gubernatorial proposal for a footprint-scale-in-revenue increase (– and –). We measure the variable of "existing revenue burden" as the estimate of the percentage of "revenue" available to the governor stated as a percentage of statewide personal income. The higher the percentage of the burden, the more reluctant the governor will be to further increase it. Every increase in a tax, fee, or charge must come at some marginal political cost relative to the vote gain for new or continued political spending (Downs 1957). Further, the higher the existing burden, relative to other states and other times, must sharpen the governor's calculations as to likely vote gain. Stated differently, there are sharply diminishing vote returns to marginal increases in the already high-revenue-burdened states.

Variables (6 and 7): The higher the revenue collected by the income and sales taxes and, respectively, the tax shares of the income or sales tax as a percentage of total resources, the less likely there will be positive changes, respectively, in these two taxes (– and –). A governor comparatively calculates across revenue streams, and as these two taxes increase as a percentage of total resources, her calculations might well suggest, "look elsewhere" for new revenue. Put differently, while there are diminishing political returns to high aggregate revenue burdens increasing over time, there are also diminishing returns to increasing already-existing taxes that exist as a high tax share as a percent of resources. Further, increasing already high burdens of the income or sales tax might put the state at an economic disadvantage relative to adjacent nearby states.[20] Resource shares are measured as "tax as a percentage of resources."

Further, (8) the greater the expected surplus in dollar terms and as a percentage of total resources, per the time of the gubernatorial message, the less likely a proposal for increased taxes (– and –). NASBO publishes the "balance" estimate in the spring issue. The "balance" ranges in nominal dollar terms from a –$5.855 billion in 2009 in CA to a surplus of $10.8 billion in CA in 2007. Stated as a percentage of "resources," Oregon in 2003 led the way with a projected deficit of –28%, while Texas in 200 × had a 42% surplus forecasted. We expect that increases in resource scale are likely the greater the deficit, and shrinking the size of the state taxes is likely as the surplus swells.

And (9), as a state's budget stabilization fund shrinks in dollar terms and as the percentage of the prior year's budget stabilization fund decreases, that is to say, the greater the drop in the value of the fund over the prior year, more taxes will be proposed (+ and +). The "budget stabilization" or "rainy day" funds are revenues set aside to tide a state over short-term dips in resources (Rose 2008). Inevitably, there will be conflict over the meaning of the "short term," but nevertheless, sharp falls in rainy day funds signal leaders and followers of doubts in the capacity of current revenue programs to finance the state, thus increasing in the size or scale of revenues proposed.

Political determinants

For governors as elected officials, the political factors of party, ideology, and the preferences of the individual governors mediate changes in size and direction in taxes. Governors' revealed preferences in taxing – both in scale and distribution – would be shaped by (10) gubernatorial Democrats. Alt and Lowry (1994) stipulate that the Democratic Party is the "high demand" party for public goods and the Republicans are the "low demand" party. Further, we argue that the political parties differ on tax distributional issues, with the Democrats favoring redistributional taxation (the income tax) and the Republicans favoring greater distributional equity among persons via consumption taxation (the sales tax). Given that, Democratic governors are more likely to propose increases in scale in taxation and more redistributive taxation (Klarner, n.d.) (+ and +), while we expect the opposite from Republican governors.

As well, (11 and 12) greater scale changes in taxes and greater redistributive taxation will be proposed when a Democratic governor is coupled with unified Democratic party control of the states' legislative chambers (+ and +).[21] The opposite will be true of unified Republican control.

(13 and 14) Governors who are themselves characterized as "liberal/conservative" will recommend greater/lesser scale and redistributional tax changes; that is (+ and +) (Dominguez, Frisbee, Winters 2009).[22] We have data for the states and a subset of time (1990–2006) on informed respondents' judgments regarding the personal political positions of American governors. Democratic governors who are judged to be more liberal will likely push for more redistributive taxation (+ and +), while more conservative Republicans will prefer less on both counts (– and –).

(15) More taxes and more redistributive taxes will be proposed in the first year of the gubernatorial term (+ and +) (Mikesell 1978; Nelson 2000; Case 1994). The "first year effect" operates, we suggest, as the conflation of three symmetric forces: (a) the first year is the most distant from the next election reckoning and thus appears to be the safest for imposing new costs on voters. Second, (b) the first year follows a campaign where commitments are publicly expressed regarding new programs and new spending that needs to be financed. And, (c) the first year of a gubernatorial term

follows the terminal or last year of the prior governor's term, where the incumbent may well obscure heightened spending that must some time come due in the face of her reelection campaign or that of her successor.

(16) The least amount of tax and redistributive changes will occur in the last, pre-election year of the governor's term (– and –). The electoral incentives are, of course, the obverse of the "first year." And, whatever programmatic innovations occurred in the early years of the governor's term should now be in place and "delivering" her campaign promises.

Analysis

Table 6.1 displays the results for the full model for the "fiscal footprint" variable of the sum of all new tax proposals by American governors. Important results consistently appear across four different analyses. In columns (1) and (2), we examine the effects of the proposed determinants of the simple dollar size of gubernatorial new tax proposals. In the first two columns, labeled "Economic, Institutional and Political variables," we assess the partisan and institutional control variables while controlling for a set of plausible covariates. As predicted, we find that unified Republican control of states' political institutions consistently results in cutting taxes. The opposing effects of Democratic control are consistently positive, albeit small and insignificant for Democratic governors, but significantly positive for Democratic unified control. The opposite is true for unified Republican control, negatively and significantly so. The effect of year "1" of an administration also has the predicted positive taxing effects. This finding conflicts with results of Rainey, Stout, and Winters (2014), where the timing variables had little to no effect on enacted tax changes. The unanswered question here is whether these dependent variables of proposals have timing qualities while, in the end game of enactment, timing washes out.

Columns in (2) ("...with Gubernatorial preference variables") add the separate variables of estimated spatial positions of Democratic and Republican governors. Neither increasing gubernatorial liberalism among Democratic governors nor increasing conservatism among their Republican counterparts appears to have any effects. The main effects of unified control by each party remain strong and in the predicted direction. We can conclude that in assessing the simple dollar amounts of taxes proposed by governors of each of the two parties, their personal position, as more or less liberal or conservative, appears to play little role in formulating their tax proposals.

In both models (1) and (2), assessing nominal dollar amounts of proposed taxes, only four of our eight economic and institutional control variables were significant. In assessing tax dollar amounts proposed (1), state

TABLE 6.1 Baseline Analysis of the Sum of all Gubernatorial Proposed Taxes

	(A) Sum of all Tax Proposals in Nominal dollars *All states, all yrs. N = 1298* *All states, 1990-on, N = 909*				*(B) Sum of all Tax Proposals as % of Total Revenue* *All states, all yrs. N = 1298* *All states,1990-on, N = 909*			
	Econ. Institut. & Pol.		*.with Gubernatorial*		*Econ. Institut. & Pol.*		*.with Gubernatorial*	
	Variables Coeff.	*Preference Variables Std. Error*	*Variables Coeff*	*Preference Variables Std. Error*	*Variables Coeff.*	*Preference Variables Std. Error*	*Variables Coeff.*	*Preference Variables Std. Error*
Economic variables								
1) Total statewide population (+)	−0.00004***	0.0000	−0.00004***	0.0000	−0.0000001	0.000000	0.0000001	0.000000
2) Total statewide income (+)	0.0018***	0.0002	0.0018***	0.0002	0.000004*	0.000002	0.000004*	0.000002
3) Yearly change in popul. (+)	21	20	20	20	0.06	0.16	0.06	0.16
4) Yearly change in income (+)	1.52	5.5	−1.6	5.5	−0.04	0.04	−0.04	0.04
Institutional variables								
5) Revenue as % of Pers. Inc. (−)	0.31	1.34	0.34	1.34	−0.01	0.01	−0.01	0.009

(Continued)

TABLE 6.1 (Continued)

	(A) Sum of all Tax Proposals in Nominal dollars All states, all yrs. N = 1298 All states, 1990-on, N = 909				*(B) Sum of all Tax Proposals as % of Total Revenue All states, all yrs. N = 1298 All states,1990-on, N = 909*			
	Econ. Institut. & Pol.		*.with Gubernatorial*		*Econ. Institut. & Pol.*		*.with Gubernatorial*	
	Variables Coeff.	*Preference Variables Std. Error*	*Variables Coeff*	*Preference Variables Std. Error*	*Variables Coeff.*	*Preference Variables Std. Error*	*Variables Coeff.*	*Preference Variables Std. Error*
6) Tax share of income tax (–)	–1.44	1.14	–1.4	1.14	–0.034**	0.01	–0.034***	0.009
7) Tax share of sales tax (–)	–1.55	1.34	–1.45	1.35	–0.012	0.01	–0.012	0.01
8) Expected surplus (–)	–0.18***	0.02	–0.19***	0.02	–0.0006**	0.0002	–0.0006**	0.0002
9) Change in budget stab. fund (–)	0.88	1.31	0.85	1.31	0.01	0.02	0.01	0.02
Political variables:								
10) Democratic governor (+)	17	46	6.55	57.2	0.011	0.34	0.11	0.34
11) Unified Democrat gov't. (+)	133**	48	135**	48	0.54	0.35	0.54	0.35

(Continued)

TABLE 6.1 (Continued)

	(A) Sum of all Tax Proposals in Nominal dollars All states, all yrs. N = 1298 All states, 1990-on, N = 909				*(B) Sum of all Tax Proposals as % of Total Revenue All states, all yrs. N = 1298 All states,1990-on, N = 909*			
	Econ. Institut. & Pol.		*.with Gubernatorial*		*Econ. Institut. & Pol.*		*.with Gubernatorial*	
	Variables Coeff.	*Preference Variables Std. Error*	*Variables Coeff*	*Preference Variables Std. Error*	*Variables Coeff.*	*Preference Variables Std. Error*	*Variables Coeff.*	*Preference Variables Std. Error*
12) Unified Republican gov't. (–)	–118**	46	–118**	46	–1.4***	0.36	–1.41***	0.36
13) Democ. gub liberalism (+)	–	–	-27	33	–	–	0.12	0.21
14) Repub. gub. conserv. (–)	–	–	-7	26	–	–	0.08	0.16
15) 1st year of gubern. term (+)	95.6*	39	96*	39	0.43	0.3	0.43	0.30
16) Last year of gubern. term (–)	5	37	2.5	37	0.31	0.29	0.31	0.29
Adj. r2 = F test = (16, 231)	**0.16** 15.8*** **N = 1248**		**0.16** 573 **N = 909**		0.04 3.7 N = 1248		0.04 3.7 N=909	
One-tailed t test. #= .10, *= .05								

significance of **=.01, ***=.001

population, state income, and the budget surplus were significant. Governors in well-populated states propose fewer tax increases, while those in high-income states propose more in the way of taxes. And, not surprisingly, the larger the expected surplus in the prior year's budget, the less likely that new taxes will be proposed. Our inclusion of the measure of the income tax and sales tax shares of total statewide revenues was expected to be negatively associated with tax increases. The logic is one of marginally increasing political costs by adding to already high levels of personal taxation. The two variables do consistently have the expected negative signs, but only in the case of the income tax share of revenues, when we assess increases in taxes as a percentage of revenues, is it significant.

In columns (3) and (4) of Table 6.1, in the case of the variable of proposed taxes as percentage shares of past total revenue, a similar pattern of coefficients appears, although in greatly attenuated form. Heavily populated states propose smaller tax percentage increases, while wealthy states propose more. The greater the share the income tax is of a state's revenue (in row (6)), the smaller the percentage increase asked for by the governor. Consistent with expectations, states with unified Republican control are more likely to request decreases in taxes. Turning to the equation adding the gubernatorial spatial positions (in column (4)), nothing is added by these two variables.

We would be remiss not to note the very modest total effects of models (A-1) and (A-2) in Table 6.1, with adjusted r-squares of .16 each. This becomes even more attenuated when we turn to models in Table 6.1 (B: 3 and 4) that assess proposed changes in the total taxes as a percentage of past revenues, R^2 of .04 each.

Tables 6.2 and 6.3 take up changes in the income and sales taxes, respectively. Each of the tables, like Table 6.1, is split into two halves, the columns corresponding to (1) and (2) assess changes in dollars in these two taxes as stated in nominal dollar terms, while those under (3) and (4) presents results for changes in the taxes as a percentage of total state revenues. Examining Table 6.2 for changes in the income tax as proposed by the governors, we see that the effects of total statewide population and income continue to be powerful determinants, as we would expect when we look at the diverse array of states with income tax programs. Well-populated states tend, on average, to have smaller tax proposals, while wealthy tend to have larger gubernatorial proposals. But these are also ordinary and usual controls when assessing simple dollar revenues.

Further, in looking at proposed changes in the income tax, as we expect, the greater the share the income tax is of state revenue – in row (3) – the less likely the governor is to propose increases. This finding on the income tax was foreshadowed by results in Table 6.1. This is consistent, we argue,

TABLE 6.2 Sum of Gubernatorial Income Tax Proposals

	(A) Sum of all Tax Proposals in Nominal Dollars All states, all yrs. N = 1298 All states, 1990-on, N = 909				*(B) Sum of all Tax Proposals as % of Total Revenue All states, all yrs. N = 1298 All states,1990-on, N = 909*			
	Econ. Institut. & Pol.		.with Gubernatorial		Econ. Institut. & Pol.		.with Gubernatorial	
	Variables Coeff.	*Preference Variables Std. Error*	*Variables Coeff*	*Preference Variables Std. Error*	*Variables Coeff.*	*Preference Variables Std. Error*	*Variables Coeff.*	*Preference Variables Std. Error*
1) Total statewide population (+)	-0.00003***	0.000005	-0.00002***	0.000006	-0.0000*	0.0000	-0.0000*	0.0000
2) Total statewide income (+)	0.001***	0.0001	0.0009***	0.0002	0.0000**	0.0000	0.000002**	0.000001
3) Tax share of income tax (−)	-2.05**	0.83	-1.86*	0.87	-0.018**	0.005	-0.021***	0.007
4) Tax share of sales tax (−)	0.42	0.82	1.12	0.85	0.006	0.005	0.011#	0.006
5) Expected surplus (−)	-0.13***	0.015	-0.123***	0.016	-0.0002*	0.0001	-0.0002#	0.052
6) Democratic governor (+)	-8.98	25.8	114**	46.6	-0.22	0.17	0.48	0.36
7) Unified democrat gov't. (+)	34.5	26.6	15.5	27.9	-0.022	0.173	-0.11	0.21
8) Unified republican gov't. (−)	-45.5*	25.9	-27.1	29.4	-0.394*	0.168	-0.43#	0.22

(*Continued*)

TABLE 6.2 (Continued)

	(A) Sum of all Tax Proposals in Nominal Dollars *All states, all yrs. N = 1298* *All states, 1990-on, N = 909*				*(B) Sum of all Tax Proposals as % of Total Revenue* *All states, all yrs. N = 1298* *All states,1990-on, N = 909*			
	Econ. Institut. & Pol.		.with Gubernatorial		Econ. Institut. & Pol.		.with Gubernatorial	
	Variables Coeff.	*Preference Variables Std. Error*	*Variables Coeff*	*Preference Variables Std. Error*	*Variables Coeff.*	*Preference Variables Std. Error*	*Variables Coeff.*	*Preference Variables Std. Error*
9) Democ. gub liberalism (+)	–	–	-1.86	20.1	–	–	0.056	0.153
10) Repub. gub. conserv. (–)	–	–	-71.9***	23.1	–	–	-0.411**	0.177
11) 1st year of gubern. term (+)	11.5	21.8	-1.05	23.2	-0.07	0.14	-0.142	0.177
12) Last year of gubern. term (–)	24.3	21.2	-3.67	23.2	0.20	0.14	0.033	0.177
Constant	0.60*				0.29			
Adj. r2 = **F test =**	**0.15** (10, 1061) = 19.2*** N = 1072		0.11 (12, 763) = 9*** **N = 776**		**0.03** (12, 1059) = 3.9*** N = 1072		**0.03** (12, 763) = 3.24** **N = 776**	
One-tailed *t* test. #= .10, *= .05								

significance of **=.01, ***=.001

TABLE 6.3 Sum of Gubernatorial Sales Tax Proposals

	(A) Sum of all Tax Proposals in Nominal dollars All states, all yrs. N = 1298 All states, 1990-on, N = 909				*(B) Sum of all Tax Proposals as % of Total Revenue All states, all yrs. N = 1298 All states,1990-on, N = 909*			
	Econ. Institut. & Pol.		.with Gubernatorial		Econ. Institut. & Pol.		.with Gubernatorial	
	Variables Coeff.	*Preference Variables Std. Error*	*Variables Coeff*	*Preference Variables Std. Error*	*Variables Coeff.*	*Preference Variables Std. Error*	*Variables Coeff.*	*Preference Variables Std. Error*
1) Total statewide population (+)	–0.00001**	0.000004	–0.00002**	0.000005	0.0000	0.0000	0.0000	0.0000
2) Total statewide income (+)	0.0007***	0.0001	0.0007***	0.0001	0.0000	0.0000	0.0000	0.0000
3) Tax share of income tax (–)	–0.117	0.788	–0.13	0.94	0.002	.005	0.004	0.006
4) Tax share of sales tax (–)	–0.571	1.12	–0.32	1.31	–0.002	0.0075	–0.007	0.006
5) Expected surplus (–)	–0.074***	0.01	–0.075***	0.014	–0.0002*	0.00009	–0.0001	0.0001
6) Democratic governor (+)	34.3	22.8	125.3**	42.4	–0.156	0.157	–0.31	0.34
7) Unified Democrat gov't. (+)	56**	23	51.2*	26.9	0.015	0.162	0.054	0.21

(Continued)

TABLE 6.3 (Continued)

	(A) Sum of all Tax Proposals in Nominal dollars *All states, all yrs. N = 1298* *All states, 1990-on, N = 909*				*(B) Sum of all Tax Proposals as % of Total Revenue* *All states, all yrs. N = 1298* *All states,1990-on, N = 909*			
	Econ. Institut. & Pol.		.with Gubernatorial		Econ. Institut. & Pol.		.with Gubernatorial	
	Variables Coeff.	*Preference Variables Std. Error*	*Variables Coeff*	*Preference Variables Std. Error*	*Variables Coeff.*	*Preference Variables Std. Error*	*Variables Coeff.*	*Preference Variables Std. Error*
8) Unified Republican gov't. (–)	–24	22	–20.3	27.1	0.015	0.158	–0.146	0.216
9) Democ. gub liberalism (+)	–	–	–10.4	18.1	–	–	0.045	0.148
10) Repub. gub. conserv. (–)	–	–	–59.4**	20.9	–	–	0.20	0.17
11) 1st year of gubern. term (+)	35.9#	18.9	37.5*	21.7	0.25*	0.13	0.33*	0.17
12) Last year of gubern. term (–)	–11.7	18.4	–20.9	21.7	–0.0007	0.128	0.12	0.17
Constant	**–27.2**	**60.5**	**–20.5**	**70.4**	**0.17**	**0.27**	**0.11**	**0.34**
Adj. r2 = F test =	.13 (10, 1124) = 17.85*** N = 1124		0.11 (12, 801) = 9*** N = 118		.003 (10, 1061) = 1.33 **N = 1072**		0.000 (12, 763) = 0.51 **N = 814**	
One-tailed t test. #= .10, *= .05								

significance of **=.01, ***=.001

with an argument of increasing marginal effects on electoral prospects of changes in high income tax states. The income tax in the states is far and away a political focal point of taxes. This is reflected, as well, in the negative coefficients for any expected surplus.

In the political variables for the nominal dollar proposed changes in the income tax, and looking first at the simplest model under columns (1), the variable of "unified Republican government" has a significant negative coefficient. Republican governors are emboldened in the face of full institutional control to propose cuts to the income tax. If we fold in the "sincere preference" variables, (9) and (10) in model (2), we see that the greater the personal political conservatism of the Republican governors, the greater the slash in proposed income taxes. Democratic governors, as compared with Republican governors are more likely to propose positive percentage changes to income taxes. Unified Republican control has the expected negative effects. Further, as Republican governors increase in conservatism, they are much more likely to propose income tax cuts – a "sincere preference" in action. Electoral timings ((11) and (12)) appear to have no effect. Finally, note that the adjusted r-squares in Table 6.2 are even more marginal than for Table 6.1.

Columns (3) and (4) present the result testing for the model of changes in income taxes as percent of total revenue. The population and income variables continue to be important as do the tax share of the income tax and the expected surplus. Again, united Republican control and increasing Republican gubernatorial conservatism are associated with smaller or negative increases in this measure of the income tax.

Table 6.3 assesses our model for gubernatorial proposals to change the sales tax. Columns (1) and (2), again, review OLS results for proposals to change the nominal dollar amounts of the sales tax. The population and income variables continue to powerfully shape gubernatorial proposals – heavily populated states are less likely to see sales tax proposals while statewide wealth elevates the likelihood of such proposals. The effects of the expected surplus dampen sales tax proposals. Having a Democratic governor is positively but insignificantly associated with increases in the sales tax by the governor, while unified Democratic government is distinctly and positively related. The coefficient for unified Republican government, while negative as predicted, is not significant.

Column (A: 2) sets out the coefficients for the model that include the effects of the governors' Democratic liberalism or, respectively, Republican conservatism. While the measure of personal liberalism of the Democratic governor is negative and not at all significant, its inclusion enhances the effects of possessing the governor's seat by Democrats by a sizable amount. Both that coefficient and that for unified Democratic government are positive. These two coefficients raise doubts as to the impact of our distributive hypothesis that Democratic governance would more likely favor the income tax increases and favor decreases in the consumption-oriented sales tax. Indeed, the effects, at least for nominal dollar increases, flat-out shifts our focus away from the distributive effects of taxation to the fiscal footprint hypothesis: Democratic and liberal governors more heavily favor increases in the size of government, irrespective of the ways and means of financing that growth. Their interest is in "more government" and less so in the distribution of the costs of governance. This focus on "size" vs. "distribution" is reinforced by the effects of the Republican governors' political conservatism variable: The more conservative a Republican governor is the greater interest in reducing the sales tax. Unified Republican government also has a negative coefficient, albeit insignificant. It is also the case that if there are increases in the sales taxes, increases are concentrated in the first year of the gubernatorial term.

Assessing tax proposals defined as changes in sales taxes as a percent of prior year's tax revenues, the effects are severely attenuated. High rates of existing sales taxes dampen such sales tax proposals, as does – no surprise – a budget surplus. Further, if proposals occur, they are more likely in year "1" of a gubernatorial term, as predicted. Note, however, that the equation is painfully weak with an equation F test of 1.8.

Discussion and conclusion

The net effects of the simple variable of political party affiliation of the governor on gubernatorial tax proposals are mixed and especially attenuated in the case of the sales tax. Being a Democratic governor, by our modeling strategy of a simple binary variable, is, of course the obverse of being a Republican governor. While the net effects of "Democraticness," in the case of our measure of total dollar proposed tax and revenue changes, are both positive but insignificant, they are negative and insignificant for revenue changes as a percentage of revenues collected. Just being a Democrat – or a Republican – does not, in and of itself, lead to more or less proposed changes in total taxes, fees, and charges. This is true of the variable when restated as "totals" as a percent of past revenue, as well. When, in Tables 6.2 and 6.3, we add in the measure of "liberalism" or "conservatism" for the two sets of partisan governors, the effects become quite strong with Democrats consistently proposing higher taxes – or Republicans proposing greater cuts – in their budget messages. Overall, in assessing the impact of all of the "political party" variables on budget proposals, the greater message or "take-away" is that Republicans in the governorship and Republicans in united partisan institutions are consistent with gubernatorial proposals to cut taxes.

The effects of the governor's own specific preferences – in rows (12) and (13) of Table 6.1 and (9) and (10) in Tables 6.2 and 6.3-- are much less clear. It appears that, in their taxing strategies, governors do not attempt, even in the best of all political circumstances of being in control of all branches of government, to engage in either redistributive or simple distributive taxing. Expressed gubernatorial preferences, even in the face of united partisan control, appears to be not so much that of sincere, programmatic, or ideological preference and more strategic; the simple legislative variable of unified partisan control – governor, upper, and lower houses – appears to dominate the analysis. However, when sincere gubernatorial choices appear, they appear for increasing Republican conservatism resulting in greater cuts in taxes (row 10 in Tables 6.2 and 6.3).

We include in our simple model electoral timing variables of binary variables for year 1 and 4 of an administration. We expect greater taxing in the first year and diminished in the last year, and there does appear to be some greater overall taxing in year 1 (row 14 in Table 6.1) and for proposed changes in the sales tax (row 11 in Table 6.3).

Further, our model of covariates, as specified in Table 6.1, is overly-complicated. A simpler set of controls appears more reasonable as set out in Tables 6.2 and 6.3. As well, the estimations for nominal dollar totals are better fit as compared with "tax dollars as percent of revenue." In point of fact, our estimation accounting for gubernatorial proposals expressed as percentage figures were painfully weak. Finally, we must confess that our expectations for substantial explained variance by our models were not achieved. Overall, massive amounts of variance in what governors propose for new or changed taxes remains unexplained.

Our redistributive/distributive hypothesis that might separate Democratic from Republican governors fared poorly. It appears that Democratic and Republican governors are even-handed tax increasers or cutters. Democratic and Republican governors were just about as likely to recommend an increase/decrease in the sales tax as the income tax (row 6 in Tables 6.2 and 6.3). Finally, while the personal liberalism of Democratic governors did not appear to carry much weight in their taxing proposals (rows 9 in the table), for Republicans, as gubernatorial conservatism increased, so did their tax-cutting proclivities (row 10 in Tables 6.2 and 6.3). Further, they appeared to be even-handed in their approach to cutting taxes – just as likely to cut income as sales taxes.

Notes

1 The economic logic of the need for "starving the beast" follows from the fiscal illusion from government spending and taxation as set out in *Democracy in Deficit* by James Buchanan and Richard Wagner.
2 I attribute the phrase to Anthony Downs, *Economic Theory of Democracy* (1957), pp. 55–62.
3 The more modern version was enunciated by Mitt Romney in 2012 as "the 47%."
"There are 47% of the people who will vote for the president [Obama] no matter what. All right, there are 47% who are with him, who are dependent upon government, who believe that they are victims, who believe the government has a responsibility to care for them, who believe that they are entitled to health care, to food, to housing, to you-name-it. That that's an entitlement. And the government should give it to them. And they will vote for this president no matter what...These are people who pay no income tax."
Accessed from David Corn, "SECRET VIDEO: Romney Tells Millionaire Donors What He REALLY Thinks of Obama Voters," *Mother Jones* magazine, September 17, 2012.
4 The "norm" appears among the only state without a binding constitutional or statutory rule, Vermont, which, nevertheless, routinely balances its budget over its two-year budget cycle, which yields its well-respected AA+ S&P bond rating.
5 An overview of the Kansas experience is provided at https://www.theatlantic.com/politics/archive/2017/02/the-republican-blowback-against-sam-brownback-kansas/517641/.
6 The plausible political rationale for this finding is that even in a year with a "surplus," a state might well need extra monies to meet new demand for the following year's expenditures; thus, a revenue "increase" occurs even in the face of a budgetary "surplus." Further, the mere fact of the "surplus" may embolden the governor and legislature to be expansive, per the argument regarding Vermont as set out in Chapter 2 of this volume.
7 Gubernatorial and legislative staffers routinely prepare just such "schedules" for use by their principals. Winters reviewed a one-page memo from the VT governor's office listing, by tax, fee, and charge, some thirty or so revenue line items of the amount expected to be derived from a "one unit" increase (or decrease) in each source in millions of dollars of revenue for the state.
8 Alt and Lowry (1994, 2000) use the concept of "fiscal scale" as a term for a measure of total budget outlays. We chose a term that more suggests the fiscal "impression" on voters of government.
9 This leads to the next natural question: Once a governor "proposes" a schedule of tax changes, when and under what legislative conditions is it passed, altered, or literally "disposed of?"
10 We have data on six more taxes, fees, and charges, but the income and general sales taxes comprise the largest share of state government taxes and are the obvious candidates for gubernatorial and/or legislative changes.
11 We think of policy "disposition" as the public policy analogue to the idea of a policy "mood" or general preferences of relevant populations (Stimson, McKuen, and Erikson 1995).
12 Specific changes in "statutory rates of sales and/or income taxation" are an ever-declining fraction of all changes in these two taxes in the American states (see Rainey Stout, and Winters 2014).

13 The Jacoby and Schneider policy analyses (2009) can be faulted on another ground related to our study; see Chapter 1 of this volume. An epistemological prior in every quantitative analysis of spending and taxing politics in the American states ought to distinguish between choosing to analyze "*state* spending and/or taxing" and "*state and local* spending and/or taxing" and defend their choice. Our analysis examines only those taxes, fees, and charges that are state-only related. States will, from time to time and typically via local request, legislate permission for local, county, and town governments to enact local taxing provisions; however, we examine here only changes in statewide revenue programs – programs for which governors and legislators assume credit or blame. It appears that in the Jacoby and Schneider research, they also employed "state-only" measures of spending, which biases their work as a function of the nature of the division between state spending and local spending. For example, in their research, New Hampshire appears as the third most "collective-regarding" of the states, which it simply is not. If the very large amounts of local spending in New Hampshire and in other states were factored into their analysis, we suspect that quite different results would have emerged and New Hampshire would have plummeted to at or near the bottom in their measure.

14 While Vice President Richard Cheney once claimed that "Ronald Reagan proved that deficits don't matter anymore" (accessed December 6, 2016, at https://en.wikiquote.org/wiki/Dick_Cheney), others (Keech 2013, xiv) worry that at the national level "the emergence of large annual deficits and the increasing national debt" is a byproduct of a natural electoral aversion to taxing (xiv).

15 We note that state income taxes are variably "progressive." Some have tax progressions or gradations by income; others are a simple percentage rate of a flat tax. But even the flat tax, e.g. in Massachusetts, comes encumbered with exemptions and deductions that favor those in lower income brackets.

16 As calculated by the author (Winters) from data in the 2012 *Statistical Abstract of the United States* per Section 8 on "state and local government finances" and accessed November 15, 2016, at http://factfinder.census.gov/faces/tableservices/jsf/pages/productview.xhtml?src=bkmk.

17 In the analysis of these two taxes that follows, those states with no general sales tax (Alaska, Delaware, Montana, New Hampshire, and Oregon) and those without a personal income tax (Alaska, Florida, Nevada, New Hampshire, South Dakota, Tennessee, Texas, Washington, and Wyoming) are excluded from the respective data sets.

18 Technically, data are available for 1987 as well. Our sense, in examining this first year of data collection, was that the data were incomplete; thus. we began in year 2 of NASBO's data.

19 Our data on gubernatorial proposals for changes in state taxes are drawn from the spring and fall issues of *Fiscal Survey of the States*, published by the National Association of State Budget Officers (hereafter NASBO). The "revenue resources" variable typically occurs in columns (3) or (4) and is the sum of the beginning balance for the state, interim "adjustments," and expected revenue from existing programs.

20 A nice geographic example of the impact of high sales taxes on economic goods is the distribution of Home Depot stores in NH, VT, ME, and MA, where the general sales tax rates are, respectively, 0%, 6%, 6.25%, and 5.5%. For example, as a byproduct of selective shopping by VT consumers, there are no Home Depot stores closer than 50 miles to the NH border.

21 We delete Nebraska from the data set as a one-chamber legislature and putatively nonpartisan.

22 We have data on the personal spatial ideological position of governors from 1990 to 2006+ only (Dominguez, Frisbee, and Winters 2009). Winters and colleagues (Frisbee, Dominguez, and Winters 2012) developed a mailed survey that asked 1450 respondents distributed across the fifty states in a three-round mailed survey to rank gubernatorial candidates for each election between 1990 and 2006 and each party on an ideological space (-3 being the most liberal, +3 being the most conservative, and 0 being that of the average American voter). Respondents were also asked to place the average voter from their state on the political spectrum so that we could account for a state's political leanings. The surveys were sent to 1450 potential respondents across the fifty states. At least twenty surveys were sent to respondents in each state. State-by-state lists of respondents were drawn up by the authors from web-based information and basically were divided between political practitioners and academics. Political practitioners were party activists, journalists, and others involved in political work (e.g. executive directors of non-profits or policy organizations). Academic respondents were found by looking at the websites of colleges or universities within the states and finding faculty who studied American state and local politics. One-page (two-sided) surveys were sent to each respondent twice over an eight-week period, along with one email. Respondents could reply using "snail mail" and a hard copy of the survey, or they could email their responses back to an email account created especially for the survey. About 600 usable surveys were returned. The smallest number per state was at 5 for South Dakota. Nevertheless, the correlations of the assessments of the ideological placements on the –3 to +3 scale for even this small N state exceeded .90.

In our request to a respondent, we asked:

"The project needs a set of estimates on a common political scale of the ideological or philosophical positioning of your state's gubernatorial candidates since 1990. By "political space," as you will see from the enclosed questionnaire, we simply want you to indicate where your state's gubernatorial candidates fall along a scale that goes from –3 (most liberal) to 0 (your understanding of the "space of the average American voter") to +3 at the most "conservative," or at points in-between, such as +0.67. Please think of ideology as if it were a "taxing and spending" trait; moving from those who advocate a significant expansion in the role of the state by new spending and likely new taxes (at –3), through those who are *status quo* oriented (at 0, the middle of American voters), to those who desire significant cutbacks in programs, the size of state governments and, thus, reduced taxes (at +3)."

Our purpose was to gain evaluations on all *primary candidates*, but as a by-product, of course, we also have the estimate for the winner, the incoming governor for our purposes. Responses did vary widely by states, with SD at five responses and TN and GA had six responses. By contrast, NH, MD, and CA had Ns of responses > 20. Even with their few responses, the intercorrelation matrices of respondents' evaluations for SD, GA, and TN averaged .90, .97, and .82, respectively – all at appreciative and reliable levels. While our survey ended with the candidates for the 2006 election, the values for governors elected that year were extended for the duration of their gubernatorial service. This is consistent with the behavior of our respondents. Once a respondent coded a governor as a "2," for example, that coding value systematically characterized the respondent's coding for each successive election. It was as if no governor ever changed his/her mind.

PART III

Non-obvious taxing and spending

7

THE OBSCURE TAX OF CORRUPTION IN THE AMERICAN STATES[1]

Richard F. Winters and Amanda Tomlinson

Introduction

Most Americans believe that political corruption is a personal failing of the individual public servant, a view that is reinforced by the press with its focus on individual figures prosecuted on a case-by-case basis.[2] However, we demonstrate, as others have,[3] that corruption is peculiarly distributed; not every government – the American states in our analysis -- has its "fair share" of corrupt officials.[4] Put directly, an "individualist" understanding is not adequate in explaining public corruption; some states are more corrupt than others.[5] If the distribution of corrupt officials is maldistributed, if some states have higher fractions of this public "bad" than others, then specific conditions may act to heighten or dampen rates of public wrongdoing. While it may be the case that, on average, individuals in Virginia or Florida are less honest and, therefore, more "corruptible" than those in North Dakota or Vermont, and thus the governments draw from significantly different pools of (dis)honest individuals for public service, we are more comfortable with an explanation that looks at varying conditions and contexts of the U.S. states in accounting for variations in corruption. What makes corruption relevant is its cost, either directly by extracting governmental resources for unauthorized gain or by the indirect "theft of services," diverting governmental actions for unauthorized uses.

Corruption in the American states

In a 1960s article, James Q. Wilson writes that political corruption was the "shame of the American states" (1966).[6] Wilson argues that U.S. state

DOI: 10.4324/9781003606291-11

governments are particularly vulnerable to public corruption by comparison with local governments or the wealthier federal government. The federal government has higher levels of administrative professionalism; Washington draws the best and brightest of administrators alongside more professional and reelection-minded politicians who are more mindful of the consequences of their and others' misdeeds. Further, there is putatively greater review and monitoring of subordinates' actions by Washington's leaders. The links between politicians and bureaucrats may be better "buffered" in Washington by, for example, oversight Congressional committees, which diminish corruption. Further, national politicians are subject to greater scrutiny by the centralized, professionalized national press, as well as by large numbers of resident Washingtonian interest and watchdog groups.

States, according to Wilson, may be uniquely prone to corruption: State officials may be subject to less voter scrutiny because voters are more poorly informed about the actions of state officials. Many state capitals are located at some geographic distance from the states' larger metropolitan areas, which further attenuates press coverage of misdeeds. Thus, it may be no accident that state officials in Annapolis, Springfield, Jefferson City, Tallahassee, and Baton Rouge have national anecdotal reputations for political corruption. State government officials and bureaucrats handle more discretionary money than their local governmental counterparts and, even, conceivably, those of the federal government. One of the by-products of the development of the modern American federal system of governance is that an extraordinary amount of money is funneled through state capitals via the states' own revenue sources, which is then matched, on many occasions, by federal grants and contracts. State officials control, or have a hand in the distribution of, a sizable fraction of public monies spent on governmental purchases of domestic goods and services. In addition to the sheer amount of intergovernmental transfers, the bulk of federal largesse is contributed by out-of-state taxpayers, which may further diminish state officials' inhibitions in dipping into the state's public till, matched, as it is, by out-of-state taxpayers. "[M]en steal when there is a lot of money lying around loose and no one in watching" (Wilson, 1966, p. 31).

Wilson argues that local governments are vulnerable, but less so than state governments. Put simply, there is less to misappropriate, and typically local officials are more likely to be subject to closer scrutiny by local press and voters. The New England experience suggests that there may be greater scrutiny of officials' actions by local voters in local elections, and that scrutiny is heightened as the size of local government shrinks and the population becomes more homogeneous.[7] Both Bryan (2004) and Wilson argue that local voters more closely monitor local politicians because local politicians' actions directly affect local tax rates. Further, any self-aggrandizing display of local corruption may be more obvious to local citizens.

The meanings of corruption

Corruption, for our purposes, is an official's concealed private misappropriation of a public right for direct gain to self (see also Nye 1967, Rose-Ackerman 1975, Shleifer and Vishney 1993, Treisman 2000, Gordon 2009).[8] Gunnar Myrdal (1968) unpacked the proximate links between public officials and corruption: there is high value associated with officials' control over the power to positively or negatively coerce individuals.[9] State-issued licenses are required to positively perform certain acts. State permits are necessary in order to engage in many transactions, and state-issued grants of money support and advance local projects. Further, while we ordinarily view a corrupt act as a "positive" one – the public official has to do "some thing for some one" in order to obtain the illegal rewards – there is also the power *to do nothing*, to overlook violations of regulations. In this case, individuals bribe officials for governmental inaction. Myrdal argues that bureaucratic and political control over valuable rights "adds greatly to the incentives for, and the rewards of graft and corruption." Governmental control over the "rights to coerce positively and negatively" constitutes the resource base for corruption.[10]

Among the net perverse effects of corruption are tax costs. Corruption is a non-statutory tax on citizens by "upping the costs" of public activity, a public cost increase that has not been formally approved by governmental action. Further, as Shleifer and Vishney (1993) note, the "imperative of *secrecy* makes bribery more distortionary than taxes" (600, italics in the original). Cross-nationally, corruption appears to dampen economic activity, not only for reasons of corruption acting as if it were a further monetary "tax" on action, but also for reasons that corruption encumbers dealings with heightened transaction costs and the complicated ambiguities of the means to enforce a corrupt bargain (Mauro 1995; Ades and di Tella 1999; Treisman 2000). Corruption in the states may also result in dampened growth in income, employment, and median home prices (but see Glaeser and Saks 2004).[11] Corruption exacts non-monetary costs as informal transactions multiply. Further, while Hibbing and Theiss-Morse (1995, 2000) conclude that the American public accepts the outcomes of politicians' actions, nevertheless citizens have profound doubts about the process of getting to those actions. It is not a great leap of inference to argue that some part of Americans' anxieties about the quality of the political process revolves around uncertainties about whether and who paid whom, how often, how much, and when, in order to get something done, undone, ... or not done.

The political analysis of corruption

Studies typically focus on the likely causes of corruption, such as the impact of judicial resources; whether poverty or economic growth fosters corruption; or whether cultural factors such as other crime rates affect corruption propensities (Meier and Holbrook 1992, Schlesinger and Meier 2002). Traditional political factors of "size of government, bureaucracy and rent-seeking" and the impact of party and electoral competition (Hill 2003) also may lead to corruption variations for reasons of varying political "observability, transparency, and trust" (Alt and Lassen 2003, 342).

In an early study, Welch and Peters (1978a, b) surveyed several hundred state senators in twenty-four American states, asking legislators how best to measure corruption, and concluded by asking about their perceptions of corruption in their state.[12] Weak findings existed for lower tolerance for corruption among women legislators, among freshman members, liberals, and urban legislators. The industrial east, midwestern, and southern states had higher perceived corruption, while states in the mountain, prairie, and New England regions were lower.[13]

Dincer and Johnson (1983) and David Nice (1983) first analyzed the data from the Public Integrity Section of the Department of Justice on annual convictions for corruption.[14] Johnson (1983) examined early data from reports from all eighty-five substate U.S. districts (the courts of original jurisdiction) and discovered that the underlying district political cultures and states' level of political participation affect corruption conviction rates. Nice (1983) also found that the predominant "moralistic" political culture and education levels in states dampened corruption rates.

Meier and Holbrook (1992) conducted the most wide-ranging examination of the causes of corruption convictions from 1977 to 1986, marshalling twenty-two variables analyzed in clusters of judicial resources, historical/cultural, electoral/political, and bureaucratic/structural. They winnowed the list to eight variables that appeared best related to convictions, and of these, gambling arrests, government employment, and percent urban were positively related, while factors of percent college graduates and interparty competition were negatively related.[15] The authors were not entirely satisfied with their own analysis, and in a subsequent study, Schlesinger and Meier (2002) reexamined the variables using 1986–1995 DoJ data and discovered few persistent causal factors. However, a factor analysis discovered three significant underlying state-by-state traits, which they labeled "cosmopolitan" states (with more prosecutions), "traditionalist" states (also more prosecutions), and states with "low social capital" (also more).

In an earlier paper, we took Meier and Holbrook's analysis one step further (Maxwell and Winters 2003) and reexamined four of their models, fifteen variables in all, for the next panel of U.S. DoJ corruption data, the 1987–2000 data set, also analyzed in this article. Cluster by cluster, the only variables that consistently accounted for prosecution variation in the 1977–1986 period and also in the 1987–2000 period were percent urban, percent college graduates, voter turnout, and gambling arrests. When we pitted identical final sets of variables for the two period data sets (those in Table 6 of the Meier and Holbrook paper), the only consistent predictor was the negative impact of voter turnout on statewide corruption convictions.[16]

Hill's analysis (2003) is consistent with a political/electoral understanding of the causes of corruption convictions. He focused on measures of interparty competition in the states which should "increase the likelihood of the exposure of or punishment for corrupt acts," in our conceptualization, the "detection" of corruption (613). Hill employed Meier and Holbrook's 1977–1987 conviction measure and found that a measure of democratization that is a composite of party competition and electoral turnout rates is negatively related to convictions while controlling for other important factors such as government size, urbanism, and median income.

Adsera, Boix, and Payne (2003) confirmed a socio-political understanding of the causes of corruption. In their analysis of cross-national as well as cross-American-states data, rates of public malfeasance are diminished by regular, free elections and by how well informed voters are about political choices. The credible threat of the loss of power via the electoral process disciplines honesty among officials, which is further reinforced by the belief that well-informed voters more closely monitor officials' behaviors. In the American states, they examine the same dependent variable that we employ here and conclude that "... having reliable and efficient politicians derives from the presence of politically active, well-informed, sophisticated electorates" (480).

Cross-nationally, Mauro (1993) as well as LaPorta et al. (1999) claim that ethnic fractionalization, heterogeneity, or, as we put it in this examination, social diversity, also positively affect rates of corruption. Glaeser and Saks (2004) examined the states and concluded, consistent with Adsera *et al.*, that their results "...are remarkably similar to those at the country level" (p.3). Higher levels of income and education dampen corruption rates, while racial heterogeneity is positively, albeit more weakly, related.[17]

Our measure of political corruption

The Public Integrity Section of the U.S. Department of Justice brought 17,800 corruption cases spread across the fifty states in its first twenty-four years. Do the DoJ numbers appear to be a reasonable proxy for "real corruption?" Put differently, how would we know that we are adequately measuring a real trait of public corruption? We would be encouraged if there was stability in corruption convictions in the states as if the numbers per state appear to equilibrate.

Corruption, if the Department of Justice data is a good proxy for the *de facto* statewide trait, does not distribute itself in obvious ways.[18] The typical state averaged about 15 prosecutions per year, but this ranged from one per year in Vermont to nearly eighty per year in New York. As this suggests, the conviction rates vary by size of state; highly populated states with their many more officials have many more cases of corruption. At the limit, over the quarter century, New York has recorded 2000 such convictions, while Vermont trails with a scarcely appreciable seventeen.

The most frequently used approach in measuring corruption, and the one we employ here, is to link corruption convictions with the number of elected officials. Illinois, as is widely known, is the outlier at the upper end of the distribution of officials, averaging about 42,000 officials *per annum* over the 1977–2006 period. Hawaii is the opposing outlier, averaging about 180 officials per year.[19] Next lowest in officialdom are Delaware and Rhode Island, with 1100 officials. If we divide the number of convictions by the number of officials, we get an ordering of states with Florida at the top of the heap and Vermont at the bottom. There does appear to be some face validity to the five most corrupt states in convictions per number of elected officials: Florida, Virginia, Maryland, Louisiana, and South Carolina. Perhaps the list of the five "least corrupt" makes even more intuitive sense: Vermont last, then North Dakota, Nebraska, New Hampshire, and Iowa. We would prefer, of course, to have the number of all elected *and unelected* public officials, which is the universe of the Public Integrity Section's statutory province. However, the number of elected officials may be a good proxy for the number of all governmental officials.[20] The number of convictions per thousand officials is strongly curvilinear, and we adopted the formulation used by others in the literature (Meier and Holbrook 1992, Schlesinger and Meier 2002, Adsera and colleagues 2003, and Hill 2003) that the most appropriate measure of Justice Department-indicated public corruption is the *log of the number of convictions per 1,000 elected officials in a state.*[21]

A state that, by conventional wisdom (see fn 5), should appear high on the list, Illinois, in fact, ranks 25th. But the median figure for Illinois may mask a more profound regularity. Illinois has 30% more elected officials than the 2nd-ranking state, Pennsylvania. While political corruption should be linked positively to the number of officials, very large numbers of officials may veil public malefactors. Thus, the middling numbers of the Illinois convictions may imperfectly reflect an underlying higher real rate of undetected corruption. This may be due to an exhaustion factor at the

Federal Attorneys' offices in Illinois despite its three federal judicial districts, as the number of potential malefactors increases with the number of officials.[22] Many acts of official corruption in Illinois may be too trivial for federal judicial action.[23] Nevertheless, we expect corruption convictions per 1000 officials to fall with rising numbers of governments but to fall with diminishing decrements. Our model, discussed below, accounts for this by using the number of governments and the number of governments squared as independent variables in explaining corruption per numbers of elected officials.[24]

We further test for internal validity by the consistency of the measure. Meier and Holbrook (1992) examined the data using the years 1977 to 1986. The simple correlation between their and our measure (for the 1987–2006 period) is +.85. If we average the convictions per 000 officials for the six 5-year periods from 1976 to 2005, the interperiod correlations average +.66. However, the correlations average +.89 for the four periods from 1985 to 2005, indicating that after an initial set of years, an equilibrium figure of prosecutions per year by state seems to become established. Further, corruption convictions over time in states appear to be relatively stable processes. For thirty of the fifty states, the simple average figures for each state for the twenty-four-year period appear to be the best guesstimate.[25] No states show a decrease in convictions over the two-plus decades. States that have the steepest rates of increase are Florida, Missouri, California, Washington, Ohio, and Texas.[26] A handful of small states show great relative increases – an increase of two cases per year in Wyoming and Idaho, and with North Dakota and Washington increasing between 1 and 2 cases per year.

Boylan and Long (2003) created a second measure of state-by-state corruption estimates via a mailed questionnaire to close observers of the political scene – statehouse reporters. They measured state-by-state corruption via recording statehouse reporters' responses to six questions on statehouse practices, e.g. "what percentage of state employees file fraudulent expense reports" (425). The correlation between our 1987 and 2000 measures of convictions and the Boylan and Long (2003) scores of reporters' perceptions is +.57. This measure was employed in Alt and Lassen (2002) and was also analyzed, alongside the convictions measure, in an earlier version of this manuscript; see Maxwell and Winters (2006).[27]

A model

We argue that the determinants of corruption follow from the likelihood of its "commission" and "detection" (Becker 1968). We propose a model that focuses on seven indicators of four across-state traits that shape the likelihood of the commission of corrupt acts and their likely detection.

1 Corruption rates vary negatively with "*numbers of 'corruptible' governmental bodies*" – falling as the numbers of governments in states rise. Stated at the limit, states with few governmental bodies are likely to have high rates of corruption prosecutions per 1000 elected officials.[28] The relationship, we believe, will be non-linear. States that have particularly large numbers of governments, Illinois and Pennsylvania, for example, will have fewer convictions, but more than states with modest numbers of governments. Thus, we expect a *negative sign from the linear term and a positive sign from the squared term*, reflecting the distribution of values at the tails. Why so? In the case of the DoJ measure, we do not believe that the US Department of Justice distributes its attorneys for cases on "public integrity" to the states based on numbers of governments; rather, they are probably distributed as a function of the general caseload. If so, Minnesota, with its 3500 governments and, thus, many "elected officials," will probably have a number of U.S. Attorneys overseeing public integrity cases roughly equal to states of similar size, such as North Carolina and Florida, each with about 1000 governments – 30% of the number of Minnesota governments. The potential caseload of possible corruption may be many times higher in Minnesota due simply to the larger numbers of governments. We would expect, however, that Minnesota, with its many more governments, will have fewer corruption convictions when stated, as we and others do, as proportional to the number of officials. There may be a simple legal behavioral explanation as well. As the number of governments increases, the likely scale of corruption – the gains from the corrupt act – becomes smaller and thus of less interest to the prosecutorial ambitions of energetic U.S. attorneys.

The distribution of our DoJ corruption measure by the number of governmental units appears in Figure 7.1 along with the linear and quadratic fits of the underlying distribution. Note the linear relationship is predictably negative – as the number of possible corruption locales increases, as measured along the horizontal axis, conviction rates fall. However, that masks a relationship of a rising rate as the U.S. DoJ confronts the reality of politics in Illinois, Texas, and Pennsylvania. A simple model predicting the corruption rates with the variable of "number of all governments in the state" and its "square" yields the expected negative for the linear term and positive for the quadratic.[29]

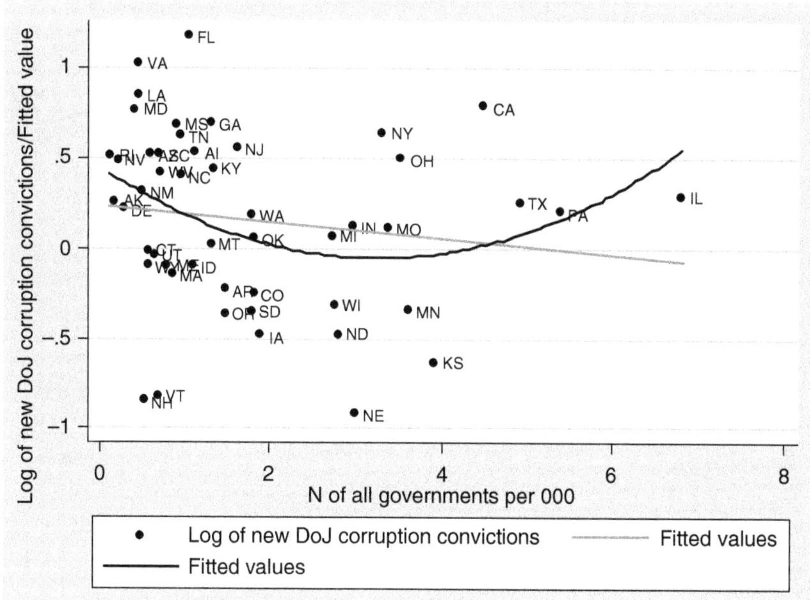

FIGURE 7.1 Department of Justice Convictions by 000s of Governments in State.

Figure 7.1 indicates that states with few and states with large numbers of governments are more prone to corruption convictions than states with "middling" numbers of governments.

2 A "commission" factor: The "*greater the size of state population*" the greater the corruption. As size increases, the public treasury will appear to the corruptible official to be more and more a common pool into which officials can dip with barely observable consequences and, thus, appear to hurt no one. If so, we suspect that there may be an opposing effect, that "*smaller states*" will have markedly lower levels of corruption. In small states, corruption may pose such a perceived threat to the "idea" of the "state" as a publicly idealized, homogeneous, comprehensible "community" that the power of the "idea" serves to deter officials. Those in small states may well understand their position as being in the employ of the commonwealth of all and thus have higher internalized norms of self-restraint. To steal from another in the smaller "all" is, in effect, to steal from those much like oneself. Therefore, we expect a positive sign for the variable of the size of population and a negative sign for the squared term indicating the sharply lower levels

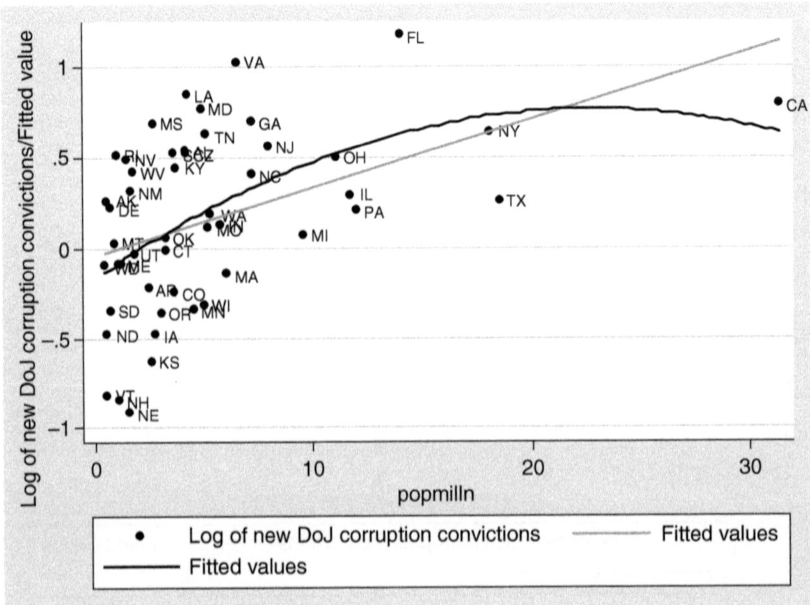

FIGURE 7.2 Department of Justice Convictions by State Population in Millions

found among states with small populations. The confirmatory scatter plot of population size and the log of corruption convictions appears in Figure 7.2 along with a curve that best approximates its quadratic fit.[30]

Figure 7.2 indicates that more populated states have disproportionate numbers of corruption convictions and smaller states have disproportionately fewer corruption convictions.

3 We pursue a parallel line of argument and resurrect a *form* of J.Q. Wilson's original observation about the ethnic makeup of a state and suggest another "commission" factor. States with high levels of "*demographic diversity*" will have correspondingly high levels of corruption.[31] As diversity in the states increases, contributions via taxes to the public treasury are collected from a variety of constituencies – ethnic ones in our conception.[32] Corrupt officials can rationalize dipping into the public fisc by arguing that they are primarily skimming from the many unlike themselves.[33] Diversity rationalizes corruption as extraction from others unlike the self.[34] Graphic and regression diagnostics suggest that this is a simple linear relationship – as the heterogeneities of states' populations grow, as ethnic groups become more discrete and less like one another, corruption rises.

4 Finally, states with "*civic-minded, well-informed political cultures,*" as measured by high percentages of college graduates and a Census Bureau-derived measure of high levels of individual-level civic involvement,[35] will have lower rates of corruption for reasons of both "commission" and "detection." Well-educated citizens, we believe, are less tolerant of corruption. Well-educated citizens are better informed and more likely to wreak electoral vengeance on public malefactors and their sponsors/colleagues. High levels of civic involvement may also lead to closer ties between citizens and officials and likely constrain officials to be more open and transparent in their dealings with the public.[36]

Model results

We expect that our seven-variable model will account for substantial variation in the log of the 1987–2000 sum of DoJ convictions per 1,000 elected officials. We also report on a time-series, cross-sectional, fixed effects (for time) with panel-corrected standard errors in the analysis of the data. We expect that our model will hold when examining twenty-four years of data across 49 states.[37] Finally, we also test for the misspecification hypothesis by re-examining a set of hypotheses advanced by Alt and Lassen (2003) that American states with especially transparent political institutions, e.g. open primaries, easier initiative and referenda provisions, etc., will also be states where corruption "detection" is enhanced, and thus corruption should be attenuated.[38]

The simple OLS test for the DoJ model appears in Column (I). The overall results are impressive. As the number of governments in the states rises, corruption convictions fall. We explain this with reference to scarce Department of Justice resources that must be spread over a larger number of possible corruption sites in states with large numbers of governments. Alternatively, as the numbers of governments grow in these states, the possible benefits of corruption fall, so there may be less incentive for dipping into the public till. Alternatively, large numbers of governments necessarily draw out large numbers of amateur and part-time officials – both elected and unelected – with an unknown consequence, but conjecturally positive, on the probability of corruption. The size and significance of the coefficients, negative in the linear term and positive in the squared term, indicate this curvilinear effect. States with small numbers of governments have higher appreciable corruption conviction rates per 1000 elected officials, and the rate of convictions falls among those with larger numbers, but at a declining rate. As Figure7.2 suggests, it begins to rise again with particularly large numbers of governments as corruptible bodies. The coefficients for these two measures are significant in both the simple OLS test and in the unreported results of an analysis with robust standard errors.

We further hypothesized that the population size of the states would have non-obvious effects. Officials in states with large populations might be more tempted to corruption given the anonymity of their position in a large, multi-division, multi-level organization and, thus, the appearance of the diminished impact of their personal corruption on the state. Officials in very small states may have a greater sense of the proximity of their own corrupt activities on the public treasury and the negative impact on the public interest of, for example, their extra-legal activity. We also believe that a corollary trait is that officials in small states may have a heightened sense of being engaged in common activities that gives meaning to the notion of the commonwealth of all, and that sense may decline with rising population. If true, we expect a positive sign for the simple population variable and a negative coefficient for the quadratic, squared term. In the OLS test, both coefficients are sizable and in the predicted positive and negative directions, and each is significant in the unreported robust regression estimates as well.

We also argue that the likelihood of corruption rises in American states as the states' populations become more diverse. Our proxy measure for the more general trait of social "diversity" is a nine-element Herfindahl index of ethnic *homogeneity*. The results of the OLS regression argue that as the states' *ethnic homogeneity* rises, corruption rates fall. We believe that this is a particularly robust finding. This highly positive relationship holds when calculated with either the Black or Hispanic percentages of the states' populations excluded and the Herfindahl index recalculated, and when both are excluded. The relationships hold as well in a regression that includes the variables of percentage Black in the population and the percentage Hispanic in the population along with a now-seven-element Herfindahl index. Further, the seven-element homogeneity index is significant and in the correct direction, while neither the Black nor Hispanic variables are significant. *We argue, contrary to Wilson (1966), that no single ethnic element of an index of homo/heterogeneity accounts for corruption rates. The strong case can be made for the impact, not of any particular ethnic group's impact on heightened corruption, but instead the combined effect of diversity.* States that have many population components appear to have greater corruption rates, irrespective of the identity of the array of ethnic groups that comprise the population.[39] Our explanation for this is simple: in a state with a heterogeneous population, any single official will perceive his or her act of malfeasance as largely affecting a population that is unlike the self. Diversity diminishes officials' moral constraints that might limit exploitation of the commonwealth. In diverse states, the population appears less "common" to the corrupt official.[40]

Finally, we argue, as do others before us (Hill 2003; Alt and Lassen 2003), that a participant, well-informed population should lead to public honesty. We measure this (1) via the percent of the states' populations that are college graduates and (2) by a direct measure of the proportion of the states' populations that claim to have volunteered in some kind of civic activity. In the simple OLS model, the education variable is a strong predictor of corruption rates, while the civic involvement variable is weaker, albeit significant at.10 level.[41] In an unreported robust regression, both factors are strongly related to corruption in the predicted direction – falling as the educated fraction of the electorate rises and falling as the rates of popular civic involvement rise. In both the simple OLS model and its robust equivalent, our seven-variable model accounts for 72% of the variance in the dependent variable.

The Department of Justice data on convictions is available on an annual basis from 1976 to 2000, so a time-series cross-sectional (TSCS) design is feasible. Further, state population figures, and thus their squares, are available annually. The numbers of governments and the squares, as well as college degrees as a percent of the population, are available only on the decennial census years. For these variables, we began with the 1970 Census data and interpolated the annual figures between 1977 and 1980. Beginning with 1981, we used the same interpolation method to generate annual figures for this decade, and we followed a similar methodology for the years between 1990 and 2000. A truncated measure of ethnic homogeneity is also available on a decennial basis, reliably so for Black, Asian American, Hispanic, and "other." Our measure of "civic involvement," however, is available only for the 1990 period. Our solution was to generate a TSCS data set of annual data from 1977 to 2000 for the log of the conviction rate per 1000 officials and for the state population figures and the squares. We added the annually interpolated data on governments, college degrees, and a Herfindahl diversity measure based on the above-mentioned four ethnic population components for the years between the decennial censuses of 1970, 1980, 1990, and 2000. Our civic involvement measure was entered identically for each state for each of the twenty-four years. We also added, per convention, dummy variables for each time period less one. State-by-state fixed effect variables could not be added because of the invariance over time of our civic involvement variable. We employed a Prais-Winsten regression with panel-corrected standard errors with an assumption of a first-order autocorrelation.[42] Our results appear in Column II of Table 7.1 and are supportive of our original model: States with large populations have more corruption; states with small populations have much less. States with smaller numbers of government have more corruption, but states with particularly large numbers have proportionally

TABLE 7.1 Models of Corruption in the American States

	I. Simple OLS	*II. Time Series.*	*III. OLS w/ DOJ*
	Using log of DoJ measure	*Cross-Sect. DoJ measure*	*Robust s.e. using w/ pol. transp. vars.*
(1) The N of governments:			
(a) Number of all governments (–)	–.39*** *(0.08)*	–.0009*** *(0.0002)*	–.38*** *(0.09)*
(b) N of all governments sqrd. (+)	036*** *(0.014)*	.00000008** *(.00000003)*	.04*** *(0.014)*
(2) Size and very small size			
(c) Population in millions (+)	.11*** *(0.02)*	.372*** *(0.03)*	.124*** *(0.03)*
(d) Population in millions sqrd (–)	–.002** *(0.0006)*	–.009*** *(0.0016)*	–.004** *(0.002)*
(3) Socio-ethnic homogeneity			
(e) index of ethnic homog (–)	–.0002*** *(0.00008)*	–.0003*** *(0.00007)*	–.0002** *(0.0007)*
(4) A civic, well-informed population:			
(f) Percent college graduates (–)	–.043*** *(0.011)*	–.125*** *(0.024)*	–.057*** *(0.01)*
(g) Civic involvement (–)	–9.58# *(5.74)*	–50.3*** *(12.9)*	–18.5*** *(5.81)*
Other variables:			
(5) Metropolitan population (+)			–0.0026 *(0.0031)*
(6) Real income growth p.c. (-)			–0.00003 *(0.00002)*
(7) General real tax revenue, p.c. (+)			0.00002 *(0.00003)*
(8) Direct initiatives (+)			0.115 *(0.09)*
(9) Direct initiatives, threshold (+)			0.0046 *(0.01)*
(10) Camp. Expend. Restrictions (+)			0.031 *(0.087)*
(11) Open party primaries (+)			0.08 *(0.071)*
Constant: Adjusted R sqd. = F tests:	2.6*** 0.72 (7, 41) = 18	Wald chi²(30) = 629*** 0.47 (N = 1176)	2.74*** 0.72 (11,36) = 12

= significant at .10, one-tailed test; * = significant at.05, etc.
significance is sufficient for scholarly purposes.

greater. And corruption as a dynamic process is lower in states with civically involved populations, those with well-educated populations, and in states that are ethnically homogeneous.

A somewhat different picture emerges when we add Alt and Lassen's core controls to a prediction of the DoJ data, as in Column III. None of their hypothesized factors of metropolitan population, per capita real income, and real tax revenues were significant. Because their education measure of high school diploma percentage is inferior to our measure of percent college graduates, we included the latter in this test. We conclude that their core controls degrade the model based on the DoJ corruption conviction rates.

Also, in panel III, we employ our seven control variables analyzing the DoJ measure and examine the added impacts of indicators of political transparency as employed in Alt and Lassen (2003) and Adsera et al. (2003). None of the variables that measure enhanced political transparency, and thus ease of voter control, appears to affect prosecution rates. Our own set of factors (a) through (g) continues to have predictable impacts.

Conclusion

In an earlier paper (Maxwell and Winters 2003), we carried out a good faith replication of Meier and Holbrook (1992), and we concluded that there was little of causal consequence that we could confidently carry forward. Instead, we posed the *tabula rasa* question: What factors should reasonably and proximately relate to variations in statewide corruption? The question led us to focus on some of the manifest observables of the states, such as the number of governments, the size and diversity of states, and their social and political qualities, such as civic involvement and education, that could be reasonably related to factors that elevate the probability of "commission" of corrupt acts, and therefore likely frequency, or the "detection" of corruption, which should act as a disincentive and thus attenuate corruption.

We are encouraged by the results that we obtain. Whether one adopts a point of view that is methodological in origin or more analytic, the sheer number of governments in the states and its square appear to shape the dependent variable as we and others set it out. Increasing the numbers of governments affects not only the disposition to corruption (more corruption for reasons of the size of the "pot") but also its observation, impact, evaluation, and consequence. Illinois may have a reputation for being a corrupt state because it has so many arenas for public corruption to occur.[43] But nevertheless, not all of these will rise to the attention of, nor be cause for action by, the three offices of the U.S. Attorney districts. Some will be handled via the Illinois state criminal codes, a data set that we do not have. Alternatively, it may be the case that as the numbers of governments increase, bringing government closer to the people and involving greater numbers of local officials, government becomes more transparent, and thereby attenuating corrupt activities.

The states' increasing size and heightened diversity appear to loosen internalized norms constraining official acts. Put simply, small size and socio-political homogeneity heighten identification among officials and citizens in the community, precisely the kinds of contexts where corruption will be less likely. We also find support for the classical political economy lesson (Adsera et al. 2003; Hill 2003; Boylan and Long 2004) that corruption is dampened in states with well-educated and highly involved citizens. What also matters is the nature of the population in the states. Population heterogeneity heightens corruption. The simplest reason is the public goods explanation that moral restraints are attenuated in states with diverse populations. Our mixed findings should be of interest, as well. Contrary to Alt and Lassen (2003), the core political economy variables of metropolitan population and per capita real income and real tax revenue are not significant in predicting corruption convictions. Finally, many conventional measures of political transparency and control at the state level do not appear to be good explanations of corruption convictions after controlling for factors in our model.

Notes

1 Earlier versions of this chapter were presented at the 2004 meeting of the Midwest Political Science Association; as part of the Morton-Kenney Lecture series at Southern Illinois University, Carbondale; at the 2005 meetings of the American Political Science Association; at the 2006 meetings of the Southern Political Science Association; and at an American Politics Seminar at Dartmouth College. We have profited from comments of Nelson Kasfir, Deborah Brooks, John Carey, Linda Fowler, Michael Herron, and Ronald Weber. Winters thanks members of the Department of Political Science at Southern Illinois University-Carbondale for inviting him to present the initial results of this analysis as part of the Morton-Kenney Lecture Series. The comments of Jason Barabbas, Jennifer Jerit, David Kenney, Frank Klingberg, and Bill Lawrence of SIU-C were especially helpful. Winters particularly thanks the late Professor Jerome Mileur of the Department of Political Science at the University of Massachusetts Amherst, for his generous support of the Morton-Kenney lectures at our *alma mater*. I also acknowledge the very useful 2012 conversation that I had with the late Lee J. Radek, former head of the U.S. Department of Justice Section on Public Integrity.

2 The "personal failing" observation was forcefully advanced in conversation with the first author by Prof. Frank Klingberg on October 7, 2005, and likely reflects Klingberg's longtime observations about Illinois politics. The first-named author, raised in Illinois, in fact, doubts that Illinois is the most corrupt state in the Union. That reputation was sourced, I believe, from four of its governors since 1968 having served time in prison for corruption. If you believe, as Klingberg does, that the "fish rots from the head," then Illinois is

profoundly corrupt. The data examined here belies this generalization. On the other hand, long-time attorney for various gambling interests and then-mayor of Las Vegas Mayor Oscar Goodman pointed out the more general, collective view: "There's a tendency on the part of the people to think politicians are inherently corrupt..." (*New York Times*, December 15, 2003, p. A21. Press treatments focusing on ex-Governors Otto Kerner (D-IL), Dan Walker (D-IL), George Ryan (R-IL), and Rod Blagoyevic (D-IL) reinforce this personal view. Two earlier governors, Len Small and Williams Stratton, were tried but acquitted for crimes committed during their governorship. More recently, Michael Madigan, longtime Speaker of the Illinois House, is due to stand trial on corruption charges in 2024.

3 See Wilson (1966), Welch and Peters (1978), Nice (1983), Meier and Holbrook (1992), Meier and Schlesinger (2002), Adsera (2003), Hill (2003), and Glaeser and Saks (2005).

4 The number of convicted corrupt public officials (defined shortly) *relative to population* varies tenfold across the American states. The numbers of corrupt officials *relative to the number of elected officials* in the states range 120-fold, while corrupt officials *relative to the number of governments* in the states vary by 1–166.

5 When Winters informed his spouse that he had been invited to talk at Southern *Illinois* University in Carbondale on corruption in the states, she responded, perhaps betraying her New Hampshire sensibilities, "exactly what can *you* teach *Illinois* about *corruption*?" Corrupt failings of Illinois officials figure prominently in David Kenney's biography of Illinois Governor William G. Stratton (1990) and centrally so in Robert Hartley's biography of former Illinois State Senator and Secretary of State Paul Powell (1999), a fellow Southern Illinoisan. Kenny focuses on the Hodges corruption case in the Stratton administration and Stratton's own brush with the law while in retirement.

6 Many popular stories of political corruption are typically couched at the level of state and urban governments – Louisiana in Robert Penn Warren's *All the King's Men* (1946), Boston and Massachusetts in Edwin O'Connor's *The Last Hurrah* (1956), New York, New York in William Riordon's *Plunkitt of Tammany Hall* (1948), Providence and Rhode Island in Stanton's *The Prince of Providence* (2003), and Illinois in Hartley's *Paul Powell of Illinois: A Lifelong Democrat* (199) and Kenney's *The Political Passage: The Career of Stratton of Illinois* (1990).

7 The New England town meeting form of government probably reaches the limit of greatest voter scrutiny; see Frank Bryan's very useful analysis of heightened personal participation in town meetings in *Real Democracy* (2004).

8 For a comprehensive survey and legal analysis of governmental corruption, see Henning and Radek (2011).

9 Myrdal (1968).

10 Myrdal (1968), p. 932.

11 However, neither Glaeser and Saks (2004) nor the authors (2006) in a replication and extension of Glaeser and Saks found any impact of corruption on levels or changes over time in several relevant traits of economic activity in the U.S. states.

12 Welch and Peters' "scale of corruption" quizzed state senators on three survey items: (1) the use of public monies for private travel, (2) the abuse of a committee assignment or chairing the state's appropriations committee so as to enable purchase of land, and/or (3) the promise of campaign contribution for "voting the right way." State senators considered these items as valid indicators of political corruption by elected officials.

13 However, by aggregating the results of quizzing senators from, for example, Connecticut, Maine, and Massachusetts into one regional assessment, Peters and Welch were lumping together the reactions of respondents from diverse states with likely quite varying state-by-state results.

14 In 1978, after the Watergate episode, the U.S. Congress passed, and Jimmy Carter signed into law, the "Ethics in Government Act." The passage of the law was in part a reaction to rising anxiety over campaign finance and, in part, a response to continuing anxiety over corruption in government. One provision of the 1978 Act was to establish in the U.S. Department of Justice a separate Section on Public Integrity to prosecute federal, state, and local officials on corruption charges. According to the Act, the Section is to publish annually the number of elected officials by state convicted for "criminal abuses of the public trust by government officials." For the most recent editions of their annual report, see http://www.usdoj.gov/criminal/pin.html.

15 Another factor was also negatively related to corruption convictions: the greater the number of state legislative functions for which computers were available. Computer usage for budgeting and auditing performance, for example, was hypothesized to enhance legislative monitoring and oversight and thus should dampen corrupt activities. However, this measure was available from the *Book of the States* for only two biennia (1986–1987 and 1988–1989) and was badly right-skewed. In Schlesinger and Meier's (2002) reexamination of the data for the 1986–1995 period, the computer variable was not significant, nor was it significant in our replication.

16 Maxwell & Winters' reanalysis (2003) is available from the author at rfw@dartmouth.edu.

17 Two reports look at a different measure of statewide corruption – a cross-sectional average of journalists' impressions of corruption in their state capitals. According to Boylan and Long (2003), having better-informed voters, proxied by education levels, was an especially telling predictor of low levels of "perceived" corruption. Budget size and distributive goods were poorer predictors, and the crime rate was the least well related to journalists' estimates of corruption. Alt and Lassen (2003) also employed the Boylan and Long measure and control for what they label the "core" factors of metropolitan population, real income per capita, percentage of population with a high school diploma, and general real tax revenue per capita. In assessing seventeen multivariate models controlling for the "core," they focus on factors that should enhance voter control in political agency relationships (e.g. initiatives, open primaries, etc.) and on a variety of political structure variables and economic opportunity variables.

18 About 5% of the DoJ data by state by time period were missing or incomplete. Our rule of thumb was to interpolate by averaging the leading two and lagging two observations surrounding the missing value. Where the missing data was either at the leading edge (1976) or last edge (2000), we used the average of the next two, 1977 and 1978, or the preceding two (1999, 1998) for the missing data.

19 We drop Hawaii because the paucity of their officials wildly skews the results – any number of convictions divided by only a couple of hundred elected officials will be very high. This is consistent with the literature (Meier and Holbrook 1992, Meier and Schlesinger 2002, Hill 2003, Adsera et al. 2003).

20 John Carey points out in conversation with the senior author that this may be a weak, if possibly incorrect, assumption. Large numbers of unelected "officials," i.e. appointees and bureaucrats may be found where there are relatively fewer elected officials.

21 Glaeser and Saks (2004) used corruption convictions per 1000 population.
22 Belying this administrative argument, Illinois is one of the nine states with three separate federal judicial districts, each with its complement of prosecuting attorneys. To us, more districts implies more judicial resources and thus more capability in searching for and rooting out corruption.
23 A different causal argument suggests that corruption may go down as the numbers of officials in a state increases. As the number of officials – potential malefactors – increase, first, the likelihood of other public officials aware of or monitoring for corruption in others may go up. Further, as the numbers of governments go up, the relevant size and policy domains of the governmental constituencies must shrink, and the costs of colluding go up as well, suggesting that large numbers of governments may well dampen corruption. We suspect, however, that causality goes in the opposing direction: as the numbers of governments and, therefore, officials, grow, the likelihood of corruption increases, but the *rate of convictions* per N of officials falls.
24 The simple correlation between the *number of governments* and the *number of elected officials* in the states is .90. Our dependent variable is corruption convictions per 1000 elected officials.
25 Put differently, no significant linear relationship with time appears over the twenty-four-year period for the measure for thirty of the fifty states.
26 Illinois displayed the ninth-largest increase over the twenty-five years of data.
27 Other Boylan and Long questions asked about the numbers of recent news stories about corruption, perceived local prosecutorial priority of corruption cases, best journalistic guesstimates about the relative frequency of corruption among public employees and among legislators, and journalists' best guesstimate of where the state would rank among the American states on corruption, and so on. Three states had no responses – New Hampshire (possibly too few reporters in residence in Concord, N.H.), Massachusetts, and New Jersey. Oregon had only one response. Some states had substantial numbers of responses – twenty-five from California and twenty-two from Ohio. Nevertheless, we are anxious about the error associated with journalists' judgments as the numbers of responses dwindle into the single numbers. Note that Boylan and Long's survey asks in-state observers to rate own-state corruption. One byproduct of this method is that, for example, Utah's journalists rate their state's corruption much as Illinois' journalists rate the "Land of Lincoln," a peculiar combination in our distant understandings. We chose not to include the analysis of the Boylan and Long measure in this paper because we are unconvinced of its utility in our application. First of all, we explore our model's ability to account for variations in corruption across states and across time. The Boylan-Long measure was generated via a one-shot (1998–1999) survey. Second, the intertemporal stability across the states of corruption convictions reassured us of the convergent validity of this measure. Third, we remain anxious about the respondent selection effects at work in the Boylan-Long methodology. Two of the three states with no responses from statehouse reporters were Massachusetts and New Jersey. Our worry is that the typical responses from MA and NJ reporters upon receiving their questionnaire were, respectively, "YaGottaBeKiddingMe ...Right?" and "FuhGeddaBoutIt." If so, we share the authors' concerns that reporters might systematically exaggerate upwards or downwards the actual prevalence of corruption (p. 424), that is to say, those who responded were those who were likely to respond in consistent, albeit not necessarily accurate, ways.

28 At the lower limit, Rhode Island has 128 governmental bodies, Alaska 176, Nevada 212, Delaware 281, and Maryland 416. At the upper limit, Illinois has 6,810 governmental units, Pennsylvania 5397, Texas 4919, California 4495, and Kansas 3918.

29 The simple OLS equations are:

Log new conviction per 000 officials = –.31 N of all governments + .05 N of governments^2

(s.e. = .14) (s.e. = .024) $R^2 = .10$

30 The curvilinear relationships between the log of corruption convictions and states' populations and between the log of corruption and the number of governments (in Figures 1 and 2) are not materially affected by the outliers in each – California and Illinois, respectively. Retaining vs. dropping CA in the regressions with population and population squared imperceptibly affects the results, while dropping IL actually increases the curvilinear nature of the relationship between the numbers of governments per state and the distribution of corruption convictions. Regressions similar to those reported in fn. 25 above confirm, albeit more weakly, the curvilinear relationships in the measure.

Log new conviction per 000 officials = .08 population in millions –.002 popul. in millions^2

(s.e. = .028) (s.e. = .001) $R^2 = .25$

31 Our ethnic homogeneity index is a nine-element Herfindahl index of state-by-state ethnic composition and was constructed from data obtained from Barone and Ujifusa's *Almanac of American Politics* (1994) on the percentages of states' populations that were Black, Hispanic, Asian-American, and Native American; and from the 1990 U.S. Census on the percentage of the population that claimed English, German, Irish, Italian, and a summary percentage of "other European" ancestry. This and other measures novel to this study, as well as the data set, can be obtained from the senior author.

32 Ethnic diversity, we (weakly) argue, is a proxy for other dimensions of diversity, e.g. religious, economic, and occupations.

33 Unlike Wilson, our argument is *not* that some ethnic groups – the Italian-American and Irish-American communities in his analysis – are prone to corruption, but rather that the presence of a highly diverse community of many ethnic groups leads to greater corruption. As our subsequent analysis demonstrates, there is no relationship between, for example, the statewide fractions of Black or Hispanic and corruption. It is the case, we argue, that the manifold presence of many ethnic groups relates to corruption.

34 A similar argument is in Lassen (2003).

35 Constructed by the authors from a 1989 Current Population Survey of the U.S. Department of Commerce. The texts of the questions, according to the CPS codebook, were "Last week, did [you] do any unpaid volunteer work?" and "For what type of organization did [you] do most of [your] unpaid volunteer work?" The options for responding were "hospital or other health organization," "school or other educational institution," "social or welfare organization," "*civic or political organization*," "sport or recreational organization," "church or other religious organization," and "other type of organization." (See p. 8–17, May 1989, *Current Population Survey, Multiple Job Holdings, Flextime and Volunteer Work*. U.S. Department of Commerce, Bureau of the Census, ICPSR

Study #9472. Note that the rate of civic involvement varies fourfold across the states, from about 1% in TN, GA, KY, and NY to better than 3.5% in ID, OR, NE, and WY.

36 Simple graphic and regression analysis indicates that both of these factors relate linearly and negatively with the conviction measure of corruption.

37 The N of 1176 equals 49 states × 24 time periods. Hawaii is, again, excluded for reasons of paucity of elected officials. The annual DoJ data is also modeled as the log of the number of convictions per 000 elected officials. The statistical routine was STATA's rreg. The single fixed effect was for time. Our Census Bureau-based measure of "civic involvement" did not vary across the states over the time period.

38 Note that they analyzed the Boylan and Long (2002) measure.

39 Alt and Lassen (2003) and Knack (2002), in an associated article of interest, argue for the impact of specific ethnic groups. Knack uses the common variable of percent African-American as a measure of population heterogeneity, while Alt and Lassen use the percent of the states' populations Scandinavian in family origin. Our results strongly argue that ethnicity in the states is strongly mediated as a function of diversity, not from the presence of one group or another. On this issue, also see Hero and Tolbert (1996).

40 Documentation on the estimations discussed in this paragraph, as well as the unreported robust estimations, can be obtained from the author.

41 Following the analysis by Hill (2003), we included in an unreported test (obtainable from the author) a measure of statewide Congressional turnout and the Ranney index of interparty competition. Neither was significant, and both were inferior to the impact of our civic involvement variable on corruption. Hill generously provided us with a measure of Elazar's state-by-state "moralism index," which we also included in an unreported test to no effect. In a further effort to isolate a cultural trait, we included a measure of the distribution of born-again Christians by state (as constructed in Winters and Rygorski, in this volume), also with no effect.

42 Analysis was carried out using the xtpcse command in STATA with correlation (psar1).

43 Two other observations about the first-named author's home state of Illinois. Many years ago in a newsletter titled *Comparative American State Politics,* I published a short essay that measured and attempted to explain "An American States' 'Navel-Gazing Index.'" I was prompted to generate this measure by my visits to the locally renowned "Dartmouth Bookstore," which had a "books of local interest" display. I continued to be struck that this display – 300 yards from the New Hampshire-Vermont border – had two books on Vermont for every one book about New Hampshire, despite the fact that New Hampshire had an older, larger history and was twice the population of Vermont. I then visited the newest edition of *Books in Print* and counted for each state the books published for or about the state. And, sure enough, Vermont did have many more such books in print; Vermont is in the upper quartile and New Hampshire in the third quartile. Among the fifty states, after controlling for size, population, date of entry into the Union, and so on, Virginia had the top rank ... Illinois was at the bottom. Maybe what I did not account for was Illinois' "normality." In the May 19, 2024 edition of the *Washington Post* (page G4), Andrew Van Dam and associates did a statistical analysis of some thirty different measures of states' populations and discovered that, sure enough, Illinois was the "most normal state in the Union."

8

PREFERENCES MATTER

How charitability preferences as expressed by behavior affect spending and, therefore, taxing[1]

Richard F. Winters and Daniel Rygorsky

American governments redistribute substantial resources via public, tax-supported welfare programs from those who are better off to those who are in need. The now-historic Aid to Families with Dependent Children (AFDC) and the post-1996 Temporary Assistance to Needy Families (TANF) are the classic examples and are analyzed here. There are also charitably supported, private-sector organizations, such as Habitat for Humanity, United Way, the American Cancer Society, and the American Red Cross, that coordinate help from donors to those who are in need. While the *nominal* aggregate amounts of Americans' private donations to the poor have grown over time,[2] *real* private giving to the poor as a percentage of personal income has been steadily dropping. Further, organized private direct cash aid to the poor has just about disappeared.[3] Rose-Ackerman (1986) argues that the organizations supported by private giving to the poor now complement direct government aid at the margins via job help, counseling, support services, disaster relief, legal help, and so on. There is widespread support for the observation that direct monetary support to the poor will come to be largely a governmental effort relying on the coercive tax system so that all who can will pay, and, perforce, all will become charitable to the poor.[4] And as expected through the last several decades, the total amount of public aid grew steadily in nominal and real terms, and as a percentage of personal income.[5] There is an equally compelling observation that the private sector support for the poor and those who are in need has also grown, but these services offer complementary assistance to the direct cash aid of the federal, state, and local governments.

DOI: 10.4324/9781003606291-12

Our purposes in this chapter are fourfold. A growing literature (Erikson, Wright, and McIver (1989); Berry et al. (1998); Brace et al. (2008); Gray et al. (2004)) relates variations in highly generalized statewide voters' preferences with variations in state policy choices. States with "liberal" electorates elect leaders who adopt liberal policy sets. A smaller, but, for our purposes, more relevant literature creates narrower, finer estimates of state-by-state "micro-preferences" for particular governmental goods and services and relates these measures to the adopted public policies (Plotnick and Winters (1985, 1990); Brace et al. (2004); Johnson (2001); and Norrander (2000, also, see 2001). What is striking about this literature is its variability in findings. Norrander (2000) persuasively relates past and current opinion on capital punishment to death penalty rates in the states. Plotnick and Winters (1985) fail in their efforts to relate statewide preferences for private giving to statewide welfare generosity.[6] Brace and colleagues note a simple and perverse negative relationship between preferences for more welfare spending as derived from a large number of GSS surveys and actual statewide spending,[7] while Johnson (2001) notes that statewide positive racial attitudes boost welfare outlays. In this chapter, we generate a new measure of individual preferences for giving to the poor – *a direct behavioral measure of generosity – and this personal preference measure powerfully relates to cross-sectional measures of governmental welfare outlays and to changes in these measures in the presence of a strong model explaining welfare as public redistribution.*

Second, our novel state-by-state indicator is that of the public's directly expressed behavior as preference for helping the poor. Our argument is simple: states where the populations give "a lot" in donations to an array of private charities – state-by-state donations to eleven national charities that assist the poor and needy – will also express this generosity with their political votes and voices and elect and pressure officials to translate their charitability preferences into allied generous cash-welfare policies.[8] Put differently, they vote/devote their private and public actions; state voters that are privately generous are also publicly generous.

Third, we hypothesize that our behavioral-preference measure (a) will be positively related, *ceteris paribus*, to the cross-sectional estimates of public aid, pre- and post-TANF reform, but also (b) to changes in public generosity. Traditionally in this literature, analysts have accounted only for cross-sectional variations in welfare generosity. Welfare generosity as measured typically in the literature is that of the "welfare guarantee," which is best characterized as resulting from a "sticky" political process.[9] But changes do occur over time. In the eight years that span pre- and post-TANF reforms of 1986, nine states cut their guarantees, nineteen states showed no changes, and twenty-two states showed increases.[10]

Fourth, we hope to toss a brickbat at a widely circulated and *utterly inappropriate measure of* "charitability." Every year, articles appear that rank the states on "charitability." All rely on U.S. Internal Revenue Service data on charitable deductions on personal income tax returns.[11] This statistic hopelessly conflates *religious* giving with *secular* giving. We believe that individual religious giving is "giving" to those very much like "self." The obvious positive outlier here is Utah, which is routinely recorded as the most charitable state. This, of course, reflects the extraordinary giving of believers to the Mormon Church. Secular giving, both private and public, which we analyze shortly, most closely exemplifies what we consider to be genuinely selfless giving, the nearest idealization of the Maimonidian penultimate rank of "givers unknown to the recipient and beneficiaries unknown to the giver."[12]

Public and/or versus private aid to the poor

Growing *public* redistribution ought to crowd out *private* charitability. Using accessible statistics, in 1966 public aid accounted for about 1% of real personal income. By the late 1990s, it had grown fourfold. Over the same period, "private giving to human services" fell from .33% of real personal income in 1966 to a low of .13% in the late 1980s, and it had crept up to .25% by 2006.[13] Put differently, in 1966 public aid exceeded private help by 3 to 1; in 2006, that ratio had increased to 16 to 1, with real public aid rising while real private aid fell and then rose. *Giving USA* also arrays several classes of giving by "end-use," e.g., education, international affairs, arts & culture. Of the eight classes of "end-use," only "giving for human services" indicates a real decrease for the period. This is consistent with the temporal crowding-out hypothesis. As American governments stepped in to help the poor, previous donors to human service organizations were "freed up" from having to help the poor; they could then move down their schedule of preferences for spending, conceivably, their next best charitable choice, and help with that effort, rivalrous as it is with help for the poor. We agree that there is a general, national, temporal, albeit partial crowding-out, thus a negative relationship between the national total private giving and total national public aid over time.

The hypothesis of "crowding-out," complete and otherwise

There appear to be strong theoretical reasons why public efforts on behalf of the poor will crowd out counterpart private efforts. Warr (1982) predicts dollar-for-dollar crowding-out of private donations by public transfers. As evidence, Roberts (1984) points to statistical data collected from the 1930s that show that as the level of public transfers increased, private donations fell sharply (143). Abrams and Schmitz's (1978) data on the growth of total governmental social welfare transfers and total private contributions show that while both have grown, private contributions have done so at a slower rate, indicating that over time government transfers have been shouldering a larger, although not exclusive, share of the "social welfare burden[.]," a claim that is consistent with our evidence. As they note, an "interdependent utility" model would predict only partial crowding-out based on

> the assumption of interdependent utility functions between contributors and recipients.... If the utility which the contributor received from donations is a function of the utility of the recipient, then increases in government transfers... would lower the recipient's marginal utility of an additional contribution.
>
> *(31)*

This decrease in the recipient's utility means that added contributions by the giver mean less and less to the poor, and this, therefore, suggests that the contributor's marginal utility from an additional contribution is also decreased. As a result, higher government transfers cause individuals to reduce their charitable donations and to increase their consumption of other goods – including other kinds of charitable "goods" – until their marginal utilities are equated. But this would not necessarily mean that all donors would stop giving; there will likely be a reservoir of charitable donors who still receive utility from further private contributions, believing either a government shortfall of money, a governmental misdirection of effort, or the existence of unsupported complementary services, thus resulting in only partial crowd-out.

Another perspective also predicts only partial crowding-out – the "better to give than to receive" hypothesis. In this model, the utility function of the contributor is independent of the utility function of the recipient. Andreoni (1988; 1989; 2006; 2007) argues that individuals also receive utility – a "warm glow" – from the simple act of giving. There is vast participation in the charitable sector, with 85% of all households making some kind of donation, which suggests an individual-level factor of "wanting to give." All empirical studies of the relationship suggest that government "donations" to the public good only incompletely crowd out private donations, with each government dollar given resulting in a decrease of anywhere from five to twenty-eight cents in private donations (1988, 58).

Rose-Ackerman (1986) suggests other rationales for partial crowding-out. Governmental grants to private social service organizations will increase private charitable donations in a number of possible ways. Matching grants from government to private aid agencies can increase individual charitable giving by lowering the "price" of donations. Also, under this model, the governmental regulatory policies that accompany fixed-sum grants are seen by donors as a valued ideological constraint on the private organization and thus will increase donations by raising the marginal benefits of private donations. Additionally, government grants could increase donations by forcing managers to adopt ideological positions that are favored by potential donors.[14] We conclude that public crowd-out of private charitability is lumpy and partial. Some acts of government completely crowd out private activities, and organized cash aid to the poor is the best example. Other public activities fractionally affect private charitable activities.

While crowding-out of private charitable giving by government welfare spending may occur across time at the aggregate level, an opposing argument suggests that at the spatial level of the American states, there might be a positive relationship between levels of private and public generosity. We argue that local public redistribution is driven by the same impulse as private secular charitability.[15] States that are generous in their help for the poor are likely to be states with a rich infrastructure of private organizations that supplement, prop up, and help the poor. Put differently, well-organized public efforts that help the poor (generous welfare programs, for example) are both determined by and generate counterpart private organizations that are also supportive of the poor (Rose-Ackerman 1996; Plotnick and Winters 1985). Public generosity at the subnational level may well result not in "crowding-out," but "drawing-in." We argue, further, that states vary along a secular-sacred dimension, and as religious organizations weaken in number and fealty, secular public and private redistribution rises.

By the crowd-out logic, however, states in a federal system that generously support the poor with high per-family "aid level," e.g., Massachusetts and Vermont vs. penurious states such as Louisiana and Texas, would also be states with penurious citizens in their private, charitable giving.[16] We argue the *opposing hypothesis* that, disaggregated across the states, *private generosity is positively correlated with public generosity*.[17] Our central proposition, then, is that there is a latent trait of generosity preferences that varies across the states and that positively links private and public charitability. If so, we expect a state-by-state measure of private generosity will be *positively* related to the statewide public measure of generosity, the opposite of that predicted by the crowding-out hypothesis. The privately generous, in states by their giving behavior, lead to high levels of private help and lend political support for higher taxes that lead to more generous welfare guarantees.[18] If so, private giving should be an appropriate measure in any general model predicting public spending on redistribution as a proxy for the public's interests in helping the poor. Furthermore, we argue that this across-state, positive private-public link is consistent with a negative relationship between the two at the national, aggregate level. While national private giving to the poor has fallen across time across all states, we argue that the fall is proportionate so that those states that began with high private and public rates of generosity continue to have high rates relative to other states.

If public and private giving is positively related across the states, what accounts for the relationship? We argue that states' populations vary in their "tastes" for assistance to the poor. If so, these variables fall within the broad set of other political "taste" variables, e.g., for increased "welfare spending" (Brace et al. 2002), or for "generalized statewide liberalism" (Erikson et al. 1996), or generalized "citizen" and/or "institutional liberalism" (Berry et al. 1998).[19] However, our measures are direct, demonstrable generosity behaviors. If so, they are more specific and precise measures of the statewide collective individuals' interests in supporting particular private and public efforts. And to the extent that they are direct "pocketbook" measures of contributions above and beyond what the public sector offers to the poor, we might label them as *sincere* measures of the *public demand for redistribution.*

Measuring the traits of statewide charitability

Our statewide behavioral indicator of "charitability" is estimated via data on voluntary donations to eleven private organizations. Letters were sent to thirty large, nationwide – and immediately recognizable – American charities devoted to "human service" causes seeking information about their state-by-state distributions of giving. We obtained data from eleven of the charities: the American Lung Association, Habitat for Humanity, the American Cancer Society, the American Kidney Foundation, the American Diabetes Foundation, the American Red Cross, Disabled Veterans of America, the American Heart Association, CARE, the International Rescue Committee, and the United Way of America.[20] The logic in use that we employed was that the larger the number of charities for which we gathered data, the better our measure would be of capturing an underlying fundamental trait of across-state personal generosity.

We requested the charity data sets for two or more consecutive years scattered over the period from 1989 to the mid-1990s. To achieve partial correction, we averaged the state-by-state annual giving data from each so as to generate one state-by-state "total giving" measure per charity.

Two further corrections were necessary: Our eleven charitable "total giving" amounts per state obviously are strongly affected by states' population size and level of personal income – big states and wealthy states give more in the aggregate. Therefore, we developed state-by-state measures of "how deep into the pockets" the states' givers reached. Put directly, while the wealthy in some states may have deep pockets, some states' wealthy may have short-armed penuriousness. Therefore, for each charity's total giving for each state, we divided the amount donated by (1) population and then (2) divided this small quotient by statewide per capita income. This procedure yields an estimate of the now-miniscule fraction of individual income that the average person donated to each charity in each state.

We expect that all eleven organizational giving measures will be positively correlated with one another, and that appears generally to be the case, as displayed in Table 8.1. We tried various factor analytic combinations of charities, but in the end, we decided simply to use all of the data with the exception of the charity "org4," the giving of which was nearly perfectly correlated with its neighbor "ORG3."[21]

Table 8.1 indicates that, among the fifty states' populations, "giving" to the ten charities that we assess all correlates positively with one another.

We obtained our first measure of charitability by factor analysis of the now-ten charities listed in capitalized form in Table 8.1. The first principal factor extracted from the analysis accounted for 35% of the common variance.[22] States with positive scores demonstrate greater charitable giving, and those scoring negatively have lower than typical giving. At the limits are the least charitable, Louisiana, with a weighted giving estimate of –2.88, and the most charitable, Vermont, with a giving estimate of +8.[23] No strong geographic patterns are evident in the table (see the Appendix to this chapter for the state-by-state scores), as states from the various regions are scattered throughout the table. Among Southern states, for example, Louisiana, Texas, and Mississippi are among the country's least charitable states (as are West Virginia (45th of 48), New Jersey (44th), and Illinois (43rd)), while their Southern neighbors, Florida, North Carolina, Georgia, and Virginia, rank 12th, 14th, 17th, and 22nd among charitable states.[24]

Our second measure of charitability simply added up the small amounts that citizens of each state, per capita and expressed as a fraction of personal income, gave to the charities. However, because the total amounts given to the American Red Cross and to the United Way dwarf by a factor of 15 that given to the other charities, our charitable giving sum is measured by only donations given to the eight smaller charities.

TABLE 8.1 Intercorrelations Among Measures of Charitable Giving

Charities	*ORG1*	*ORG2*	*ORG3*	*org4*	*ORG5*	*org6*	*org7*	*ORG8*	*ORG9*	*ORG10*	*ORG11*
ORG1	1.00										
ORG2	0.25	1.00									
ORG3	0.52	0.39	1.00								
org4	*0.52*	*0.43*	*0.99*	*1.00*							
ORG5	0.34	0.25	0.34	0.35	1.00						
ORG6	0.47	−0.02	0.10	0.10	0.37	1.00					
ORG7	0.42	−0.01	0.24	0.24	0.48	0.77	1.00				
ORG8	0.57	0.35	0.36	0.37	0.34	0.70	0.65	1.00			
ORG9	0.16	0.51	0.21	0.23	0.08	−0.11	−0.09	0.12	1.00		
ORG10	0.20	0.28	0.44	0.44	0.39	−0.11	0.01	0.00	0.11	1.00	
ORG11	0.10	0.31	0.39	0.39	0.18	−0.49	−0.29	−0.13	0.17	0.64	1.00

Explaining the links between secular and public charitability

A simple extension of the crowding-out hypothesis argues that states with generous public aid programs would have less private help relative to less publicly generous states. We argue, in opposition, that there is a "fundamental spatial trait" to giving, which is further reinforced by the "drawing-in" hypothesis. In either case, it is a *ceteris paribus* argument, and the control variables need to be spelled out.

Dependent variables: Our initial dependent variable is the simple *1994 and the 1996 values of the maximum monthly AFDC benefit for a 3-person family authorized by state legislation.*[25] We believe that the legislative guarantee is the simplest and most reliable estimate of statewide decisions that measure intentional, legislated generosity. The historic AFDC "guarantee" of support for the three-person family is a legislative decision about how much state monies will be appropriated to gain a federal match. Put directly, the guarantee is a state-made decision that *best* measures statewide public generosity (Plotnick and Winters 1985, 1990). In addition, the 1994 and 1996 state-by-state legislative guarantee figures are the most proximate measure of public generosity in time relative to our measures of secular dollar and time generosity. Our second dependent variable is the *TANF 2000 and 2003 welfare guarantees for a three-person family*. The correlation between the AFDC and TANF benefits is a +.95.[26]

Independent variables: We believe that the determinants of welfare spending fall into several broad classes reflecting the impacts of race and ethnic diversity; recipient traits; economic resources and costs; the interests of social classes and groups; and finally, the collectively measured "tastes" for welfare spending as proxied by our and others' measures.[27]

Welfare spending is affected by racial and ethnic relationships in the states.[28] (1) As the *Black percentage of all recipients of assistance* in a state grows, we would expect that welfare spending will fall (Plotnick and Winters 1985; Soss et al. 2003; Fong and Luttmer 2009). As the percentage of blacks on welfare rises in states, the incentive to be generous falls among the majority, non-Black voting populations and their representatives. Aiding a group that is unlike the majority population is a more difficult "political sell." However, we expect that the fraction of the states' voters that is Black will positively affect the guarantee. While high fractions of Black recipiency may drive down generosity, the voting power of the Black population will have the opposing effect of supporting the value of the guarantee (Plotnick and Winters 1985). (2) As the *percentages of the states' populations that are themselves Black* rise, holding other factors such as the percentages of recipient populations that are Black constant, public generosity will rise. Higher percentages of Black populations would be associated with political efforts to expand the use of governmental resources to aid the poor. Further, as the percentages of states' populations that are Black increase, the interests of Blacks are more likely to be represented in state legislatures, as more state legislators are likely to be Black, and the remaining legislators will have larger Black constituencies to whom they are responsible.

Related to race, but albeit analytically distinct, is the impact of ethnic heterogeneity on the size of the guarantee. Hero and Tolbert have written extensively about the impact of racial diversity (Hero and Tolbert 1996), while Plotnick and Winters (1985) and Johnson (2001) directly test for its effects. (3) States with high levels of "ethnic heterogeneity" will have higher levels of welfare generosity.[29] As heterogeneity in the states increases, as the state's political community becomes more diverse, the welfare community – recipients, human services providers, and the private-side beneficiaries and suppliers – becomes just one more set of groups pressuring for their fair share of the governmental expenditure pie. Politicians in the diverse states are prone to "capture" by these groups as they assemble electoral and re-electoral coalitions (Stigler 1971).

Our second general set of factors focuses on traits of the recipient population that should impact the size of the benefit. (4) The percentage of AFDC households headed by a single parent, the *unmarried fraction of recipients*, should be negatively related to the guarantee. Frohlich and Oppenheimer (2000) put it, "[i]ndividual choices to help others are mediated by judgments of moral worthiness" (106). Plotnick and Winters (1985) argue that simple moralism drives this effect. Higher rates of single-parent families and out-of-wedlock births fall within the ambit of moral considerations, and voters and legislators may be less willing to generously support "morally suspect" families. Another recipient trait variable is a measure of the relative burden of the welfare population. (5) As the *percentage of state's population receiving welfare assistance* grows, the willingness of the rest of the population to shoulder generous benefits shrinks, and the guarantee will be smaller.

The third class of causal factors affecting generalized public generosity falls broadly within the economics of public welfare. (6) As the fraction of the monthly aid checks distributed to recipients and borne by states' taxpayers falls, and a concomitant *share assumed by other jurisdictions* such as county governments rises, i.e., the "local share," one might expect the states' legislators to be more generous. In New York, for example, the guarantee is set by the state legislature in negotiation with the governor, yet county governments carry one-half of New York state's obligation. Thus, responsible statewide officials can obtain generous benefits while providing only 25¢ out of every increased AFDC dollar; another 25¢ is borne by local governments, and the last half is borne by the federal matching grant.[30] (7) *Statewide wealth* ought to be positively associated with public aid generosity. Wealthier states should find it easier to raise tax monies sufficient for generous support; states made up of individuals, precisely because of their wealth, who are better positioned to forego consumption for taxation so as to help the indigent.

Further, the federal government matches the AFDC amount appropriated by state governments at a rate that varies from 50¢ per state dollar in wealthier states to 80¢ per state dollar in poorer states. (8) As the *states' share of the AFDC cost* increases from 25¢ per dollar spent in Arkansas, for example, to 50¢ (in NY) per dollar, the variable of "price" measures the state taxpayer cost of aid to the poor and should be reflected in lower AFDC payments. However, because the federal matching grant is based importantly on the distribution of personal income across the states, the strong negative correlation between "personal income" and "price-to-state-taxpayers" (-.73) creates an estimation problem.[31] An associated economic factor is the impact of the size of the guarantee of bordering states. Several studies have assessed the impact of the value of the "neighbors" guarantee on one's own state's benefits with the assumption that nearby states share many traits, including regional costs of living, as well as the diffusion of information about what nearby states offer (Berry et al. 2003). (9) We hypothesize a positive association between states' guarantees and the *average of their neighbors' guarantees adjusted for each state's costs of living.*

Hill and colleagues (1995) also employed measures of the states' tax effort and tax capacity. Tax effort measures the burden that states make in levying taxes on citizens – high effort suggests willingness to tax for public goods; thus, we would expect (10) that high *tax efforts* positively affect welfare choices. The generalized taste for public goods as expressed via the levels of taxes collected will be reflected in welfare spending. Revenue capacity is more directly related to what is possible in the states. Wealthy states, such as New Jersey, have high revenue capacity, but so also do states that, with large natural resource reserves, are assessable via severance taxes. Thus, like personal income, (11) *revenue capacity* should be positively related to welfare help.

Our fourth broad class of factors is the impact of social class or interest groups supporting or attenuating welfare claims. Numerous measures of groups and classes have been constructed.[32] These statistics array the number of human services organizations calculated relative to population – a measure of the density of human services organizations by state. However, in assessing these measures, all were inferior to two simple indicators derived from data now available on the numbers and kinds of organized groups in the American states.[33] (12) As the *number of* "for profit" *organizations per 1000 population* (as classified in Gray and Lowery 2001) rises, so also should either indifference to or opposition to public aid rise. Business and professional organizations have no great stake in public assistance, and many may actively oppose positive efforts by state governments to assist the poor (Lowry 2004). These "voices" would be rivaled by (13) the smaller *numbers of* "welfare" *and* "women's" *groups* (also classified by Gray and Lowery 2001), many of which may have "generous public assistance" as part of their political agenda. Finally, state electorates vary widely in the representation of income classes as voters. (14) Following Hill and Leighley (1992), we expect that an *electorate with an upper income* bias would negatively impact welfare generosity.

Fifth, states' populations will vary in their "taste" for helping. In an effort to further plumb the set of political variables as controls, we (15) compiled the *average of the year-to-year percentage of polled voters by state who claimed to be* "liberals" *less the number citing* "conservative."[34] Further, (16) because the level of welfare payments in a state is a "sticky" figure and resistant to change, we expect that there will be a long-term equilibrium in payment levels that would likely be affected by the *number of recent unified Democratic governments divided by the number of Republican governments in each of the states*. Further, (17) a policy "taste" measure that integrates economic as well as political choices might be found in tax progressivism. The simplest and most direct such measure that we found is the *level of the highest assessed rate applied to residents in states' income taxes*. States with no income taxes, e.g., New Hampshire, would score "0" on such a scale, and those with a flat rate, e.g. Massachusetts, would be pegged at the fixed rate. The higher the rate, the higher the progressivism, which we expect to be matched on the outlay side via more generous welfare benefits.

Finally, our two main measures of interest – charitable giving and also "taste" variables – are (18) *charitable giving*, the factor-analytic-based measure of charitability as discussed above, and (19) *the sum of charitable giving*, a direct indicator of giving to eight smaller, but nationwide, charitable organizations. Finally, because we are examining two years of data on welfare (20), we also include a *dummy variable for either 1997 or 2000.*

Testing for the impact of charitable giving on welfare spending

Four models, as set out in Table 8.2, test for the effects of observed private giving on public aid, other factors determining the level of such aid held constant. Model (1) is a direct test of the impacts of our factor-analytic measure of secular giving on the AFDC welfare guarantee in the 1990s. Model (2) substitutes the "sum of charitable giving" for the factor analytic measure and relates this measure to the AFDC 1994 and 1996 period. Model (3) applies the factor score measure for the 2000 and 2003 TANF welfare guarantee,

TABLE 8.2 Private Charitability and Public Redistribution

	AFDC Measures				*TANF Measures*			
	1994 & 1996: Factor Scores for Char. Giving		*1994 & 1996 Giving Sums to Eight Charities*		*2000 & 2003 Charitable Giving*		*2000 & 2003 for Sums to Eight Charities*	
	Coeff.	*Std. Error*	*Coeff.*	*Std.Error*	*Coeff.*	*Std. Error*	*Coeff.*	*std.error*
Race & diversity:								
1) % Recipients black	–1.92*	.92	–1.56#	.86	–1.48	1.10	–.57	1.13
2) Black as % state population (+)	2.14	2.33	.82	2.20	–1.78	2.80	–3.83	2.92
3) 1990 Ethnic heterogeneity (+)	.03#	.01	.01	.01	.03#	.02	.02	.02
Traits								
4) % Recipients single parent. (–)	–2.21	1.45	–1.94	1.36	–1.68	1.81	–1.92	1.82
Economics								
5) Recipients as % population (–)	1.21	5.65	5.02	5.30	9.51	7.14	11.40	7.30
6) % AFDC local share (+)	–1.17***	0.45	–2.46***	.50	–1.60***	.56	–3.17***	.69
7) Deflated per capita inc. (+)	0.02***	0.00	0.01***	0.00	.01	.01	.01	.01

(*Continued*)

TABLE 8.2 (Continued)

	AFDC Measures				*TANF Measures*			
	1994 & 1996: Factor Scores for Char. Giving		*1994 & 1996 Giving Sums to Eight Charities*		*2000 & 2003 Charitable Giving*		*2000 & 2003 for Sums to Eight Charities*	
	Coeff.	*Std. Error*	*Coeff.*	*Std.Error*	*Coeff.*	*Std. Error*	*Coeff.*	*std.error*
8) Price (-)	–44.60	149.60	108.00	133.00	---	---	---	---
9) Avg. of neighs.' "guars."	.08	.10	.06	.10	–.02	.13	.02	.13
10) Tax efforts (+)	1.68**	.67	.81	.64	2.32**	.86	1.26	.88
11) Tax capacity (+)	1.56	.98	.78	.90	1.91#	1.08	1.69#	1.09
Support								
12) For profit org. 000 pop. (–)	–607.10***	105.90	–430.30**	180.40	–688.00***	244.00	–527.00*	239.00
13) Welfare/women's Per 000 (+)	4581.90***	1680.20	5011.00***	1567.00	5230.00**	2066.00	6464.00***	2096.00
14) Upper class elect. Bias (-)	–.62**	.18	–.62***	.17	–.85***	.23	–.83***	.23
Taste for helping:								
15) Liberals less conserv. in state (+)	–2.53	2.04	–2.09	1.96	1.54	1.16	1.54	15) Liberals less conserv. in state (+)

(*Continued*)

TABLE 8.2 (Continued)

	AFDC Measures				*TANF Measures*			
	1994 & 1996: Factor Scores for Char. Giving		*1994 & 1996 Giving Sums to Eight Charities*		*2000 & 2003 Charitable Giving*		*2000 & 2003 for Sums to Eight Charities*	
	Coeff.	*Std. Error*	*Coeff.*	*Std.Error*	*Coeff.*	*Std. Error*	*Coeff.*	*std.error*
16) Dems - reps in state gov't (+)	.10	.150	–.03	0.13	.19	.19	–.02	.18
17) Highest income tax class (+)	.07#	.037	0.08**	0.03	.04	.04	.08#	.04
18) Charitable giving (+)	35.10***	8.80	---	---	52.60***	10.90	–	
19) Sum of char. giving (+)	---	---		59825***	16695	–	–	
Time								
20) Year 1996 0r 2003 (–)	–13.7	12.6	–10.9	11.7	–3.82	8.04	–3.8	8.07
constant	137.5	158.8	125.94	145.25	319.86	197.47	310.12	197.86
Adj. r^2 = Root MSE. =		0.87 46.6		0.90 43.4	0.81 59.7		0.81 59.8	

Dependent variables: In eqs. 1 and 2, 1994 and 1996 deflated values of the three-person family AFDC guarantee; in eq. 4 and 5, 2000 and 2003 TANF guarantees for the three-person family. Unstandardized regression coefficients with standard errors. N = 96. # = sig. at.10; * = sig. at.05, etc. one-tailed tests.

while Model (4) uses the sum of charitable giving measure on the TANF measure. Because TANF welfare programs are partially financed via block grants to the states, we dropped the "price" variable from the estimations.

The fundamental message of our four tests is straightforward: Spatial measures of private giving are strongly and positively related with public aid even in the presence of a powerful set of rival predictors. If there is a spatial crowding-out, the coefficient of "charitable giving" should be negative. On the other hand, if charitability can be represented either as "drawing-in" and/or as an inherent trait of the population of the states, as we argue, then the coefficient should be positive – as it is. The factor-analytic measure of financial charitability is correctly signed and significant in all models. The alternative measure, a simple summation of giving to eight of the more modest-sized charities, also has the expected positive and strong association in all models. Consistent across the models, our two measures of personal charitability have positive impacts on welfare assistance. We conclude, therefore, that states' populations who want to help the poor demonstrate personal help for the poor on the private side through giving to private charities and on the public side via supporting high levels of guaranteed aid for the poor and indigent. The variation is expressed privately, publicly, and jointly.

Our other findings are generally consistent with the literature. As the size of the recipient population that is Black increases, generosity of state aid typically falls. This, in part, is offset by the increases in the size of the Black population in the state, which boosts welfare help in the early time period. Note that the percent Black component of the population is negatively related to the TANF guarantee, while the politically helpful fraction of the Black community generally adds to AFDC generosity. As hypothesized, as the fraction of Blacks on the welfare rolls increases, this diminishes others' interests in being helpful, more so with AFDC but less so with TANF.[35] Ethnic heterogeneity, as hypothesized to enhance political bargaining, increases the size of the guarantee.

As the fraction of the recipient population that is unmarried rises, state generosity falls. All the relevant coefficients are negative in the four models, although none reach appropriate significance levels. Contrary to expectation, the size of the recipient population relative to the total population is always positively related to the size of the guarantee.

The analysis of the economics of welfare yields interesting results. Consistently, as the local share of the guarantee increases, a cost-sharing practice that exists for ten states at rates that vary from 5% to 50%, the size of the guarantee falls. Per capita income, as expected, was strongly and positively related to the AFDC guarantee. In the TANF period, it continued to be positive, but at half the impact with the same standard errors, and now falls into insignificance. Statewide wealth in the modern era appears to have diminished impact on welfare generosity. The "price" of welfare, the states' share of state and federal welfare payments, also did not display the expected direction in model (2) and had large standard errors. The impact of states' neighbors had, in models (1) and (2), the expected positive impact, albeit at an insignificant level.

Both tax capacity and tax effort were positively and typically significant determinants of the guarantee. Higher welfare benefits are a part of the product of the breadth of states' efforts: states with rich tax bases and states that choose to exploit those bases for governmental effort are more generous to the poor. Consistent across all of the models were the impacts of our interest group and social class measures. States with well-organized "for profit" interests have lower welfare outlays. However, states with higher numbers of groups with putatively greater stakes in helping the poor – "welfare" and "women's" groups – have higher benefits.

Our more general measures of political beliefs and practices variables fare poorly in the models. The balance of liberalism and conservatism in the states' electorates has little impact. Further, the long-term balance of Democratic vs. Republican party control of the state houses has little impact. However, consistent with our "tax effort" variable, having a progressive, and therefore extractive, income tax rate, the more generous is its welfare program. Finally, as the dummy variables indicate, the 1996 AFDC and 2000 TANF guarantees are lower in real dollar terms than their 1994 and 1998 counterparts.[36]

Explaining change in the guarantees[37]

As noted earlier, some twenty-eight of the states changed the nominal value of the guarantee from 1996 to 2003. Five states decreased the amount, and twenty-three increased the guarantee. We hypothesize that in this period of policy change, those states with higher TANF guarantees will more likely be states with high levels of expressed generosity per our giving measures. Thus, in a simple model of change, we expect, *ceteris paribus*, each of the two charity measures will be positively related to the value of the TANF guarantee, controlling for prior values of AFDC and other variables.

We can plausibly create a model of political change for some of the relevant factors as set out in Table 8.2. Per our belief in the stickiness of the welfare policy process. we expect that the value of the 1993 guarantee would be strongly related to the value of the 2003 TANF guarantee. We expect that the size and change in some of the important racial traits of the states will also relate to the change in the guarantee. High levels of Black recipients for 1994 will likely be reflected in scaled-back TANF guarantees. Further, as the percentage of recipients that are Black increases, we hypothesize lowered guarantees. However, as the size of the states' populations that are Black themselves

TABLE 8.3 Using Private Charitability to Account for Change in Public Redistribution

Change in AFDC to 2003 TANF Guarantees					
(1) with Factor Scores Scores for Char. Giving					*(2) 1994 & 1996 Giving Sums to Eight Charities*
		Coeff.	*Std. Error*	*Coeff*	*Std. Error*
1) Guarantee 1994	(+)	1.1**	0.13	1.1	0.1
Race & diversity:					
2) 1994 % Recipients black	(–)	0.24	0.66	0.23	0.66
3) 1994 Nonwhite as % state population	(+)	.13	0.62	0.12	0.6
4) d in Nonwhite as % state pop. (1994 to 2003)	(+)	0.49	0.99	0.48	0.98
Recipient trait:					
5) 1994% Recipients single parent.	(–)	-1.25	1.80	-1.2	1.7
Economics:					
6) Recipients as % 1994 population	(–)	1.44	13.5	1.2	13.7
7) d in recipients as % population (1994 to 2003)	(–)	-2.46	16.9	-2.8	17.1
8) 1994 per capita inc.	(+)	-0.01	0.0	-0.0	0.0
9) Change in per capita inc. (1994 to 2003)	(+)	0.0	0.0	0.0	0.0
Party					
10) N of years unified democ. party ctrl (94 to 03)	(+)	4.1	2.9	4.1	2.9
11) N of years unified repub. party ctrl (94 to 03)	(–)	1.5	3.1	1.5	3.1
Taste for helping:					
12a) Factor scores of charitable giving	**(+)**	**0.2**	**9.0**	**–1320.8**	**12509.5**
13b) Sum of giving to eight charities	**(+)**				
constant		100.2	89.9	98.2	89.
Adj. r^2 =		0.87		0.87	
Root MSE.=		47.8		47.8	

Dependent variables: In eqs. 1 and 2, the values 2003 TANF guarantees for three-person family. Unstandardized regression coefficients with standard errors. N = 48. # = sig. at .10; * = sig. at .05, etc. one-tailed tests.

changes, reflecting increased voting and legislative power, it would likely be associated with higher TANF guarantees. We would expect that high rates of 1994 recipiency would lead to little or no change in the TANF guarantee. On the other hand, statewide wealth as measured by per capita income and changes in that should lead to greater generosity. Over the relevant time period, two simple political measures of partisan control should generate opposing effects: the number of years of unified Democratic control should lead to higher guarantees, and unified Republican control to no change or decreases. And, finally, our simple mid-1990s measure of statewide private charitability should both be positively related to higher TANF guarantees.

The fair summary of the results in Table 8.3 is that of disappointment. The guarantee is sticky – the AFDC 1994 figure does predict the 2003 TANF figure, but little else is of consequence. Every single other predictor falls well short of statistical influence, and that includes our measure of private generosity.

Conclusion

If the preferences of citizens for charitability are revealed in their observed practices of giving to the needy, then this paper has established links between generalized citizen preferences for help for the poor in private organized giving of money and its public expression in the statewide public AFDC program. Charitability preferences are, as we have defined them, privately and publicly expressed, as originally expressed in Plotnick and Winters (1985, 1990). Where Plotnick and Winters failed in that article was including the IRS data that is badly tainted with religious giving – religious giving is giving to those who are just like the giver, hardly a Maimonidian ideal.[38]

Secondly, we have established the validity of our general measures of private giving. While more charities could be added to the composite measure, and/or better data could be gathered on charities that are more directly linked to the conceptual base of "human services," it is precisely the consequence of crowding-out that makes such charities difficult to find. Further, we believe that our aggregate preferences-for-charity measures hold up well in a multiple regression test in explaining public redistribution. Assessed within a fairly rigorous model, our indicators of private preferences and practices held up well.

What did not hold up so well was accounting for the change in welfare generosity to the preferences for giving. The lack of explanatory power may be due to the stickiness of public generosity. States may be reluctant to change the guarantee in the short term, yet the transition from AFDC to TANF surely provided a setting for welfare adjustments. Finally, we do not have a dynamic measure of charitable preferences. It may be the case that those states that cut the guarantee were states where voters readjusted their own private charitable giving. To the point, we have only one measure of difference.

APPENDIX 8.1 State-by-state factor scores on CharGive and VolntARC

By state:	*CharGive*	*VolntARC*		*Rank order*		*CharGive*	*VolntARC*
Alabama	–1.59	–2.04	Vermont	6.31	Washington	3.80	
Alaska	–0.98	1.83	Hawaii	5.30	Wisconsin	2.87	
Arizona	2.07	–0.34	Delaware	3.84	Oregon		2.82
Arkansas	–0.90	–2.13	N. Dakota	2.43	Wyoming	2.39	
California	–0.10	–0.38	Florida	2.16	Nebraska	2.33	
Colorado	–0.75	0.64	Arizona	2.07	S. Dakota	2.08	
Connecticut	1.57	0.43	Connecticut	1.57	Iowa		1.84
Delaware	3.84	–0.66	Minnesota	1.36	Alaska		1.83
Florida	2.16	–1.45	Maine	1.27	Vermont	1.80	
Georgia	0.30	–2.14	Ohio	1.18	Maine		1.77
Hawaii	5.30	–1.00	New Hampshire	0.97	N. Dakota	1.61	
Idaho	–0.57	1.31	Pennsylvania	0.87	Idaho		1.31

(*Continued*)

APPENDIX 8.1 (Continued)

By state:	*CharGive*	*VolntARC*		*Rank order*		*CharGive*	*VolntARC*
Illinois	−0.72	−0.27	Maryland	0.83	Minnesota	1.24	
Indiana	−0.87	−0.83	Virginia	0.73	Montana	1.18	
Iowa	−0.57	1.84	Oregon	0.64	Kansas		0.78
Kansas	0.32	0.78	Missouri	0.54	Colorado	0.64	
Kentucky	−1.38	−1.36	Washington	0.39	Virginia	0.49	
Louisiana	−4.13	−1.35	Kansas	0.32	Connect.	0.43	
Maine	1.27	1.77	Georgia	0.30	Michigan	0.02	
Maryland	0.83	−0.59	New York	0.11	Ohio		−0.12
Massachusetts	−0.80	−0.47	Nevada	0.05	Oklahoma	−0.15	
Michigan	−0.98	0.02	S. Dakota	0.00	Pennsylvania	−0.21	
Minnesota	1.36	1.24	Wisconsin	−0.03	Illinois	−0.27	
Mississippi	−2.11	−2.22	California	−0.10	New Mexico	−0.27	
Missouri	0.54	−1.20	New Mexico	−0.31	Arizona	−0.34	
Montana	−1.08	1.18	Rhode Island	−0.45	California	−0.38	

(Continued)

APPENDIX 8.1 (Continued)

By state:	*CharGive*	*VolntARC*		*Rank order*		*CharGive*	*VolntARC*
Nebraska	−1.17	2.33	Idaho	−0.57	Texas		−0.44
Nevada	0.05	−1.37	Iowa	−0.57	Mass.		−0.47
New Hampshire	0.97	−0.61	Illinois	−0.72	Maryland	−0.59	
New Jersey	−1.69	−0.92	Colorado	−0.75	New Hamp.	−0.61	
New Mexico	−0.31	−0.27	S. Carolina	−0.76	Delaware	−0.66	
New York	0.11	−1.72	Tennessee	−0.78	Utah		−0.71
N. Carolina	−1.33	−1.10	Massachusetts	−0.80	Indiana	−0.83	
N. Dakota	2.43	1.61	Indiana	−0.87	New Jersey	−0.92	
Ohio	1.18	−0.12	Arkansas	−0.90	Rhode I.	−0.96	
Oklahoma	−1.42	−0.15	Michigan	−0.98	Hawaii		−1.00
Oregon	0.64	2.82	Alaska	−0.98	W. Virg.	−1.00	
Pennsylvania	0.87	−0.21	Montana	−1.08	N. Carol.	−1.10	
Rhode Island	−0.45	−0.96	Nebraska	−1.17	Missouri	−1.20	
S. Carolina	−0.76	−1.54	Utah	−1.20	Louisiana	−1.35	

(Continued)

APPENDIX 8.1 (Continued)

By state:	*CharGive*	*VolntARC*		*Rank order*		*CharGive*	*VolntARC*
S. Dakota	0.00	2.08	N. Carolina	–1.33	Kentucky	–1.36	
Tennessee	–0.78	–1.69	Kentucky	–1.38	Nevada		–1.37
Texas	–1.88	–0.44	Oklahoma	–1.42	Florida	–1.45	
Utah	–1.20	–0.71	Alabama	–1.59	S. Carol.	–1.54	
Vermont	6.31	1.80	New Jersey	–1.69	Tennessee	–1.69	
Virginia	0.73	0.49	Texas	–1.88	New York	–1.72	
Washington	0.39	3.80	Mississippi	–2.11	Alabama	–2.04	
W. Virginia	–2.19	–1.00	W. Virginia	–2.19	Arkansas	–2.13	
Wyoming	–2.50	2.39	Louisiana	–4.13	Mississ.	–2.22	
Wisconsin	–0.03	2.87	Wyoming	–2.50	Georgia	–2.14	

Notes

1 This chapter is a "follow-on" to two papers published with Robert Plotnick of the University of Washington (1985, 1990). The first-named author is grateful to Prof. Plotnick for the collaboration. This chapter reflects, in part, that collaboration.
2 In *nominal dollars* by decade since 1975, individual Americans contributed $28.56, $71.69, $123.68, and $260.28 billion, respectively, to non-profit organizations (*Giving USA 1999; 2006*). Using "giving to human services" in the *Giving USA 1997* (pp. 200–203) as the proxy for private monetary giving to the poor, $2.94 billion was donated for human services in 1975, $8.5 billion in 1985, $11.7 billion in 1995, and $25.36 in 2005.
3 This reallocation of private giving is widely accepted; see Roberts (1984) for the argument.
4 See Mueller (1989, 1990), Chapters 23 and 29, respectively, for analyses of the public logics for welfare.
5 Total all-government nominal spending on "public aid" appears to be the best aggregate measure of all direct spending on "welfare." According to the *Statistical Abstract* (1999, p. 386; and in 2006, p. 358, equal to the sum of "public assistance medical care" and "income maintenance benefit payments"), this totaled $49 billion for 1975 (obtained from an earlier volume in the comparable table), $104 billion for 1985, $254 billion for 1995, and $404 billion for 2003.
6 Plotnick and Winters' measure was a poor proxy for citizen preferences for giving to the poor. We utilized factor scores derived from two measures: (1) "[state-by-state] contributions to United Way charities per capita and [2] charitable deductions claimed on federal income tax returns as a percentage of adjusted gross income (468)." The two measures, perversely so, are negatively correlated with one another and probably reflect the very sizable reporting of contributions to church and religious organizations in the IRS data. Not surprisingly, this disparate factor loading of the two measures did not relate at all to public giving.
7 They note it as the "AFDC monthly payment 1995," which we assume is either the average payment or one of the measures of the guarantee.
8 For a compatible theoretical treatment of preferences for redistribution, see Alesina and Giuliano (2009); also, for an individual-level analysis, see Alesina and La Ferrara (2005).
9 The simple correlations across adjacent years for the 1984 to 2003 series of AFDC and TANF "guarantees" never fall below .95, and the simple r between the 1984 AFDC and the 2003 TANF guarantees is .92.
10 Hawaii, Oklahoma, and Connecticut cut the most, while Wisconsin, New Mexico, and West Virginia increased the most – not your usual array of states.
11 An example: https://www.ksl.com/article/50072337/utah-ranked-most-charitable-state-in-us-in-2020-new-study-finds.
12 See https://www.chabad.org/library/article_cdo/aid/45907/jewish/Eight-Levels-of-Charity.htm?gclid=Cj0KCQjw6pOTBhCTARIsAHF23fKWvDG0Kt7kH06tK7tlO1TTeNwix3Fu-DCDxCXbl0pt0S-KeP8WyZIaArwHEALw_wcB.
13 Calculated by the authors. Total federal, state, and local public aid was compiled from the series of *Statistical Abstracts* for the appropriate years until 1995 using the column labeled "public aid" in the table ordinarily titled "Social welfare expenditures under public programs" (see, for example, Table 607, p. 386 of the *Statistical Abstract of the U.S. 1999*). We continued the series for

the 1996–2000 years by summing the categories of "public assistance medical care" and "income maintenance benefits payments" in the 2006 *Statistical Abstract of the U.S.*, Table 528. The nominal monetary data were deflated using the series of deflators for the annual personal consumption expenditure obtained from the *Economic Report of the President, 2008*, using Table B-7. Private giving, also deflated, was measured using data from "giving to human services" in *Giving USA 2006*, p. 206.

14 Schiff (1985) and Steinberg (1993) review the economic literature on government and private crowding-out.

15 We use "secular" in the classic sense of non-ecclesiastical. Most data analyses of total charitable giving conflate two unlikes – giving to religious organizations and secular giving to non-religious, non-profit organizations. The distinction between the two is not just between sacred vs. secular, but, more importantly, secular giving is more likely to be anonymous giving to others who may well be *unlike* the giver, while religious charitability can best be thought of as giving to others who are probably very much *like* oneself.

16 The impetus for this research rested on a bet between the two authors on this point. Rygorsky wagered that generous welfare states would have low private giving; Winters bet the opposite: Winters won.

17 As Plotnick and Winters previously hypothesized. In fact, the simple correlation between our measures of private charitable giving and public giving to the poor via the AFDC or TANF family guarantees (defined shortly) is .43 and .46, respectively.

18 We recognize that our argument is fundamentally individualistic and that it would be better tested at the individual level via survey research. However, no survey exists that adequately measures individual *social-welfare generosity* that could be aggregated to the state level so as to ascertain links with *generous public policy*. It is not sufficient to quiz individuals about their private preferences for private and public assistance to the poor. We are interested in their behavior, both privately in terms of personal generosity and publicly in terms of public policies adopted by their legislators and governors. We believe that the test of the sincerity of opinion preferences for charitability will best be tested via a measure of their private actions – direct, pocketbook charitable contributions.

19 There are a couple of related literatures. A small and dated political science literature, spawned by Banfield and Wilson (1971), centers on the concept of "public-regardingness." Except for a flurry of reactions and critiques, it has received little attention in the literature (see Wolfinger and Field 1966, and Lupsha 1975 and citations therein). A second, more distantly related literature is the voluminous one generated by Robert Putnam's "bowling alone" hypothesis (Putnam 2000, but see Uslaner's (2002) excellent critique). Putnam notes that while "[a]ltruism ... is by some interpretations a central measure of social capital ... [d]oing good *for* other people, however laudable, is not part of the *definition* of social capital...." (117; emphasis in the original). A more current thread crosses the disciplines of politics and economics in the empirical and formal analysis of self- and other-regarding behaviors (see Andreoni 1988, 1989, 2006, 2007; Warr 1982, and Roberts 1984). A review of other-regarding elements in moral and political reasoning is Frohlich and Oppenheimer (2000). Kristin Monroe (1996) and Alexander Field (2001) survey the social, economic, and political analyses of altruism from their respective fields of political science and economics. Matt Ridley (1996) presents a popular survey of "the origins of virtue." Fehr and Fischbacher (2003) review the behavioral and sociobiological sciences literature examining human altruism.

20 Five of the eleven largely provide services for the medically needy, and per the earlier discussion of crowding-out, none of the charities can be said to deal simply and directly with directly cash-assisting the "poor." We argue, nevertheless, that giving to these charities with their helping orientations is a reasonable proxy for "giving to the needy."

21 We assume, although we did not confirm, that the two charities worked in concert with one another via sharing donor lists.
Scores for each state were then calculated by the equation: CharGive = 0.39*ORG1 + 0.28*ORG2 + .35*ORG3 + 0.38*ORG5 +.34*ORG6 + .44*ORG7 + .36*ORG8 + .13*ORG9 + .16*ORG10 + .08*ORG11. We suspect, but do not know, that ORG4 and ORG3 share donor lists.

22 We were surprised at the extreme score for Vermont. Vermonters ranked 1st in per capita giving as a percent of personal income in four of the ten charities, second in two, fourth, and sixth in one each, and 22nd and 24th in giving to the American Red Cross and United Way campaigns. Interestingly enough, these last two charities were the biggest and most national of our charities. It's as if Vermonters calculated … "my giving would make more sense in smaller and less well-known … and maybe more local … organizations."

23 The simple correlation between CharGive and a dummy for the south is -.29.

24 The data for the 1994, 1996, 2000, and 2003 AFDC/TANF guarantee for the three-person family is drawn from the 2004 *Green Book*, Table 7–10. All figures were temporally and spatially deflated using the Berry-Fording-Hanson annual deflators drawn from ICPSR, study 1275. We chose the *Green Book* published figures because of their accessibility to us and to others and their frequent use in the literature. Russell Hanson and Carl Klarner have noted that these figures are not perfectly "clean."

25 Our numbers of cases for examining the 1994–1996 and 2000–2003 guarantees equal 96. No Berry-Fording-Hanson adjustments for spatial differences in the "cost of living" are available for Alaska and Hawaii, and we dropped them from the analysis. We doubled the sample size in an unsuccessful effort to disentangle the confounding effects of the "price" of the guarantee from statewide personal income. Measures of the guarantee and per capita disposable income were spatially and temporally deflated for each of the time periods. The values for the other variables remained the same in the two-year spans.

26 Our thinking here very much mirrors that of Plotnick and Winters (1987, 1990).

27 Throughout our results, our tests for the simple variable of the "south" indicated zero impact; thus, we did not include it.

28 Our ethnic homogeneity index is a −1*a nine-element Herfindahl index of state-by-state ethnic composition and was constructed from data obtained from the 1994 *Almanac of American Politics* on the percentages of states' populations that were Black, Hispanic, Asian-American, and Native American; and from the 1990 U.S. Census on the percentage of the population that claimed English, German, Irish, Italian, and a summary percentage of "other European" ancestry. The most diverse states are NY, NJ, CA, and IL, while the least diverse states are WV, KY, NH, and VT.

29 Ten states had some sort of match with other local governments in 1994 and 1996.

30 The simple correlations between per capita income and the variables of price to the state and the guarantee are -.73 (I with P) and .64 (I with G). The relationships between income, price, and the guarantee are quite erratic. In a simple model pooling observations from 1980, 1985, 1990, 1992, and 1994

(available in the 1998 *Green Book*, with state-by-state price and the guarantee data in Tables 7.16 and 7.14) using control variables of population, dummies for four regions, and a year variable, the correct signs for price (-) and income (+) appear. In the disaggregated year-by-year regressions, however, per capita income is always related positively to guarantee, while price is contraindicated positive for the 1980 and 1985 data and correctly, albeit insignificantly, negative for the 1990, 1992, and 1994 data.

31 See Plotnick and Winters (1985) for numbers of professional social workers per 1,000 population and Robert Lowry's (2004) state-by-state data on the size of various kinds of groups. Using IRS-supplied Form 1990s, the Urban Institute has amassed an enormous storehouse of data on American charitable organizations. The Urban Institute's monograph, *Viewing nonprofits across the states*, provides state-by-state numbers of 503(c) public charities, and the percentage of these devoted to support of human services can be obtained. The report can be obtained at: http://www.urban.org/PERIODCL/cnp/cnp_1.htm; see, for example, Table 1, columns 1 and 6.

32 See Gray and Lowery 1996 and 2000 for a discussion of the data. The data is available at "multi-state lists 1997" at: http://www.unc.edu/depts/polisci/lowery_page.html/.

33 The most widely applied measure of state-by-state liberalism is the Erikson-Wright-McIver (1989) measure of voters' liberalism as aggregated from numerous *New York Times* polls. In our case, we used the average of the percentage of liberals from 1983 to 1993 for our analysis of the 1994 and 1996 AFDC guarantee and the average from 1996 to 2003 for our analysis of the TANF guarantee. Berry and colleagues (1998) used interest group measures of federal legislators aggregated by state as another set of measures of the liberalism of citizens and statewide officeholders. Brace and colleagues (2002) generalized nine specific measures of ideological preferences from multiple waves of the General Social Surveys, one of which sought responses to "country spending on welfare?" as either "too much," "about right and DK," or "too little." In the end, we found none of these to be helpful in accounting for welfare generosity. None of these indicators were statistically significant in any of our models of welfare generosity, and all but one generated t statistics less than +/– 1. The Brace et al. measure with a negative sign (t = –1.03) is consistent with their unexpected result of the negative relationship between their measure of "too little" welfare spending and the 1995 AFDC monthly payment (Brace et al. 2002, Table 7, p. 183.)

34 For a review and analysis of the impact of race on the AFDC and TANF eras of welfare politics in America, see Schram et al. (2003).

35 This likely reflects a well-known characteristic of the last two decades of welfare policy-making in the American states: Over time, state budgets were balanced in part by not adequately adjusting year-to-year welfare aid levels to changes in the cost of living; see Moffitt (1990).

36 For Table 3, variables number (1), (7), (8), (9), and (10) were obtained from the "UKCPR_National_Data_Set_10_12_09-2" data set at the University of Kentucky. Variables (11) and (12) were calculated by the author from the political variables from that data set. The "race and diversity" measures and that of "recipient trait" were derived from various editions of the "Green Book."

37 We consider the private giving to national charities as idealized gestures of the 2nd level of charitable giving according to Maimonides' eight levels of charity; see (https://www.chabad.org/library/article_cdo/aid/45907/jewish/Eight-Levels-of-Charity.htm).

PART IV

Assessing the consequences of taxing via individual-level data

9

THE INDIVIDUAL POLITICS OF TAXES AND THE VOTE[1]

Brian G. Stults and Richard F. Winters

Introduction

Given that taxes are raised frequently in the American states,[2] we should have increasing confidence in answering the queries of whether, and if so, when and under what conditions do gubernatorial candidates face electoral retribution for taxes that increased during their term of office. Over the past two decades, answers to this question have differed. Early evidence (Pomper 1976, Hansen 1983) based on highly aggregated measures suggested that the relationship was weak. Better measures of legislated changes in tax rates also suggested weak retribution (Eismeier 1983). Separating brand-new programs vs. changes across sales and income taxes indicated variable impact by type of tax and weak overall impacts (Kone and Winters 1993). Niemi and colleagues (1995) argued that the impact of changed tax rates on individuals as assessed in thirty-five pooled 1986 gubernatorial exit polls was significant. However, the net effect on the voter was small, and the individual effects found in such a single election analysis could be substantially biased.

We pool exit poll data of gubernatorial elections for eighteen years for forty-three states.[3] Pooling permits the addition of "fixed effects" for each state and for each election year, with the result that time-invariant, statewide, and electoral period effects are factored out. Further, our model contains a more comprehensive set of control variables and sets of "contextual conditions" that allow for answers to queries of when and under what conditions do taxes electorally impact. Pooling individual-level, cross-sectional data and adding key controls reduces the probability of omitted variable bias, thereby obtaining better estimates of the "true" effect of tax hikes on the vote.

DOI: 10.4324/9781003606291-14

We argue that endogeneity is the *fundamental* problem associated with determining the effect of tax hikes on the vote. Because governors are interested in furthering their political careers, attaining reelection, or helping their party's successor candidates for office, governors' decisions on whether to raise taxes are related to the upcoming, projected vote share. If tax changes have the potential to render uncertain incumbents' hopes, then governors will likely seek non-tax solutions to their need for revenue – budget cuts, increased fees, charges, etc. This will be true as the prospects for electoral victory shrink. If so, then the effect obtained from a regression analysis will be biased: it will only take into account the effect *when a tax change is observed*. Thus, we expect the data on tax changes to be severely truncated in electorally problematic/competitive conditions, precisely the most interesting situations of all. The effects of tax changes will be markedly different from that which would be observed if tax changes occurred exogenously, *as if they were essentially unrelated to electoral consequences*.

The usual solution to this problem of "instrumental variables" will not work in this situation because we believe that no suitable instrument is available.[4] We offer a second-best strategy of putting regression results in context through interaction effects, as we will describe more fully shortly. Theory suggests what groups of governors might have the most to fear from raising taxes and, as such, would engage in the most strategic behavior. In an indirect way, the use of interactions permits us to map out those situations that are characterized by a relatively high degree of endogeneity and to separate out those situations in which endogeneity is most likely to plague the model from those situations in which it is less likely to be an issue. We argue that our technique highlights, but does not resolve, endogeneity.

Our "mapping" strategy suggests that the political context (Books and Prysby 1992; Brace and Jewett 1995; Stonecash 1996) may be a key determinant of individual vote choice and election outcomes, yet many empirical studies fail to place the major results – typically couched as regression coefficients – within relevant contexts. Powerful examples of hypothetical contextual effects arise at the aggregate level. Electoral timing should affect voter retribution; thus, tax hikes in periods of rising unemployment will be more severely punished at the polls. At the individual level, we might expect high-income voters to be more sensitive to changes in the income tax. Many authors have discussed the role of context in the politics of taxation (e.g., Hansen 1983; Winters 1996), but these discussions were rarely accompanied by direct empirical investigation.[5] The implication, then, is that the gubernatorial tax-vote relationship should be reexamined using an empirical model designed to ascertain whether the tax-vote relationship is conditional on the political and economic environments as well as on the characteristics of the voting population. To do so requires data that merges measures of individual-level voting behavior (315,000 voters) that vary across electoral contexts (forty-three states) and time/electoral periods (228 gubernatorial campaigns from 1982 to 2000).

This chapter is organized as follows. The section "Assessing the impact of state taxation on gubernatorial voters" reviews the literature on the impact of taxation on gubernatorial vote outcomes. Section "If taxes impact, when are governors likely to tax?" reviews the likely determinants of under what conditions governors are likely to propose and get taxes changed. These conditions generate the problem of endogeneity, because proposing new taxes and getting them enacted must surely be related to the prospects of electoral victory, *a priori*. The endogeneity issue is described in the section "The endogeneity problem," and we propose a "second best" response. Section "A model of voter retribution" proposes a contextually rich, across-state, across-time model of voter retribution for tax changes. The section "Data and operationalization of the individual-level models" describes our data and the operationalization of the model. Section "Further specifications regarding methods and econometrics" describes a number of measurement and econometric issues in the study. Section "Testing the models" describes the results of the models' tests. We conclude in Section "Conclusions."

Assessing the impact of state taxation on gubernatorial voters

Our analysis of the impact of taxation on the vote occurs within the bounds of a largely agreed-upon set of determinants of the vote. At the aggregate level, researchers show that national effects dominate gubernatorial contests (Peltzman 1987; Kenney 1983; Holbrook 1987). Chubb (1988) demonstrated that aggregate gubernatorial election outcomes are affected by state economics, but national forces – and particularly evaluations of the president's handling of the economy – are more important.

At the individual level, Svoboda (1995) found that voters' evaluations of the state economy significantly affect vote choice. Strong national-level findings resulted from the use of aggregate economic indicators rather than respondents' perceptions. Stein (1990), using 1982 exit polls, demonstrated that responsibility for economic conditions is assigned to the president, not to the governor, and that punitive effects are concentrated on incumbents of the president's party. Hansen (1999) used time-series poll data from eight states from 1967 to 1997 and found that high unemployment resulted in higher disapproval of the governor's job ratings, but consistent with the asymmetric effects literature, lower unemployment was not rewarded.

Atkeson and Partin (1995) found that the electoral success of senators depends on the success of the president, following a national referendum hypothesis, while the success of governors depends on perceptions of state economic conditions, but not personal economic circumstances. With an incumbent Republican president, they claimed that incumbent Republican governors (but not open-seat Republican candidates) were punished more sharply (but, see Carsey and Wright 1998a, 1998b).

Governors may be punished by political context. Voter accountability is stronger for unified government, and voters may have party-specific expectations regarding taxing and spending. Republican candidates lose votes if their party is held responsible for increases in the size of the budget, but Democratic candidates do not (Besley and Case 1995b). MacDonald and Sigelman (1999; also see Poterba 1994b) found that a governor is held responsible for tax increases and the health of the state economy only in an election year.

A great deal of scholarly research has been devoted to separating the effects of electoral retribution from changed taxes vs. changes in economic conditions. Harris (1959) found that governors were "getting the daylights knocked out of them for simply trying to make ends meet." Cowart (1973) argued that the governor has "borne the stigma of increased tax rates" (also, see Ranney 1965; Turett 1971; Beyle 1983). Pomper (1968, 1976) concluded that governors who increase taxes were not significantly hurt at the polls. Pomper observed that governors performed better if they taxed earlier in their terms rather than later. Pomper also found that in more competitive states, voters were more likely to support tax increases and larger spending. Eismeier (1983) concluded that there were electoral risks associated with higher taxes in the 1950–1980 period, but these risks were not overwhelming (379).[6] Governors who raised taxes also appeared not to lose their party's nomination in their reelection bid. Hansen (1983, 177) found that among survey respondents in 1980, 15% surveyed mentioned taxes as a criterion in their voting decisions. Moreover, 31% of occasions of new sales taxes and 22% of new income taxes were followed by the defeat of the incumbent or the party's candidate. She concluded that while there is "some risk ... involved in passing broad-based taxes ... the imposition of [such] taxes does not constitute political suicide" (166).

Recent research reports (Jewell and Morehouse 2000) suggest that taxes are often listed as a major issue in gubernatorial contests, especially when the incumbent had promised not to raise taxes (187). Carsey (2000) argued that the 1993 campaign in New Jersey hinged on framing the tax issue. Sanders (1988) argued that the argument is too simple: the public is interested in more benefits paid with less taxes, but also may have more complex preferences: the elderly may push for greater services (and thus taxes), while younger groups want exactly the opposite (MacManus 1995, but c.f. Rhodebeck 1993).

Different taxes may have differing levels of visibility and associated electoral punishment (Burnori 1998, 191–192). Changes in the income tax will be punished because it places the burden on "well-educated, informed, politically responsive, upper- and middle-class citizens" (Downs, 1960), yet the sales tax is opposed by well-organized commercial and retail interests. Mikesell (1998) noted, "the consumer sees the [sales] tax being levied on each purchase and thus is aware of its cost to him or her... The tax can be starkly transparent" (17). Low-income earners have been shown to be resistant to the regressive sales tax (Phares 1980). However, excise taxes may provide a way for governors to raise revenue with less public attention. Consumers may be unaware of taxes on alcohol, gasoline, and cigarettes (Winters 1996, 335–336) and are more likely to be galvanized by the personal income and sales taxes (339).

Three articles are central to our argument. Kone and Winters (1993) studied the aggregate results from 407 gubernatorial elections from 1957 to 1985 and found that enacting brand-new income or sales tax programs harmed the incumbent's party in the subsequent election, although this effect was not significant. However, incremental changes in existing sales tax programs were found to have a significant impact.

Niemi and colleagues (1995) analyzed exit polls for thirty-four gubernatorial elections in 1986. State and national economic factors were found to be significant predictors of the personal vote – including taxation. Indeed, there was punishment associated with each increment of taxation. They also find evidence that bad economic conditions and more tax increases are correlated with governors' decisions not to run for reelection. The study suffers from limits that originate from its single cross-section design. They measure change in the national economy with subjective evaluations by the respondent – they interact with an evaluation of the state of the economy with whether the voter judged the economy to be a "salient" issue. Unlike overtime changes in unemployment or real disposable income, these are subjective questions that are influenced by partisan predispositions or the already-determined vote choice, thereby making them poor proxies for economic change. In fact, in a single cross-section, there is no national economic change at all. Finally, using a single cross-section meant that Niemi and colleagues could not use state fixed effects.

Besley and Case (1995a) first treated the relationship between taxation and vote choice as an endogenous one, determined simultaneously, and that the effects of a tax may differ depending on circumstances. Using various income groups and their respective average tax liabilities, they craft models that control for changes in state income, state unemployment rate, and state debt. However, they do *not* include relevant political controls used in previous studies of taxation and voting behavior. They find that an increase in taxes diminishes the probability of voting for an incumbent, but if neighboring states raise taxes at the same time, the effect is offset. To account for possible endogeneity problems, tax effects are instrumented with year effects and demographics (changes in the proportion of elderly and the young), and the original results stand. The lack of political controls creates a potentially serious problem: The demographic instruments are surely correlated with the error term in vote choice, making them poor instruments. While their attempt to resolve the endogeneity problem is admirable, their success is questionable. Their instruments fundamentally proxy for a tax *when it must be enacted to maintain balanced budgets* and not for when a tax is voluntary. The difference may be thought of as fiscal health in the former situation as opposed to increased services as a political preference of the incumbent administration in the latter.

If taxes impact, when are governors likely to tax?

Information asymmetries exist for leaders and voters. Governors and their advisers will be uncertain of the impact of a proposed tax change. Actions such as opinion polls, elite consultation, party caucusing, and media trial balloons are undertaken to diminish uncertainties (Hansen 1999). Leaders' information on electoral consequences is ultimately imperfect, so there is an incentive to choose an option that affords the opportunity to hedge. This is particularly so because voters, too, are imperfectly informed – perhaps more so than candidates because voters are "rationally ignorant" (Downs 1957). Opportunistic politicians (Brennan and Buchanan 1980) will structure taxes in such a way so as to acquire the greatest impact with the least visibility.

We assume that governors will attempt to satisfy their personal preferences, the most notable of which is future electoral success. However, state executives generally act as though raising rates represents a serious political risk (Berry and Berry 1992; 1994). As such, governors attempt to enact taxes only at times when a "political opportunity" presents itself, represented by a likely low level of electoral retribution or a situation in which exogenous factors leave the governor no choice but to raise taxes. The situation is further complicated by the political and economic climate within a state that can affect a governor's ability to pass legislation. In general, then, tax rate increases are a likely product of the interaction of three types of factors: a governor's personal preferences, exogenous economic and legal factors, and the political climate.

Personal Preferences: Personal preferences include reelection concerns, desire to pursue higher office, and the governor's ideology – all of which combine to form a spatial "ideal point" for each governor. The relative weights that each governor places on ideology, reelection, and other personal preferences are unknown; they cannot be directly observed, would be difficult to measure in any case, and only can, at best, be inferred from gubernatorial actions.

Ideology: Governors may have a preference between tax programs, and in our case, the choice is between changing the sales, income, or sin taxes. The incidence or burdens of these taxes vary by income, so we might expect that the likely electoral reactions to the tax choices of a governor by income class will be reflected in the chosen tax instrument of change. Lower socioeconomic class voters devote more resources to consumption and less of their income to savings and investment and thus should be more sensitive to changes in sales and excise taxes (Winters 1996). Higher income voters might oppose changes in the income tax because they save and invest more and are "taxed twice" on income (first via the income tax and then on the interest and dividends). Further, because income tax systems are often graduated into brackets, higher income individuals may also face higher average rates. Further, tax increases "purchase" public goods. Some public goods valued by some governors, e.g. roads and highways or a balanced budget, may be inferior goods for governors with a taste for redistributive policies. A governor sets expenditures and revenue collections so as to maximize the chances of winning the next election (Downs 1957, 1960). Incumbents seek to maximize a weighted sum of expected votes, where those weights are determined by voter characteristics (Hettich and Winer 1988).

Winning elections, either one's own reelection or a future office, or increasing the likelihood of the election of the successor of his/her party is a well-established motive (Mayhew 1974). As a result, whether taxes are increased likely depends on how those taxes will affect a sitting governor's electoral bid. Further, voter retribution is likely linked to the timing of the tax change. Berry and Berry (1992) found support for an election cycle hypothesis for the timing of tax changes, particularly in contrast to competing explanations of tax increases. Mikesell (1978) found that the less visible excise taxes are more likely to be used as revenue sources in an election year (but see Hansen 1983 and Chapter 9 in this volume). It is probably easier for a governor to engage in "bracket creep" than to institute a brand new income or sales tax (Davies 1986, Penniman 1976; but, cf. Kone and Winters 1993). Governors expect that increases in existing taxes will not carry the same level of electoral retribution as the imposition of new taxes or large rate hikes in existing taxes. On the other hand, having a larger than average number of rate increases, even if each of those increases was small in magnitude, would render the then-incumbent governor vulnerable to charges that she is a "taxer."[7]

Exogenous economic and legal factors: The explanation for tax increases with the most empirical support is enactment in response to economic downturns. The *fiscal health* explanation (Berry and Berry 1992, 1994) argues that short-term fiscal crises require tax increases to raise the necessary funds. The existence of a fiscal crisis may make it more politically palatable to raise taxes (Hansen 1983, 150–157). There are directional effects here, which may be asymmetrical: If a state is experiencing economic *growth*, then it may increase taxes, particularly those that are progressive (Berch 1995). The hypothesis posits that as a state's economic well-being increases, taxation will increase as a function of an increased ability to raise revenue through taxes (Barro 1986, 53). Further, development leads to increased demand for public services (Berry and Lowery 1987) and for public services needed to manage new and changing interdependencies, especially those spawned by urbanization (Berry and Berry 1992). Constitutional constraints and super-majority requirements may shape the need for tax increases (Poterba 1996). Some states have formal provisions limiting debt as well (von Hagen 1991). As a result of these formal constraints, raising taxes may be the only way for a governor to balance the budget by the end of the fiscal year.

The political climate: Finally, there is a set of factors that may best be described as the political climate. *Unified party government* makes it easier for programs to be enacted because the barriers created by partisanship are eroded (Poterba 1994b; Alt and Lowry 1994; Hansen 1983). It may matter *which party* is in control (Gilligan and Matsusaka 1995; Berch 1995; Roemer 1999, and Chapters 3, 4, 5, and 6 of this volume). Finally, *party strength* is distinct from party control. Certainly, whether the government is unified, the percentage of seats held by each party in the legislature, and the quality of the candidates all proxy for party strength, but they do not measure the influence of the state party apparatus on policymaking. At the gubernatorial level, Morehouse (1997) discovered that strong parties and strong gubernatorial influence over the legislature eased gubernatorial agenda passage. Collectively, scholars have referred to the litany of explanations for taxation as "political opportunity" hypotheses (Howe and Reeb 1997). Berry and Berry (1992) concluded that governors increase taxes at times when the politicians can shield themselves from the political costs (737). "Our multivariate model of tax innovation suggests that even if the adoption of a new tax does not guarantee electoral defeat for a governor, politicians act as if such an adoption will spell defeat" (736). It is a combination of internal and external, political and economic conditions that form such windows.

The endogeneity problem

228 elections were held in forty-three American states between 1982 and 2000. In fifty-five of these elections, no changes in the rates or brackets of income, sales, or sin taxes occurred during the governors' term preceding the election. Furthermore, twelve states observed no income tax changes during the two decades, and ten states had no changes in the sales tax. Such states cannot contribute directly to the estimation of the relevant tax coefficients. The simplest explanation is that there would be no way to disentangle the "effect of no tax increases" in the state from the state fixed effect.[8] In essence, the coefficient on the tax variable is really the effect of tax increases on the vote only for a "marginal" group, i.e., voters in those states where a tax increase occurred at some point during the decade.

An example illustrates a corollary point. Suppose that in half the states, an incumbent running for reelection would expect, given conventional statewide "wisdom," to take a 5% hit for increasing tax rates. Some governors are willing to bear this burden because they are strong candidates, while others have no choice but to increase taxes for fiscal reasons. Suppose that in the other half of the states, voters are much more tax-averse, and, as a result, a tax increase would cause an incumbent to take a 10% hit in a reelection bid. Relative to the previous set of states, the proportion of governors willing to undertake tax hikes in these states would be considerably smaller. Risk-averse governors in tax-averse states in the midst of fiscal crisis might try to cut expenditures before passing an unpopular rate hike. Governors in this second group will be less likely to increase tax rates, and therein lies the problem. Because of the added fear of electoral retribution in the electorally sensitive states, some governors who otherwise would have raised taxes at one point in time will choose not to do so. At the limit where taxes scared off all such governors, the electoral retribution effect in these states cannot be estimated because the tax measure has no variability. As a result, the regression fails to reveal the increased punishment in these states which would have occurred if taxed, and the coefficient is attenuated away from its "true" value. Strategic behavior on the part of reelection-minded incumbents acting within tax-sensitive contexts introduces this problem.

The usual approach to deal with an endogeneity problem is with an instrumental variables (IV) or two-stage least squares (2SLS) approach.[9] We argue that the IV/2SLS approach, while theoretically and mathematically appealing, is not a reasonable solution in our cases. The IV method has three stringent assumptions: the existence of endogeneity; the instrumental variables are strong; and the exogeneity of the instruments themselves. Because IV is a less efficient estimator than OLS, failure to satisfy these key assumptions will yield results that are both biased and inefficient – an even worse outcome than which would have been obtained with OLS. Some analysts appear to have failed to test their data to ensure that each of these assumptions is met. Others have used instruments that are clearly correlated with the main dependent variable, as was the case with Markus (1988), who estimated a model of vote choice and wanted to resolve the measurement error within the variable for the respondent's personal financial situation. Markus instrumented for financial situation with the respondent's age, sex, and education, as well as information regarding the respondent's experience with unemployment and income, all factors likely related to the vote. In fact, our model employs as control variables (as do most vote models) some variant of all of Markus's "instruments" and finds them all to be significant. As such, Markus's instruments were inappropriate.

Finding a valid instrument for tax increases is problematic. In Besley and Case (1995a), state tax changes were instrumented with state demographic variables (changes in the proportions of elderly and young individuals in the state's population) and year effects. While Besley and Case employed overidentification tests and determined that the demographic variables should not be eliminated from the second stage, there are several problems with their approach. First, their failure to reject the null hypothesis may have been a function of the small number of observations – 85 observations with 13 independent variables in the structural model. Second, they reported no tests of the *strength* of their instruments. If the joint *F*-statistic on these instruments is less than 10, then while they may be significant in the conventional sense, they would not be sufficiently so to obtain consistent parameter estimates. Third, their model is sparing in its use of control variables; while they controlled for changes in income, debt, and unemployment for the state and the state's neighbors, *no political controls* were included. Omitted variable bias is a real possibility. Had the model included a comprehensive set of political controls as well as national economic variables, then it may indeed have been the case that age changes would have appeared to be significant predictors of the gubernatorial vote.

A more serious problem comes from considering what the IV estimates really are measuring. As we noted earlier, the IV estimator determines the effect for a particular marginal population or group. In Besley and Case's model, there are two marginal groups – one for each set of instruments. The first group is all of the states clumped together at a particular time; this aggregation arises out of the use of year effects. The second group is those states undergoing major demographic changes in terms of the age of the population. In the first group, tax changes are a response to national conditions and tides; in the second group, the tax changes are a response to changes in the services that the electorate demands or the electoral preferences of different age groups. In essence, the effect of tax changes on the vote is probably being measured for the *marginal groups where taxes are a fiscal necessity*. This is very different from an exogenous increase in tax rates.

We claim that there does not appear to be an apparent, appropriate instrument for tax increases. The closest possible option would likely be a set of institutional and legal variables, such as the stringency of balanced budget provisions (Poterba 1996) or court decisions that impose a tax onto a state. However, these variables may be indirectly correlated with the vote, as the governor will behave strategically, determining expenditures and services offered so as to maximize his or her utility. This does not mean, however, that analysts must simply accept endogeneity on the tax issue as a given. As we explained in the introduction, there need not be a single effect of a tax change on the vote; rather, one can imagine a set of effects conditional on other explanatory variables. Providing sufficient numbers of such conditional "contexts" allows us to map out the endogenous and the exogenous space indirectly, thereby allowing us to make interesting inferences without relying on the IV estimator.

A model of voter retribution

The public has shown sophistication with respect to assignment of functional responsibility in holding governors responsible for changes in state economic conditions (Stein 1990). As the chief executive with the responsibility for management of the purse strings, the governor receives more publicity and media attention than other elected officials. Gubernatorial accountability has increased in recent decades with presidential and gubernatorial decoupling, with 80% of the states now in the midterm or off-year. Further, there should be little voter confusion as to whether tax changes are state or federal. While an individual's perceptions of local and state economic conditions may be affected by the health of the national economy, the same effect would not be expected with respect to taxes. Sales taxes are clearly imposed by states and localities, and individuals separately file federal and state income taxes. Finally, changes in state tax rates are relatively rare (Berry and Berry 1992), and when increases do occur, they are often visible and sometimes climactic (Kone and Winters 1993; Niemi et al. 1995). While voters are usually interested in the results of economic policies rather than the actual policies themselves (Kiewiet and Rivers 1985, 370), the case of taxation may be an exception. Intense media coverage and the saliency of the issue ensure that tax increases will be prominent in public discourse. Further, the opposing party and its candidates have a powerful incentive to expose the taxing actions of the incumbent.

There are compelling reasons to believe that increases in taxation will harm the sitting governor or the party nominee. However, some might take issue with this hypothesis for two reasons. First, as was noted earlier, taxes are also the mechanism through which the governor provides programs that garner votes and support. Kone and Winters evaluate the claim:

> [e]ven when benefits funded by tax increases do become visible, the distributions are demographically selective or spatially limited leading taxpayers to perceive that many of their tax dollars are being used to finance programs which assist other constituencies. In any case, because the benefits of many expenditure policies are remote in time, preventative in nature, and collective in consequence, they are not properly appreciated by voters when compared to the immediacy of tax burdens.
>
> *(1993, 27)*

In short, taxes may help particular segments of the population and garner group votes; a backlash from the remainder of the population would be expected. This is precisely because tax increases are visible to the electorate; were they not, a governor could curry favor with each group and "hide" these actions from the rest of the public. Furthermore, there is inefficiency associated with any governmental action: the nature of bureaucracy mandates that the value of inputs will be greater than the value of outputs.

The second reason that some might believe that tax hikes would not be punished is contextual. The governor's hand may be forced into taxation. Rarely does a governor raise one of these major taxes because he or she wants to provide some particular program or policy. Indeed, a superior strategy for a governor would be to determine what existing programs garner the least political support and eliminate them, thereby freeing up resources. More often, it is the case that a tax increase is seen as a no-win situation but a fiscal necessity. The political opportunity hypotheses developed earlier provide a range of ways in which a governor may be able to raise taxes without incurring electoral costs. Thus, it is not altogether clear that tax increases will always convey election-day punishment. Nevertheless, given the logic above, we hypothesize: *(H1) Increases in taxes negatively affect the vote for the incumbent or the nominee from the incumbent's party.*

Electoral retribution should also be examined as conditional on sets of statewide contextual factors. If the public properly assigns electoral responsibility to political agents, then it follows that an incumbent governor would be held liable for presiding over a tax increase to a much greater extent than the successor candidate of the incumbent's party. Therefore: (H2) *An incumbent suffers a greater electoral penalty for tax increases than do nominees of the incumbent's party who run for the office of governor.*

Previous models have implicitly assumed that the effect of tax hikes on the vote is symmetrical for Republicans and Democrats – a testable proposition. Additionally, while Republican voters are traditionally associated with higher incomes and Democrats are associated with lower incomes, this yields another prediction: an increase in the income tax should alienate a key Republican voting bloc, while an increase in the sales tax should alienate a Democratic bloc. If so, (H3) *(a) the effects of tax increases on the vote for Republican incumbent governors and Democratic incumbent governors are not symmetrical. (b) Republican governors are penalized more than Democratic governors for enacting an income tax increase. (c) Democratic governors are penalized more than Republican governors for enacting a sales tax increase.*

This hypothesis has a rival: As partisanship is the most predictive factor in the gubernatorial vote, it may be the case that a voter's partisan predispositions affect whether he or she will punish the incumbent. Specifically, if the voter is Republican and his or her Republican incumbent governor raises taxes, the voter's partisanship may overwhelm dissatisfaction. Thus, strong partisans may not jump to support the candidate of the other party, even in the face of disliked taxation. This poses the following: (H4) *(a) Republican voters are less likely to punish Republican governors and more likely to punish Democratic governors for a tax increase, and (b) Democratic voters are less likely to punish Democratic governors for a tax increase.*

Voters are likely to be differently affected by changes in different taxes, and their vote should reflect such impacts. The income and sales taxes are widely thought to be two taxes with quite different impacts on income classes. Therefore, we argue: (H5) *(a) Higher income individuals are more likely to punish an incumbent administration (or the* nominee *from the incumbent's party) for an income tax increase than are lower income individuals, (b) and while lower income individuals are more likely to punish a sales tax increase.*

Because research suggests that governors are held responsible for economic conditions, regardless of whether those conditions are within their control, it is possible that gubernatorial political liability increases for tax increases in years of fiscal crisis. In parlous economic times, voters can ill afford to give up more income. Further, a tax hike would serve as a symbolic reminder of the failure of the governor. Thus, (H6) *governors who raise taxes when unemployment is rising in the electoral year will be punished more than those governors who raise taxes in times of falling unemployment.*

Data and operationalization of the individual-level models

Our study exploits exit poll data that is collected biennially at polling sites across the nation.[10] For the period from 1982 to 2000, we pool the Voter News Service (VNS (1994, 1996, 1998, and 2000 elections)), Voter Research and Surveys (1990, 1992), the ABC/*Washington Post* (1982, 1984, 1986, 1988), and CBS/*New York Times* (1984, 1988) surveys. Exit poll data is, for example, the only systematic data that satisfies conditions of large numbers of voters per state (usually from 750 to 2500 voters) and sampled serially across the period with an appropriate sampling model.[11] Actual VNS procedures elicit two kinds of voter "ballots," a "long" or national form and the "short" forms for the states that include many of the questions from the national forms as well as some questions specific to the politics of that state. Aggregating the data from the state and national forms and from earlier VR&S, ABC, and CBS polls yields about 315,000 observations of gubernatorial voters. However, because potentially relevant control variables such as respondent ideology, education, and income only appear on some versions of the questionnaires, the number of voter observations varies in parts of this study.[12]

Our model is of the following form:

$$v_{ist} = \alpha T_{st} + \beta E_{st} + \gamma P_{st} + \lambda X_{it} + d_s + f_t + \varepsilon_{ist}$$

where v_{ist} is the vote choice of individual i in state s at time t, T_{st} is a vector of relevant tax variables (including interactions with other variables in some specifications), E_{st} is a vector of economic conditions at the state and national levels, P_{st} is a vector of political conditions at the state and national levels, X_{it} is a vector of characteristics of the individual voter, d_s is a vector of state fixed effects, f_t is a vector of year fixed effects, and $\varepsilon_{\_ist}$ is the error term.

Dependent Variable: The dependent variable is the respondent's *vote for governor*, coded 1 if he or she voted for the Democratic candidate and 0 if he or she voted for the Republican candidate.[13]

Independent Variables: The five sets of independent variables are the fixed effects, our three tax variables, economic conditions, political conditions, and individual characteristics. Because the individual characteristics are derived from categorical variables, those control variables are incorporated through the addition of dummy variables.

Fixed Effects: To account for over-time national trends in the vote for governor, year fixed effect dummies for each of the election years are included. Additionally, forty-three state fixed-effect dummies are incorporated, which account for time-invariant but state-constant aspects of the political culture in the American states that give one party a natural edge (Stimson 1985).

Tax Variables: We created a database that noted whether, in the electoral term for each governor, the state had an increase in the personal income tax rate or bracket, an increase in the sales tax rate, or increases in the tax rates on cigarettes, beer, and gasoline. Unlike Niemi et al. (1995), who aggregated these and a number of other excise tax increases into a single composite variable, the income and sales tax variables were coded separately for this study, while the excise sin taxes were aggregated, thereby examining the electoral effects specific to each of the three types of taxation. The number of increases in the tax during the electoral period was multiplied by +1 if the incumbent is Democratic and –1 if the incumbent is Republican. Weighting the tax variable by party of the governor provides directionality. In our case, an increase in the sales tax, weighted as it is positively with a Democratic governor in office, will have a negative impact on the dependent variable of the individual Democratic vote. Most existing research (Eismeier 1983, Kone and Winters, 1993, Niemi et al., 1995) measures the tax variables by the number of legislated occasions the tax was increased. Measuring the tax variables by the number of rate increases ensures that only those effects that are due to governmental action are being picked up by the model.[14] By contrast, for example, tax revenues or tax collections as a percent of income may change in response to changes in state and national economic conditions.

Economic Conditions: Classical models of retrospective voting suggest that voters reward incumbents for increases in real per capita disposable income and punish incumbents for increases in unemployment (Chubb 1988; Peltzman 1987; Holbrook 1987; Stein 1990). Measures of the *percentage change in national unemployment* and *percentage change in national real per capita disposable income* from the year prior to the election to the year of the election are included. The variables are weighted by the presidential party in power variable.[15]

Voters also respond to state-level economic conditions when choosing between candidates for the governorship (Chubb 1988; Atkeson and Partin 1995; Svoboda 1995; MacDonald and Sigelman 1999; Howell and Vanderleeuw 1990). Our model includes *percentage change in state unemployment*, weighted by gubernatorial party in power, as well as the state-level *percentage change in real per capita disposable income,* weighted by the gubernatorial party in power variable.

Political Conditions: Evaluations of the sitting president have also been found to affect the vote for governor (Simon 1989; Peltzman 1987;

Stein 1990; Piereson 1975). While some have argued that coattails are decreasing in importance (Tompkins 1984, 1988, Chubb 1988; Jewell and Olson 1988), few dismiss the effect outright (e.g., Tompkins 1988). Several studies in the last few years have found presidential evaluations to be important determinants of the gubernatorial vote in the 1990s (Carsey and Wright 1998a; Carsey 2000). Mondak and McCurley (1994) argued that coattail voting depends on the context of the election as well as the characteristics of the individual voter. Our model includes a dummy variable for *presidential approval,* which is coded +1 if the respondent approved of the sitting president (or, in the case of an election year, voted for him) and 0 otherwise. Relevant interactions are included to weight the presidential approval variable by the presidential and gubernatorial parties in power. Because the data are taken from exit polls, the results should be insulated from the question order effects of presidential approval ratings on gubernatorial approval that have been found by some researchers (see Alspach 1991).

Incumbency has been found to be a highly significant factor in the vote for governor (e.g., Cowart 1973; Jewell and Morehouse 2000). Stein (1990, 40) found incumbency to be "modestly helpful for forecasting gubernatorial elections." As partisan attachments loosen, incumbency should play an increased role (Romero and Sanders 1994). Incumbency offers the indirect advantage of a great deal of visibility, even more so than some national-level offices (Squire and Fastnow 1994). It is easier for incumbents to raise money (Jewell and Morehouse 2000, 165). Furthermore, it appears that an incumbent governor is likely to be held accountable for past performance more than another representative from his or her party (Atkeson and Partin 1995; Jewell and Morehouse 2000, 191; Niemi et al. 1995). Three dummy variables for incumbency are included: whether the *incumbent is a Democrat,* whether there is an *incumbent Democrat running*, and whether there is an *incumbent Republican running*. These variables are interacted with several variables in the model, including the tax variable, as explained below.

Finally, some governors elected with a "mandate" are stronger candidates than others and, thereby bring political "tides" to bear on the next election. We include the *Democratic percentage of the vote in the previous gubernatorial* contest (Niemi et al. 1995; Hansen (1999). We include variables for candidate-specific characteristics: *candidate age* (Besley and Case 1995a), *candidate gender* (Delano and Winters 2002), and *candidate quality rating* for both the Democratic and the Republican nominees (Squire 1992).

Individual Characteristics: Analysts continue to establish that an individual's partisan identification affects the individual vote for governor

(Jewell and Olson 1988, 207; Jewell and Morehouse 2000, 181; Squire 1992; Svoboda 1995; Atkeson and Partin 1995). The dynamics of partisanship in gubernatorial contests may change with time (Piereson 1977) and may not be the same across state electorates (Jackson and Carsey 1999). We employ dummy variables to denote whether the respondent identifies as a *Democrat*, a *Republican*, or an *Independent.*[16]

Our measure of the respondent's *income* needs explanation. Much of the literature on electoral choice has treated income as a dichotomous variable, used mostly as a qualitative control in multivariate methods (see, for example, Axelrod 1972, 1982, and 1986; Stanley et al. 1986; Stanley and Niemi 1993). The VNS surveys provide categorical measures of income, but the exact categories vary across years. Additionally, because of inflation, the effect of a particular value of income in one year cannot be treated the same as the effect of the same nominal income in a later year. Our procedure to resolve these difficulties involved two steps. The respondent's income was recoded as the mean of the category that he or she selected. For example, if the respondent selected the income category "$50,000-$75,000," his or her income was recoded to be $62,500. Top-coded earnings (e.g., "$100,000 or more") were multiplied by one and a half. Second, we deflated these figures to 1990 dollars. The income variable was expressed in thousands of dollars, resulting in rough cross-election equivalence and suitability for use in a pooled cross-sectional design.

Other demographic variables have been found to affect the individual vote. Voters' *age* is particularly important for this study given that the elderly benefit disproportionately from some state programs such as welfare (MacManus 1995; Rhodebeck 1993). Other research has uncovered the effects of *race* and *gender* on exit poll voting (Delano & Winters 2002). These demographic variables had categorical formats on the VNS surveys, and as such, they were employed as a series of dummy variables.

Further specifications regarding methods and econometrics

The binary nature of the dependent variable in the exit poll analysis suggests that a probit or logit model would be more appropriate; however, the coefficients of a linear probability model are more easily interpretable. Several tests were run to compare the key coefficients among the logit, probit, and linear probability models, and the substantive findings did not appear to be dependent upon the choice of model. Thus, it would appear that the choice of model, at least in this instance, is not tremendously important.

Pooling only states and years: A pooled cross-sectional design presents a number of statistical obstacles (see Stimson 1985 for an overview). First, observations within each state exit poll are likely to be correlated with each other, a problem that can be solved through the addition of state fixed effects. However, a problem arises from the fact that state fixed effects, by definition, will constrain the effect to be the same across time. As such, there may be "common group effects" that *are* time-variant, and as a result, the combination of state and year fixed effects may fail to capture the entire relationship. An example would be some exogenous shock $_{st}$ that occurs in a particular state in a particular year and affects the vote but does not affect the vote in any other periods/states. This is a problem that exists when the independent variable (in this case, taxation) is more highly aggregated than the dependent variable. One approach to solve the common group effects dilemma would be to use fixed effects at the level of "state-year" units. However, because the tax change variables only vary with state-year, the addition of such fixed effects would prohibit identification of the tax coefficients. Thus, we chose to "cluster" the standard errors by state-year while including the state fixed effects. In effect, this makes the standard errors behave as if a random effects estimator were employed. This approach was employed in each of the models.

Interaction Terms and Weighting By "Party in Power*:*" In previous studies of elections (e.g., Bloom and Price 1975) and gubernatorial contests in particular (e.g., Chubb 1988; Kone and Winters 1993; Niemi et al. 1995; Lowry et al. 1998), a standard coding scheme is employed to measure the dependent variable. For individual-level data, the dependent variable is dichotomous, coded as +1 if the respondent voted for the Democratic candidate and 0 for a Republican vote. The problem with this choice of dependent variable is that it does not measure incumbency directly. That is, if one expects an incumbent to be punished if unemployment increases, the model encounters a problem: an increase in unemployment will appear to have a positive effect on the vote for the Democrat if there is a Republican incumbent, while that same increase will appear to have a negative effect on the vote for the Democrat if there is a Democratic incumbent. Including a simple measure of change in unemployment, then, is clearly inappropriate. As such, scholars have interacted with these variables with "party in power" terms. If the original variable was a national condition, then it was multiplied by +1 if the president was a Democrat and –1 if the president was a Republican. Similarly, if the original variable was a state-level condition, then it was multiplied by +1 if the incumbent governor was a Democrat and –1 if the incumbent governor was a Republican.

While this scheme is intuitive and does force the effects to operate in the correct *directions*, it is also improper on two levels. First, it fails to account for party-dependent effects (e.g., if Republican incumbent governors were to be punished more for an economic downturn than their Democratic counterparts). And, as the literature on "asymmetric effects" suggests, these effects are sizeable (Bloom and Price 1975). A more serious problem is that the introduction of these interacted variables creates a misspecified model due to omitted variable bias. If the "party in power" variable is not included in the model (and, in the case of the existing research, it sometimes is not), the interaction term will be biased, and potentially seriously so.[17]

To summarize, if the public assigns responsibility for political or economic conditions in a rational way, then the effects of such retribution may vary based upon the party of the president and the party of the governor. For national-level conditions, this situation is dealt with by using six variables: (1) the independent variable as it was recorded, without any weighting; (2) a dummy variable for the party of the incumbent president; (3) a dummy variable for the party of the incumbent governor; (4) an interaction between the independent variable and the presidential party dummy; (5) an interaction between the independent variable and the gubernatorial party dummy; and (6) a three-way interaction between the independent variable, the presidential party dummies, and the gubernatorial party dummy. For state-level variables, the same basic procedure is followed, but those categories involving the dummy for the party of the president are excluded. While this general approach of adding interactions to account for more complicated dynamics can reduce the efficiency of the parameter estimates, those estimates will be unbiased. In general, this approach is used for the control variables at the individual level. The tax variables, however, employ the simple multiplication by +1 and –1 scheme. This is to keep the interpretation of the important coefficients as simple as possible.

A Comment on Fixed Effects: Including year and state fixed effects adds a twist to the analysis. For reasons of multicollinearity, in a model that includes year fixed effects, any control variables that change in value only by year cannot be added. Similarly, in a model that incorporates state fixed effects, any variables that take on values that are time-constant but specific to each state also cannot be added. Within a linear regression, any continuous variable that takes on k values can be represented as well or better through the inclusion of $k - 1$ dummy variables. Further, if the relationship between the dependent variable and the independent variable in question is even slightly non-linear, then the non-parametric approach will actually yield a higher R^2 value.[18] Several of the variables that are listed in the preceding sections, e.g. the national-level measures of percent change in real disposable income and unemployment, would exhibit this collinearity problem with respect to the year dummies. As a result, the "main effects" of these variables were not included when the regressions were run. However, these variables can still be *interacted* with the "party in power" variables as described previously and then added to the model without generating collinearity.[19]

Testing the models

Because we employ a linear probability model at the individual level, there may be questions of how precisely to interpret the coefficients. The obvious and intuitive way to conceptualize them is as the average change in voters' probabilities of voting for the candidate given that the governor raises the tax in question. This change is measured in terms of percentage points.[20] A reasonable-sounding interpretation, albeit an inappropriate one, is that the coefficient indicates the direction and size of impact on the electoral margin that the incumbent will obtain. This is an incorrect way to conceptualize the dependent variable, which is, after all, a description of individual behavior, but if the number of voters is large, it should be a close approximation.

Note that nearly all of the models code the tax variable using the scheme that is usually employed in the literature – multiplying the number of increases by +1 if there is a Democratic incumbent governor and –1 if the incumbent administration is Republican. Under certain conditions, this choice of coding will miss the underlying party-specific differences in electoral retribution, but it also makes interpretation of the coefficients relatively straightforward and simple.

Table 9.1, Two Basic Models; Table 9.1 presents the cumulative results of two basic specifications of the tax-vote relationships. Row (A) represents the results of a series of regressions using the simplest of all tax change measures, one identical to that used by Niemi et al. (1995), which is the sum of all tax changes per administration weighted by the party of gubernatorial control. The variable ranges from a –10 (Nebraska in 1982) to +7 (North Dakota in 1988). The typical respondent experienced a very minor tax change. The standard deviation for the "all tax change" variable is 3 such changes. Rows (B), (C), and (D) disaggregate the tax change variable into its component changes in income, sales, and "sin" taxes with the associated coefficients "right-justified" in the cells. The associated R^2 for the respective equations in rows (A) and for (B), (C), and (D) are contained in rows at the bottom of the table and labeled "R^2 for 'all tax' equation" and "R^2 for the 'three tax' equation."

Column (1) displays the simple regression coefficients associated with the party-weighted tax variables in explaining the gubernatorial vote. In its most aggregated form, in Row (A) the sum of all changes in taxes has a strong, positive relationship with the vote. The R^2 for the equation, as denoted in the row titled "(A) R^2 for 'all tax' equation," is .002. At its simplest, taxes appear to benefit the taxing party at the polls.

However, working along row (A) to the right, we add sets of control variables. In row (A) and column (2), the variables for time (9 binaries) and

TABLE 9.1 The Effects of Taxation Increases on the Vote

	(1)	*(2)*	*(3)*	*(4)*	*(5)*	*(6)*	*(7)*
	Bi-var Regr.	*Add State/yr.*	*Add Incumbency*	*Add Pres Approval*	*Add Econ Factors*	*Add Voters Traits*	*Add Cand. Quality*
(A) Sum of All Taxes Mn = .09; sd = 3; mn/mx = −10/7	.0077** (.0003)	.0042 (.0025)	−.003 (.003)	−.004 (.003)	−.003 (.003)	−.003 (.003)	−.001 (.003)
(B) Income tax Mn = .0; sd = .69; mn/mx = −2/3	0.014** (0.0015)	0.019 (0.017)	0.005 (0.014)	0.0000 (0.013)	−0.0007 (0.014)	0.003 (0.012)	0.006 (0.012)
(C) Sales tax Mn = −.03; sd = .69; mn/mx = −2/3	−0.031** (0.0015)	−0.044** (0.010)	−0.029** (0.011)	−0.034** (0.011)	−0.036** (0.011)	−0.030** (0.010)	−0.016 (0.010)
(D) Sin Taxes Mn = .13; sd = 2.2; mn/mx = −8/5	0.015** (0.0005)	0.013** (0.005)	0.003 (0.005)	0.005 (0.004)	0.005 (0.004)	0.003 (0.003)	0.0011 (0.003)
(e) State & year fixed effects	No	Yes	Yes	Yes	Yes	Yes	Yes
(f) Incumbency variables	No	No	Yes	Yes	Yes	Yes	Yes
(g) Presidential approval variables	No	No	No	Yes	Yes	Yes	Yes

(Continued)

TABLE 9.1 (Continued)

	(1)	(2)	(3)	(4)	(5)	(6)	(7)
	Bi-var Regr.	*Add State/yr.*	*Add Incumbency*	*Add Pres Approval*	*Add Econ Factors*	*Add Voters Traits*	*Add Cand. Quality*
(h) National and state economy variables	No	No	No	No	Yes	Yes	Yes
(i) Respondent characteristics: partisanship, ideology, age, gender, race, income, education	No	No	No	No	No	Yes	Yes
(j) Candidate characteristics: gender, age, quality	No	No	No	No	No	No	Yes
N	313847	313847	313847	313847	312467	276537	274939
R^2 for "All Tax" equation	0.002	.02	.03	.22	.22	.35	.35
R^2 for "three tax" equation	0.004	.02	.03	.22	.22	.35	.35

Coefficients denote the increased probability of voting for the Democratic candidate for each year the incumbent increased the tax rate for each tax. The tax variables are the number of times the tax was raised in the electoral period, multiplied by +1 if the incumbent governor is a Democrat and –1 if the incumbent is a Republican. Models include the respective sets of controls as set out in rows (d) through (i).

= $p < .10$; ** = $p < .01$, *p = <.05. The complete set of tables can be obtained by contacting the second author.

states (42 binaries) are added. The "all tax" coefficient remains positive but is now insignificant. Adding the Republican and Democratic incumbency variables along with the time and state binaries (in row (A) and column (3)) now turns the coefficient into its expected negative value, and the R^2 rises slightly. Adding the presidential approval/presidential vote variable (in column (4)) inserts a generous dose of partisanship into the equation, and the R^2 rises appreciably. Further, the variable for "all tax" change begins to equilibrate at the level of –.003, but it is statistically insignificant. The implication of the coefficient is simple: A standard deviation change in the value of the "all tax" variable, that is to say, for a Democrat, adding three tax changes of any kind to the revenue complement in the state will cost the Democratic candidate about 1% of a change in the voters' probability of support. Three new Republican tax changes, by complement, will gain Democrats the same percentage of the vote probability. As we add further sets of controls in columns (5) through (7), the values of the coefficients not only remain steady at the –.004 to –.001 rate but also remain as insignificant coefficients. While row (A) captures the effects of any and all tax changes, there is no *a priori* reason to expect that the political costs of each type of tax change will be identical. Kone and Winters (1993) detected greater punishment at the aggregate level of changes in the sales taxes. Rows (B), (C), and (D) display the results of changes in each of the three tax components. With no controls and no rival variables other than the other tax variables, as reported in row/column (B/1), the income tax is, contrary to expectation, positively and significantly related to the vote probability, while changes in the sales taxes (C/1) are negatively related to the responsible gubernatorial party vote. Changes in sin taxes (D/1) are, also perversely, positively related to the vote. The R^2 is, for practical purposes, zero. The pattern of positive signs for income and sin tax changes and negative signs for the sales tax holds as we begin to add sets of controls.

Columns (2) through (7) report the relationships between changes in each of the three taxes and the vote as we systematically add sets of control variables. By adding gubernatorial incumbency variables, as set out in column (3), we now factor in political party effects – either with a Democratic incumbent or a Republican incumbent in the race – and a pattern of coefficients is established that is basically maintained until the final column: each sales tax change dampens voter preference on the order of 3% to 4%, while changes in other taxes have negligible impacts. Only in column (7), when the estimates of the quality of the Democratic or Republican gubernatorial candidates are added, does the sales tax variable drop marginally to a level of not quite significant. Strong, high-quality candidates can ameliorate the impact of tax changes. Or, as the endogeneity logic would argue, strong, high-quality candidates are able to risk tax changes.

In the end, these results provide new perspectives on electoral retribution. We suggest three possible interpretations: one of tax "timing"; the second, the cost of political information; and, third, a coding issue. While the tax-summation measure (in row A) picks up voter retribution, only the sales tax changes seem to have consistently negative and generally significant effects upon the vote probability for the incumbent or the party's nominee. This argues that an increase in sales taxes is more salient than an increase in the income or sin taxes. The reasonable explanation might have to do with the fact that citizens encounter the sales tax on an everyday basis, while they deal with the income tax just once a year when filing returns or seem unable to notice the particular excise levies on various "sins." Another distinction is that the income tax code is more complex due to the presence of exemptions and deductions, and thus it is more difficult for voters to ascertain the effect due to a legislated tax change. It also implies an incentive for politicians to tinker with the complex income tax code.[21] This latter explanation implies that the coefficient on the income tax is subject to omitted variable bias of code complexity and voters' informational barriers. Third, if the income tax statutes are so complex that legislated changes defy candidates' and voters' ability to identify and clarify their electoral implications, then an alternative coding strategy might be considered – going to the sources, such as state legislative leaders, and quizzing them regarding the "political" meaning of what appears to us to be simple, straightforward, and easily identifiable changes in the tax code as set out, for example, in the biennial *Book of the States*. Finally, changes in sin taxes have little electoral impact.

Table 9.2, *Party, Incumbency, Taxation and the Vote:* Row (A) of Table 9.2 presents the results of the "sum of all taxes" measure on voters' decisions. Predictably, in column (1), which repeats the finding set out in column (7) of Table 9.2, the coefficient is negative, albeit insignificant, and suggests that a one standard deviation change in the taxing practice of an administration, e.g., from "0" or no tax changes during the prior four years to "3" Democratic-sponsored changes, would result in about a 1% loss in the probability of a favorable vote. Consistent with our argument to this point, we split the sample of voters into those with incumbents defending their tax records vs. open seat races – open for reasons either of term limits or voluntary departures, as we do in row (A), columns (3) and (4). While the coefficient associated with races with both incumbents and nonincumbents has the expected negative sign, there are sizable standard errors suggesting that many incumbents overcome their tax records.

Rows (B) and (C) disaggregate the sample into races that defend a Republican taxing record (in (B)) and Democratic taxing records (in (C)), and then races with incumbents vs. open seats. Asymmetries in signs

TABLE 9.2 Party, Incumbency, and Taxation on the Vote

Nature of population	*(1)*	*(2)*	*(3)*	*(4)*	*(5)*	*(6)*
	All Voters, All Races	*All Voters, All Races*	*Races with Incumbent*	*Open Seats*	*Races with Incumbent*	*Open Seats*
(A) The sum of all increases in income, sales, and sin taxes. Mn = .08; sd = 3; min/mx = –10 to 7	–0.001 (0.003)	–	–0.003 (0.006)	–0.004 (0.005)	–	–
(B) The sum of all increases in income, sales, and sin taxes made by *Republican administrations.* Mn = –1.1; sd = 1.8; min/mx = –10 to 0	–	–0.0040 (0.0050)	–	–	–0.002 (0.007)	–0.010 (0.009)
I The sum of all increases in income, sales, and sin taxes made by *Democratic administrations.* Mn = 1.2; sd = 1.7; min/mx = 0 to 7	–	0.0024 (0.0045)	–	–	–0.005 (0.009)	–0.0002 (0.008)
N	274939	274939	154155	120784	154155	120784
R^2	.35	.35	.34	.39	.34	.39

Coefficients denote the increased probability of voting for the Democratic candidate for each year the incumbent increased the tax rate for each tax. The tax variables are the number of times the tax was raised in the electoral period, multiplied by +1 if the incumbent governor is a Democrat and –1 if the incumbent is a Republican. All models include controls based upon the following variables: state and year fixed effects; the party of the incumbent; whether the incumbent is running; the respondent's partisan identification, ideology, age, gender, race, income, and education; percentage change in national and state unemployment; percentage change in national real disposable income; presidential approval; previous Democratic margin; candidate characteristics of age, gender, and quality ratings.

= $p < .10$; ** = $p < .01$, *$p = < .05$. The complete set of tables can be obtained by contacting the second author.

(although neither coefficient is significant) occur on both counts. Looking first at column (2), Republican candidates defending the party's taxing record advantage their Democratic opponents by about.4% per taxing action. Because the tax variable ranges from a value of "–10" for the most taxing Republican governors to "0" for those Republican governors who raised *no* taxes, the fewer the taxes raised by the Republican, the more disadvantaged was the Democratic gubernatorial nominee, thus the negative sign of the coefficient. Perversely, the positive coefficient in Row (C), Column (2) indicates that Democratic taxers appear to be advantaged by taxing.

Columns (5) and (6) further isolate those candidates most and least burdened by tax changes. The weak appear to be (insignificantly so) open-seat Republican candidates who are defending their fellow partisans' taxing record as those most crucially affected. A standard deviation change in tax policy for such open-seat Republican challengers, a move from no change to "2" tax changes, implies a 2% vote loss. However, none of these coefficients are statistically significant.

Table 9.3, ***Party, type of tax changed, and incumbency:*** Table 9.3 parcels up the data by responsible incumbent party, by type of tax changed, and by nature of the political defense – an incumbent in the race vs. open seat races. Table 9.3 represents nine separate regressions testing for the effects of responsible political party control on subsequent voter retribution. The striking impression is that Republican candidates are more likely to be punished for taxing actions, and Democrats appear to be more likely to be advantaged by voters for taxing actions. Further, there are asymmetries between taxes in terms of relative punishment, with the sales tax, again, standing out as the retribution-prone tax change.

Among "all races," as set out in column (1), increases in income taxes by Democrats are not punished. No coefficient associated with taxing actions approaches significance, and two of the three are positive. For Republicans, income and sales tax changes have negative signs, and the coefficient for changes in the sales tax strongly suggests a heightened likelihood of voting against the Republican.

Columns (2) and (3) divide the races into those with active defenders of records – races with incumbents vs. open seats with two challengers, one of whom may be endeavoring to bob and weave away from his/her party's taxing record. The evidence suggests that there is little retribution wreaked against Democratic taxers. For incumbent Democrats, all of the coefficients are weak, and one has the wrong sign. For nonincumbent Democrats, it appears that they may even gain in voter approval in the face of additions to the sales taxes imposed by their fellow partisan from the previous administration. The evidence for Republicans is more mixed.

TABLE 9.3 Party, Incumbency, and Taxation on the Vote

	(1) *All Races*	*(2)* *Races with Incumbents*	*(3)* *Open Seat Races*
(a.1) Democratic increases in # of income taxes. Mn = .03; sd = .6; min/mx = 0 to 3	.011 (.016)	–.0002 (.0346)	.009 (.014)
(a.2) Republican increases in income taxes. Mn = -.4; sd = .6; min/mx = –2 to 0	–.006 (.016)	.0095 (.0266)	–.040# (.021)
R^2	.35	.34	.39
(b.1) Democratic increases in # of sales taxes. Mn = .28; sd = .56; min/mx = 0 to 3	.009 (.013)	.022 (.031)	.046** (.014)
(b.2) Republican increases in sales taxes. Mn = -.4; sd = .6; min/mx = –2 to 0	–.033** (.011)	–.071* (.034)	–.0007 (.0167)
R^2	.35	.34	.39
(c.1) Democratic increases in # of sin taxes. Mn = .1.6; sd = 1.4; min/mx = 0 to 5	–.0014 (.0050)	–.013 (.008)	–.015 (.012)
(c.2) Republican increases in # of sin taxes. Mn = –1.67; sd = 1.44; min/mx = –8 to 0	.0008 (.0068)	.0003 (.0083)	–.002 (.014)
R^2	.35	.34	.39
N	274939	154155	120784

Coefficients denote the increased probability of voting for the Democratic candidate for each year the incumbent increased the tax rate for each tax. The tax variables are the number of times the tax was raised in the electoral period, multiplied by +1 if the incumbent governor is a Democrat and –1 if the incumbent is a Republican. All models include controls based upon the following variables: state and year fixed effects; the party of the incumbent; whether the incumbent is running; the respondent's partisan identification, ideology, age, gender, race, income, and education; percentage change in national and state unemployment; percentage change in national real disposable income; presidential approval; previous Democratic margin; and candidate characteristics of age, gender, and quality ratings.

= p <.10; ** = p <.01, *p = <.05. The complete set of tables can be obtained by contacting the second author.

Of the six coefficients for the three taxes by incumbent and nonincumbent, two reach some level of statistical significance. Nonincumbent Republicans are punished for their party's income tax record, while incumbent Republicans are strongly punished for a sales tax change. One sales tax change nets a 7% loss in the probability of an expected Republican vote for the sales-taxing incumbent.

Among "all races," as set out in column (1), increases in income taxes by Democrats are not punished. No coefficient associated with taxing actions approaches significance, and two of the three are positive.

Table 9.4, the *State of the Economy:* The last statewide contextual factor that we examine is the economic climate of the state at the time of the election. The state of the economy should have a significant impact upon the voters' reactions to when and which taxes are increased within a state. Our measure of fiscal health is the change in the statewide unemployment rate for the year before the election. In the face of the good news of falling unemployment (columns 1, 2, and 3), voter retribution for tax changes should be dampened. If unemployment is rising (columns 4, 5, and 6), on the other hand, bad-news voters may have heightened macroeconomic concerns and should be more likely to punish those who tax. Table 9.4 arrays our data and tests for these hypotheses.[22]

Column (1) examines for all races the good news conditions when unemployment is falling. We include a stacked series of interaction terms. Rows (a), (b), and (c) set out the net direct impact of the changes in the three taxes. Row (d) interacts the falling unemployment rates with Democratic Party governorship. Rows (f), (g), and (h) in a three-way interaction code races as to type of tax change under conditions of falling unemployment by Democratic Party gubernatorial control. No clear, simple effects occur. The net effects of tax changes (rows a, b, and c) appear to be attenuated by the added contextual factors. In the case of falling unemployment, none of the first-order tax coefficients is significant, nor are any of the added interaction variables of falling unemployment times the Democratic party control variable. In fact, the interaction term of "falling unemployment X Democratic administration" has a contrary negative sign.

The next two columns split all races into those with defending incumbents (2) and those that are open contests under the "good news" condition. No clear effects occur for incumbents. However, in open seat contests, Democrats appear to be damaged by past income tax and sin increases but benefited by changes in the sales tax.

Column (4) examines for all races the impact of tax changes under the "bad news" of rising unemployment. Again, no clear message appears among the broader tax variables, rows (a), (b), and (c). By decomposing the tax changes during rising, good times (columns 5 and 6), we discover

TABLE 9.4 Good Times vs. Bad Times and Taxation Increases on the Vote (Standard errors in parentheses)

Reactions to changing taxes by varying economic climate and incumbency and open seats (Standard errors in parentheses)

	"Good times" with falling unemployment			*"Bad times" with rising unemployment*		
	(1) All races	*(2) Races w/ incumbent running for reelection*	*(3) Races w/o incumbent running for reelection*	*(4) All races*	*(5) Races w/ incumbent running for reelection*	*(6) Races w/o incumbent running for reelection*
(a) Effect of increasing income tax	.016 (.015)	.008 (.043)	.007 (.012)	–.011 (.017)	–.003 (.03)	–.054** (.014)
(b) Effect of increasing sale tax	–.010 (.012)	–.034 (.035)	.010 (.012)	–.011 (.013)	–.041 (.044)	.068** (.025)
(c) Effect of increasing sin tax	–.002 (.005)	–.005 (.008)	–.005 (.006)	.002 (.005)	.0003 (.01)	–.011 (.007)
(d) Falling UE * Dem Gov Pty	–.018 (.018)	–.027 (.031)	.003 (.027)	–	–	–
(e) Rising UE * Dem Gov Pty	–	–	–	–.011 (.016)	.03 (.03)	.040 (.039)
(f) Income tax changes * Falling UE*DEMPTY	–.021 (.022)	.02 (.05)	–.042# (.025)	–	–	–
(g) Sales tax changes * Falling UE*DEMPTY	–.007 (.016)	–.045 (.046)	.061** (.016)	–	–	–

(Continued)

TABLE 9.4 (Continued)

Reactions to changing taxes by varying economic climate and incumbency and open seats (Standard errors in parentheses)

	"Good times" with falling unemployment			*"Bad times" with rising unemployment*		
	(1) All races	*(2) Races w/ incumbent running for reelection*	*(3) Races w/o incumbent running for reelection*	*(4) All races*	*(5) Races w/ incumbent running for reelection*	*(6) Races w/o incumbent running for reelection*
(h) Sin tax changes * Falling UE*DEMPTY	.009 (.009)	.009 (.013)	–.029# (.015)	–	–	–
(i) Income tax changes * Rising UE*DEMPTY	–	–	–	.04* (.02)	.104# (.057)	.072** (.019)
(j) Sales tax changes * Rising UE*DEMPTY	–	–	–	–.005 (.018)	–.028 (.055)	–.048# (.025)
(k) Sin tax changes * Rising UE*DEMPTY	–	–	–	–.003 (.007)	–.014 (.014)	–.0006 (.010)
N	274,939	154,155	120,784	274,939	154,155	120,784
R^2	.35	.40	.39	.40	.40	.39

Voters who identify themselves as independents and "other" are excluded. The baseline category is self-identified Republicans. Coefficients denote the increased probability of voting for the Democratic candidate for each year the incumbent increased the tax rate for each tax. All models include controls based upon the following variables: state and year fixed effects; the party of the incumbent; whether the incumbent is running; the respondent's partisan identification, ideology, age, gender, race, binary variables for the upper one-third and lower one-third of states' last year change in unemployment rate weighted by Democratic party affiliation of responsible governor, education; percentage change in national unemployment; percentage change in national real disposable income; presidential approval; previous Democratic margin; and candidate characteristics of age, gender, income, and quality ratings.

# $p < .10$; * $p < 0.05$, ** $p < 0.01$

that income tax changes by Democrats are positively rewarded by voters, both for incumbents and nonincumbents. That is to say, in hard economic times, Democrats appear able to defend a rise in the income tax – a tax likely to hit, or at least that can be represented as "likely to hit," the better-off. Changes in sales taxes appear marginally to be punished, while sin tax changes appear to have little or no effect.

Table 9.5 Voter Characteristics – Income: We turn to the question of whether electoral retribution depends upon the characteristics of the voter, which we accomplish by means of interaction terms. Employing interactions at the individual level when the variable of interest has a number of categories presents a dilemma. Examples of such variables include education and income. Because income in the VNS study is coded using ordered multichotomous schemes, we converted the variable into a continuous one – albeit with some degree of measurement error, as explained earlier on page 18. For our purposes in Table 9.5, we created two binary variables for income – one for those in the upper one-third of the income distribution and a second for those in the lower one-third.[23] These binaries were then interacted with the number of occasions for which each, say, wealthy voter's income, sales, or sin taxes were increased during the prior incumbents' terms. The same procedure was carried out for the personal income, sales, and sin tax binaries for the lower third of the income distribution.

Table 9.5 displays the results for our analysis for all races (in column 1); for races where incumbents were defending their records (column 2), and for all open-seat races (in column 3). Looking first at "all races," the effects of changes in taxes retain their rough pattern of signs and relatives sizes. No effects appear for the income tax; negative effects for the sales tax changes at about a 2% loss ($t = 1.75$); and a negative effect of sin tax changes. Rows (d) and (e) contain the coefficients and associated standard errors for the simple income binaries, and, as expected, wealthier voters were less likely to vote Democratic and lower income voters more likely.[24] Rows (f) through (h) contain coefficients associated with being in the indicated income class multiplied by the number of indicated tax changes. In the case of "all races," wealthy voters appear to vote counter-intuitively: on behalf of incumbents/parties that increase the income tax, opposing those who increase the sales tax, and favoring changes in sin taxes. Lower income voters oppose those who increase their income and sales taxes and favor – significantly so – those who finance government by means of increases in the sin taxes, also not an intuitive finding, as gas, alcohol, and cigarette taxes fall disproportionately on those at the lower ends of the income distribution.[25] Note that the values of the interaction term for "lower income class*Δin sin taxes" vary from –8 to +5.

TABLE 9.5 The Effects of Voters' Incomes and Taxation Increases on the Vote
(Standard errors in parentheses)

Individual income and reactions to taxes (Standard errors in parentheses)			
	(1) All races	*(2) Races with incumbent running for reelection*	*(3) Races without incumbent running for reelection*
(a) Effect of increasing income tax	0.0040 (0.012)	0.023 (0.028)	–0.006 (0.015)
(b) Effect of increasing sale tax	–0.021# (0.011)	–0.059 (0.037)	0.025 (0.017)
(c) Effect of increasing sin tax	–0.0043 (0.0034)	–0.007 (0.008)	0.025** (0.0089)
(d) Binary variable for upper one-third of income distribution	–0.006# (0.0033)	–0.0009 (0.0046)	–0.010** (0.004)
(e) Binary variable for lower one-third of income distribution	0.0096** (0.0033)	0.011** (0.003)	0.011* (0.005)
(f) Interaction: upper one-third * N of income tax change	0.0045 (0.005)	0.013# (0.007)	–0.003 (0.007)
(g) Interaction: upper one-third * N of sales tax change	–0.0039 (0.006)	–0.001 (0.011)	–0.003 (0.006)
(h) Interaction: upper one-third * N of sin tax change	0.0029# (0.0017)	0.0025 (0.0019)	0.002 (0.002)

(Continued)

TABLE 9.5 (Continued)

Individual income and reactions to taxes (Standard errors in parentheses)			
	(1) All races	*(2) Races with incumbent running for reelection*	*(3) Races without incumbent running for reelection*
(i) Interaction: lower one-third * N of income tax change	−0.009 (0.007)	−0.019# (0.010)	0.005 (0.010)
(j) Interaction: lower one-third * N of sales tax change	−0.0057 (0.0056)	0.015 (0.010)	−0.009# (0.005)
(k) Interaction: lower one-third * N of sin tax change	0.0044** (0.0018)	0.0009 (0.0025)	0.006** (0.002)
N	274210	172867	137089
R^2	.401	.407	.394

Voters who identify themselves as independents and "other" are excluded. The baseline category is self-identified Republicans. Coefficients denote the increased probability of voting for the Democratic candidate for each year the incumbent increased the tax rate for each tax. All models include controls based upon the following variables: state and year fixed effects; the party of the incumbent; whether the incumbent is running; the respondent's partisan identification, ideology, age, gender, race, binary variables for the upper one-third and lower one-third of income distribution, education; percentage change in national and state unemployment; percentage change in national real disposable income; presidential approval; previous Democratic margin; candidate characteristics of age, gender, and quality ratings.

= $p < .10$; *$p = < .05$, ** = $p < .01$.

Columns (2) and (3) display the analysis for races with and without incumbents. For races with incumbent defenders-of-record, general retribution in the face of sales tax increases is marginally heightened, but so is the standard error. For races with incumbents defending their tax records, none of the interaction terms are consistently significant. Coefficients which appear to be the best predictors are those associated with income tax changes and high-income voters' reactions – positively so ($t = 1.73$) – and the opposing impact on low-income voters ($t = -1.93$).

The analysis of the impact on open seat races of tax changes is not particularly clarifying. Changes in sin tax changes are rewarded (see row c) and particularly so among low-income voters (row (k), column (3)) in open seat races. The other sizable coefficients are associated with the contrasting impacts of the upper and lower income binaries on the vote. In summary, there is no compelling evidence for the expected pattern of voting self-interest; indeed, the lack of evidence merits rejecting the hypothesis that higher income citizens support the sales tax while lower income citizens support the income tax.[26]

Table 9.6, Partisan *Identification:* One of the common ways in which our two parties are painted is that the Democratic Party favors "tax and spend" politics while the Republican Party prefers fiscal restraint. If this is an accurate description of reality, then it might follow that self-identified Democrats might be more willing to accept taxes than self-identified Republicans. Table 9.6 shows three specifications designed to investigate this proposition. The interaction term in this model is the number of taxes raised, weighted by the party in power and multiplied by +1 if the respondent identified himself or herself as Democratic and 0 if he or she identified with the Republican Party. For these models, those respondents who identified themselves as either independent or "other" were the excluded class.

None of the specifications of the interaction terms was significant. However, it is notable that while small in effects, Democratic voters appear to punish an income tax increase (column (1) and row (b)) while rewarding sales and sin tax increases relative to their Republican counterparts (column (1) and rows (d) and (f)). This is a puzzling result. Theory and conventional wisdom would suggest that Republicans earn higher incomes and thus would be disproportionately hurt, dollar-for-dollar, by an income tax relative to a sales tax. Similarly, it is often thought that Democrats may support income tax programs, which place a great deal of the burden on high-income citizens, in order to obtain funding for social programs. The results from the models in Table 9.6, even though not significant, suggest that this logic should be reconsidered. It is true that the size of the standard errors relative to the magnitudes of the coefficients means that even the direction of the effects cannot be inferred in

TABLE 9.6 Partisan Identification and the Effects of Taxation on the Vote (Standard errors in parentheses)

Individual partisanship and reactions to taxes (Standard errors in parentheses)			
	(1) All races	*(2) Races with incumbent running for reelection*	*(3) Races without incumbent running for reelection*
(a) Effect of incumbent/ incumbent party increasing income tax	.005 (.016)	.018 (.032)	–.022# (.012)
(b) Added effect if respondent is Democrat	–.006 (.015)	–.008 (.024)	.011 (.017)
(c) Effect of incumbent/ incumbent party increasing sales tax	–.024* (.012)	–.048 (.037)	.022 (.018)
(d) Added effect if respondent is Democrat	.0005 (.013)	–.007 (.026)	–.0007 (.015)
(e) Effect of incumbent/ incumbent party increasing sin taxes	–.005 (.004)	–.004 (.007)	–.023** (.009)
(f) Added effect if respondent is Democrat	.005 (.004)	.0015 (.005)	.006 (.005)
N	274210	154155	120784
R^2	.40	.40	.39

Voters who identify themselves as independents and "other" are excluded. The baseline category is self-identified Republicans. Coefficients denote the increased probability of voting for the Democratic candidate for each year the incumbent increased the tax rate for each tax. All models include controls based upon the following variables: state and year fixed effects; the party of the incumbent; whether the incumbent is running; the respondent's partisan identification, ideology, age, gender, race, income, and education; percentage change in national and state unemployment; percentage change in national real disposable income; presidential approval; previous Democratic margin; candidate characteristics of age, gender, and quality ratings.

= $p < .10$; ** = $p < .01$, *p = < .05. The complete set of tables can be obtained by contacting the second author.

any meaningful sense. However, it is also true that were the effect suggested by theory to be pronounced, the magnitudes of the coefficients would be sufficiently large to overwhelm the standard errors. This clearly does not happen in any of these specifications, and as a result, it is fair to conclude that the conventional wisdom that Democratic voters are more conducive than Republicans to the politics of taxing and spending needs reevaluation. It may be the case that Democrats are more favorably inclined to spend but averse to taxing – not at all an unexpected set of opinions to hold – especially if the typical Democrat were hopeful that that "fellow behind that tree, over there" would be the one most likely to be taxed.[27] There also may be an alternative explanation for the odd results. It could be that because the model does not account for whether the incumbent candidate raising taxes is a Democrat or a Republican, there is omitted variable bias.[28] The unreported disaggregation of the races, as we do in columns (2) and (3), does not appear to clarify the issue.

Conclusions

We sought evidence for whether and under what conditions voters in gubernatorial elections respond to various kinds of tax increases when signed into law. Our data would appear to be the most comprehensive set available yet – forty-three states, 228 elections, and 315,000 voters – for testing claims of voter retribution. There is evidence from other studies of the modest impacts of taxing on the vote at the aggregate, election outcomes level, as well as among a cross-section of voters at a specific time period. Our results reconfirm the modesty of the impact of tax increases on voters' behavior. Further, we can reasonably assert that the impacts are vanishingly small, albeit not zero.

When sales, income, and sin tax changes are combined into a single indicator, given proper controls, there appears to be an overall negative, but insignificant, effect. When the taxes are examined tax-by-tax, the sales tax emerges as the most electorally sensitive. We stipulated a set of conditions that might exacerbate or dampen retribution – by incumbent vs. open seat races and by party. Incumbents plausibly should be held to a higher standard of responsibility for tax actions by voters, while the open-seat, responsible-party successor might artfully dodge retribution. However, the evidence suggests that no clear distinction occurs among voters. Further, when all taxes are lumped together, no across-party distinctions appeared, either. The lack of evidence for incumbents is consistent with our view of forward-thinking, strategic-calculating politicians.

When the lumped tax changes are cleaved into the three components of sales, income, and sin and examined by incumbent/open-seat and by party, a not-obvious pattern begins to emerge: both incumbent and open-seat Democrats appear to be much less vulnerable to tax changes, while both incumbent and open-seat Republicans appear more vulnerable. A further distinction that is maintained throughout our analysis is that changes in sin taxes appear to least impact voters.

One contextual condition that might sensitize voters to tax changes would be the state of the economy. We expect that voters are more likely to punish "taxers" in bad times of rising unemployment and be more sparing in punishing during good times. There was no evidence of such a pattern in our sample of states, elections, and voters. Indeed, the most robust finding reinforced our impression that Democrats appear to be better able to dodge tax-related retribution from voters.

Our final analyses focused on individual-level traits by asking whether voters by income or by party appeared more electorally sensitive to tax changes. Changes in the sales tax appeared to be weakly and negatively sanctioned by upper- and lower-income voters, while changing the sin taxes appeared to gain lower-income voters' support. Upper income voters, contrary to reasonable expectation, appeared weakly favorable to income tax changes. No particular effects appeared when voters were examined by party.

Notes

1 An earlier version of this paper was delivered at the 2004 annual meetings of the Southern and Midwest Political Science Associations. Prior versions, based on data from 1990 to 1998, were presented at the 2002 annual meetings of the Southern, American, and Midwestern Political Science Associations and at the 2002 Conference on State Politics and Policy at the UW at Milwaukee. We appreciate the helpful comments and useful suggestions of all of the conference and panel participants.
2 In the forty-three states from 1979 to 2000, income, sales, and sin tax (beer, gasoline, and cigarettes) changes totaled 540 discrete changes, respectively, 72, 76, and 392.
3 Our three-way N is 228 elections and about 315,000 voters in forty-three states. Hawaii and Alaska are excluded because Voter News Service does not canvas their exiting voters. We also exclude the off-year elections in New Jersey, Virginia, Kentucky, Louisiana, and Mississippi. The "independent" gubernatorial administrations, Weicker in CT and King in ME, were also not included.
4 Besley and Case (1995a) attempt such, unsuccessfully, in our opinion.
5 We exclude Carsey's excellent analysis of campaign dynamics (2000) from this generalization.
6 Eismeier coded his tax variable for legislative changes as opposed to the change in revenue collected. This technique, which we adopt, more accurately taps

into changes in the tax code for which the governor can reasonably be held accountable.

7 There is another problem associated with rate increases of the same tax. If the demand for the good or goods being taxed is elastic, the marginal gains in revenue will decline as the rate increases. As a result, politicians must consider how voters will react to the tax not just politically but economically as well.

8 However, observations from states in which taxes are not increased still affect the coefficients on other controls in the model. There is almost always some non-zero correlation between the tax and control variables; thus, the tax coefficient must adjust until a least squares solution is obtained.

9 The IV and 2SLS estimators are essentially the same. The only difference is that 2SLS will underestimate the coefficient standard errors. The reason is that IV takes into account the fact that the endogeneity correction (the predicted values for the first-stage regression) is being *estimated*, while 2SLS treats it as if it were *known*. Contemporary statistical programs will do the IV calculation and obtain the correct standard errors. In both cases, the coefficients will be identical; only the standard errors will differ.

10 Hawaii and Alaska were not included in this study, nor were those with odd-year elections: New Jersey, Virginia, Kentucky, Louisiana, and Mississippi. For 1996 and 1998, some telephone surveys to account for absentee and early voters in California, Oregon, and Washington were conducted.

11 VNS, for example, chose a probability sample of voting precincts to represent different geographic areas across the state and the vote by party. Precincts were chosen with a probability proportionate to the population size in each state. However, in some states with large minority populations, some precincts were sampled at a higher rate than others. The procedure was such that each voter in a state had an equal likelihood of having his or her precinct chosen, and the exit polling was conducted throughout the day so as to give all voters an equal probability of being interviewed.

12 We are particularly interested in exploiting the interactions between state-level contextual variables and individual-level survey variables. Our contextual conditions, such as state and national economic data, predominantly come from the Census Bureau's *Statistical Abstracts* as well as volumes of *Book of the States*. Estimates of state-level unemployment figures are derived from data sets from the Current Population Survey (CPS). The data on tax increases is derived from relevant volumes of *Book of the States* as well as the Tax Foundation's annual publication *Facts and Figures of Government Finance and the Monthly Publication of the Federation of Tax Administrators*. Complete documentation on data sources can be obtained from Winters at rfw@dartmouth.edu.

13 Votes for third-party candidates were excluded from the analysis. All votes cast in the 1998 Maine and 1994 Connecticut elections (Independent incumbent governors Angus King and Lowell P. Weicker, respectively) were excluded as well because the incumbents were third-party candidates. There is no straightforward way to map electoral retribution against third-party incumbents.

14 The legislative focus forces us to distinguish what a "legislated" tax change is. States often pass tax laws that are designed to take effect in the next fiscal year, so the researcher is confronted with the question of whether to code the tax hike as occurring at the time of passage or the time when it took effect. For our purposes, tax variables were coded according to the date they took effect. This is because it is expected that the most proximate effects of tax increases on voters will begin to occur at that time.

15 Weighting the economic variables assumes that the impact of, for example, a 1% increase in national unemployment in the early 1980s will have the same (positive) impact on the possible Democratic vote for governor as a 1% drop in unemployment during the Clinton administration.
16 Those who characterized themselves as "other" composed the excluded category. While voters' ideology has been shown to have a significant effect on the gubernatorial vote, especially when the competing candidates are ideologically far apart (Jewell and Morehouse 2000, 185), we chose not to include the VNS measure of ideology. The Voter News Service asked voters about their ideology in only one-half of the elections. We chose to maximize cases rather than maximize variables. Education was a personal characteristic asked only of voters in a fraction of the elections and not included in our analysis.
17 Using the "weighted" variable and the "party in power" variable is only one of several structurally similar possibilities that would be correct. Equally legitimate would be a model including the main effect, a dummy variable for the party in power, and an interaction term. We employ this latter specification for weighting the control variables.
18 Of course, a non-parametric approach can also quickly absorb degrees of freedom, thereby resulting in less efficient parameter estimates.
19 While this statement is true in the simplest sense, the conclusion does not hold in very complex models such as the one used here. Because certain variables only vary by year, such as the change in unemployment or real wages, they take on relatively few values. When these variables are interacted with the dummies that represent the parties in power, the explanatory power of the interactions is quickly exhausted. The result is that most statistical programs will begin to drop some of these interactions, making it difficult to estimate the effects associated with the original set of variables.
20 What this means is that if the coefficient is, for example, –0.05, then the voter will be five percentage points less likely to vote for the incumbent. So, if the voter would have had a 60% probability of voting for the incumbent if there had been no tax increases, then the same voter would have a 55% probability of voting for the incumbent if there had been a single tax increase. The changes in percentage points, distinct from changes in percent, should not be confused.
21 Note that the numbers of income tax and sales tax changes were roughly equal in our data set.
22 We drop from the regression the two continuous variables of statewide unemployment changes*Democratic governor and national unemployment changes*Democratic president.
23 As we noted earlier, the income variable has been transformed by an across-time price deflator.
24 The original transformed income variable was not included in the regression.
25 This finding squares with an oft-observed characterization of legislators about their poorer constituents – they favor changes in sin taxes over all others (personal conversations with the second author).
26 Another interpretation may be helpful in terms of ascertaining why the results are contrary to theoretical predictions. Because the correlation between income and education is quite high, it may be the case that the interaction terms are tapping into respondents' educational status as well. Those individuals with a great deal of education may be more likely to oppose regressive taxes because they realize that these taxes are imposed predominantly on those citizens who are least able to pay. This might lead such individuals to oppose the sales tax and support the income tax, which would be consistent with the results from this table.

27 A characterization of voters and tax politics attributed to Senator Russell Long (D-LA).

28 A similar test was conducted on a much smaller subset of elections of the impact of liberal and conservative ideological self-identification in the presence of changes in income, sales, and sin taxes through use of dummy variables of ideological position*changes in taxes. No consistent impacts occurred. While liberal and conservative voters are strongly related (pro- and con-) with the Democratic vote for governor, even in the presence of similar partisan identification factors, the impact of their ideological preferences was not heightened in the presence of tax changes.

PART V

Electoral consequences of taxation are attenuated via electoral strategies

10

"GOVERNOR QUITS!" THE STRATEGIC PERSONAL & POLITICAL ECONOMY OF FOREGOING RE-ELECTION

Richard F. Winters and Melissa Rich-Marroncelli

Introduction

Voters, candidates, and analysts may misjudge how frequently gubernatorial officeholders choose to relinquish their opportunity to seek reelection[1] – "quitting" in our terms – and may fail to appreciate the importance and political content of quitting.[2] For modern American governors, quitting occurs as frequently as does election defeat. While the recent record suggests a defeat rate of about 24% (Squire and Fastnow 1994), historical figures for 1978–1996 show an equal-sized "quit" rate for the modern era of 24%. The net effect is that if 24% quit and a quarter of the remaining 76% are defeated at the polls, only about 57% of eligible governors run for and win an additional term. Put differently, the result of self-inflicted and electorally inflicted mortality is that slightly more than one-half of eligible American governors choose to run and, then, win reelection.[3] An alternative perspective is that if one wants to account for the fates of modern American political executives, one must account for both electoral defeats (primary and general elections) and self-chosen fates (quitting).

The 1986 gubernatorial elections, as analyzed in Niemi et al. (1995), may suggest a typical set of gubernatorial electoral contours. Of the twenty-four elections where the incumbent could run for another term, one incumbent was defeated in a primary challenge (Sheffield of Alaska), two had interesting and nontrivial primary competition (Clinton vs. Faubus in Arkansas and Sununu vs. Easton in New Hampshire), while another two were defeated in the general election (White of Texas losing to Clement and

DOI: 10.4324/9781003606291-16

Earl of Wisconsin losing to Thompson). But, in 1986, six of twenty-four incumbents *quit* before the primary quest for renomination, and, we argue, some probably quit for politico-economic reasons. The six quit before any election was held, before voters had a direct chance to express their opinions, and in advance of the filing date for their party's primary.

In addition to documenting the unexpectedly large number of quitters, we argue the political content of quitting. More often than is conventionally appreciated, giving up the chance to run for reelection is done after the realization that winning an additional term would be unlikely or would come at great personal and organizational cost. If so, then the causal logic that explains aggregate electoral defeats of governors should explain incumbents' quitting as well. In this paper, we find that the incumbents' unpopular tax policy choices, the years in office, and the difficult-to-defend, poorly performing state economic records do, in fact, impact gubernatorial quitting.

Our analysis comes in the context of emerging studies of voting behavior and electoral outcomes in the American states that focus on contested gubernatorial race. Analysts have not pushed their studies backwards in time to the primary election or to quitting behavior as important determinants of the electoral outcome, but as Herbert Simon's well-known conjecture suggests, shaping the alternatives (quitting) importantly configures the contestants-as-alternatives, which shapes the ultimate outcome. Quitting behavior, as Niemi and colleagues (1995) suggest, may also, in part, account for the widely observed attenuated effects between changing statewide economic conditions and public policy changes (such as taxation) and the gubernatorial vote. If incumbents who are vulnerable for reasons of statewide fiscal policy decisions and economy issues are more likely to quit, then the weaker-than-expected findings may be an artifact of a sorting process weeding out the vulnerable incumbents in advance of the general electoral contests. The attenuated effects of "taxing on voting" (see Chapter 9), therefore, are a by-product of quitting. Finally, governors may constitute the best set of political executives for the scientific study of when and under what conditions executive incumbents walk away from office. We all know that personal reasons such as illness (George Wallace), personal failings (Jim Guy Tucker), and the threat of impeachment (Evan Mecham) account for some semi-voluntary departures; we ask whether there are more general and more difficult to establish traits – politico-economic in nature – that more systematically account for quitting.

Our argument: Political scientists ordinarily believe that democratic accountability of incumbent executives is importantly shaped by voters' general election or primary election judgments (Key 1966; Fiorina 1981; Hibbing 1991). A few studies have looked at accountability and primary election outcomes as ways in which voters make short-term judgments and send signals regarding officeholders' records. Dramatic primary election challenges to incumbents occur with some frequency at the state levels.[4] Yet, no one has systematically examined the record for pre-electoral judgments of the sort that ask, under what conditions will an eligible governor, one constitutionally permitted to seek reelection, decide not to run for reelection? We test the hypothesis, across states and across time, that governors "quit" for a variety of state- and national-level political and economic reasons that constitute a strategic explanation of quitting – governors depart because of cloudy reelection prospects assessed pre-electorally.

Some scattered evidence appears for the hypothesis. Niemi et al. (1995) discovered that, for the twenty-four non-term-limited 1986 gubernatorial elections, incumbents were more likely to remove themselves from competition when their respective state economies had performed below average and when their states had enacted more than the typical number of tax increases during their terms in office (p. 941). These findings, based on the performance of six of twenty-four governors eligible for reelection, argued for the increased importance of state-level economic and taxation factors in predicting gubernatorial election outcomes, as poorly performing departing governors are "removing potential targets from voter retribution" (p. 941). Although their suggestion was interesting, their evidence was less convincing given the small numbers of six quitters among twenty-four governors for one election cycle of unknown typicality.

Consider the following broader array of gubernatorial fates for an expanded 1978–1996 data set: Of the 270 gubernatorial elections held, 57 were open seats due to statutory or constitutional term limits, leaving 213 incumbent governors eligible to run for reelection. Putting aside the four suspensions or removals,[5] three deaths, and one plausible illness,[6] the six who left in the mid-term for various political appointments and their "short-term" successors[7] leave 193 incumbents, of whom 47 (24%) chose, at the end of their term of office, not to run for reelection.

Gubernatorial elections are vital elections in the American democracy because of their unique ability to combine state and national-level political and economic concerns. As "state executives," these politicians may be held liable for national-level acts of the president, probably most acutely so when the governor and president are of the same party (Stein, 1990). Likewise, as the state executive, these politicians are accountable for problems or successes in their respective states. It would stand to reason, then, that a strategic gubernatorial incumbent, when making his or her decision about whether he or she should run for reelection, would consider conditions at both the national and state levels when making his or her decision.

Chubb (1988) claims that assignment of economic responsibility in state legislative and gubernatorial elections increasingly depends on factors outside of the state, such as the state of the national economy and the perceived success of the president in managing it. While he acknowledges that state economic conditions have a significant, though small, impact on gubernatorial election outcomes, he concludes that "If gubernatorial elections tum on economic performance, it is generally the performance of the president in managing the national economy that really matters" (149). Simon (1989) similarly argues that the impact of presidential support is strong enough to affect "the aggregate results of gubernatorial elections" (301). Simon and colleagues (1991) maintain that the success of a sitting president may be beneficial to members of the president's party at all electoral levels (1188). Stein (1990) argues that voters do not hold their governor responsible for their state's economic problems and that they "assign responsibility for their personal and the state's economic well-being to the national government and specifically to the president and his party" (44). According to his "restricted in-party culpability explanation," voters may vote for or against the governor of the president's party to send a message to the president about her handling or mishandling of the economy (51). Brace (1993) supports this notion of assigning minimal responsibility to governors for fluctuations in the state economy: "state politicians are not notably rewarded or punished for their management of state economies," and governors, specifically, are only "minimally responsible" for differences in state economies between their states and surrounding states (121).[8]

At the opposing end of this discussion are those who consider state-level factors to be important in determining the outcomes of gubernatorial elections. Governors are accountable for the performance of the state economy and, statistically, are relatively less affected by the performance of the national economy (Squire and Fastnow 1994). Atkeson et al., for example, respond to Simon et al.'s (1991) with the claim that "...governors, as chief executives of their respective states, are held responsible for the health of their state economies and are not generally shown to be liable for fluctuations in presidential approval" (1995, 105). Part of this difference may be attributed to the fact that Simon et al. considered factors at the aggregate level while Atkeson/Partin examined voter choices as exhibited through survey data. This is a recurring problem in political science research: the preferences of individual voters as conveyed through polls and surveys often appear poorly or imperfectly reflected in aggregate election results.[9] Our study is conducted at the aggregate level. If our hypothesis is correct, though, and governors presiding over states which are having economic problems remove themselves from the electoral competition, then this phenomenon may help explain the conflict between the national vs. state roles and the lack of continuity between survey and aggregate findings. Perhaps voters would have more sharply assigned responsibility to incumbent governors whose states' economies were performing poorly had these incumbents actually run for reelection. Quitting with the resulting new nominee of the incumbent party may attenuate voters' blaming behaviors. Stein (1990) provides further evidence of voters' awareness of governors' efforts to protect their state from the effects of national and subnational economic swings. The assignment of economic responsibility between governors and senators during the 1982 gubernatorial and senatorial contests is apportioned with 15.4% of American voters assigning responsibility for the state's economic problems solely to the governor, while 18.4% assigned responsibility for their state's economic problems to both the president and to the governor (41).

Others claim that changes in state-level public policy factors, such as taxation, ought to be predictive of an incumbent's success or failure in his or her reelection bid. However, the state economy/taxation effect, while statistically significant, barely seems to affect the actual electoral outcomes for governors. Kone and Winters (1993), for example, find small effects for tax policy variables – a small 2% decrease in the governors' share of the general election vote among those governors who had initiated general, broad-based tax increases during their tenure. On the other hand, perhaps their dampened findings, as Niemi and associates would argue (1995), simply reflect the loss of the high-taxing end of the gubernatorial distribution simply because of gubernatorial "quitting."

Another consideration in a study of quitting and reelection is executive incumbency. Incumbent governors who seek reelection win reelection about 76% of the time, a reelection rate for governors far less certain as compared with members of Congress. Senators win reelection about 85% of the time (Squire et al. 1994, 707), and the commonly accepted figure for House members is well above 90% (Jacobson and Kernell 1981). The power of incumbency varies with the nature of the office in question, executive vs. legislative, and may well have a varied effect at the national versus the subnational level (Atkeson and Partin 1995; Squire and Fastnow 1994). Squire and Fastnow claim that voters hold governors to be more responsible for the performance of the state economy than U.S. senators. Governors are more vulnerable to election defeat than senators because governors receive more media attention than senators, resulting in more public scrutiny of governors (718). Squire and Fastnow also found that citizens know more about their governors than their senators, and, according to survey research, also seem to like their governors less (708–709). Gubernatorial challengers are more effective and often better liked than senatorial challengers, making reelection more risky for incumbent governors than for incumbent senators (714). Lastly, gubernatorial challengers also receive more media attention than senatorial challengers (713). This increases the likelihood of a gubernatorial challenger mounting an effective, credible campaign and decreases the likelihood of an incumbent governor succeeding as a shoo-in in gaining reelection. These factors are likely to make the avoidance of retribution from voters and thus a successful reelection more difficult for governors. Therefore, governors are likely to be more responsive to the preferences and desires of their constituents than senators (718). We extend the argument that the factors that seem to increase the electoral vulnerability of governors should logically increase the likelihood of their *not* seeking reelection.

How best to explain quitting

"Running" or "Not running" is the dichotomous decision of an incumbent governor to run for reelection in the 1978–1996 period: not run (=1) or yes run (=0). Of the 193 reelection-eligible governors, as defined earlier, 47 quit. We employ multivariate probit analysis in explaining the quit/run choice of incumbents.

The following factors are hypothesized to influence the quitting choice:

1 As the conditions of the states' economies change as measured by:

   a the number of jobs gained increases, the likelihood of quitting decreases (–).
   b As real personal income increases, quitting should decrease (–).
   c As the unemployment rate in the state increases, so should the probability of quitting (+).
   d The second differences of the above three factors of changes in jobs (–), income (–) and unemployment (+) should also be related to the likelihood of quitting.
   e As more people move into a state, measured simply by population growth, indicating the state's increasing political-economic attractiveness, quitting should decrease (–).

2 The number of taxes that increased while the incumbent was in office should be related to quitting (+).
3 The incumbent' s historic election success should lead to a lower probability of his/her quitting (–).
4 The literature suggests that the causal effect of the number of years in office at the time of decision is somewhat ambiguous. While longevity in office is an indicator of gubernatorial success, talent, skills, and experience, all of which suggest decreased quitting, it is also the

case that longevity may create accumulating grievances that increase the likelihood of quitting. We sign on to the "cumulating grievance" hypothesis, and the causal direction for this variable will be positive (+).

5 Party may have varying effects on quitting. We make no prediction (+/–).
6 Increases in the Gallup Poll presidential approval should encourage the president's party associates to seek reelection, thus lowering the probability of their quitting (–)
7 As the presidential party's (PPP) weighted national rate of unemployment rises, the likelihood of a common-party incumbent quitting also rises (- for GOV*PPP).
8 As the party-weighted national personal income rises, the interest of that party's incumbents in quitting should fall (- for GOV*PPP).

The complete description and sources for the data appear in the Appendix section. We now more fully discuss our set of expected determinants of "quitting."

Taxes: The tax variable is a measure of the total number of tax increases in each state for each gubernatorial term in the data set. The mean number of tax increases per term was 2.5; while among quitting governors, the mean was 3.5 tax increases per term, a distinction which is consistent with Niemi et al.'s (1995) conclusion concerning incumbent governors in 1986 – as incumbents accumulate more tax increases during the term, he/she is more likely to forego reelection.

Number of years in office/past success: Squire found that the effects of the preceding election and the number-of-years-in-office were insignificant in predicting the profile[10] of challengers to the incumbent (Squire 1992, 135). On the other hand, Schlesinger finds that the number of years an incumbent has served in office affects how well he or she fares in seeking reelection. He suggests that governors "accumulate grievances from the electorate, which damage their prospects for reelection with the passage of time."[11] Over the 1978–1996 period, the variable for the number of years in office extends from two to twenty years in office. We anticipate that as the number of years an incumbent has served in office increases, so should the likelihood of quitting. Further, as the incumbent's share of the total vote in the last election increases, his or her estimation of the total vote in the upcoming election should increase, and the probability of quitting, then, should decrease.

Gallup presidential approval variable[12]: As presidential approval decreases, this should increasingly disadvantage the incumbent governors of the president's party, and such party-cohort incumbents should be less likely to seek reelection. Simon, for example, suggests that "the impact of presidential support in gubernatorial elections is both statistically significant and substantively important" (1990, 301). If Simon's claim that there is a "systemic accountability extend[ing] to gubernatorial elections" (301), then it is reasonable to conclude that the Gallup poll approval ratings for the president may significantly affect a governor's decision to seek reelection.

Party: We test if there are differences between the decisions of incumbents of different parties on deciding whether to run for reelection (Democratic incumbents = 1; others = 0). The way in which the parties are perceived, for example, may influence the severity of the economic situation in the state, and, therefore, the decision of the incumbent. As Jacobson discusses in his study of House elections, Democrats are often associated with the ability to create a fair budget and tax system and are often considered more capable of dealing with social problems like unemployment, etc. On the other hand, Republicans are associated with traits such as economic efficiency and the ability to maintain low taxes (1990, 112). Taxing, for example, may be more politically harmful for Democrats than for Republican governors due to the perception of Democrats as higher "taxers" than Republicans in general.

"Economic" variables: The "economic" variables included two types of measures, direct and indirect. Among the direct measures of economic activity in the state were the four variables that measured national and statewide changes in unemployment and real per capita personal income. The national measures were weighted by the party holding the presidency. The indirect measures of economic activity included changes in the state population and changes in the number of people employed in the state. An increase in the population of the state or the number of people employed, while a possible result of many factors, may, in part, indicate increased migration to that state because of perceived heightened quality of life in that state, thereby boosting incumbent popularity. Conversely, a decrease in the population of the state or a slowing of job growth may indicate a decline in the overall health of the state economy; incumbents from these states should be more likely to quit.

The economic variables were measured in three ways. All economic variables were recorded at three chronological times: the election year (ey), one year prior to the election (ey_{-1}), and two years prior to the election (ey_{-2}). "First differences" were calculated between each pair of years: one between ey and ey_{-1} and the other between ey_{-1} and $ey_{-2.}$ The rationale for the two first difference measures is that a significant fraction of "quitting" occurs well before the election, most often in the first quarter of the election year or even earlier. Thus, any economic analysis of a quitting decision occurring early in an election year might be better captured by using difference data based on years "2" and "3" of a four-year term.

Where necessary, these changes were transformed into the percentage change based on the previous year (for the population variable and for the number of people employed variable) so that differences across differently populated states would be equalized and not subject to the differences based on state size. We also obtained the "second difference" of these variables. The "second difference" variables are measures of the overall size of change in the increase or decrease of the variables over the course of the term between the election year and up to two years prior.

Per capita personal income: We expect that the probability of quitting is inversely related to income gains and changes in income gains. Our measure of personal income is based on statewide real per capita income adjusted for nationwide changes in the value of the "personal consumption expenditure."

Unemployment change: Increases in state unemployment will be positively related to the probability of quitting. Similar first and second differencing operations occurred for our statewide measure of personal employment plights.

Population change: States experiencing greater than average population percentage gains do so, in part, for political reasons, indicating population tides that move and shift in response to better than average politico-economic climates. We expect that the differences will be negatively related to quitting.

Number of people employed: We expect that positive gains in the percentage of the number of people employed will also be inversely related to quitting. Booms in employment make for buoyant governance. Although the data are not conclusive, it is possible that voters cast votes retrospectively with regard to their personal income status and the current unemployment and job rates in their state, and prospectively with regard to how their state may fare in jobs. Both appraisals of the state, retrospective and prospective, may result in a credit-giving or blaming response by the electorate, both of which may be directed towards the governor. There is some evidence that voters may vote according to such prospective evaluations. The idea of a prospectively voting electorate is discussed, for example, by MacKuen et al., who conclude that, with regards to the president and national economic conditions, "voters respond prospectively to the likely economic future" (1992, 607).

The multivariate probit results: In the probit analysis, we fashion three tests for the effects of economic and political variables on the probability of an incumbent governor quitting. Model (1) assumed that the time period most relevant to consideration was the election year and the year

TABLE 10.1 Probit Estimates of Quitting for All Eligible Incumbents

	Expected Sign	*(1) st Differences at ey–ey$_{-1}$ Coeff. (Std. Error)*		*(2) 1st Difference at ey$_{-1}$–ey$_{-2}$ Coeff. (Std. Error)*		*(3) 2nd Difference Coeff. (Std. Error)*	
Dep. Var.: probability of quitting							
(1) d state RDPI (ey–ey$_{-1}$)	–	–.0004*	(.0002)				
d state RDPI (ey$_{-1}$–ey$_{-2}$)	–			004	(.00028)		
2nd d state RDPI				–.0006*	(.0002)		
(2) d state UE (ey–ey$_{-1}$)	+	.085	(.133)				
d state UE (ey$_{-1}$–ey$_{-2}$)	+			.055	(.147)		
2nd d state UE	+					–0083	(.105)
(3) d state JOBS (ey–ey$_{-1}$)	–	–.012	(.052)				
d state JOBS (ey$_{-1}$–ey$_{-2}$)	–			–. 057	(.047)		
2nd d state JOBS	–					.022	(.032)
(4) d state POPUL (ey–ey$_{-1}$)	–	.022	(.088)				
d state POPUL (ey$_{-1}$–ey$_{-2}$)	–			.073	(.121)		
2nd d state POPUL	–					.022	(.032)
(5) # TAXES increased	+	.152**	(.054)	.160**	(.054)	.158**	(.039)
(6) LAST ELECTION%	–	–.001	(.015)	–.00008	(.014)	–.003	(.015)
(7) YRS in office	+	.161**	(.038)	.161**	(.037)	.156**	(.04)
(8) PARTY	+/–	.145	(.129)	.17	(.13)	.175	(.135)

(*Continued*)

TABLE 10.1 (Continued)

	Expected Sign	*(1) st Differences at ey–ey_{-1} Coeff. (Std. Error)*		*(2) 1st Difference at ey_{-1}–ey_{-2} Coeff. (Std. Error)*		*(3) 2nd Difference Coeff. (Std. Error)*	
(9) GALLUP APPROVAL	+	.002	(.009)	.006	(.010)	.004	(.010)
(10) d nat'l RDPI (ey–ey_{-1})	–	.017	(.217)				
d nat'l RDPI (ey_{-1}–ey_{-2})	–			–.0015*	(.0008)		
2nd d nat'l RDPI	–					.0017**	(.0008)
d nat'l UE (ey–ey_{-1})	+	.0008	(.0008)				
d nat'l UE (ey_{-1}–ey_{-2}	+			–.010	(.257)		
2nd d nat'l UE	+					.171	(.264)
Number of observations	=	193		193		193	
Model chi^2	=	43.57**		45.49**		50.97**	
Prob.> chi^2	=	0.0		0.0		0.0	
Log Likelihood	=	–84.2		–83.2		–80.5	
Pseudo R^2	=	.21		.21		.24	

*Where ey = election year; ey_{-1} = year prior to election; ey_{-2} = two years prior to ey; ** $p < .01$, * $p < .05$, one-tailed test; std. errors in parentheses.*

prior to it; model (2) focused on one and two years prior to the election year; and model (3) is the "2nd difference" model. Model (1) assumes that all governors – runners and quitters – have relatively good information about economic and social performance as measured for the election year (ey) and prior years (ey_{-1} and ey_{-2}). Alternatively, model (2) argues that governors will use the first three years of real information about their administrations, relevant data based on the years "two" and "three" of the four-year term (ey_{-1} and ey_{-2}).

Irrespective of modeling time, there are two important and predicted results as set out in the probit results in Table 10.1: increases in the number of taxes have a profound negative impact on the likelihood of running again, and, as the number of years the incumbent has served increases, so also does the likelihood of quitting. Changing taxes and fiscal stresses and political aging take their tolls. There are two further effects of note, one predicted, the other not. The second difference of positive statewide income news boosted the chances of running for reelection, as predicted. On the other hand, the second difference of national income growth was positively related to quitting – a contraindicated and inexplicable finding.

There is a further result: of the two "first difference" models with significant effects of state and national income, there was no clear way of distinguishing between model (1), based on the contemporary election year information, and model (2), based on data that assumed political-economic knowledge of the earlier years of an administration. While model (1) has the correct sign and significant coefficient for statewide income, the sign for changes in national income is insignificant with a sign contrary to prediction (positive). Opposing this is model (2), where the model indicates that as US income grows, governors are less likely to quit, yet the statewide indicator is insignificant and of the contrary (positive) sign.

A weak but informative understanding of our model comes about from examining simply the predicted pattern of the signs of the independent variables, which, by and large, are consistent with our expectations, although most variables are not significant. For example, changes in statewide income are, for the two "first difference" models, negative, as predicted, indicating that as state economies prosper, incumbent governors are less likely to quit. Changes in statewide unemployment in the two "first difference" models have predicted positive, although not significant, relationships with quitting, indicating that increases in unemployment are problematic for the reelection-minded governors. Percentage changes in states' jobs are negatively and predictably related to quitting in the two "first difference" models. However, a contra-predicted finding is that growing populations are unexpectedly and positively, although not significantly, related to quitting. Further, as expected, as the incumbent' s last general election percentage margin of victory grows, the likelihood of quitting shrinks, but again, this variable was not significant. Quitting is also weakly and insignificantly related to Democratic Party incumbency.

Conclusion

Our findings have implications for conceptions and current understandings of democratic accountability. Contrary to conventional academic literature (Chubb 1988; Kone and Winters 1993), we affirm Niemi and colleagues' arguments that incumbent governors are vulnerable to electoral judgments resulting from their mishandling of their state's economy and/or for presiding over a greater number of tax increases. However, the reconciliation between our results, those of Niemi and colleagues', and the conventional results of Chubb, Kone, and Winters are clear. The behavioral expressions for officeholders of political-economic vulnerability are as telling before election as at election time. Governors who perceive themselves as most vulnerable to primary challenge or election defeat for taxing/economic reasons choose to remove themselves from competition, thereby avoiding the risk of defeat at the polls. Governors presiding over the poorest economies and/or seen to be responsible for the greatest number of tax increases will be concentrated disproportionately within the pool of gubernatorial "quitters."

Further, if "potential losers" are "quitters," then the simple act of "quitting" may account for the observed weak or highly attenuated relationship between the economy, changing taxes, and the aggregate general election vote as reported by Chubb (1988) and Kone and Winters (1993). In effect, the observed relationship at the final electoral phase is attenuated because the distribution of running governors is truncated at its most egregious, poorly performing end by the pre-election quitting of the highly vulnerable. This would leave only those with the better political-economic records running for reelection. By doing so, such quitters avoid voters' punishment for the tax increases/economic misfortune that have taken place during their last term of office.[13] This line of argument holds that gubernatorial quitters are accountable for their performance: Governors who pass more taxes and have poorer-than-average state economic conditions and strategically decide to forego reelection are doing precisely what the electorate would have done had they chosen to run, depriving them of their seat in office. We extend accountability to the pre-election level. We emphasize one other property of quitting. The frequency of quitting exceeded our expectations and those of other informed observers. According to our results, the 24% rate of gubernatorial quitting equals the historic rate of defeat.

Precisely because the singular executive is the focus of so many different political forces, we must think of quitting as a causally complex, interactive phenomenon. If a cautionary message of this research is causal complexity, then a corollary statement is that we, as students of American state politics, bring comparative advantage to this study. Students of state politics have the ability to move back and forth between various levels and methods of analysis, and therefore, we are, by subfield, best able to tease out interesting causal tests. This current research is based on a simple aggregate theory of why state executives quit, but we believe that this statistical analysis inadequately captures the complexity of quitting. We must now tum to the question of how the incumbents themselves, their associates, and opponents understand their quitting behavior. And, with the expanding number of exit polls, we also can assess the legacy of blame that voters may hold for the exiting governor. The simple study of quitting in the states, then, holds the prospect of yielding first-step benefits of knowledge gained that needs further exploitation by means of multimodal, multi-methodological approaches to the study of comparative state politics

Appendix A: data notes and sources

1 The region of each state for the Gallup approval rating percentage was taken from one of the following 4 regions: East, West, Midwest, or South. States were assigned to a particular region based on their placement in the *Gallup Poll: Public Opinion.* Delaware: Scholarly Resources Inc., 1993, XXV.
2 Incumbents who held the seat prior to the given election are considered here. The elections which took place during each year from 1978 to 1996 were determined from the *Book of the States,* vols. 20–31. Lexington, KY: The Council of State Governments, 1974–1997.
3 Dates on which incumbents "quit" were taken as the date on which an incumbent announced that he or she would not seek reelection in the upcoming election. These dates were taken from Lexis/Nexis News Data; from various *New York Times* newspaper articles; and from Scammon, Richard M., and Alice V. McGillivray, (eds.), *America Votes,* vols. 13–21, Washington: Congressional Quarterly, 1978–1994.
4 The filing dates for all state primaries were taken from "State Filing Deadlines and Primary Dates for House, Senate and Governor." *Hotline Weekly* 8 (January 1996): p. 8.
5 The tax variable is the simple count of the number of tax increases in sales, personal income, corporate income, motor fuel, tobacco, and alcohol during the incumbent' s term of office. For states with four-year

terms, the total number of tax increases includes the total tax increases for the election year and three years prior; for two-year-term states, the total number of tax increases includes the total for the election year and one year prior. These data were taken from the taxation chapters of *Book of the States,* 1974–1997, separately coded by the authors, and differences reconciled. All tax increases, new taxes, surcharges, and surtaxes were coded as the "number of tax increases." (6)

6 The number of years served by the incumbent at the end of the current term; the incumbent governor's last election percentage of total vote; the total number of votes cast in the last election; the total number of votes cast in the upcoming election; and the "independent" vote percentage for governor of the last election, if applicable, were all taken from *America Votes.* Total votes cast in the 1996 election were taken from *Congressional Quarterly* 54, no. 45 (November 9, 1996): 3250–3257.

6 The presidential approval rating was taken for the corresponding regional estimate of each state (see above "region" variable description) in January or February of the election year. These ratings were taken from the following sources: "Do You Approve/Disapprove of the Way that (President_) is handling his job as President?" *The Gallup Opinion Index,* Princeton: American Institute of Public Opinion, 1977–1981, no 143–184; *The Gallup Report,* Princeton: The Gallup Poll, 1982–1989, no. 185–291; *The Gallup Poll Monthly,* Princeton: The Gallup Poll, 1990–1996, no 291–365.

7 Data for the state population variable were taken from "Estimates of the Resident population of States and Components of Change." *US Bureau of the Census, Current Population Reports: State Population Estimates, by Age and Components of Change.* Washington, DC: US Government Printing Office, 1977–1984, nos. 726–970. and from the "Resident Population of the States," *US Bureau of the Census, Statistical Abstract of the US.* Vols. 98–116. Washington, DC, 1978–1996.

8 Data for the state unemployment rates, the number employed of the civilian labor force in the state, and per capita personal income were taken from the *US Bureau of the Census, Statistical Abstract of the US,* vols. 98–116, Washington, DC, 1978–1996.

9 Data for the national unemployment were obtained from the *Economic Report of the President, 1997,* Table B107, titled "civilian unemployment rate, and hourly compensation, major industrial countries, 1970–1996," column 1.

10 Data for real (chained 1992 dollars) per capita national annual disposable national income were obtained from the *Economic Report of the President, 1997,* Table B29, column 4, titled "total and per capital

disposable personal income... in current and real dollars, 1959–1996." The 1996 annual figure was calculated as the average of the increments between 1996:1 and 1996:2 and 1996:2 and 1996:3 added to the 1996:3 figure.

11 Data for the employed variable for the number of people employed in the state for 1994 and 1995 were taken from US Department of Labor, *Employment Status of the Civilian Noninstitutionalized Population 16 Years of Age and Over by Region, Division, and State,1994–1995 annual averages.*, Washington, DC: US Bureau of Labor; accessed January 1997 and available from http://bls.gov. The "civilian labor force" was defined as those employed members of the non institutionalized population in each state above the age of sixteen.

12 Data for the unemployment rates per state and the number of employed people per state in 1996 were taken from the January figure in the US Department of Labor, *Civilian Labor Force and Unemployment By State, not seasonally adjusted,* 1996–1997, prepared by the Bureau of Labor Statistics, US Department of Labor, Washington, DC, 1997; accessed January, 1997 and available from http://stats.bls.gov/news.release/laus.to2.htm.

13 Data for the resident population in the state for 1996 were taken from the US Bureau of the Census. *Estimates of the Population of the States: Annual Time Series, July 1, 1990.* Prepared by the State Population Estimates Program, Population Division of the US Bureau of the Census, Washington, DC: US Bureau of the Census, 1 July 1990–1 July 1996. Accessed January 1997 and available from http://www.census/gov/population/estimates/state/ST9096TI.txt.

14 Data for statewide disposable personal income were obtained from *US Bureau of the Census, Statistical Abstract of the US,* vols. 98–116 (Washington, DC, 1978–1996). Additional data for 1995 and 1996, not available in the *Abstract*, were taken from the US Bureau of Labor Internet page. All measures of statewide personal income were adjusted for changes in the value of income by deflating annually using the index of "personal consumption expenditure" taken from Table B-3, p. 304, *Economic Report of the President, 1997.* For a discussion of such adjustments, see Berry et al. (1996). The 1996 figure used was the expected 1996 annual value based on the values published for quarters II and III.

APPENDIX A-1 Voluntary Quits Per Year, Per State

Quits by year	*State*	*Party*	*Governor*
1978	Arkansas	Democrat	David H. Pryor
N = 36	Maine	Independent	James B. Longley
Quits = 4	Oklahoma	Democrat	Richard Kneip
1979, No quits, N = –2			
1980, No quits, N = 13			
1981, No quits, N = 2			
1982	Alabama	Democrat	Forest H. James
N = 35	California	Democrat	Edmund G. Brown, Jr.
Quits = 7	Iowa	Republican	Robert Ray
	Michigan	Republican	William G. Milliken
	Minnesota	Republican	Albert H. Quie
	New York	Democrat	Hugh L. Carey
	Wisconsin	Republican	Lee S. Dreyfus
1983, No quite, N = 4			
1984	Rhode Island	Democrat	Joseph Garrahy
N = 14	Utah	Democrat	Scott Matheson
Quits = 3	Vermont	Republican	Richard Snelling
1985, No quits, N = 1			
1986	Alabama	Democrat	George Wallace
N = 36	Arizona	Democrat	Bruce Babbitt
Quits = 6	Colorado	Democrat	Richard Lamm
	Idaho	Democrat	John Evans
	Nebraska	Democrat	Robert Kerry
	Wyoming	Democrat	Ed Hershler
1987	Mississippi	Democrat	Williams Allain
N = 4; Quits = 1			
1988	Montana	Democrat	Ted Schwinden
N = 10	New Hampshire	Republican	John Sununu
Quits = 2			
1989, No quits, N = 2			
1990	Alaska	Democrat	Steve Cowper
N = 36	California	Republican	George Deukmejian
Quits = 9	Connecticut	Democrat	William O'Neill

(Continued)

APPENDIX A-1 (Continued)

Quits by year	*State*	*Party*	*Governor*
	Illinois	Republican	James Thompson
	Massachusetts	Democrat	Michael Dukakis
	Oklahoma	Republican	Henry Bellmon
	Oregon	Democrat	Neil Goldschmidt
	Texas	Republican	William P. Clements
	Vermont	Democrat	Madeleine Kunin
1991, No quits, N = 1			
1992	Montana	Republican	Stan Stephens
N = 12	North Dakota	Democrat	George Sinner
Quits = 8	Utah	Republican	Norman H. Bangerter
	Washington	Democrat	Booth Gardner
	New Hampshire	Republican	Judd Gregg
1983, No quits, N = 2			
1984	Alaska	Independent	Walter J. Hickel
N = 37	Connecticut	Independent	Lowell Weicker
Quits = 8	Idaho	Democrat	Cecil D. Andrus
	Kansas	Democrat	Joan Finney
	Oklahoma	Democrat	David Walters
	Oregon	Democrat	Barbara Roberts
	Wyoming	Democrat	Mike Sullivan
1995	Louisiana	Democrat	Edwin W. Edwards
N = 3, Quits = 1			
1996	New Hampshire	Republican	Stephen Merrill
N = 11, Quits = 2	Washington	Democrat	Mike Lowry

APPENDIX A-2 Types of Quitters

Early and midterm quitters, difficult to model politico-economic records, progressive ambition (N = 8):			
Arizona	Democrat	Raul Castro	apptd. Ambassador
Arkansas	Democrat	Bill Clinton	run for U.S. president
Idaho	Democrat	Cecil Andrus	apptd. Secretary of Interior
Minnesota	Democrat	Wendell Anderson	U. S. Senate

(Continued)

APPENDIX A-2 (Continued)

Early and midterm quitters, difficult to model politico-economic records, progressive ambition (N = 8):			
Nevada	Democrat	Richard Bryan	U. S. Senate
Wisconsin	Democrat	Patrick Lucey	apptd. Ambassador
Wisconsin	Democrat	Martin Schreiber	succeeded Lucey in Senate
Minnesota	Democrat	Rudy Perpich	succeeded Anders in Senate
Died/illness/removed/resigned from office (N = 12):			
Alabama	Democrat	George C. Wallace	illness
South Dakota	Republican	George Mickelson	died
Connecticut	Democrat	Ella Grasso	died
Vermont	Republican	Richard Snelling	died
Alabama	Republican	Guy Hunt	resigned
Arizona	Republican	Evan Mecham	resigned
Maryland	Democrat	Marvin Mandel	resigned
Arkansas	Democrat	Jim Guy Tucker	resigned
Arizona	Republican	Rose Mofford	succeeded Mecham
Maryland	Democrat	Blair Lee	succeeded Mandel
Alabama	Democrat	Jim Folsom	succeeded Hunt
South Dakota	Republican	Walter Miller	succeeded Mickelson
Progressively ambitious quitters			
Arkansas	Democrat	David H. Pryor	U.S. Senate
Oklahoma	Democrat	David L. Boren	U.S. Senate
California	Democrat	Edmund G. Brown	run for U.S. president
Arizona	Democrat	Bruce Babbitt	run for U.S. president
Nebraska	Democrat	Robert Kerry	U.S. Senate
New Hampshire	Republican	Judd Gregg	U.S. Senate
Kansas	Democrat	Joan Finney	U.S. Senate
Wyoming	Democrat	Mike Sullivan	U.S. Senate
South Dakota	Democrat	Richard Kneip	apptd. Ambassador
New Hampshire	Republican	John Sununu	White House appt.
Flat out quitters (N = 37)			
Alabama	Democrat	Forrest H. James	
Iowa	Republican	Robert Ray	
Michigan	Republican	William G. Milliken	
Minnesota	Republican	Albert H. Quie	

(*Continued*)

APPENDIX A-2 (Continued)

Early and midterm quitters, difficult to model politico-economic records, progressive ambition (N = 8):			
New York	Democrat	High L. Carey	
Wisconsin	Republican	Lee C. Dreyfus	
Utah	Democrat	Scot M. Matheson	
Vermont	Republican	Richard Snelling	
Wyoming	Democrat	Ed Hershler	
Connecticut	Democrat	William O'Neill	
Massachusetts	Democrat	Michael Dukakis	
Texas	Republican	William P. Clements	
Vermont	Democrat	Madeleine Kunin	
Montana	Republican	Sam Stephens	
Utah	Republican	Norman Bangerter	
Connecticut	Independent	Lowell Weicker	
Oklahoma	Democrat	David Walters	
Oregon	Democrat	Barbara Roberts	
Louisiana	Democrat	Edwin D. Edwards	
Washington	Democrat	Mike Lowry	
Maine	Independent	James B. Longley	
Rhode Island	Democrat	Philip W. Noel	
Rhode Island	Democrat	Joseph Garrahy	
Colorado	Democrat	Richard Lamm	
Idaho	Democrat	John Evans	
Mississippi	Democrat	William Allain	
Montana	Democrat	Ted Schwinden	
Alaska	Democrat	Steve Cowper	
California	Republican	George Deukmejian	
Illinois	Republican	James Thompson	
Oklahoma	Republcian	Henry Bellmon	
Oregon	Democrat	Neil Goldschmitdt	
North Dakota	Democrat	George Sinmer	
Washington	Democrat	Booth Gardner	
Alaska	Independent	Walter J. Hickel	
Idaho	Democrat	Cecil D. Andrus	
New Hampshire	Republican	Steve Merrill	

APPENDIX A-3 Means, Standard Deviations, Minimums and Maximums (N = 193)

	Means	*Std. Devs.*	*Minimum*	*Maximum*
1) # of TAX increases	2.5	2.1	0	10
2) # YEARS in office	5.5	3	2	20
3) Incumbent's ast % VOTE	55.9	7.5	33.1	83.2
4) PARTY of incumbent; D = 1, R = –1	.2	1	–1	1
5) GALLUP APPROVAL weighted	1	11.9	–29	29
6) POPULation:				
(a) 1st Difference (ey-1-ey) in %	1	1.6	–4.4	6.9
(b) 1st Difference ey-2-ey-1) in %	1.3	2.6	–13.2	4.8
(c) 2nd Difference	–.3	2.6	–3.4	15.7
7) UE Unemployment				
(a) UE at ey	6.5	2.2	2.2	14.3
(b) UE at ey-1	6.4	2	2.5	13.1
(c) UE at ey-2	6.6	2	2.4	12.4
(d) UE 1st Difference (ey-1-ey) in %	.09	1.39	–3	4.7
(e) UE 1st Difference ey-2-ey-1) in %	–.1	.9	–3.1	2.2
(f) UE 2nd Difference	.2	1.4	–4.1	4.9
8) Number employed				
(a) N of EMPLOYEE at ey	2143985	254914	160000	14100000
(b) N of EMPLOYEE at ey-1	2111047	2505666	152500	13900000
(c) N of EMPLOYEE at ey-2	2058295	2435835	145000	13800000
(a) 1st Difference (ey-1-ey) in %	1.7	2.9	–8.3	10
(b) 1st Difference ey-2-ey-1) in %	2.6	3.4	–3.4	22.2
(c) 2nd Difference	.2	1.4	–22.8	11
9) RDPI Real disposable p.c. income				
(a) RDPI at ey	13523	4388	61832	5151
(b) RDPI at ey-1	11276	74375	55402	5151
(c) RDPI at ey-2	2058295	2435835	145000	13800000

(Continued)

APPENDIX A-3 (Continued)

	Means	*Std. Devs.*	*Minimum*	*Maximum*
(a) 1st Difference (ey-1-ey) in %	756	416	-508	2179
(b) 1st Difference ey-2-ey-1) in %	739	350	-982	2207
(c) 2nd Difference	17	567	-2179	2130
10) PARTY (Dem = 1)	.6	.5	0	1
11) National UE% at ey	6.9	1.4	5.4	9.7
(a) UE% 1st difference	6.9	1.4	5.4	9.7
(b) UE 1st difference at ey-1	-.19	.53	-2.1	2.1
(c) UE 2nd difference	.28	.9	-2.2	1.8
12) National real p.c. income at ey	16759	1516	14662	19153
(a) National real p.c. income 1st diff.	276	256	-185	975
(b) National real p.c. income at ey-1	205	150	-185	975
(c) National real p.c. income 2nd diff.	71	268	-630	697

Notes

1 The analysis of legislative, mostly Congressional, quitting behavior is better established; see Hibbing (1991). The logic of the argument applies to the U.S. presidency as well. In the last half century, of the eleven presidential incumbents eligible to run for reelection, four had serious, or at least interesting, primary challenges: Johnson in 1968, Nixon in 1972, Ford in 1976, and Carter in 1980. Quitting behavior and similar causal logics also appear at the presidential level: two of the post-war presidential elections were infused by "strategic quitting" – Truman in 1952 and Johnson in 1968. There are also Nixon parallels among our nation's governors.

2 Of the dozen or so well-informed political scientists who responded to our casual and sort-of-random e-mail query of "what percentage of otherwise eligible incumbent governors will choose *not* to run for reelection, instead choosing to quit the race?" all but one chose a percentage lower than the actual percentage. The typical "prediction" was at the 5–10% levels, well below the 24% actual figure. One political scientist, only halfway joking, responded, "No governor ever just quits!" Actually, a truthful observation. The observation hinges on the meaning of "just"; many quit as we observe for "just" reasons –national partisan trends, the local economy, tax actions, etc.

3 Beyle (1992b) compiles similar rates for governors, albeit for a different time period. For interesting case analyses of these kinds of gubernatorial elections, see Beyle (1992a).

4 We have in mind here the American state politics literature on the "divisive primary"; see, for example, Kenney and Rice (1984) and Dominguez, Frisbie, and Winters (2017) for reviews of the literature.

5 The "Nixon parallels" of Mecham of AZ, Mandel of MD, Hunt of AL, and Tucker of AR.
6 Grasso of CT, Mickelson of SD, and Snelling of VT; and the illness of Wallace of AL in 1986.
7 We deleted six governors (Anderson of MN, Bryan of NV, Clinton of AR, Lucey of WI, Castro of AZ, and Andrus of ID) who left office prior to the end of their terms because it was difficult to figure out how precisely to measure their midterm political-economic records and the records of their short-term successors.
8 What has not been adequately addressed in analysis of national vs. state economy effects is the question of "so what?" Put differently, as a mental experiment: As one conjures up gubernatorial elections over time, and where the national economy increasingly comes to influence state electorates, but consider where and when state economy effects systematically diminish in impact, then, at what point does the performance of the state's economy begin to diminish as a campaign issue that candidates exploit? Our answer is that the state-only effects would have to become vanishingly small before the state economy issue no longer importantly focuses the attention of gubernatorial candidates. If deemed positive, governors claim credit for their states' economic performance, small or large and irrespective of the causal claims as to national- vs. state-determined effects. And, vice versa, incumbents must defend their record that will be exploited by the challenger if their states' economies falter ... large or small.
9 This is consistent with the oft-observed distinction between aggregate analysis of national economic performance and Congressional reelection outcomes vs. survey analysis of Congressional voters and personal economic outcomes, an insight first observed and accounted for by Kramer (1983). Chapter 9 of this volume (with Stults) is an exception by melding both state and national aggregate political factors into an analysis of individual voting in gubernatorial races across states and across time.
10 The "profile" of a candidate in Squire's work refers to a challenger's political office experience, with the highest-profile candidates being ex-governors, members of Congress, and statewide elected officials.
11 Joseph Schlesinger, *Ambition and Politics* (Chicago: Rand McNally, 1966), as cited in Jim Seroka, "Incumbency and Reelection: Governor v. U.S. Senators," *State Government* (Summer, 1980), p. 161.
12 The Gallup Poll presidential approval rating was weighted in the following manner. Each state received the approval rating for its corresponding national region (e.g. Alabama was accorded the rating given to the "South") and recorded as positive or negative deviations from 55% (for a similar calculation, see Frey and Schneider 1978). This figure was established as the "benign" figure, indicating neither harm nor gain resulting from approval/disapproval. As the president's popularity grows in excess of 55%, we hypothesized that fellow-party gubernatorial incumbents benefit. If the president was a Democrat, as in 1978–1980 and 1993–1996, then this deviation from the approval rating was multiplied by 1 for all Democratic governors, by –1 for all Republican governors, and by zero for Independent governors. This results, for these periods, in a benefit for gubernatorial Democrats if the presidential approval rating was greater than 55% and a benefit for Republicans if the approval rating was less than 55%. The same procedure with opposing values was carried out for governors during the Republican presidential period in 1981–1992.
13 This assumes that state electorates do not hold the party nominee-successor of the "quitting" governor as responsible for the state's political economy as they would have held the incumbent, or, if responsible, then only at a diminished level.

11

"FORGET ABOUT ALL THAT 'READ MY LIPS' STUFF, OK?"

The short history of gubernatorial election and re-election strategies in the face of new tax programs[1]

Richard F. Winters

Introduction

The 1990 tax-related actions of George H. W. Bush and his subsequent election loss raised questions about how changing taxes may affect the subsequent electoral fortunes of incumbent executives or their successors.[2] Political scientists have not, with a handful of exceptions, systematically assessed the consequences of policy innovations such as new taxes – either new programs or significant changes in existing programs – on the elections which follow. Nor have analysts examined ways in which candidates' choices and actions exacerbate or attenuate the electoral consequences of significant policy changes such as brand-new broad-based tax programs. It is safe to assume that candidates believe that the effects of new taxes on the vote are mutable; otherwise, few major tax programs would get put into place. Politicians are correct: the evidence indicates that the actions and behaviors of tax advocates and opponents shape the electoral verdicts in ways that produce outcomes that range from powerful affirmation of the new taxes to equally powerful voter rejection. The frequent elections for American governors and the twenty-five adoptions of new and broadly based tax programs over the 1950s–1980s decades provide a fruitful area for research on the determinants of voter judgements in these regards.[3]

The wisdom of politicians: Conventional wisdom among politicians and activists has tax innovation associated with electoral retribution. From national elections to the most local, the often forcefully posed question by electoral challengers to "taxers" is "Are you getting your money's worth?" and it is often knowledgeably and ruefully answered by

DOI: 10.4324/9781003606291-17

candidates who face financially burdened voters with tax-related aphorisms such as "they never vote you in; they vote you out."[4] To activists, the logic of retribution appears to be inexorable. Voters will and do punish "taxers" for policy changes that negatively affect their income and for which officeholders are responsible.[5] This is particularly so, politicians will argue, because information on tax policy changes is "free," easily obtainable, and rapidly conveyed to voters via the media as an important political issue prodded along by political forces opposing the new taxes. Electoral incentives draw attention to tax policy decisions. Opponents of tax-raising incumbents will inevitably question the worth of tax increases and endeavor to differentiate themselves from the officeholders' taxation policies. Tax opposition can prove politically lucrative in the short run because of the high political visibility of tax changes. Even in the long run, the tangible benefits of tax increases (e.g. new highways, more policing, expanded educational facilities) take time to manifest themselves. Tax increases are put into place now in order to finance expenditure programs, many of them with drawn-out, remote, and often geographically concentrated benefits. Even when benefits funded by tax increases do become visible, their distribution is selective or spatially limited leading taxpayers to perceive that many of their tax dollars are being used to finance programs which assist other constituencies. Thus, because the benefits of many expenditure policies are remote in time and/or preventative in nature, they are not properly appreciated by voters when compared to the immediacy of changing tax burdens (Downs, 1960).

States may also have less crowded agendas where tax and fiscal issues may dominate the state political agenda, unlike the national agenda, where domestic economic concerns compete with foreign and defense policy for attention. States also employ numerous taxes, levies, fees, and charges, so it is typically the case that in every two- or four-year period, one, two, or more of the state's revenue programs get changed or a new tax or charge is adopted. Further, the number of states and the economic competition between them for mobile businesses and wealthy voters make for increased sensitivity to the tax burden within the state relative to neighboring states. Although many taxes affect the voters' immediate circumstances, I argue that they should be particularly cognizant of the broad-based and conspicuous personal income and sales taxes levied in the American states. Some suggest that the progressive income tax will evoke more electoral punishment since it places a greater burden on upper class citizens who are well-educated, informed, and politically responsive. On the other hand, although it is regressive in nature, the sales tax is encountered more frequently in day-to-day life (Downs, 1960). Both taxes examined in this chapter are the most prominent personal taxes levied by states.

A possibly counterintuitive wisdom: Politicians are not necessarily helpless in confronting the tax task; they can, under certain conditions, shape the electoral consequences of daring, taxing moves. They believe they can turn history around. Three weeks before his defeat, incumbent Republican Governor and sponsor of the new Illinois income tax, Richard Ogilvie, noted, "Governors who impose income taxes always lose, but I intend to be the exception."[6] This view of candidates actively shaping the conditions of their elections or re-elections may account for the counterintuitive finding of political scientists who have investigated the issue of tax-related electoral retribution (Pomper, 1968; Turett, 1971; Sabato, 1978; Eismeier, 1983) and who suggest marginal effects of taxing on the vote. Gerald Pomper concludes that "...contrary to the rules of political folklore, governors who lead in increasing taxes do not suffer at the polls significantly." (Pomper 1968, pp. 133–134). In support, Turett's (1971) analysis of 43 elections with incumbents running for re-election in the 1960s failed to detect any significant correlation between rates of change in tax burden and electoral success. Eismeier (1983), who examined 389 elections in the 1950–1980 period, more cautiously argued that "governors, gubernatorial candidates and state parties that urged higher taxes faced greater risks of electoral defeat. Yet "these risks are not overwhelming in all cases" (p. 379). On the other hand, Sabatato notes more anecdotally that "tax policy after 1960 is the most prominent issue in gubernatorial politics that results in incumbent defeats" (p. 110).

The results of the multivariate analysis by Kone and Winters (1993) of 407 gubernatorial elections between the years 1957 and 1985 support both the candidates' views of the expected negative effects of innovating a sales or income tax program on voting and the scholars' ambivalences. The adoption of either a new income or sales tax program costs the incumbent governor or the nominee of the "taxing" party, respectively, 2% or 2.4% at the polls, after controlling for rival determinants of the gubernatorial vote. This finding of a tax-related vote cost confirms the conventional wisdom of political activists. Yet the standard errors of these coefficients have values of about "3," that is to say, a distribution of errors that normally indicates "no significant finding." Or, more conventionally put, the statistics suggest that while, on balance, new taxes cost votes, no inevitable costliness results. Some governors put programs in and subsequently lose the election, the rueful example being Ogilvie, thus confirming political folklore; others enact new taxes and subsequently win with large margins, e.g. tax innovators John Volpe of Massachusetts and Deane Davis of Vermont. Thus, the scholarly ambivalences.

The uncertain findings regarding the electoral fate of taxing governors are reflected in Table 11.1. Of the ten incumbent governors who passed new taxes and who again ran in the general election for re-election, six were re-elected. Of the six re-elected, half were returned with increased electoral margins. And of thirteen non-incumbent nominees of what I shall call the "tax-vulnerable" party," nine were elected to hold the governors' chairs for their "taxing" party, while four went down to defeat representing the then-governors' and taxing party.

Some observations: incumbents are vulnerable to re-election problems (60% reelection); less tainted party successors do better (70% of "tax-vulnerable" nominees elected). While it appears that the marginally safer course for the tax-vulnerable party of the then-incumbent governor is to run an attractive successor to the "taxing" governor, we do not know whether the enhanced success of non-incumbent candidates of the tax-responsible party (70% vs. 60%) is greater or lesser than what would be expected as compared to a similar set of candidates absent the tax baggage handed to them by their party's predecessor.

A third observation: Table 11.1 only shows the fate of those running in the general election; it ignores those defeated in primary battles (Robert Smylie of Idaho and Price Daniel of Texas, as examples) and other diverted political careers (George Leader of Pennsylvania, Gaylord Nelson of Wisconsin) or tax-wrecked careers (Richard Ristine of Indiana). Thus, assessing the costs of taxation by examining only general election statistics imperfectly reflects real electoral effects.

A fourth observation: The analysis also ignores the political careers of those who put into place new broad-based taxes and chose not to run for re-election, Frank Licht of Rhode Island being a prominent case. The taxers who choose not to run again raise the question of causality: Do they not run because of taxation, or do they tax in the knowledge that they do not intend to run again? The former is the "sacrificial lamb" hypothesis, the latter the leader who throws self on to the sword.

Fifth, the simple electoral statistics of change from prior election year, as indicated in Table 11.1 for incumbents, are misleading because they ignore factors other than "last outcome" in explaining the gubernatorial vote. Factors such as party, the economy, and other statewide races ought to be controlled for in realistically assessing the impact of taxes. Thus, the need for a general model of the vote from which residuals of the main equation can be produced.

Finally, in any general statistical model, there will be errors in attribution that can be quite profound. Ristine's 1964 Indiana gubernatorial loss to Roger Branigin is an exquisite example. Democrat Branigin won his party's nomination. He was preceded in office by Democrat Matthew Welsh, who passed a new sales tax.[7] Its passage, however, was crucially aided by the decisive vote cast by the then-presiding officer of the Indiana Senate

TABLE 11.1 Winning and Losing via Taxes

I. A. Among elections after passing an **income tax**, those ... Incumbents **winning** were: (with changes in margins (ELECT$_2$-ELECT$_1$) in %votes	1970, K. Curtis; –3% (Dem., ME) 1974, M. Shapp; –2.7% (Dem., PA) 1976, B. Byrne; –10.6% (Dem., NJ)
I. B. Incumbents **losing** were (with changes in margins (ELECT$_2$-ELECT$_1$) in %votes	1970, N. Tiemann; –16.7% (Rep., NE) 1972, R. Ogilvie; –2.2% (Rep., IL) 1974, J. Gilligan; –5.7% (Dem., OH)
I. C. Non-incumbent nominees of tax responsible party **winning**	1964, H. Smith (Dem., WV) 1970 W. Millikin (Rep., MI) 1974 P. Noel (Dem., RI)
I. D. Non-incumbent nominees of tax responsible party losing:	(none)
II. A. Among elections after passing a **sales tax**, those ... Incumbents **winning** were: NY) (with changes in margins (ELECT$_2$-ELECT$_1$) in %votes	1966, N. Rockefeller; –.8% (Rep., 1966, J. Volpe; +12.4% (Rep., 1970, D. Davis; +1.5% (Rep., VT)
II. B. Incumbents **losing** were (with changes in margins (ELECT$_2$-ELECT$_1$) in % votes	1958, Russell; –13% (Rep., NV) 1962, N. Tiemann; –16.7% (Rep., NE)
II. C. Non-incumbent nominees of tax responsible party **winning**	1958, Lawrence (Dem., PA) 1962, J. Connally (Dem., TX) 1962, Reynolds (Dem. WI) 1963, Breathitt (Dem., KY) 1964, Branigin (Dem., IN) 1965, Samuelson (Rep., ID)
II. D. Non-incumbent nominees of tax responsible party **losing:**	1966, Sorenson (Dem., NE) 1969, Battle (Dem., VA 1969, Meyner (Dem., NJ) 1970, Head (Rep., MN)

in a tie vote – the tie-breaking "yea" was made by the then-Lieutenant Governor and *Republican* Richard Ristine, who subsequently won the Republican gubernatorial nomination. By my statistical rule of thumb, Democrat Branigin inherited the "taxer" label from his Democratic predecessor Welsh. Yet the election was largely won by Branigin's disavowal of the tax and his heaping of responsibility on Ristine's shoulders, where, by reasonable voter calculations, it ought to rest.

I find that the effects of taxes on voting, especially the adoption of new tax programs on the electoral process and outcome – not necessarily just the vote – are quite profound and, most frequently, negative. The history of tax innovations ranges at best – as seen by the incumbent or his party – from the need for incumbents' hyperkinetic campaign activities working to overcome the electoral burden of their tax acts, e.g., Nelson Rockefeller in 1966, Deane in Vermont, and Volpe in Massachusetts, to, at worst, wrecked political careers, e.g. Gilligan of Ohio, Russell of Nevada, Smylie of Idaho, Leader of Pennsylvania, and Ristine of Indiana. Career wreckage is obscured if one relies on statistical analysis alone. And statistical analysis cannot measure energies and other resources invested in campaigns necessary to surmount the vote costs of new tax programs, campaign commitments that would not have been invested absent the new taxes. Further, because scholars have not yet modeled it precisely enough (thus the weak or ambivalent findings), the candidate-activist view of tax retribution is the more accurate one. The sizable standard errors indicate misspecification; the statistical models of the scholars are problematical.[8] However, some governors can be profound tax innovators and subsequently prosper, but because they are the exceptions, they deserve separate discussion later in this chapter.

Among the twenty-three elections following the adoptions of new sales or income tax programs, many such elections have large positive residuals and appear to be won by the skillful, "profit-from-adversity" governors. They won handsomely despite the fact that they (if they were re-elected incumbents) labored under the burden of having been directly associated with adopting a brand-new sales or income tax program. Or, if they were the nominee of the party of the then-incumbent, they are associated with the new tax program via party responsibility. Conversely, other gubernatorial candidates appear to enhance adversity – losing votes (but not necessarily the election[9]) by an amount greater than what one would expect even accounting for the electoral impact(s) of new tax(es) passed in their administration or their predecessor's administration. In our general equation of state gubernatorial voting, their elections, their candidacies have large negative residuals. They can be thought of as political "duffers," failing in their election campaigns at a rate greater than the average among similarly burdened governors/candidates. A regression equation allows me to identify which candidate did better or worse than expected.

In a general overview of the twenty-five races with a qualitative assessment of the electoral consequences of new taxes, I explore possible non-statistical or not-yet-quantified factors which shape the electoral consequences of new tax adoptions. Finally, I examine the campaigns where adversity was overcome and incumbents won despite new taxes. There must be particular factors and the strategies and tactics of the successful incumbents which interact with the events of the campaign to produce victory. In explaining the performance of the "skillful," relatively *ad hoc* variables or rules of thumb are adduced to explain re-election success. The empirical "tests" for these explanatory factors are news accounts and interviews with the candidates, journalists, historians of the states and other experts.

Tax policy and American state politics

Electoral support for the gubernatorial nominee of a party is a function of a set of politico-economic forces that can be modeled at the aggregate level.[10] Such forces are hypothesized to be:

- changes in national economic indicators;
- changes in state economic indicators;
- the balance of party forces within the state;
- national, gubernatorial office, and other electoral "tides"; and,
- changes in tax policy.

I employ multivariate regression within a pooled, cross-sectional data set of all gubernatorial elections from 1957 to 1985 to predict the percentage of votes that a Democratic gubernatorial candidate should receive based on the results of political and economic variables and tax policy variables that are hypothesized to influence the vote.

Dependent variable: The dependent variable is the percentage of the two-party vote received by the Democratic gubernatorial candidate.

Independent variables: Factors that directly influence the vote:

Voters respond negatively to year-to-year increases in (1) *national unemployment* and positively to increases in (2) *national personal incomes*.[11] Voters also likely respond to aggregate measures of economic conditions that closely represent their personal plights – state economic conditions. Our model includes year-to-year changes in (3) *state personal income* and changes in (4) *state unemployment*. Often, one region of the nation is blessed with economic prosperity, while another suffers economic decline. While such an event may well be attributable to national policy decisions, the visible state governors may be vulnerable in this regard. Further, while national figures provide a popular gauge of national well-being, state indicators may be good proxy measures of voters' own economic circumstances.

I lack data on party identification for the states in the three decades of the study. The model, therefore, includes a proxy measure of (5) *Democratic partisan strength in the states* constructed as a floating average of the Democratic percentage of the Congressional elections in the state for the three prior electoral periods. The virtue of this partisan floating average is that it represents a relatively current approximation of a party's strength while based on non-gubernatorial races and averaging distortions that might arise from a single election.[12]

Incumbency may have a significant political "tide-like" effect. The present governor has already established name recognition. The incumbent has access to the resources which, through patronage and policy, can enable him or her to generate the support of important constituencies. The executive is the most visible state official. His or her share of television time and newspaper coverage typically exceeds that of the challenger. Further, incumbent governors have the advantage of symbolizing the status quo.

Many voters will not take the time or effort to familiarize themselves with the proposals of the challenger if they are content with the way things are. Nonetheless, the increasing demand for services on the one hand and threats of taxpayer retribution on the other create a situation in which incumbency might well be a disadvantage for candidates in gubernatorial elections.[13] Hence we assume that (6) *Democratic Party incumbency* is an important variable and that it will have a positive impact on the number of Democratic votes received.

There may be cross-sectional, 50-state effects that characterize each electoral period.

Such (7) *50-state electoral tides* may reflect direct and indirect presidential effects, e.g. Democratic successes in 1964, or they may reflect the "temper of the times," e.g. Democratic defeats in 1978. For whatever reason, Democratic gubernatorial nominees across the country can be expected to fare better or worse at some times as compared to others. Therefore, I include an average Democratic gubernatorial success variable, which is calculated for each state as the average value of the percentage obtained by all other Democratic gubernatorial nominees running on that date.

The model also takes into account the unique influence of a federal system. National races have an impact on concurrent statewide elections. The excitement of the national contest, for example, may stimulate greater voter turnout; hence, an increase in the number of Democratic gubernatorial votes may be anticipated in a Democratic presidential election year. An examination of our data reveals that of the 407 elections in question, 141 were coterminous with presidential elections. I account for the presidential influence in the simultaneous gubernatorial contests by including the (8) *percentage of the two-party vote received by the Democratic presidential contender* in the given state. And a binary variable indicating a (9) *presidential year* is also included.

There may be simple secular effects that occur across (10) *time.* A step-level variable for year is included.

Finally, I include several measures of the tax policy variables.[14] In the first set of regressions, using simple binary variables, those key electoral occasions when a (11) *new sales* or (12) *new income taxes* are implemented. I expect that the coefficients associated with these variables will be negative as evidence of electoral retribution. In another regression, simple binary variables are added for three key conditions that may shape the electoral performance of incumbent governors as set out in Table 11.1: A simple binary variable (13) for all *Republican governors who institute a new income tax;* another binary variable (14) for all *incumbent Democrats who instituted new income tax programs;* and a final variable (15) for all *Republicans running who instituted a new sales tax program.* If tax punishment is occurring in the regressions, then the signs for the variables (13)–(15) ought to be positive, negative, and positive, respectively.

This may be an appropriate time to set out which elections were coded as "tax related." Table 11.2 sets out the elections where new income taxes and new sales taxes might have been an issue. Eleven elections were coded as those which followed the adoption of a general personal income tax. The figure indicates which Democratic candidates were coded as "vulnerable," either because they were incumbents or because they were trying to follow in the footsteps of a Democratic governor responsible for the new taxes.

Regression model: With 407 gubernatorial elections in the fifty American states[15] from 1957–1985,[16] the general regression specification we estimate is *%Democrat for Governor* = $BW + TX + SY + e$, where *%Democrat for Governor*= the percentage of the two-party vote obtained by the Democratic gubernatorial nominee; B is a vector of coefficients associated with the set of independent variables just discussed; T is a vector of coefficients associated with specifications of the tax innovation variables as discussed; and S is an unreported fixed effect vector of 49 dummy variables, one associated with each state (with the 50th represented by the value of the constant).[17]

Results: Table 11.3 displays the results of the regression equation for all states for the period testing the hypotheses discussed above. Enacting new income and sales tax programs, as reported in lines 11 and 12, has negative coefficients indicating a 2–2.4% vote loss among the fifty states for Governors who enact new tax programs. Yet the coefficients have sizeable standard errors indicating that, on balance, new tax programs, as predicted, are penalized by voters, but that there are many cases of governors who pass new programs and are held blameless by the voters at the polls. Or, even more intriguingly, it is likely, given the standard error, that some governors are able to gain at the polls relative to the figure expected by their tax policy and predicted by the other variables in the equation.

TABLE 11.2 Tax-Related Elections, 1957–1985

Income tax passages: election dates, states, and subsequent electoral outcomes

1961 legislation, 1964 election: West Virginia; Smith** (DD) over Underwood (R).
1967 legislation, 1970 election: Michigan; Millikin (RR) over Levin## (D).
1969 legislation, 1970 election: Maine; Curtis**[14] (DI) over Erwin (R)
1965 legislation, 1966 election: Nebraska; Tieman (R) over Sorenson** (DD)
1967 legislation, 1970 election: Nebraska; Exon## (D) over Tieman[13] (RI)
1971 legislation, 1974 election: Ohio; Rhodes (R) over Gilligan**[14] (DI)
1969 legislation, 1972 election: Illinois; Walker## (D) over Ogilvie[13] (RI)
1971 legislation, 1972 election: Rhode Island; Noel** (D) over DiSimone (R)
1971 legislation, 1974 election: Pennsylvania; Shapp**[14] (DI) over Lewis (R)
1976 legislation, 1977 election: New Jersey; Byrne**[14] (DI) over Bateman (R)

Sales tax passages: election dates, states, and subsequent electoral outcomes

1955 legislation, 1958 election: Nevada; Sawyer (D)# over Russell (RI)[15]
1956 legislation, 1958 election: Pennsylvania; Lawrence (DD)** over McGonigle (R)
1961 legislation, 1962 election: Texas; Connally (DD)** over Cox (R)
1961 legislation, 1962 election: Wisconsin; Reynolds (DD)* over Kuehn (R)
1960 legislation, 1963 election: Kentucky; Breathitt (DD)* over Nunn (R)
1963 legislation, 1964 election: Indiana; Branigin (DD)** over Ristine (R)
1965 legislation, 1966 election: New York: Rockefeller[15] (RI) over O'Connor (D)#
1966 legislation, 1966 election: Massachusetts; Volpe[15] (RI) over McCormack (D)**
1966 legislation, 1966 election: Idaho; Samuelson (RR) over Andrus (D)#
1967 legislation, 1966 election: Virginia; Holton (R) over Battle (DD)**
1967 legislation, 1969 election: New Jersey; Cahill (R) over Meyner (DD)**
1969 legislation, 1969 election: Minnesota; Anderson (D)# over Head (RR)
1967 legislation, 1970 election: Nebraska; Exon (D)# over Tiemann[15] (RI)
1969 legislation, 1970 election: Vermont; Davis[15] (RI) over O'Brien (D)#

Where (D) = Democrat and previous incumbent was a Republican;
(R) = Republican and previous incumbent was a Democrat;
(DD) = Democrat and previous incumbent was a Democrat;
(RR) Democrat and previous incumbent was a Democrat;
(DI) = Democrat incumbent;
(RI) Republican incumbent;
** = Democrat candidate coded as tax vulnerable;
= Republican candidate coded as tax vulnerable.
[13] = candidacy coded as "+1" in variable (13) as Republican with new income tax;
[14] = candidacy coded as "+1" in variable (14) as Democrat with new income tax;
[15] = candidacy coded as "+1" in variable (15) as Republican with new sales tax;

TABLE 11.3 A Model of Gubernatorial Voting

Variables	*(1) Means (std devs.)*	*(2) Means (std devs.)*	*(3) Means (std devs.)*	*(4) Means (std devs.)*
1. Δ U.S. Unemployment %*PPIP	2.55** (.74)	−1.65** (.57)	−1.69** (.57)	−.72 (1.07)
2. Δ U.S. Income*PPIP	−.002 (0.02)			1.24 (2.7)
3. Δ State Pers. Income*GPIP	−.001 (.0015)			.61 (4.5)
4. Δ State UE rate*GPIP	−.20 (.41)			−.04 (1.37)
5. Democratic %of the vote	.326** (.09)	.40** (.08)	.40** (.08)	54.92 (12.13)
6. Democratic incumbent	2.54** (.60)	2.21** (.56)	2.21** (.56)	.22 (.98)
7. Gubernatorial tide	−.163 (.114)			54.69 (5.9)
8. Democratic Presidential%	.025 (.052)			12.82 (21.7)
9. Presidential year	.48 (.2.47)			.407 (.492)
10. Time	.006 (.071)			25.13 (8)
11. New income tax * GPIP	−2.0 (3.21)	−2.29 (3.2)	−.98 (4.76)	.007 (.163)
12. New sales tax * GPIP	−2.41 (2.87)	−2.46 (2.88)	−4.61 (3.59)	.007 (.215)
13. Republican w/ new income tax			6.46 (9.32)	.005 (.07)
14. Democrat w/ new income tax			−1.21 (7.15)	.01 (.1)
15. Republican w/ new sales tax			−6.73 (6.1)	.012 (.11)
Constant	40.96	29.79	29.87	
Multiple r	.68	.68	.69	
Adjusted multiple r	.36	.39	.39	
S.E.E	9.8	9.8	9.8	
Dependent variable = Governor % Democratic vote			54.71 (12.6)	

The equations reported in column (3) include all of the significant regressors from the first two regressions plus the binary variables for the three conditions of party of incumbent governor and instituting new sales or income tax programs. As expected, when the incumbent Republican puts into place a new income tax program (n = 13), the Democratic challenger receives almost 6.5% more votes at the polls, signaling typical voter retribution. However, note that this binary variable has a positive value for just two races – Tiemann of Nebraska and Ogilvie of Illinois – and the widely different results in those races (a rout of Tiemann and a close race for Ogilvie) results in the large standard error. When a Democrat puts in a new income tax program, again, the predicted effect is a much smaller loss of 1%, but, again, with a huge standard error. Perversely, though, in the case of Republican governors who put in new sales tax programs and run for reelection (e.g. Volpe, Davis), they tend to do better, much better (6.7%), than expected in running against their Democratic challengers, but with inflated standard errors. None of these results resolve the issue in favor of either the politicians' view of candidacies put in harm's way by new taxes or the scholars' view of the questionable nature of the causal link between taxes and retribution.

Our causal representation of the electoral result in gubernatorial elections was more complicated than just tax variables; thus, an examination of the other hypothesized effects on the vote is appropriate. In brief, our floating average measure of partisanship, Democratic Party incumbency, and national unemployment have consistent and predictable effects on the vote. Our other expected causes do not. Time, represented as a simple step-level variable, has a trivial effect on the Democratic party share. How well other governors fare via the average of other gubernatorial races in a governor's electoral environmental – (7) *Gubernatorial tide* – is also insignificant and with the wrong – negative – sign. Democratic presidential elections and other governors' Democratic successes, while positively affecting the Democratic gubernatorial vote, do not seem to have a consistent effect on gubernatorial successes.

The effects of party-weighted economic variables on Democratic successes are a perplexing set of results. While Chubb (1985, 1988) found that the party-weighted second difference of national per capita income had a significant impact on the Democratic share of the vote, our party-weighted measure of the first difference of income does not indicate electoral effects. The coefficient is of the wrong sign and not significant.

Both Peltzman (1987) and Chubb (1986) report insignificant effects of state-only economic variables. Both used only measures of income change. We also inserted Department of Labor estimates for state unemployment (reported in line 4). However, neither of our party-weighted variables for state economic performance – income (in line 3) or unemployment – affects the party vote. Note that if we use equation (2) as the standard prediction equation, then the effects of the tax policy variables are comparable in significance to the standard variables of incumbency (6), party (5), and national economic conditions (variables 1 and 2).

Residual analysis: We now turn to analysis of the residuals in beginning an election-by-election examination of the determinants of gubernatorial taxing successes and failures. Using the reduced set of variables as reported in column (3),[18] I generate the residuals of the twenty-five gubernatorial elections which followed the adoption of either or both new general sales and income taxes. For convenience of analysis, I have separated them into displays by new income and new sales tax as presented in Tables 11.4 and 11.5.

Table 11.4 reports the residuals for all new income taxes by election by the Democratic figure, with the tax-responsible candidate underlined. For the income tax, the residuals range from the negative figures for Kenneth Curtis (Democrat of Maine running in 1970) and Philip Noel (Democrat of Rhode Island running in 1972). Both obtained about 5% less share of the vote than would be predicted knowing the factors outlined in column 3 of Table 11.3 plus the 49 state-by-state variables. Note that both Curtis and Noel won re-election as the incumbent in Curtis' case. The reader should be reminded of the interpretation of the residual. Given the 2% standard vote loss expected of Curtis as an "income-taxer" and the predicted effects of party, incumbency, and national economic conditions, Curtis gained 5% fewer votes than expected. He won, however, by one-tenth of a percent. More direct losers were the next two candidates, Sander Levin, who ought to have beaten William Millikin, who was running to succeed his party standard-bearer (and taxer George Romney), and Philip Sorenson, who lost to Norbert Tiemann, who capitalized on the taxing predilections of the then-incumbent, Democrat James Morrison.

At the opposing end, Democrat Roger Branigin of Indiana (in his 1964 race against Ristine) ran about 7% higher than one would expect, while Democrat Brendan Byrne running for re-election nearly gained that bonus.

A number of campaigns gained about what one would expect given the extant conditions plus the adoption of new taxes. The most exquisite election "wash" must be incumbent Democrat John Gilligan's 1974 losing race to James Rhodes in Ohio. Gilligan's loss by less than .5% suggests that Ohio's new income tax cost him the election, when 2% was the average tax-loss figure for such governors – just enough to lose the election. Another election where the Democrats did about as well as expected by the model included the winning election by Smith of West Virginia.

The residuals from the sales tax as presented in Table 11.5 indicate greater spread. Robert Meyner lost in New Jersey to William Cahill by 14% more than would be expected knowing party, national economic conditions, incumbency, and tax policy. Edward McCormack lost by a similar percentage to the incumbent "taxer" – John Volpe. What makes these two races interesting

TABLE 11.4 Residual Analysis of **Income-Tax-Affected Elections:** Unexpected Gains and Losses at the Polls

+ signifies gains post-tax; - as losses post-tax; quantities indicate gains/losses in vote % different than predicted:	
-10	
-9	
-8	
-7	
-6	
-5	*Curtis* beats Erwin, 1970, Maine
	Noel beats DeSimone, 1972, Rhode Island
-4	*Millikin* beats Levin, 1970, Michigan
	Sorenson loses to Tiemann, 1966, Nebraska
-3	
-2	
-1	
	Gilligan loses to Rhodes, 1974, Ohio
0	*Smith* beats Underwood, 1964, West Virginia
	Shapp beats Lewis, 1974, Pennsylvania
1	Walker beats *Ogilvie*, 1972, Illinois
2	
3	Exon beats *Tiemann*, 1970, Nebraska
4	
5	*Byrne* beats Bateman, 1977, New Jersey
6	
7	
8	*Branigin* beats Rastine, 164, Indiana
9	
10	
Tax-responsible candidate underlined.	

is that Meyner, a former incumbent, lost to a Republican while inheriting the taxing party mantle from his party's incumbent, Democrat Robert Hughes. On the other hand, Republican John Volpe was the taxing incumbent, who overcame the tax burden and obliterated McCormack's challenge. John Connally's 1962 Texas gubernatorial race was also almost lost, as Connally did nearly 10% worse than expected. And Democrats Leo O'Brien and Cecil

TABLE 11.5 Residual Analysis of Sales-Tax-Affected Elections: Unexpected Gains and Losses at the Polls

+ signifies gains post-tax; - as losses post-tax; quantities indicate gains/losses in vote % different than predicted:	
–14	*Meyner* loses to Cahill, 1969, New Jersey
–13	
–12	McCormack loses to *Volpe*, 1966, Massachusetts
–11	
–10	
–9	*Connally* defeats Cox, 1962, Texas
–8	
–7	O'Brien loses to *Davis*, 1970, Vermont
	Andrus loses to *Samuelson*, 1966, Idaho
–6	
–5	
–4	*Breathitt* beats Nunn, 1963, Kentucky
–3	
–2	
–1	*Battle* loses to Holton, 1969, Virginia
	O'Connor loses to *Rockefeller*, 1966, New York
	Reynolds beats Kuehn, 1962, Wisconsin
	Lawrence beats McGonigle, 1958, Pennsylvania
0	
1	Exon beats *Tiemann*, 1970, Nebraska
2	Anderson beats *Head*, 1970, Wisconsin
3	
4	
5	Sawyer beats *Russell*, 1958, Nevada
6	
7	
8	*Branigin* beats Ristine, 1964, Indiana
9	
10	
11	
12	
13	
14	
Tax-responsible candidate underlined.	

Andrus also did much worse than expected against their opponents, who should, at least formally, be thought of as "taxers." Those who gained a higher percentage of votes than expected given the record are, again, Roger Branigin of Indiana and Grant Sawyer of Nevada, who ran about 9% and 5% higher, respectively, than expected.

Taxing fate, or "pushing behind the statistical curtain"

Tables 11.6 and 11.7 indicate some of the direct and second-order effects on electoral outcomes of adopting new tax programs. The substantive point of the figures is to portray the likely causal consequences of new tax programs. Such effects are likely to be seen in terms of candidate fates, primary losses, campaign changes, and altered candidacies, and voter behaviors. I conclude in the final column of the two tables with some summary judgment of the impact of new tax programs on the electoral outcome. The evidence for these figures – and, therefore, I emphasize the tentative nature of the conclusions in the characterizations – is my reading about the elections and interviews and discussions with candidates, their staffs, academics, and other "informed" individuals.

The summary judgements regarding Tables 11.6 and 11.7 are as follows:

- Of the twenty-three elections following new sales and/or income taxes, the adoption had a major impact on about 60%, 14 of 23 elections.
- New taxes had "some impact" in two elections, Pennsylvania in 1958 and New Jersey in 1966.
- The adoption seemed to be a minor part of the campaign or not an issue at all in seven campaigns – Nevada, 1958; Michigan, 1970; Virginia, 1969; Minnesota, 1970; West Virginia, 1964; Minnesota, 1970; and Pennsylvania, 1974.
- Of the twenty-three elections, we can conclude that the political careers of eight incumbents ended largely because of the income tax: Smylie of Idaho and Daniel of Texas. Ristine of Indiana, Morrison of Nebraska, Gilligan of Ohio, Ogilvie of Illinois, and Licht of Rhode Island.
- At least one incumbent's career was substantially diverted – Gaylord Nelson of Wisconsin.

"Coming to grips" with new taxes and coming out on top

Governors know that taxes hurt electorally. In addition, they conventionally know (in some sense) that new tax programs will probably hurt them the most. A number of our results belie conventional wisdom. Why should this be so? If the chances for punishment are high for new tax programs, then the political investments governors must make in attenuating these effects are going to be proportionally, if not multiplicatively, higher.

TABLE 11.6 The Effects of Adopting a New Income Tax Program (with Winner in Bold)

State/ Candidates	*Is Candidate Tax Responsible?*	*Main Effects, If Any*	*Second Order or Contingent Effects*	*Net Effects*
Nevada, 1958 election				
Sawyer (D)				"Not an issue"
Russell (RI)	Yes	2 term governor defeated		"Not an issue"
Idaho, 1966 election				
Smylie (RI)	Yes	Primary loss of incumbent governor		ends his electoral career
Samuelson (R)	Via party, but...	Disavows party's sales tax; Challenges incumbent, wins primary	Rallies conservatives, faithful, anti-taxers	Major impact
Andrus (D)	No	2nd nominee of Dems.; Early favorite faced party Split	Unable to capitalize on Repub. Split.	Major impact
Texas, 1962 election				
Daniel (DI)	Mixed	Indecision on taxes, large # of primary opponents; loses	3rd term weariness; anti-incumbent.	Major impact; ends political career
Connally (D)	Via party but...	Split the party, enters primary and wins	Sharpens Dem split in Texas L vs. C	Major impact; Smallest Dem victory in years

(*Continued*)

TABLE 11.6 (Continued)

State/ Candidates	*Is Candidate Tax Responsible?*	*Main Effects, If Any*	*Second Order or Contingent Effects*	*Net Effects*
Cox (R)	No	Mounts credible challenge	New tax as important part of challenge	Major impact
Pennsylvania, 1958 election				
Leader (DI)	Mixed	Party is split. Lt. Gov runs and attacks admin; Leader loses U.S. Senate race of Hugh Scott	Incumbency issues in primary races	Substantial
Lawrence (D)	Via party but…	Intra-party conflict		Some impact
McGonigle (R)	No	Tax as campaign issue		Some impact
Indiana, 1964 election				
Branigin (D)	Via party but…	New Dem, tax is issue; Ristine held responsible. He was key Senate vote for tax.	Obscures Democ. Party role in tax; His Democ. Party predecessor responsible	Major issue
Ristine (R, incumbent Lieut. Gov.)	No, but…	Cast key Senate vote; Held personally responsible; Bears brunt of criticism	Campaign for new tax	Major impact; ends his career
Wisconsin, 1962 election				
Nelson (DI)	Yes	Foregoes race for 2nd term.; Vetoes 1st bill, signs 2nd.	Spits Democ. Party Coalition. Labor Opposed.	Major impact on Nelson

(*Continued*)

TABLE 11.6 (Continued)

State/ Candidates	*Is Candidate Tax Responsible?*	*Main Effects, If Any*	*Second Order or Contingent Effects*	*Net Effects*
Reynolds (D)	Via party	Att. General under Nelson; somewhat responsible.		Some impact
Kuehn (R)	No	Some party energizing effects		Some impact
Kentucky, 1963 election				
Breathitt (D)	Via party	Democ. Primary with ex-Gov. B. "Happy" Chandler.	Accelerates attrition in Democ. Party ranks.	Major impact
Nunn (R)	No	Increased party unity and energy	Conflates anti-tax with anti-Civil Rights sentiments in Kentucky at the time.	Major; Best Republican showing
New York, 1966 election				
Rockefeller (RI)	Yes	Two term incumbent; responsible for new sales tax sentiment	Accelerates public weariness with NR incumbency; Other issues: recent divorce	Major impact
O'Connor (D)	No	Could not effectively mobilize around anti-tax sales tax	Weakens already weakened candidacy	Some impact

(Continued)

TABLE 11.6 (Continued)

State/ Candidates	*Is Candidate Tax Responsible?*	*Main Effects, If Any*	*Second Order or Contingent Effects*	*Net Effects*
Massachusetts, 1966 election				
Volpe (RI)	Yes	Tax issue energized Volpe's administration. Sales tax "popularized." JV as activist, wears out Legislative opposition.	Confirmed JVs "hands-on" reputation	Some impact
McCormack (D)	No	Could not energize an anti-tax coalition	Weakens already weakened candidacy	Some impact
Virginia, 1969 election				
Holton (R)	No	Capitalizes on Democratic Party splits	Agreement on need for new taxes in party and state.	Little impact.
Battle (D)	Via party	Tax issue one of many factors factionalizing Virginia Democrats		Little impact.
Nebraska, 1970 election				
Tiemann (RI)	Yes	Republican anti-tax primary opposition, damaged NT's general election candidacy.	Anti-tax conflated with gun control and farm issues	Profound loss; defeated incumbent.

(*Continued*)

TABLE 11.6 (Continued)

State/ Candidates	*Is Candidate Tax Responsible?*	*Main Effects, If Any*	*Second Order or Contingent Effects*	*Net Effects*
Exon (D)	No	United Democrats		Profound; anti-tax key to victory
Minnesota, 1970 election				
Anderson (D)	No			Appeared to be a marginal issue
Head (R)	Via party			Marginal issue.
Vermont, 1970 election				
Davis (RI	Yes	Dominated campaign activity; important issue	Memorable ad campaign	Major impact
O'Brien (D)	No	Initial issue edge slowly evaporated	Eventually "new" sales tax becomes a "no-win" issue for O'Brien	Some impact

TABLE 11.7 The Effects of Adopting a New Sales Tax Program (With Winner in Bold)

State/ Candidates	*Is candidate Tax Responsible?*	*Main Effects, If Any*	*Second-order or Contingent Effects*	*Net Effects*
West Virginia, 1964 election				
Smith (D)	Via party			Not an issue
Underwood (R)	No			Not an issue
Michigan, 1970 election				
Millikin (R)	Via party			Not an issue
Levin (D)	No			Not an issue
Maine 1978 election				
Curtis (DI)	Tax as major issue	Justifies via program outlays	–	Major, direct impact
Erwin (R)	Questions wisdom of tax	Presents alternative budget	–	
Nebraska, 1966 election				
Morrison (DI	Yes	Defeated in U.S. Senate race.	ends political career	Major impact
Sorenson (D)	Via party	Referenda on ballot on income and prop taxes	Linked to Sorenson	Major impact
Tiemann (R)	No	Fresh face, banker, Businessman, and landowner		Major impact

(*Continued*)

TABLE 11.7 (Continued)

State/ Candidates	*Is candidate Tax Responsible?*	*Main Effects, If Any*	*Second-order or Contingent Effects*	*Net Effects*
Ohio, 1974 election				
Gilligan (DI)	Yes.	Tax as major issue	Justifies via outlays and new programs	Profound effect
Rhodes (R)	No	Critical of new taxes	Presents alternative budget	Major effect
Illinois, 1972 election				
Ogilvie (RI)	Yes	Tax issue became key; Personally responsible; Divisive issue; Weak prim opp. gets 20%		Major impact; ends political career
Walker (D)	No	Fresh campaigner.; Walks State; Opposes Ogilvie *and* Chicago Daley machine.	–	Major impact; Key to victory.
Rhode Island, 1972 election				
Licht (DI)	Yes	Does not run for 3rd term	Says “two terms is enough”	Informed analysts suggests that that tax ends his career
Noel (D)	Yes, via party	Tax as an issue	–	Major impact

(Continued)

TABLE 11.7 (Continued)

State/ Candidates	*Is candidate Tax Responsible?*	*Main Effects, If Any*	*Second-order or Contingent Effects*	*Net Effects*
DeSimone	No	Tax was an issue	–	Major impact
Pennsylvania, 1994 election				
Shapp (DI)	Yes	Tax was an issue	"saved state from bankruptcy"	Minor impact
Lewis (R)	No		criticizes "waste and inefficiencies."	Minor impact
New Jersey, 1977 election				
Byrne (DI)	Yes	New tax as the issue	Dominates. Byrne establishes value of state spending.	Major impact
Bateman (R)	Yes	New tax as the issue	Questions need for new taxes; Campaigns on savings, cuts, efficiencies	Major impact

Because they expect the punishment, governors will make sure that all possible efforts are made to limit the electoral impact of new tax initiatives. This is likely to appear, for example, as a matter of timing. Pass new taxes early in one's administration, a la the Florio administration in New Jersey. Or, create bipartisan coalitions for new tax initiatives that limit between-party sniping. Or, governors wait until the state fisc is in such hopeless straits that a public consensus converges on the wisdom of new taxes. Or, like Deane Davis of Vermont, governors use electoral stratagems, by hook or by crook, and turn what ought to be a barnyard mess into chicken salad at the polls. What do the success stories have in common, or, in particular?

Classic risk-taking at the tax-margins – Kenneth Curtis of Maine: Young, activist Democrat, Kenneth Curtis, narrowly defeated incumbent Governor J. H. Reed in the 1970 election, campaigning on behalf of his "Maine Action Plan." Two years later, some of the costs of action came due, and Curtis pushed for and won a general income tax. The tax passed the House and the Senate by the margin of one vote, votes cast by the Republican leadership in the two chambers.[19] After passage, the state was sharply divided on the issue of the wisdom of the new broad-based tax and the political future of its incumbent Governor. Curtis faced a single primary opponent, a perennial political gadfly, Plato Truman, in the primary. Truman's anti-Curtis strategy was simple – plaster Maine with billboards that have the simple message: a huge STOP sign with the logo "Stop Curtis' Taxes." Truman won about 40% of the vote and it was obvious that the classic political drama was about to occur: political retribution wreaked on the incumbent, and the state of Maine would return to a more sensible Republican administration, whose nominee was a long-time party activist and the decisive winner of the Republican primary, James Erwin.

Early polling results also indicated that Curtis was in trouble and that Erwin had a commanding lead. Erwin's lead was so sizeable early in the campaign and public reaction to Curtis was so hostile that the incumbent had to tum his physical campaign strategy dramatically around. Early in the campaign, Curtis could not mingle in crowds or walk plant floors or anywhere where crowds might gather. Heckling inevitably resulted. Plant gates provided streams of one-on-one encounters or small groups where Curtis could "show his face." Curtis knew his task was to turn around his low poll ratings (30% favorable vs. 70% for Erwin).[20]

Yet, there was trouble in the Republican ranks, also. Republican leadership votes were decisive in advancing the income tax bill to Curtis's desk, and they refused to endorse Erwin's anti-tax stands. Erwin sought the legislative leadership out in advance of the vote and asked them not to give Curtis the chance to campaign on behalf of an already-passed tax, "Make him campaign on the basis of the tax that he wants to pass. Don't give him the opportunity to campaign on something already on the books."[21] Erwin was serving his second term as the Republican and majority choice for the legislatively chosen Attorney General of Maine. In the next ten weeks, Curtis gathered up just enough votes to return – a 469-vote margin.[22] He did it with the classic campaign of an activist. Curtis presented the Maine income tax (the state already had a 5% sales tax) as a "fair tax." Equity considerations appeared to weigh heavily in the minds of voters, and many responded to appeals of simple justice.[23] More to the point, the income tax, then a year old, could also be presented as a "fear tax." Important to the political arsenal of the incumbent is spreading the message that present streams of benefits would be jeopardized if the already-instituted tax were repealed. The appeal can be made convincing to any number of discrete constituencies – educators, university students, the elderly, indigents, farmers, and so on. While it is the case that many benefits of government are "remote and preventative" (Downs 1960), the sophisticated and skillful campaigner will make state government benefits immediate and crucial to the present welfare of voters – or, at least, appear to be. The more skillful campaigner can make it appear that each constituency will bear a greater than expected brunt of the shrinkage of government. In this case, magnifying the burdens of shrinkage is the strategic obverse of the more frequently encountered campaign appeal of magnifying the benefits of future government programs. Voters are not well informed, and their fears can be magnified by their general anxieties regarding the uncertainty of the future.

The challenger to the incumbent taxer is hampered in creating a convincing response. The classic one is to appeal to claims for more efficient administration, as Erwin did. He claimed that selective cuts could be made that would cover the 10% deficit in state spending. But credibly making the claim of what to cut, where to cut, when to cut, and the harmlessness of it all is difficult for the challenger to make. The sophisticated response of the incumbent is to bore right in and ask, "where?" In a televised debate over the public TV station, Curtis asked,

Jim, whose program are you going to cut? Schools? Help for the Elderly? Where, Jim? Tell us right now where you will make these cuts.[24]

Casting the issue as shrinkage of a budget with nothing but deserving beneficiaries is a powerful rhetorical weapon of the incumbent. Erwin, in fact, did not have a detailed alternative budget plan before the voters until October. But, by that time, the tide was turning, and Erwin's reputed 20% lead was shrinking rapidly … and, in the end, gone.[25]

A "tum-around candidate?" – Deane Davis and the 1970 Vermont election: One analyst commented that Deane Davis began to lose the 1970 election in the 9th minute of his term when, in his January 1969 inaugural address, he advocated a general sales tax as a solution to Vermont's fiscal problems.[26] His own views, however, on taxes and on his own re-election chances were more optimistic. He notes that outgoing Governor, Democrat Philip Hoff, immediately after the inauguration congratulated him on his sales tax message and stated that he "was doing the right thing."[27] While others may have shared Hoff's sentiments about Davis doing the right thing, it was clearly not a majority of Vermonters once the tax was in place. In the 1969 "Governor's Day" appearance at the Vermont State Fair, Davis was soundly booed by the audience of locals. There were other events throughout his term and early in his 1970 re-election campaign that indicated that Davis was in trouble with the voters. Some campaign events had rough audiences, like the State Fair (which Davis cancelled during the 1970 campaign). Davis also faced a Republican primary challenge from his younger, more liberal, and anti-war Lieutenant Governor, Thomas Hayes.

Yet all analysts agree that Davis turned the 1970 re-election campaign around, probably in the last month, certainly in the last two weeks to win handily by 14%. It may also provide one scenario for politically surviving new taxes. Note that Davis has Vermont adopting a new sales tax in a state with an already burdensome income tax and where Vermont itself is a relatively poor state. It stood high, even prior to the new sales tax, in the rankings among states in state revenue collected as a percentage of state income. Yet Davis wins by 14%, with an increased margin of victory, and by 8% more than expected by my general statistical model. What accounts for Davis' victory?

I suggest that it is a function of a number of electoral strategies, some purposeful, others serendipitous. Davis entered office having signaled to voters in his initial election campaign that a sales tax may be necessary "as a last resort." And, while the "nine-minute honeymoon" may have been short, the worst news of his administration was upfront and public early when electoral damage can be better calculated and handled.

Second, Davis brought personal factors to bear on the tax issue that dampened public outcry. For many years he had been one of Vermont's leading citizen politicians (Barre, Vermont, city councilor, city attorney, Washington County attorney, and a Superior Court judgeship). At the time of his election, he was Vermont's leading businessman (variously general counsel for the National Life Insurance Co. of Montpelier, then president, and, finally, chairman and chief executive officer). Davis marvelously conflated politics and business; he could appeal to voters' judgements about their interest in specific government programs, and, all the while, he presented himself as a convincing, private-sector-trained businessman concerned with economy and efficiency in government. To the people of Vermont, he could present the business side – a careful assessment of the needs of the state, a cost-accountant approach to government, and a private-sector-trained wariness about government that suggests to the voters that little or nothing will get by his skeptical eye at the top. He appeared to the voters as a man who was wise even beyond his then seventy years.

Third, "blame-sharing" with the opposing party is a well-honored strategy which at times may be available to the pro-tax governor. Some conditions make for a more potent strategy of fobbing off on one's opponent part (or all) of the blame for the new tax and therefore electoral burden-sharing. After six years of Democratic rule under Governor Philip Hoff, Davis could credibly say that the sales tax was now needed in order to balance the budget that was so rapidly increasing because of the commitments of the other party's administration. In addition, a powerful claim can be made to the supporters (and the candidates) of the activist party – in this case, the Democrats – that the alternative to the sales tax was severe cutbacks in appropriations for programs and benefits that directly assist their constituencies. Thus, the opposing party's criticism is and must be muted. At the same time, Davis made forthright claims to the public that the sales tax was needed even though he, the businessman-governor, was tightening welfare rules, for example, in order to ensure that no "hippies get welfare."[28] Thus, Davis' own special tight-fisted talents were highlighted while Davis paraded the suspect constituencies of the Democrats before the voters of Vermont, thereby gaining votes from Republicans and those suspicious of traditional Democratic beneficiaries, and he could also present himself as concerned about protecting the legitimate interests of worthwhile, democratically oriented constituencies in government programs.

Fourth, the Democratic opposition was necessarily hampered. Leo O'Brien, the Democratic nominee, never obtained a purchase on the tax issue. O'Brien was closely associated with the Hoff administration, having served before the 1968 election as leader of the Senate Democrats. O'Brien was also well aware of the need for new revenue, and the strongest statement that he could make regarding the tax was to "repeal it when economically feasible." Davis' campaign retort to O'Brien and voters was "when it's economically feasible, I'll repeal all of your taxes."[29] The fly-paper quality of Democratic spending commitments and the need for a new sales tax were also unobtrusively signaled every day in the campaign. Ex-Governor Phil Hoff, the Democrat responsible for many new programs, was also running that year for the U.S. Senate seat held by Republican Winston Prouty. Thus, there was a constant electoral reminder of the link between today's need for a new tax and yesterday's governor and spending.[30]

Other conditions dampened Democratic efforts at challenging Davis and the new sales tax. Ambivalences about the past directions within the Democratic party – liberal and program-oriented vs. a more conservative, tight-fisted, and taxpayer-oriented party – were highlighted in the first-ever Democratic gubernatorial primary in the state. Hoff's Lieutenant Governor John Daley, initially indicated that he would not run (Daley was defeated by Davis in the 1968 general election), but then reconsidered and entered the primary against O'Brien. Daley was older, more conservative, and from the southern part of Vermont. Both Hoff and O'Brien were from the Burlington area. Daly appealed to non-Burlington voters, to more conservative voters, and to a more traditional ethnic wing of Democratic voters, those who were somewhat wary of the Hoff and the more liberal wing of the party. O'Brien won the primary with about 55% of the vote, and, while the closeness of the vote indicated serious cleavages within the Democratic party, the party launched the general election campaign relatively united. Daley's primary challenge had two[31] opposing effects. On the one hand, it energized O'Brien and made him known throughout the state, but it also sensitized voters – Democratic and Republican – to the political baggage that O'Brien was necessarily carrying around as the heir apparent to Hoff. And the late date of the primary election, two months before the general election, complicated the party-healing process.

Finally, there was a celebrated event in the campaign that is always posed locally as the crucial factor – the bailing-out-the-boat ad. Midway through the campaign, the Davis people unveiled an ad campaign that the incumbent was initially dubious about. It had Davis bailing out a half-sunken rowboat with an appeal to voters to return the governor to finish the job of rescuing the "ship of state" done in by others. The ad was an instant hit, as even his opponents knew instantaneously. I suspect that it was so powerful for reasons that are not often adduced, namely, that in a small, relatively socially homogeneous states, it appealed to the sense of community of Vermont voters and the felt need or willingness to contribute in order to advance the common wealth.[32]

Winning and losing candidate traits:

John Volpe won a smashing reelection victory in 1966 following the adoption of the Massachusetts sales tax. Or, Edward J. McCormack Jr. lost devastatingly at the polls to an incumbent who had just passed a sizeable sales tax. Both statements are true, and both capture the interaction of a tax issue with candidates with winning and losing personal traits. Volpe transformed taxes, what we now consider to be a "campaign negative," into a significant "positive." Volpe was favored from the start to win reelection. What were the ingredients to his success?

In his first reelection campaign for the governorship in 1964 (he had previously served as governor), Volpe signaled to the voter that he might proceed with a sales tax. Whatever negative effects such signaling might have had (similar signaling had damaged the electoral future of his predecessor,

Foster Furcolo) were vitiated by a bitter division in the Democratic ranks when then-Lieutenant Governor Frank Bellotti defeated incumbent Governor Elliot Peabody in a hotly contested primary. Volpe won this 1964 election by one-half percent.

Personal traits of John Volpe helped gain the passage of the sales tax and transform it into a positive electoral issue at the time of his next reelection. He was a widely known and highly respected businessman heading up a large construction company with operations throughout Massachusetts. Like Deane Davis, he brought the positive traits of concern for efficiency and no-nonsense business practices to politics. But, in his terms as governor, he also established a reputation as a progressive, modernist, and reform-oriented governor in an era when the path to power for Republicans in that state seemed to point in the direction of promising efficient and honest progressivism of utilizing governmental power for public interest ends. To this end, Volpe advocated a positive agenda supporting higher education, state mental health systems, and state support for local provision of welfare and other services.[33] In recalling the sales tax fight, Volpe's Lieutenant-Governor, Elliot L. Richardson, noted in a recent article, "There was no fiscal crisis as such, we just wanted to be able to do more."[34]

Establishing the public benefits of the new tax was one part of the Volpe campaigns for the tax and his reelection. It appeared to be successful – legislators speak of walking in holiday parades with people shouting at them from curbside, urging them to "pass the tax."[35] There was widespread agreement among legislators on the need for new taxes in order to support new state spending. Thus, the issue became what kind of tax is needed for required public services, rather than the trade-off between taxes and services. As evidence for public agreement, a year after Volpe's re-election in a referendum on the sales tax that was pushed by the AFL-CIO, the public supported the new tax by about a 4 to 1 vote.

A second trait: Volpe's energy and activism in pursuing the sales tax passage convinced the electorate of its worth and Volpe's likely probity and efficiency in its subsequent administration. The passage of the sales tax was largely due to Volpe's activity and resolve. The democratically controlled state legislature kept turning down Volpe's tax package, and he kept coming back with a revised version. Volpe was inexhaustible. "It was the old Chinese water-torture treatment. If they keep dropping water on your head, eventually you come around. Eventually, Volpe wore the legislature down.[36] The sales tax passed with 53% support in the House and 56% in the Senate in chambers which were 71% and 68% Democratic, respectively.

Volpe's activities were propped up by the weakness of the opposition. In 1964, the Democrats were split by the Bellotti-Peabody rivalry. In 1966, the leader of the opposition to the sales tax, Senate President Maurice Donahue, entered the Democratic battle to gain the convention nomination for Governor along with Edward McCormack. McCormack had been in a bitter, party-splitting battle four years previously with Edward Kennedy for a U.S. Senate seat. Donahue campaigned in opposition to the sales tax, but McCormack won the endorsement of the state convention by a 60% vote. McCormack subsequently won a contested gubernatorial primary by the same figure over a Kennedy partisan. But the Democratic Party was hopelessly fractured. Complicating the issue was McCormack's campaign. "He was not a strong candidate. McCormack was not inherently an attractive politician." Volpe won with about 63% of the vote and carried every county in the state.

An incumbent's "dream re-election" – Milton Shapp's 1974 victory: To the extent that Curtis's Maine victory was every incumbent's re-election nightmare, Shapp's victory was every incumbent's dream. Shapp's 1971-passed personal income tax was, to all intents and purposes, not an issue in his 1974 re-election campaign.

Shapp signaled to voters in his 1970 campaign that an income tax might be necessary. However, others had signaled the need for a new income tax program earlier, including his Republican predecessor, Raymond Shafer. Shapp's 1970 campaign was eased by conflict within the Shafer administration (Shafer could not succeed himself) over the nomination. Lieutenant Governor Broderick won the nomination over the opposition of Shafer. Like Volpe of Massachusetts, Shapp won in part because of his "outsider" qualities and the fact that he was a businessman promising efficient, honest administration of the taxpayers' dollars.

Shapp was inaugurated in June, and a graduated income tax was passed by March. In late June, the Supreme Court invalidated its graduated provisions; Shapp called the legislature back into session and had a flat tax on his desk by the first of September. The tax was put into place and did not become an issue in the 1974 election. Widespread bipartisan agreement on its need, public recognition of the "time" for the tax, the Watergate election year, and the weakness of the Republican 1974 candidate led to a Shapp victory.

Shapp's opponent that year was Andrew Lindsay (Drew) Lewis. Lewis had not held any general elective office; he was Montgomery County Republican Chairman when nominated. Lewis was a young businessman nominated, in part, to counter Shapp's outsider, businessman image. He campaigned against corruption in Shapp's administration, waste, the need for budget cuts, and the size of state government. If anything needs explaining, it is probably why Shapp did not do better. According to Table 11.1, Shapp did only about one-half percent higher than would be predicted knowing all of the particulars of Pennsylvania and the fact that he passed an income tax. There was corruption in government, and there was probably waste. And Shapp's outsider image and the joy he took in that role also antagonized other party leaders. In the year before the election, Philadelphia Mayor Frank Rizzo pledges that "Shapp will be a one-term governor.[37] A June 1973 poll indicates that Rizzo would beat all comers in the race for Governor running as a Democrat, as a Republican, or as an Independent.[38] And in 1973, the Republican Party believed that Shapp would be an "easy target.[39] My sense is that the new Pennsylvania income tax was probably not a live candidates' issue in the 1974 election, but it did activate voters and cut into Shapp's margin of victory.

"Back-to-the-future" 1964 style is expensive – Rockefeller's comeback strategy:

Conventional wisdom had Nelson Rockefeller some 25% to 30% behind Frank O'Connor by the beginning of the formal campaign. Rockefeller won with 54% of the vote. One journalist characterized Rockefeller's 1966 campaign as "the most astute, the most professional, the most imaginative, and perhaps the most ruthless this nation has ever seen."[40] Rockefeller retailed his third term in 1966, post-1965 sales tax, by selling the future and his stewardship of it.

Rockefeller won his second term with a promise of "no new taxes," in contrast to the Democratic candidate, Robert M. Morgenthau, who, he charged, would raise taxes by 75%.[41] Less than one year later, Rockefeller reneged on his promise, indicating that economic failures of the Kennedy administration had constricted expected revenue growth. In January of 1965, he proposed a budget with a 2% sales tax, calling for a $598 million increase in spending with new, promised programs in higher education, highways and mass transit, and state construction. Rockefeller embarked on a campaign of selling to voters his program of benefits of the new taxes. As Peirce put it:

> The 1966 campaign was a classic, first creating a favorable image for a candidate who started an incredible 26 percentage points behind in the poll. It began with a variety of amusing, sometimes animated commercials that plugged Rockefeller's record on issue after issue ... without ever introducing the governor himself.[42]

The campaign tactic is consistent with an agenda-setting strategy whereby an unpopular candidate must first make voters' opinions positive, not of the candidate, but of those objects/things/activities that voters can then associate with the candidate. Reduce the visibility of the unpopular incumbent by highlighting the positive images of the products of his actions, and then introduce the responsible incumbent. Once the association is made, then attacks on the opponent – "moving to slashing attack on the opposition in the final stage – is possible."[43]

O'Connor's campaign was hurt by his New York City home base, his lackluster campaign, divisions within the Democratic Party (differences with Mayor Robert Wagner) that Rockefeller skillfully exploited, and the activities of the Liberal Party, which advanced the candidacy of Franklin D. Roosevelt Jr. But my sense is that the key to Rockefeller's comeback victory was the turning of the image of his results and then the candidate.

A classic tax-based electoral battle – Byrne vs. Bateman of New Jersey:

The Brendan Byrne administration finally got an income tax bill passed by the New Jersey legislature in probably the longest, most bitter, messiest bill-passing episode of the last twenty years in American state politics.[44] A bill with a "temporary" tax was passed and signed in early July 1976. The issue was so protracted, so many actors became involved (the proximate issue was the state's Supreme Court invalidation of local property-tax financing of public schools), so many variations and options were proposed, discussed, voted up in one chamber, and then down in the other chamber, so much posturing was mixed in with electoral fears and genuine reservations about an income tax as well as strongly felt advocacy of it that the public became more than disenchanted – they were furious and enraged.[45] There appears to be no reliable figures on head-to-head matches between likely candidates early in the campaign, but there are three telling, albeit somewhat oblique, indicators. At about the time of the primaries, Byrne's approval rating among the voting public had dropped to 17%.[46] Secondly, Byrne had ten opponents in the Democratic gubernatorial primary, and as an incumbent, he won the election with only 30% of the vote. It was clear that in three years, Byrne had come a long way from first waffling on the issue of the need for an income tax in his 1973 campaign to declaring just before the election that "we don't need one." Byrne won his first term with the largest margin of any New Jersey governor and a 2 to 1 vote over conservative Republican Charles Sandman, a candidate who declared, "no income tax until hell freezes over."

From early June until November, Byrne turned the election around. What makes the feat so extraordinary is that he did it against a strong, attractive Republican, Raymond Bateman, who won convincingly against House Minority Leader Thomas Kean in a spirited primary. The Republicans came out of that election unified and confident that they were going to sweep the New Jersey elections. Not only do they not win the governorship, they lose seats in both chambers, and after Byrne won the election with 57% of the vote, an elated, energized Byrne called the lame-duck legislature back into session, which, chastened, repealed the June 1978 expiration date of the new income tax.

What were the determinants of his success? The protracted lead-up of the tax issue, the long general election campaign (June until November), the large number of debates between the two candidates, and the odd-year timing of the election (November 1977) focused public opinion on the election. Initially, public opinion was quite hostile to the new income tax. However, a number of factors and events attenuated those strong feelings. First, opinion on the issue was quite closely polarized along party lines and candidate approval lines, and that relationship began to crystallize over the campaign.

Secondly, many Jersey voters already paid income taxes to Pennsylvania and to New York. Thus, they would now be paying to another, more proximate, "own" government. Thirdly, property tax rebate checks were issued with an eye to the election timing, thus signaling some expenditure benefits for the new taxes. Indeed, some taxpayers who were already paying commuter income taxes in New York and Pennsylvania were directly benefitted by the combining of the New Jersey income tax and the property tax rebate.

A factor that was clear in other incumbent victories asserted itself here as well – challengers seem unable to present plausible, rival alternative budget schemes to voters. Bateman's alternatives, thoughtful and sophisticated as they were coming from one of the leading State Senators of the opposing party, just were not plausible, as he admitted. Much depends on the "state's economy rebounding" in order to be able to do away with the income tax.[47] By the end of October, polling had the race dead even.

Byrne had raised enough doubts in a sufficient number of voters' minds about Republican plans for replacing the income tax to neutralize the issue. But, in addition, I suspect that positive personal traits of Byrne came to bear on the final verdict as well. Byrne's rise in New Jersey politics was the classic path of the incorruptible prosecuting attorney. He first caught the eye of the public via the merchandising of his *persona,* using a taped conversation of a Jersey mobster who claimed over the wiretap that "Byrne can't be bought." Some or all of the traits of probity, resolute advocate for the income tax, veteran governor, and predictable politician are those, I suspect, that voters saw in Byrne. Byrne won with 57% of the vote in a victory that also carried Democratic politicians to success all across the state.

Conclusions

The statistical analysis in Part II examined all twenty-five tax affected actions within a general model of all 407 gubernatorial elections from the

TABLE 11.8 Four Fold Classification of Tax-affected Elections

	Winners	*Losers*
Incumbents	Curtis (Dem. ME) Shapp (Dem. PA) Byrne (Dem. NJ) Rockefeller (Rep. NY) Volpe (Rep. MA) Davis (ep. VT) 6	4
	9 Smith (Dem., WV) Samuelson (Rep., ID) Millikin (Rep., MI)	4 Battle (Dem. VA) Meyner (Dem. NJ) Soreson (Dem. NE)
Non-incumbent Nominee of the tax vulnerable party	Noel (Rep., RI) Lawrence (Dem., PA) Connally (Dem., TX) Reynolds (Dem., WI) Breathitt (Dem., KY) Branigin (Dem., IN)	Head (Rep. MN)

mid-1950s to the mid-1980s. Part III distributed these twenty-five elections according to the size of the unexplained margins of victory or loss. We attributed the size of those margins to unexamined, not-yet quantified (or quantifiable) factors, and we explored some of these factors in Part IV. Finally, in Part V, only the most successful of the handful of tax-affected elections, those where tax-aggressive incumbents were returned to office, were examined.

Table 11.8 rearranges already-presented information on winning and losing, incumbency, and tax vulnerability.

In Part V of this paper, we looked at only the upper left-hand cell of the above fourfold figure, only one-quarter of the interesting races. These successful reelections are obviously interesting races; they are, in some sense, the heroic races – races where the hard choices were made, responsibilities were faced up to, and success was gained.

The other cells are, however, no less instructive. Indeed, the upper right-hand cell – tax affected losing incumbents – may, for the professional politician, be the most interesting cell of all. Losers may be the best instructors regarding strategies that ought not to be undertaken. Finally, for sheer numbers, the lower left-hand cell may be the most interesting of all. For any number of reasons, the lower left-hand cell is interesting because it is the weightiest cell; running a successor to a tax-affected incumbent, either by choice of the incumbent or party leaders, by primary defeat, or for reasons of constitutional limits on terms is the most frequent electoral situation. Examinations of those cells will have to wait a later author

What lessons can be drawn from the present examination?

- The wisdom of both politicians and of political scientists are correct. New taxes are a losing proposition, but not invariably so.
- No surprise, incumbents responsible for new taxes are marginally more vulnerable than new party nominees.
- Republicans appear to be less vulnerable than Democrats to electoral retribution, especially in the case of sales tax adoptions. This is probably associated with Republican candidate traits (i.e. more business-like candidates) and the propensity of Republican candidates to inaugurate sales taxes as the new tax of choice and the public's perceptions of the differences between sales and income taxes.
- Except for extraordinary circumstances (Shapp, Volpe), adopting new taxes, irrespective of party or of type of tax, puts the incumbent at a steep initial electoral disadvantage.
- Personal activism of disadvantaged incumbents, a la Nelson Rockefeller and Kenneth Curtis, is a crucial variable in gaining the final electoral win. Taking the case to the voter aggressively is key.
- The classic strategy of the disadvantaged incumbent is, I suggest, that of Nelson Rockefeller. Incumbents must first frame the tax issue in terms of the positives associated with the benefits of new spending before the negative traits of the incumbent can be neutralized, positive candidate traits enhanced, and credible attacks on the challenger made.
- If, to a politician, "money is the mother's milk of politics"; to a political scientist, "money is the universal solvent of political opposition," e.g. Rockefeller. This advantages incumbents, and, I assume, Republicans.
- A coalition of intense minorities favoring reelection of the taxing incumbent can be generated via a strategy of exaggerating the burden of budget shrinkage, absent new taxes.
- The passage of time from adopting the new tax to the election does not seem to be crucial in shaping the electoral outcome.
- The signaling function of new taxes is important in vitiating the initial effects of the new tax program. While one does not have to say, like Walter Mondale, that "We need new taxes", on the other hand, "read my lips..." rhetoric must be electorally damaging.
- Bipartisan signaling, e.g. Shafer and Shapp in Pennsylvania, just about moots the tax issue.

We have endeavored to assess through a variety of techniques and based on differing sources the effects of new tax programs on gubernatorial races. The conclusion is that such effects are usually profound and usually negative. There do appear to be conditions, however, that can lead to imposing brand-new taxes in the states and positive, favorable outcomes follow for the taxing governor and/or his party. The saving grace of this last caveat is that the conditions are very often under the control of the incumbent governor.

Notes

1 I thank Deane Davis, Leo O'Brien, Paul Beers, George Goodwin, Chris Black, Mal Leary, Kenneth Curtis, James Erwin, Mary C. Harris, and Robert Kane for their time and patience in our conversations about taxes, politics, and elections.

2 What did set the Bush example singularly apart from other tax-related election consequence stories is his pre-election and widely publicized claim of "Read my lips, no new taxes!"

3 There turn out to be few voter-based analyses of state gubernatorial or legislative elections in the field of American state politics (but see Cohen, 2006; and Niemi, Stanley, and Vogel). This is especially puzzling when juxtaposed with the plethora of writings on Congressional elections (see Jacobson and Kernell for a review).

4 Nick Ravo, "Bridgeport's Novice Mayor Jolts City," in *The New York Times*, November 15, 1989, p. B-9.

5 The readers ought to be warned that, for the author, having lived in New Hampshire for forty-five years, the only state in the Union with neither a general sales nor personal income tax, the author may have accepted with too little challenge the opprobrium attached to what is, in the local lingo, the single-word, the political epithet of she's a "broadbasedtaxer." In this case, "she" is Arnie Arnesen, see https://en.wikipedia.org/wiki/Deborah_Arnie_Arnesen.

6 As quoted in the *New York Times,* October 15, 1972, p. 46. Ogilvie was wrong – of the six governors in the post-1957 period running for re-election who established new income tax programs, three lost their bids. Both Republicans sponsoring new income tax programs lost in their efforts at re-election – Ogilvie and Tiemann of Nebraska.

7 The new tax was part of a broader tax package that also quite dramatically reshaped the already existing general personal and corporate income taxes in Indiana.

8 That is to say, Kone and Winters (1993).

9 Two of the more intriguing campaigns with large negative residuals in fact had "taxing" victors, the incumbent Kenneth Curtis of Maine and John Connally of Texas, the Democratic heir apparent to his "taxing" predecessor, Price Daniel. Note that, in fact, Daniel opposed the "business-backed sales tax" (Peirce, 1972, p. 506), but nevertheless, by the statistical mechanics, I assume Daniel, and, therefore, Connally, his successor, bears the voters' blame for the sales tax adoption.

10 This model was first presented in Kone and Winters (1993).

11 All tax variables (variables 11 and 12 in the following discussion), as well as the national and state economic control variables (variables 1–4) are weighted, following Bloom and Price (1975) and Chubb (1986), by a "party-in-power" variable coded +1 if the immediate past party in power was Democratic and -1 if the party in power was Republican. National variables are weighted by the party of the incumbent president (*PPIP), while state economic and tax variables are

weighted by the gubernatorial party in power (*GPIP). The rationale for the transformation is as follows: if taxes rise during a Democratic gubernatorial administration, the Democratic vote should go down accordingly. If taxes rise during a Republican administration, the Democratic share of the vote should, by symmetry, rise.

12 Turett uses a "floating average consisting of the lowest average statewide vote for U.S. Senate and House from among the elections in question and the 2 elections immediately preceding it." He adopted a variation of a measure used by Kostroski (1973). "The years 1946–1953 allowed us the early time periods necessary to construct our floating average variable which begins predicting the 1954 elections."

13 See Ranney in Jacob and Vines (1965) and Piereson (1977).

14 All tax variables were coded using various issues of the *Tax Administrators News;* see Kone and Winters (1993) for details.

15 Most conventional analyses exclude Southern states from their analyses on the basis of "a lack of competitiveness for most of the period in question." Eismeier's methodological decision (1983) to use a win/loss measure of the dependent variable rather than predicting actual numbers or pluralities precludes him from using the Southern states. Our feeling is that although Democratic victories may be inevitable in certain states for part of the period in question, disenchantment with an incumbent administration may be apparent in a decline in the percentage of the two-party vote from one election to the next. That is, while Democratic gubernatorial candidates may always win in the South, we hypothesize that after the enactment of particular tax policies, the Democratic candidate will not win by as much. Also note that our study includes the 1970s and early 1980s, a period during which the southern states were becoming more and more competitive.

16 There are 407 independent observations in our data set, each representing one election in one of the states in the period. Because the number of gubernatorial elections per state is contingent upon the length of the gubernatorial term, implicit in the design is an imbalance in numbers of terms among the states represented in our pooled dataset. States in which governors have always served two-year terms, Vermont and Rhode Island as examples, held fifteen elections during this time period, whereas California, a state that has always had four-year terms, held only seven. Those states that switched from the two-year to the four-year term at some point in this postwar era fell between these bounds. Alaska and Hawaii were incorporated into the analysis in 1962.

17 For a discussion of fixed-effect designs, see Stimson (1985) and Sayrs (1989).

18 Along with the unreported fixed-effect vector of state-by-state binary variables.

19 Significant responsibility for drafting the final bill came from staff in the office of the Republican House Majority Leadership. The bill passed with a 2/3rds majority in both chambers, so a "broad coalition across the parties passed this bill" (telephone conversation, August 3, 1990). On the other hand, some Republicans may have voted for the bill in hopes of both gaining more money for state operations and, at the same time, saddling Curtis with responsibility for its passage and thus helping to defeat him in the forthcoming general election.

20 Telephone conversation, August 3, 1990.

21 Telephone conversation, August 2, 1990.

22 The general regression analysis has Curtis losing over 5% more votes than expected after controlling for the expected 2% loss due to the passage of the income tax.

23 Telephone interview, August 2, 1990.
24 Telephone interview, August 2, 1990.
25 A year later, a special referendum was held where the income tax was upheld by voters by a 2 to 1 margin. The Democrats made significant legislative gains in the 1972 election, and they won control of the Senate in 1974. Curtis appeared not to be damaged by the passage of the income tax in his second term. Significant changes in programs and administration were put into place. A final piece of his program – a statewide uniform tax on property – did create political havoc. Its repeal was finally engineered in a special election in 1975 during his successor's administration, Independent James Longley working with the Democratically controlled Senate and Republican House.
26 As noted in the *Rutland Herald,* October 20, 1970, page 10.
27 Interview, July 18, 1990.
28 *Rutland Herald*, September 22, 1970, p. 5.
29 His statement at a debate in Essex Junction as reported in a conversation with the author, July 18, 1990.
30 Hoff did worse than O'Brien gaining only 40% of the two-party vote in his race.
31 Interview, July 18, 1990.
32 Per the discussion in Chapter 4.
33 Chris Black, "The Sales Tax Revisited: Lessons from 1965," *Boston Globe,* Sunday, July 29, 1990.
34 Black, "The sales tax revisited....".
35 Black, "The sales tax revisited...".
36 Black, "The sales tax revisited...".
37 As quoted in the *New York Times*, February 12, 1973, p. 28.
38 *New York Times*, June 28, 1990, p. 9.
39 *New York Times*, December 11, 1973, p. 1.
40 James M. Perry, "This Rockefeller Campaign is..." *National Observer,* October 26, 1970, as quoted in Peirce, *The Megastates,* p. 49.
41 James M. Perry, "This Rockefeller Campaign is..." *National Observer,* October 26, 1970, as quoted in Peirce, *The Megastates,* p. 49
42 46 Perry, *National Observer*, October 26, 1970, p. 49.
43 Perry, *National Observer*, October 26, 1970, p. 49.
44 My selected bibliographic references to this New Jersey issue in the *New York Times* stretching from 1973 to 1977 cover seven handwritten pages.
45 The public was so angry at Byrne that Gerald Ford's most telling 1976 campaign oratory in New Jersey was a direct, invidious linkage of Byrne with Jimmy Carter. Ford carried New Jersey to everyone 's surprise, see *New York Times,* November 4, 1976, p. 33.
46 *New York Times,* November 3, 1977, II, p. 1.
47 *New York Times*, October 11, p. 1 and issue of October 16, p. 4.

PART VI

Conclusion

Politics and taxing

12

ON WHY GOVERNMENT TAXES IN THE AMERICAN STATES ARE *RATIONALLY* TOO SMALL AND POORLY DISTRIBUTED

Richard F. Winters

Introduction

Yogi Berra observed that "it's difficult to make predictions, especially about the future,"[1] and the arguments of this book are now at that cusp between what we as politico-economic analysts typically engage in, best put as "postdiction," examples of which are arguments in this volume, that is to say, after the fact generalizing about the past, versus "prediction" as to what the future *might* hold in taxation. My arguments to this point have been focused on what politicians *do* in taxing and how voters, electorates, and candidates *respond*, given the historical evidence; thus, all of our analysis to this point is explaining events after the fact, i.e., empirical postdiction. Nevertheless, I wish to conclude this volume with some thoughts about *prediction,* not only about what states' governors and legislators *are likely to do* but also about what I think that they *should do* in taxing.[2]

In brief, the arguments at this point are: Across the fifty states and across a twenty+-year period, changes in taxes in the American states reasonably cohere into three political practices: (a) redistributive taxation as represented by changes in the personal and corporate income taxes; (b) the changes in the sales tax as a tax on goods and services that are consumed by voters; and (c) changes in a broad array of licenses, fees, charges, and "other taxes" that are levied, typically, on users of some sort of quasi-public goods. It's as if politicians view taxing and revenues as a handful of silos of varying sizes and with variable-sized spigots, some running cold with few electoral consequences (e.g. federal funds, offloading

DOI: 10.4324/9781003606291-19

taxing and spending needs on to local governments) and others potentially "hot" with threatened voter retribution (increasing personal income and/or sales taxes).

Redistributive taxes are most contentious in the revenue political repertories. Contention arises, I suspect, from the conflict between (a) *equity*, that all should pay into the state, versus (b) *justice*, those who have benefitted most from the prevailing order provided by the state have a greater duty to support the system that assisted in their advantaged position, but (c) those who have *benefitted the most* also are less burdened by the increased levies. As the classic argument maintains, income has, like all valued goods, diminishing marginal value to the possessor: The N-thousands of added dollars of income to the rich person has less value to the rich man compared to that same-sized N-thousands to those of more modest means. If so, taxing the well-off burdens them less.

General *sales* as a *consumption tax* is a relatively recent adoption among the states .... Actually, among forty-five of the fifty states, only Alaska, Delaware, Montana, New Hampshire and Oregon do not have the tax. The sales tax originated in Mississippi in 1930 and quickly spread through the states in part as a response to the onset of the 1930s depression as a way to generate revenue. In the 1930s alone, twenty-two states adopted the tax.[3] The rates vary from zero in the five states above to California, with a high of 7.25% applied to sales by the state. California also allows local governments to charge a local sales tax rate for local uses, which, in California, maxes out at 4.75% locally. The effective combined rate applied across the Golden State is 8.85%. Thirty-eight states allow local governments to tack on a local sales tax.[4] One of the features of the sales tax is its "scope" variability. An example: In my current home states of Massachusetts and Virginia, newspapers are taxed in the latter and are tax-free in the former. Many states do not tax food sales, and typically, states don't tax sales of medicine. These exceptions are, of course, politically palatable as they would be levies on "necessities."[5]

Finally, the "odds and ends" of taxation, the fees, charges, licenses, and "other taxes," also seem to constitute a coherent understanding of the political world of taxing.[6] The political "logic in use"[7] of practitioners in the governor's office and the legislators in chambers seems compelling. (a) Many of these taxes, alcohol and cigarettes and tobacco, in particular, have a twofold logic: (i) the consumption of both or either has *generalized social costs*. Alcohol consumption often leads to automobile accidents, injuries, and deaths inflicted on self and others. These inflictions have social costs: police action, often judicial action, medical costs, and so on. Thus, we tax to cover the costs of the social consequences. (ii) The consumption of both is relatively *price inelastic*: I used to purchase my pack of wonderful unfiltered Pall Mall cigarettes almost irrespective of taxes in the price, and my current purchases of tequila and triple sec also are just about unaffected by increasing liquor taxes. (b) Other such taxes impose tax costs on users of public goods that are difficult to levy via individual purchasing.[8] Annual automobile registration fees and gasoline taxes are good examples; an unalterable mileage fee based on vehicle weight would be a better marker of "use." Note, however, New York has many in the city and state who do not own automobiles, thus avoiding both the gas and auto registration taxes. Nevertheless, the city user of the cab or Uber will pay a portion of the vehicle's taxation via the fee to the driver. Occupational or professional licensing falls directly onto the licensee, but the registration and licensing fees will also be passed on to the purchaser of the professional services.

Next taxing steps

An important but hardly ever expressly valued aspect of postdictive analysis is to possibly account for the conditions that form or shape the *next incremental political choice,* in my case, taxation, i.e., what will be the next set of gubernatorial recommendations or the next set of legislative/gubernatorial agreements on tax changes? Postdiction leads us to the *near-present* and leaves us with some insights, given the array of conditions and constraints, suggesting what the next set of taxing choices are likely to be. Thus, postdictive empirics, at the end, leaves us with the question of "OK, so what's next, given these initial conditions?" But while it leads to the question of what *might* we next tax, that leads to the question of *how* and *what should* we tax. The former rests on the postdictive-derived empirics; the latter questions rest on both the empirics and our *preferences*, that is to say, on our beliefs about what is good and proper in governmental action. What is *good* and *proper* in taxes are derived, per the above, from our ideas or preferences about what and how the *good* and *proper* society organizes itself. It is a *normative issue* and *not* an empirical issue.

An interesting, albeit somewhat obscure, example of what we should tax, a *normative analysis,* appeared in an October 2023 issue of the *Washington Post.* The *Post*'s three reporters and a host of research assistants posted a story on "Dying Early, America's Life Expectancy Crisis: How Red-State Politics Are Shaving Years Off American Lives." The simple but ingenious setting for the *Post* story was a comparison of past and current disease and life expectancy rates in three adjoining and demographically and economically similar counties: Ashtabula County, Ohio; Erie County, Pennsylvania; and Chautauqua County, New York. The authors, relying in part on research conducted by Jennifer Karas Montez and colleagues,[9] discover that Ohio in the 1970s had life expectancy rates near the middle of the pack of fifty states, while fifty years later Ohio had dropped into the lower fifth of the states.[10] Among the perverse rate changes occurring are greater changes in "smoking related deaths" and "motor vehicle deaths" in Ashtabula County, Ohio, when compared with similar county statistics for Erie, Pennsylvania, and Chautauqua, New York. The authors relate the drop in New York and Pennsylvania counties' smoking deaths to legislated changes resulting in much higher cigarette taxation rates in those two states, especially in comparison with Ohio's rates, thus making smoking more expensive for NY and PA residents and, by implication, diminishing tobacco use and, thus, the following falling disease rates. A similar dynamic occurred in alcohol-related deaths, such as those from auto accidents due to drunk driving. The *Washington Post* colleagues drew the obvious conclusion: If Ohio legislators and governors valued their constituents lives as much as their Pennsylvania and New York governing colleagues, then the death rates would not have fallen as they did in the Buckeye state. While it may be the case that Ohio legislators may have been more influenced by the lobbying activities of tobacco and alcohol industries than politicians in Pennsylvania and New York, it may simply be that Ohio is a "more Republican" state than Pennsylvania and New York, and, as we have noted in earlier chapters, Republicans prize low taxes and, therefore, low spending. Implicit or not-so-obvious, there is a hidden normative judgement of the journalists here: The three states' legislators and governors *should* value lives on a metric that puts the three states' constituents' lives *at the same value across these three states.* Note that this is a contestable proposition.

"What's going on" in taxing

In Chapter 1, I criticized analyses that use highly aggregated statistics of the amounts of revenue (or spending) that occurred across the states over time. But there is "a time and place for all things, large or small."[11] Figures 12.1 and 12.2 set out data from the 2024 *Economic Report of the President* (ERP) of the fractional shares of revenue collections by type of tax or revenue collected averaged for the years from 2015 to 2020. Figure 12.1 sets out the data for the federal government, while Figure 12.2 outlines the data for America's state and local governments, all data drawn from the 2024 ERP.[12] Two reactions strike me in examining these simple pie graphs. First, among federal government revenues ignoring borrowing, the individual income tax (in blue in the Figure 12.1 pie graph) amounts to nearly half of all revenue collected, while the contributions to the social security system, split between employee contributions and those of employers, amount to about 35%. In sum, these direct contributions from individuals

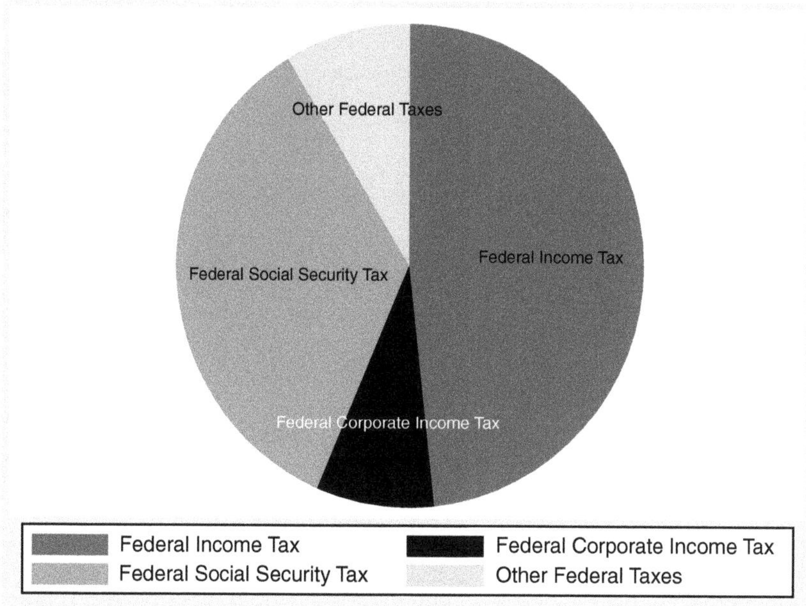

FIGURE 12.1 Federal Revenues by Class of Revenues.

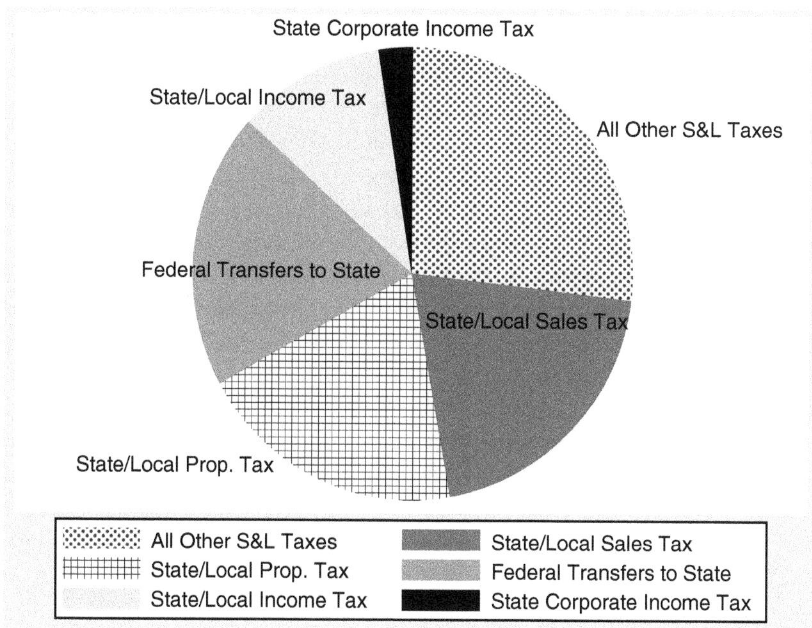

FIGURE 12.2 State and Local Revenue Shares.

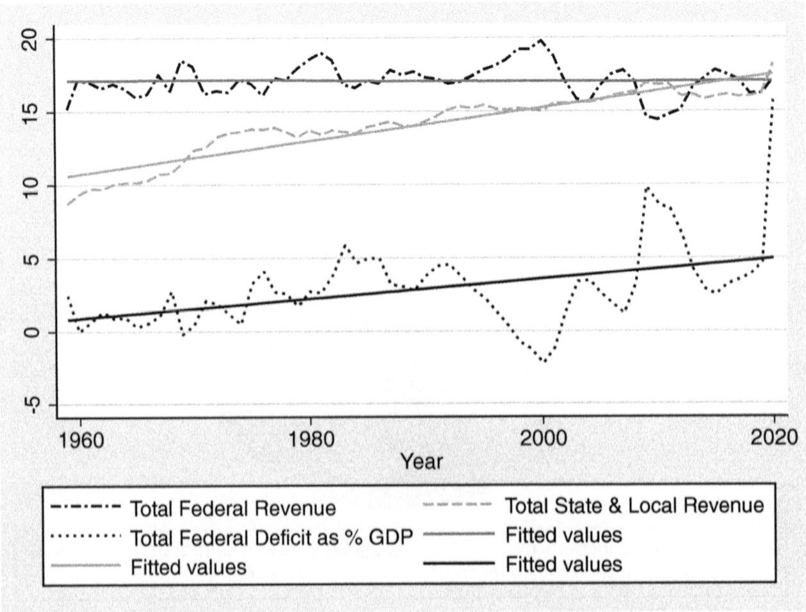

FIGURE 12.3 Federal Taxing, State & Local taxing, and Federal Borrowing, 1959 to 2020.

and businesses are over 70% of levies collected. Business taxes amount to 8% of collections, leaving other taxes at 9%.

Contrast this with state and local revenue shares in Figure 12.2. In green is that of the property tax (not directly analyzed in this volume), accounting for 22% of revenue collected. The tax is mostly a local government collection, although that varies by state; some states collect it on behalf of the local communities and distribute it by formula, while in others it is administered directly by the local community. Rotating counter-clockwise, in burgundy is the sales tax at about 22% of the total collected. In blue are the "Five Bees," the "all other" taxes of licenses, fees, charges, etc. The bright red sliver is the state corporate taxes collected, while in the grey is the personal income taxes levied by state and local governments, contributing about 15% of all revenues, and the gold are the quite sizable federal transfers to state and local governments for highways, education, health, and so on. Federal transfers of monies to support state activities for highways, welfare, health activities, etc. account for 28%. In red at the top of the figure is that of all "other income taxes" at 33%.

But the next most interesting question is how these revenue classes, both federal and state & local, changed over time. The 2024 ERP displays this data from 1959 to 2020. The sixty-year graphic time series of federal revenue sources and fifty-state revenue sources in Tables B-45 and B-50 are revealing.[13] Figure 12.3 displays the time series for all revenues collected by the federal government in the blue line with the associated yellow lowess smoothing line. The overall state and local government taxes/revenues (the middle slope, in red with the brown "lowess" smoothing line); while the green line, at the bottom of the graph, is the year-by-year federal deficit, financed, I assume, by borrowing. I include in the graph for the federal government the "taxes collected" as levies currently assessed on citizens, while the deficit/borrowing are the taxes that, in effect, we and our children and grandchildren will eventually have to finance in the future so as to enjoy our current array of federal government goods and services.

Borrowing is, in effect, a tax on our futures. No such line is necessary in graphs representing states taxing practices because states do not employ long-term borrowing to finance current year-to-year outlays. The line for state and local government taxes collected in Figure 12.3 is a straightforward and sloping upward line, increasing at about one-tenth of 1% per year of this sixty-year time frame. The federal direct taxes line (in blue) is, to all intents and purposes, near-flat to gently sloping downwards over the sixty-year period. The linear regression coefficient for year is a not-significant -.0008 ($t = -0.10$). The coefficient for federal borrowing is much higher at .051 and significant and the graph indicates both the volatility of borrowing over the six decades and its genuine rise as a source of ongoing federal revenue. The conclusion to be drawn from these comparisons and one that confirmed my earlier observations regarding the centrality of state and local spending is that the state and local *tax* line recently surpassed that of the federal government *tax* line (not including borrowing). The direct personal/corporate/other tax costs of current government spending are now roughly balanced between the states and the federal government.

Let's decompose the tax and revenue streams over time. Figure 12.4 sets out the main revenue streams of the federal government as stated in percentages of total GDP and sourced from the 2024 *Economic Report of the President*. The top and blue line, with the associated green smoothing line, displays revenues from the personal income tax from 1959 to 2020. The line appears to be ever-so-slowly growing for the first thirty years and then reaching its peak in the late 1990s, and then with drops occur in collections over the past twenty years, reflecting various legislated tax cuts. There is little in the way of a "trend" in personal income tax collections with a regression coefficient of 0.006 ($t = 1.2$). The federal personal income taxes (a) should gradually rise due to their income progressivity – as personal

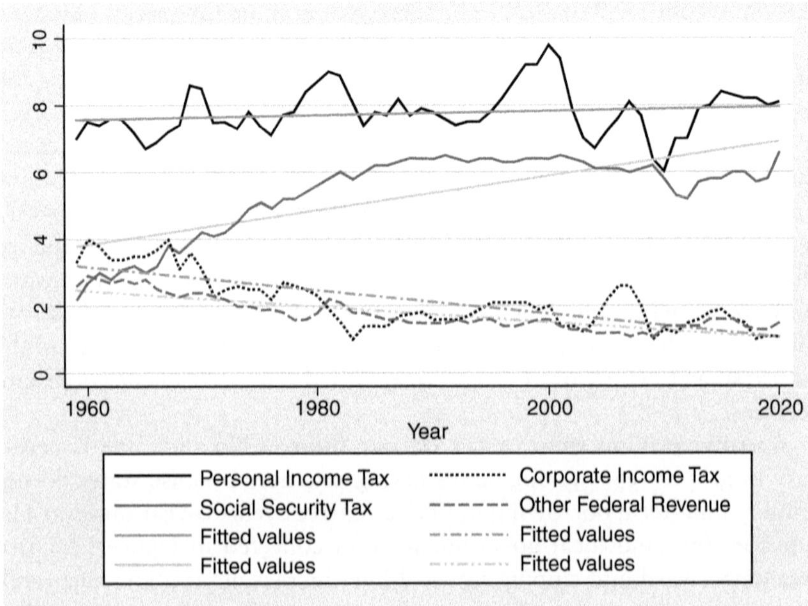

FIGURE 12.4 Federal Tax Components, 1959–2020.

incomes rise, taxpayers move into higher brackets, yielding more revenue; but (b) serial 21st-century tax cuts attempt to restore the tax to its historic (1959–1995) fraction of federal revenue, and finally, (c) the gyrations of the income tax lead to the question of "what is, in fact the *proper proportion* of such a tax to Federal revenues?"; but (d) leaving the definition of what is meant by "proper" on hold. There are two other main sources of direct federal government revenue streams: the corporation income tax and "other" federal taxes, displayed in the two closely arrayed lines in red and brown (with lowess smoothing) with the corporation tax slope coefficients of -.035 (t = 9.6) and "other" taxes, –.024 (t = –13.63). Both corporate income taxes and "other" taxes, in effect, are seriously falling over time.

But what's increasing? The partially income-based OASDI tax that supports the Social Security program has increased at .051 per year (t = 9.1), rising from about 2% of GDP collected in 1959 to a high of 6% in the early 2000s.[14] It is the case that all of these revenue streams are increasing in actual size; what Figure 12.4 sets out is which of these streams are increasing or decreasing relative to the sizes of the nation's Gross Domestic Product. In this case ... borrowing and Social Security collections are the fastest growing, while the corporation income tax is shrinking in size relative to the others.

Figure 12.5 sets out the same information for state and local spending. The Economic Report of the President outlines six main sources of state and local revenues; one source is shrinking as a percent of national GDP, relatively, while four are increasing and one is stable: Only the property tax assessed by state and local governments is shrinking relative to GDP (b = –007; t = –4.3). This reflects, I suspect, an off-loading of support for local schools and other local government programs to the state at large via statewide taxation. Sizeable increases occur in federal intergovernmental transfers to states and localities (b = .038; t = 15); "other" sources of revenues (b = .045; t = 18); the personal income tax (b = .026; t = 18); and the sales tax (b = .012; t = 8.5). The flat and low level of the fifty-state collection of the corporation income tax at a level and small in proportion makes sense; the regression estimate over time yields a coefficient of .0004 with a t = .0006. Corporation-collected taxes are essentially flatlined at a low rate.

In the states, corporations are small in number, well-organized, and able to defend, if not "definance," their present low level of tax assessment. But in the forty-five states with a sales tax, the state levies range from 4% to 7.25% per transaction, with Colorado at 3%, but with added local levies in that state, the effective rate could be as high as 8%. The sales tax collections as a percent of GDP appear to have, again, "flat-lined" recently, indicating perhaps a ceiling effect has appeared. I suspect that there is an

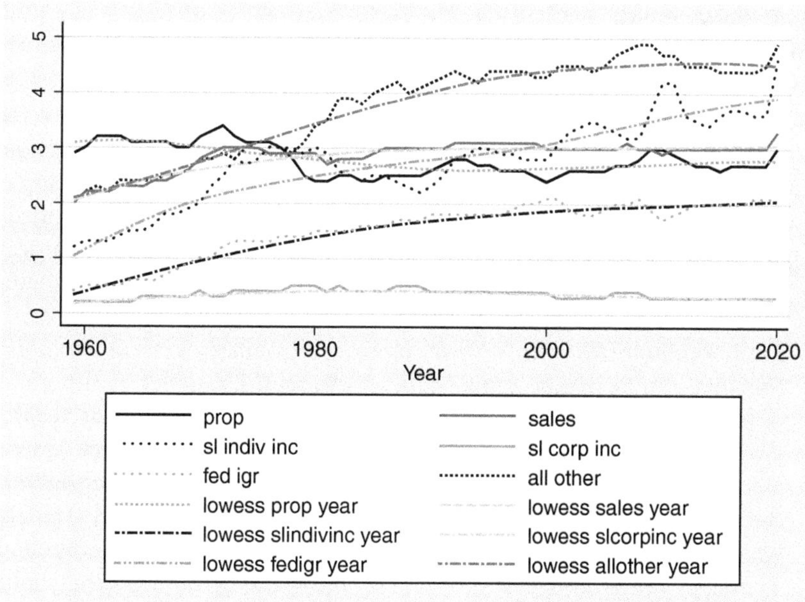

FIGURE 12.5 State and Local Tax and Revenue Components, 1959–2020.

equilibrating action at work here that makes it increasingly difficult for states to further increase their sales tax rates. The voting evidence presented in Chapter 9 is weakly supportive of a "levelling out process" at work. The *sales tax rate* is also a quite visible and manifest change in a tax; better to tinker at the margins of this tax – a "scope" tax issue – or go with changes in some other, less visible tax? However, "scope" changes are likely marginal, at best; changes in rates yield greater returns. Over the 1959 to 1980 period, the state and local combined property tax collections declined and further declined from 1980 to 2020 at a very modest rate. The personal income tax originating in the graph at 1959 at .5% relative to GDP rose to 2% by 2020. "Other" taxes comprise a sizeable fraction of state revenues at all time periods, ranging from 2% of GDP in 1950 to 5% in 2020. The revenue nexus that appears to be consistently rising source is help from the federal government. Its low point was 1959 at about 1.1% of state revenues as a percent of GDP, and it rose to 2020 to where it is 4% of such revenues.

As Lenin put it, "What is to be done?"

From my academic perspective as well as from that of the governor, floor legislator, and the appropriation and finance legislative committee member, what are the *values* that they would seek to satisfy in revenue-setting practices? Put differently, politicians in the states face an array of revenue change possibilities. What are the considerations that must enter their minds in pondering "what is to be done?"

1 *How much is needed: Chapter 4 demonstrates that* "need" *in the sense of a forecasted, oncoming budget deficit* shapes taxing recommendations and actions. The intermediate- to long-term ban on deficit financing in the 49 states (plus Vermont) constrains taxing to short- to intermediate-term actions. To paraphrase: Nothing better clears the gubernatorial and legislative minds of the threat of an imminent electoral hanging than the threat of a looming deficit.
2 *Ease of administration: Is it easy or more difficult for the state to apply this tax? Easy changes trump difficult changes.* Examples at either end of the distribution would be most states' personal income tax as "easy," since the forms typically are based on an individual's personal federal income tax and, thus, easy to calculate. Further, many states "withhold" the estimated amount owed from the individuals' wages and typically overestimate, thereby generating a payment "return" to the individual. The sales tax is also easily collected, resting as it does on the shoulders of sellers and vendors to collect and remit to the state. Nevertheless, what the bulk of chapters in this volume has demonstrated is that

increasing either the income or sales tax is a difficult task. Voters appear to be sensitive to changes in the sales tax, while it is clear that governors and legislators in the Republican Party strongly favor lowering these taxes, especially the income tax. The property tax (not analyzed in this volume) rests at the opposite, difficult end; it requires continual monitoring and assessment of sales and pricing data and hired professional appraisers to estimate the "value" of the rarely sold property and then apply the current tax rate and send out the (typically) semi-annual property tax bills.

3 *Lumpiness*: *Does the tax collected* "smoothly" *arrive in the state's coffers or does it arrive as a single or few payments?* Toward the smooth end of lumpiness in taxes would be the sales and income taxes. Even more smooth would be the many excise taxes that I, personally, have been assessed ... cigarettes (back when I smoked) and liquor taxes. The lumpiest taxation that I have experienced are, again, the property tax payments. In New Hampshire, the payment was semi-annual, and the assessment and bill arrived printed on paper of what appeared to be a near cousin of a Kleenex. In Massachusetts, it is a semi-annual payment, again printed on the flimsiest paper available. Smoothness is desirable, as adjustments to the taxation can be more easily made and surplus revenues across time can be reinvested to obtain marginally more state resources. My sense is that lumpy taxes such as the state, local, and school property taxes complicate governing, especially so at the local level.

4 *Tax numbers and revenue diversity: The federal revenue streams are few in number, while the state and local streams are larger in number.* The federal government relies typically on the personal and corporate tax bases for revenue income. The personal income tax accounts for 49% of federal taxes; corporate and business taxes, 9.4%; the personal and business social security contributions, 36.4%; and other taxes, 5.2%. State and local taxes are comprised the percent of total revenue for the personal income tax at 13.4%; the general sales tax, 16.9%; the property tax, 15.5%; corporate income taxes, 2.4%; and other taxes, 24.3%.[15] The ability of the federal government to deficit spend over the past several decades has allowed the president and Congress to basically whittle away at the tax base. The (partial) title of Graetz and Shapiro's book on the estate tax captures the widespread Washington, D.C. practice: *Death by a Thousand Cuts: The Fight over Taxing* ... captures one series of presidential and legislative attacks on federal taxing. The net effect is a slapdash application of deficit financing: levies assessed on future generations to solve our current national taxing deficit. The states are not allowed such a freedom of (mal)action. They resolve their

spending and taxing either annually or biennially. Multiple revenue streams employed by the states are a rational effort to both smooth the flows of monies into the state treasuries and also to diversify their revenue bases in such a way as to allow negative changes in one stream to be possibly offset by increases in another.

5 *Deservingness:* If voters are sensitive to changes in the burdens of financing government, then electorally attuned politicians need to devise compelling rationales for enacting tax increases. We ordinarily consider the notion of "deservingness" as associated with benefits or indulgences – veterans deserve governmental benefits given their national service; indigents deserve medical care for reasons of public charity, collective care and assistance, and so on. But the political act of raising taxes always entails public rationales of why these changes are the least bad, most defensible, and, seemingly by agreement, the most deserving of burdening. "Use" taxes or levies are the easiest to politically defend. If the state's highway department engineers persuasively convince officials of the need for more funds to repair the state's slowly degrading roadways, then politicians can defend the increased appropriations funded by increased gasoline and diesel taxes by pointing to expected new road and bridge projects. Or, if more and more electric vehicles are purchased in a state, then consider a "use tax" assessed on miles driven per annum*X (weight of vehicle), where X stands for some function increasing with increasing weight. Two easy hypotheses: (1) a separate calculation will be assessed on diesel fuel because more diesel is purchased by trucking companies that are already organized and ready to weigh in on the burdens of the increased taxation. (2) Automobile owners are unorganized, and the changes assessed against the family auto will be proportionally more burdensome than those assessed against the already organized and prepared economic interests, e.g. trucking companies.

6 *Two-faced obligations:* Fees assessed by the state, in principle, defray the cost of a reasonable governmental function that benefits both specific beneficiaries and the commonwealth (putatively) of all. Of such activities undertaken by the state, a frequently encountered and most difficult to defend is that of "occupational licensing." In one study of licensing for 102 low- to moderate-income occupations, the fifty states totaled 2749 licenses. Louisiana licensed 77 of the 102 occupations surveyed.[16] The logic in use for licensing barbers, morticians, doctors, lawyers, etc. is ensuring adequate levels of public health or safety. In principle, licensing supposedly ensures that your barber, your doctors, and your lawyer are not quacks or charlatans. However, licensing, certification, and registration entail out-of-pocket costs for the state for continual testing

for new entrants and assessments of practice for established licensees. The obvious downside of such licensing practices in the states is that the obscure boards overseeing such licensing will soon be dominated by members of the profession. What better source of campaign contributions could there be for a governor than appointing licensed members to oversee entry into their own profession? More to the point, licensing controls entry; easing entry entails more competitors, and more competitors lead to lower incomes for practitioners; ergo, appoint practitioners to the board that can deliberately shape and control the number of their fellow professionals, thereby enhancing general professional incomes.[17]

7 *Tax incidence: Governors and legislators must consider who is deserving of depriving as well as those they incline to indulge.* Louisiana Senator Russell Long is famous for observing in a meeting of the Senate Finance Committee that the individual citizen's view of the tax system is "don't tax me, don't tax you, tax that fellow behind the tree." (1) We all understand the "don't tax me" phrase; our rational preference is that someone else should be taxed for collective goods, or, even in the best of all worlds, that others be taxed for particular goods that government provides that selectively indulge "me." (2) "Also, don't tax my friend, here," my good friend should also be indulged with few burdens of financing the state. (3) The ordinary taxpayer considers the "guy behind the tree" as the unseen, unknown, vague set of individuals that can be unwittingly deprived in order to indulge "self" ... the ideal governed world of low personal tax incidences with many highly-valued, government-supplied benefits.

8 *Taxing wealth:* One of the central distinctions in this volume in between the redistributive, consumption, and user/fees/charges taxation. The issue of tax progressivity rests right at the line between redistributive and consumptive taxation. A recent authoritative paper sets out the current findings regarding progressivity in the nation and across the American states:

> First, the tax and transfer system is progressive at the federal level. Second, state and local tax and transfer systems are close to proportional, on average. Third, there is substantial heterogeneity in tax progressivity across U.S. states. Fourth, the proximate cause of this variation is the choice of tax base: states relying on sales, excise, and property taxes tend to have regressive tax systems, whereas states relying on income taxes tend to have progressive systems... . Seventh, households at all income levels who migrate from one state to another appear to be drawn to states with less progressive tax and transfer systems. But lower progressivity appears to be an especially powerful draw for very high-income movers.[18]

Why the focus on "progressive" vs. "regressive" taxes? Stasavage and Scheve (2016) outline the standard "progressivism" arguments, which appear convincing to me. The most commonly heard argument, albeit a contestable one, is centered on the *diminishing marginal value of rising personal income*. The rich will feel less pain from higher and/or increasing marginal tax rates as compared to those with lesser incomes; thus, tax the rich. On the other hand, contestants will argue that the rich in most cases have *earned* their higher incomes, and thus, the heavier burden on them for financing goods that collectively indulge all are unfair. Still, not all of the wealthy have, in fact, *earned* their wealth; there are the wealthy who inherited their wealth through no effort of their own; the outsized wealth that accrues from being a "unicorn" in an activity, e.g. Shohei Otani's ten-year baseball contract for 700 million dollars; and the windfall lucky, e.g., lottery winners. Second, there is an argument that progressive taxation is, in part, one of *compensatory assessment*. The poor, the less wealthy, will more often, for example, bear the burden of defending the country. Armed Forces conscription (when it occurs) as well as volunteerism more often engage the poor. Thus the defense economy of war and peace rests on the shoulders of the less well-off. The rich can compensate by bearing the heavier burden of a progressive tax. Stasavage and Scheve also note that there is a *moral obligation that comes from society's contributions to self* ... a "woke" argument! Many of us have enormously benefitted from public institutions. Your author was educated at an Illinois state university, a Hawaiian state university, and at graduate school at a private university, where he was well-funded by grants from various federal agencies and programs. He was vaulted, partly out of sheer luck, into a fine college teaching job. Hey, Dick Winters, maybe, it's payback time!

There appear to me to be two faces of heightened state-by-state reliance on the progressive elements of an income tax. First, it appears convincing to me. Those of us who are well-off have prospered in a system of laws, rules, norms, and practices that enabled us to succeed. Our success was, in part, due to our talents, skills, intelligence, diligence, and fortitude, but it was also due to the system that we are so embedded in that we were able to prosper. Was the balance "personal" or "systemic?" I do not know the right quantity of "balance," but I do know that my – and our – governments allowed me, enabled me, to succeed. I owe it.

Therefore, what should our states' politicians do?

One linkage between taxing practices and our normative beliefs about what ought to be done is provided by analyses such as that advanced by Anthony Downs. He led the way in considering some of the empirics of evaluating taxing and spending. While his most frequently cited book is *An Economic Theory of Democracy*, published in 1957, but not so widely cited but still most impressive to this day is his 1960 article on "Why the Government Budget Is Too Small in a Democracy." Downs argues that the taxes collected for the "correct" budget would be the ones that would be adopted if voters and leaders were *perfectly informed* about the costs and benefits of government taxing and expenditures. His analysis more generally focuses on the perfect knowledge of benefits and spending, but the argument also extends to voters and leaders perfect knowledge of the costs of programs and the incidence of the taxes assessed. However, rather than a *theory of perfect information*, or even that of *imperfect information*, we exist, per Downs, in a state of *preponderant ignorance*, where the knowledge of benefits extends only to those benefits that accrue directly to the voter, while she is more aware of the costs of all programs that fall on her via taxation. As a consequence, Downs elegantly concludes ...:

> there is ... a third state of information: preponderant ignorance. In this state, citizens are ignorant of both the items in the budget and their benefits and costs. The budget that results when such ignorance predominates differs radically from those discussed previously: it tends to be larger than the correct size because of voters' ignorance of what items are in the budget.
>
> *(1960, p. 556)*

And, "In this state, citizens' perception thresholds are so high that they are aware of only the individual policies or items in the budget that vitally affect them" (p. 545). However, because voters' incomes generally come from a single or few sources, they are more acutely aware of the tax costs that governments impose on them, especially those that directly affect their incomes, such as the direct personal income tax:

> Therefore, every citizen believes that the actual government budget is too large in relation to the benefits he himself is deriving from it. Even if he feels the optimum budget would be much larger than the actual one, he believes the actual one could be profitably reduced 'through greater economy' i.e., elimination of projects from which he does not benefit.
>
> *(p. 550)*

Is it that in any political system such as ours in the states with elected first-past-the-post, geographically based constituencies in majoritarian legislative chambers and in a representative democracy, log-rolled, omnibus spending packages that indulge most of us are inevitable? And, that the opposite is true of taxation: That no majority agreement can be reached to *increase taxes*, except for an added package of *varied tax decreases* that support particular activities that, in turn, help finance re-election campaigns for the tax-increasing legislator-voters. The evidence in earlier chapters that indicated many more "tax decreases" in the company of "much more taxation in dollars levied" is consistent with this behavior. Get needed tax increases with companion, more nominal, but targeted tax decreases where targeted decreases more often than not are "selective interests" that may assist in campaign finance.

The rising, then declining, and maybe rising once again federal income tax level is an interesting case of – at the taxing level – of this political "approach/avoidance behavior." The income tax is so fecund that it yields welcome returns to those invested with a larger "state," but it is equally the target of those with an interest in "starving the state." Republican politicians in the nation and state have focused on this tax for precisely this reason. It funds *government* and is *disliked by voters*. Reliance on the income tax is less true at state level with its myriad of taxes, but relying on diverse tax bases is a rational basis for taxing in the face of constraints on deficit financing.

Next steps

Much of the research reported in this volume covers a number of years of longitudinal analysis, but a useful step forward would be to *update the data*. A sufficient number of years of NASBO data now exists to generate analyses that span a greater number of years to test for stability in estimates of, for example, the impact of party control on taxing. My expectation would be heightened partisan differences across time under the condition of unified control and no change in the partisan effects under any condition of divided control. My expectation is that the effect of the Trump administration I is a greater focus on tax-cutting. Trump II may simply further heighten partisan differences under unified control conditions.

The NASBO group also publishes every five years a manual on *Budgetary Processes in the States* (BPS), which details *gubernatorial and legislative practices* in establishing spending and taxing actions. Political scientists should better model and understand the consequences of differing institutional constraints and facilitations on taxing and spending actions. The data published in BPS is both comprehensive and detailed and longitudinal. What we don't have a good "fix" on is which of the practices appear to relate to either gubernatorial actions or legislative determinations. Furthermore, as the publication is reissued every five years after a detailed review of current practices in the fifty states, analysts can assess some of the consequences of changing legislative organization of the budgetary process on changing taxing and spending.

A final note on next steps: NASBO's data, assessed in this volume via the *Fiscal Survey of the States*, details gubernatorial tax actions and final resolution by the governor and legislature. The semi-annual issues also contain an equivalent survey of *expenditure recommendations of governors and final legislative action*. The parallel detailed data sets – taxing and spending – lead to the obvious questions of what in taxing relates to what in spending, both in gubernatorial requests and final determinations. What requests/actions are associated with income tax decreases, and what with income tax increases? And, does the NASBO spending data also seem to agglomerate into discrete spending factors? Is there a redistributional set of spendings? Is there even something that could be generally labeled as consumption-oriented spending preferences and actions? Is there a high-demand/high-spending partisan factor in spending? And finally, what kind of budgetary REV/SPND, "swapping" behavior occurs? Are some kinds of tax increases associated with a coherent set of spending increases and vice versa? Or, is there little predictable "swapping"; rather, tax increases are related to a variety of spending agendas. It just may be that there is little in the way of predicting taxing changes given spending changes. I don't believe that that is the case, but I leave this and the many more questions posed by the NASBO data for others.

Notes

1 While typically attributed to Berra, other claims as to its origin exists. Most claims originate, oddly enough, in Denmark.

2 Two 20th-century political philosophers pose Chapter 12 arguments: In 1971, Marvin Gaye asks, "What's going on?" and in 1901, Vladimir Lenin asks, "What is to be done?"

3 https://taxfoundation.org/data/all/state/when-did-your-state-adopt-its-sales-tax/.

4 https://taxfoundation.org/data/all/state/2024-sales-taxes/.

5 And, as I note in an addendum to Chapter 2, a failure to exclude food and medicine from a proposed sales tax can prove fatal to the effort.

6 This is not quite true according to the analysis in Chapter 3. Both "motor fuel" and "cigarette and tobacco" taxes loaded on the "consumption" factor, one in the factor analysis of the gubernatorial recommendations and the other on the final legislative passage factor.

7 As in Kaplan (1964).

8 This is and will be even more so diminishing as technology allows states to impose a direct tax on users. Tolled highways are a present example of direct user fees, and a soon-to-be technological innovation such as a non-tamperable automobile mileage indicator will allow the states to tax the heavy highway users more than those who rarely drive.

9 Jennifer Karas Montez et al., "US State Policies, Politics, and Life Expectancy," *The Milbank Quarterly*, Vol. 98, No. 3 (2020), pp. 668–699.

10 This analysis draws heavily on the article, "Dying Early ..." written by Lauren Weber, Dan Diamond, and Dan Keating and appearing in the October 3, 2023, edition of *The Washington Post.*

11 Ecclesiastes 3:1.

12 The most recent data year recorded for state and local spending in the 2024 *Economic Report of the President* was 2020, thus accounting for the year analyzed for both state/local and federal taxing.

13 All data for the following longitudinal graphs have been extracted from the statistical appendices to the 2024 *Economic Report of the President,* Tables B45 and B50, accessed here: https://www.govinfo.gov/app/collection/erp/2024.

14 The "individual income base" of the Social Security tax is levied at 6.2% on the individual and maxes out at the individual income of $168,600 and is zero thereafter.

15 Revenue and tax figures are drawn from the *Economic Report of the President, 2024* accessed here: https://www.govinfo.gov/app/collection/erp/2024 and drawn from Tables B-47 and B-50.

16 See https://ij.org/report/license-to-work-3/, assessed January 28, 2024.

17 In an unpublished paper, I and two of my students collected data on variations in licensing requirements for each of the fifty states for barbers, morticians, and a few other occupations and data on occupational mean incomes using Census Bureau data. We discovered, much to our surprise, that more and heightened licensing requirements did not result in fewer practitioners as the per cent of the states' populations nor greater occupational income. Both the numbers of discrete occupational practitioners by state and the average occupational income have not been collected since by the Census Bureau.

18 From "Fiscal progressivity of the U.S. federal and state governments," by Johannes Fleck, Jonathan Heathcote, Kjetil Storesletten, and Giovanni L. Violante in Working Paper 33385 at http://www.nber.org/papers/w33385.

BIBLIOGRAPHY

Abrams, Burton A. and Mark D. Schmitz. 1978. "The 'Crowding-Out' Effect of Governmental Transfers on Private Charitable Contributions." *Public Choice* 33(1): 29–39.

Ades, Alberto and R. Di Tella. 1999. "Rents, Competition, and Corruption." *American Economic Review* 89: 982–993.

Adsera, Alicia, Carlos Boix and Mark Payne. 2003. "Are You Being Served? Political Accountability and Quality of Government." *Journal of Law and Economics* 19(2): 445–490.

Advisory Commission on Intergovernmental Relations (ACIR). 1985–1986, 1989, 1990, 1991, and 1995 issues. *Significant Features of Fiscal Federalism*. Washington, DC.

Advisory Commission on Intergovernmental Relations. 1993. *State Revenue Capacity and Effort, Information Report M-187*. Washington, DC.

Alesina, Alberto and Eliana La Ferrara. 2005. "Preferences for Redistribution in the Land of Opportunities." *Journal of Public Economics* 89(5–6): 897–931.

Alesina, Alberto and George-Marios Angeletos. 2004. *Corruption, Inequality, and Fairness*. ms. Department of Economics, Harvard University and NBER: Cambridge, MA.

Alesina, Alberto and Nouriel Roubini with Gerald D. Cohen 1997. *Political Cycles and the Macroeconomy*. Cambridge: The MIT Press.

Alspach, Steven E. and George F. Bishop. 1991. "Question-Order Effects of Presidential Approval Ratings on Gubernatorial Approval Ratings: A Research Note." *Social Forces* 69(4): 1241–1248.

Alt, James and Robert C. Lowry. 1994. "Divided Government, Fiscal Institutions, and Budget Deficits: Evidence from the States." *American Political Science Review* 88(4): 811–828.

Alt, James and Robert C. Lowry. 2000. "A Dynamic Model of State Budget Outcomes under Divided Partisan Government." *The Journal of Politics* 62(4): 1035–1069.

Alt, James and Robert C. Lowry. 2003. "Party Differences in State Budget Outcomes...." *The Journal of Politics* 65(2): 491–497.

Alt, James E. and David Dreyer Lassen. 2002. "The Political Economy of Institutions and Corruption in American States." *Journal of Theoretical Politics* 15(3): 341–365.

Alt, James E., David Dreyer Lassen, and David Skilling. 2002. "Fiscal Transparency, Gubernatorial Approval, and the Scale of Government..." *State Politics and Policy* 2(3): 230–250.

American Association of Fund-Raising Counsel. *Giving USA*. ed. by Anne Kaplan. AAFRC Trust for Philanthropy. editions 1967–1997.

American Political Science Association. Committee on Political Parties. 1950. *Toward a More Responsible Two-Party System: A Report...* New York: Rinehart.

Andreoni, James. 1988. "Privately Provided Public Goods in a Large Economy: The Limits of Altruism." *Journal of Public Economics* 31(5): 57–73.

Andreoni, James. 1989. "Giving with Impure Altruism: Applications to Charity and Ricardian Equivalence." *Journal of Political Economy* 97(6): 1447–1458.

Andreoni, James. 2006. "Philanthropy." in Serge-Christophe Kolm and J. Mercier Ythier, eds., *Handbook of Giving, Reciprocity and Altruism*, Amsterdam: North Holland, pp. 1201–1269.

Andreoni, James. 2007. "Charitable Giving" in Durlauf, Steven N. and Lawrence Blume, eds., *The New Palgrave Dictionary of Economics*, 2nd Edition.

Anton, Thomas. 1966. *The Politics of State Expenditure in Illinois*. Urbana: University of Illinois Press.

Arthur F. Bentley. 1908. *The process of government; a study of social pressures*. Chicago, IL: The University of Chicago press.

Atkeson, Lonnie Rae and Randall W. Partin. 1995. "Economic and Referendum Voting: A Comparison of Gubernatorial and Senatorial Elections." *American Political Science Review* 89(1): 99–107.

Bachrach, Peter and Morton S. Baratz. 1962. "Two Faces of Power." *American Political Science Review* 56(4): 947–952.

Barone, Michael, Ujifusa, Grant and Matthews, Douglas. 1976. *The Almanac of American Politics*. New York: Dutton, 1975.

Barrilleaux, Charles, Thomas Holbrook and Laura Langer. 2002. "Electoral Competition, Legislative Balance, and American State Welfare Policy." *American Journal of Political Science* 46(2): 415–427.

Barrilleaux, Charles and Ethan Bernick. 2003. "Deservingness, Discretion, and the State Politics of Welfare Spending, 1990–1996." *State Politics and Policy Quarterly* 3(1): 1–22.

Barrilleaux, Charles and Michael Berkman. 2003. "Do Governors Matter? Budgeting Rules and the Politics of State Policymaking." *Political Research Quarterly* 56(4): 409–417.

Barro, Stephen M. 1986. "State Fiscal Capacity Measures: A Theoretical Critique." in H. Clyde Reeves, ed., *Measuring Fiscal Capacity*, pp. 51–86. Boston, MA: Oelgeschlager, Gunn and Hain.

Baumann, Zachary D., Michael J. Nelson and Markus Neumann. 2021. "Party Competition and Policy Liberalism." *State Politics & Policy Quarterly* 21(3): 266–285.

Baumol, William J. and William G. Bowen. 1965. "On the Performing Arts: The Anatomy of their Economic Problems." *The American Economic Review* 55(1–2): 495–502.

Becker, Gary. 1968. "Crime and Punishment: An Economic Approach." *The Journal of Political Economy* 76(2): 169–217.

Berch, N. 1995. "Explaining Changes in Tax Incidence...." *Political Research Quarterly* 48(3): 629–641.

Berry, Frances Stokes and William D. Berry. 1992. "Tax Innovation in the States: Capitalizing on Political Opportunity." *American Journal of Political Science* 36(3): 715–742.

Berry, Frances Stokes and William D. Berry. 1994. "The Politics of Tax Increases in the States." *American Journal of Political Science* 38(3): 855–859.

Berry, William D. and David Lowery. 1987. *Understanding United States Government Growth: An Empirical Analysis of the Postwar Era.* New York: Praeger.

Berry, William D., Evan J. Ringquist, Richard C. Fording and Russell L. Hanson. 1998 "Measuring Citizen and Government Ideology in the American States, 1960–93." *American Journal of Political Science* 42(1): 327–348.

Berry, William, Richard C. Fording and Russell L. Hanson. 1960–2003. Cost of Living Index for the American States. ICPSR Study No.: 1275.

Berry, William D., Richard Fording and Russell Hanson. 1996. "Measuring the Cost of Living in the American States, 1960–1990," a paper presented at the 1996 annual meeting of the American Political Science Association, San Francisco, CA.

Berry, William D., Richard Fording and Russell Hanson. 2003. "Reassessing the 'Race to the Bottom' in State Welfare Policy." *The Journal of Politics* 65(2): 327–349.

Besley, Timothy and Anne Case. 1995a. "Does Electoral Accountability Affect Economic Policy Choices? Evidence from Gubernatorial Term Limits." *Quarterly Journal of Economics* 110(3): 769–798.

Besley, Timothy and Anne Case. 1995b. "Incumbent Behavior: Vote Seeking, Tax Setting and Yardstick Competition." *American Economic Review* 85(1): 25–45.

Besley, Timothy and Anne Case. 2003. "Political Institutions and Policy Choices: Evidence from the United States." *Journal of Economic Literature* 41(1): 7–73.

Beyle, Thad. 1983. "Governors." in Virginia Gray, Herbert Jacob and Kenneth N. Vines, eds., *Politics in the American States*, Boston, MA: Little, Brown, pp. 180–221.

Beyle, Thad, ed. 1992a. *Governors and Hard Times.* Washington, DC: Congressional Quarterly.

Beyle, Thad. 1992b. "Term Limits in the State Legislative Branch." in Gerald Benjamin and Michael Malbin, eds., *Limiting Legislative Terms.* Washington, DC: CQ Press, pp. 159–179.

Beyle, Thad, ed. 1994. "The Governors—1992–1993." Robert A. Silvanik. ed. *The Book of the States*, 1994–95. Lexington, KY: Council of State Governments.

Beyle, Thad and Rich Jones 1994. "Term Limits in States." *The Book of the States*, 1994–95. Lexington, KY: Council of State Governments.

Biau, Gerard, Luc Devroye and Gabor Lugosi. 2008. "Consistency of Random Forests and Other Averaging Classifiers." *Journal of Machine Learning Research* 9: 2015–2033.

Bicker, William. 1971. "The Effects of Malapportionment in the States-A Mistrial." in Nelson Polsby, ed., *Reapportionment in the 1970's*, Berkeley: University of California Press, pp. 151–200.

Birnbaum, Jeffrey and Alan Murray. 1987. *Showdown at Gucci Gulch*. New York: Random House.

Black, Chris. 1990. "The Sales Tax Revisited: Lessons from 1965." *Boston Globe*, Sunday, July 29, 1990.

Bloom, Howard S. and H. Douglas Price. 1975. "Voter Response to Short-Run Economic Conditions: The Asymmetric Effect of Prosperity and Recession." *American Political Science Review* 69(4): 1240–1254.

Boehmke, Frederick J. and Paul Skinner. 2012. "State Policy Innovativeness Revisited." *State Politics and Policy Quarterly* 12(3): 304–330.

Book of the States. Lexington, KY. Council of State Governments, various biennial volumes.

Books, John W. and Charles L. Prysby. 1992. *Political Behavior and the Local Context*. New York: Praeger.

Booms, Bernard H. and James R. Halldorson. 1973. "The Politics of Redistribution: A Reformulation." *The American Political Science Review* 67(3): 924–933.

Boylan, Richard T. and Cheryl X. Long. 2003. "Measuring Public Corruption in the American States: A Survey of State House Reporters." *State Politics and Policy Quarterly* 3(4): 420–438.

Brace, Paul, et al. 2004. "Does State Political Ideology Change over Time?" *Political Research Quarterly*. 57(4) 529–540.

Brace, Paul. 1993. *State Government and Economic Performance*. Baltimore, MD: The Johns Hopkins University Press.

Brace, Paul and Aubrey Jewett. 1995. "The State of State Politics Research." *Political Research Quarterly* 48(3): 643–681.

Brace, Paul and Melinda Gann Hall. 1995. "Studying Courts Comparatively: The View from the American States." *Political Research Quarterly* 48(1): 5–29.

Breiman, Leo. 2001. "Random Forests." *Machine Learning* 45(1): 5–32.

Brennan, Geoffrey and James M. Buchanan. 1980. *The Power to Tax: Analytical Foundation of Fiscal Constitution*. New York: Cambridge University Press.

David Brunori, ed. 1998. "State Personal Income Taxation in the Twenty-First Century." in David Brunori, ed., *The Future of State Taxation*, Washington, DC: The Urban Institute Press.

Bryan, Frank. 1974. *Yankee Politics in Rural Vermont*. Hanover, NH: University Press of New England.

Bryan, Frank. 2004. *Real Democracy*. Chicago, IL: University of Chicago Press.

Buchanan, James and Richard Wagner. 1977. *Democracy in Deficit: The Political Legacy of Lord Keynes*. New York: Academic Press.

Bureau of the Census, U.S. Department of Commerce. 1989. "Current Population Survey, Multiple Job Holdings, Flextime and Volunteer Work," Bureau of the Census, ICPSR Study #9472.

Campbell, Angus, Philip Converse, Warren Miller and Donald Stokes. 1960. *The American Voter*. New York: John Wiley and Sons.

Campbell, Colin and Rosemary. 1976. *A Comparative Study of the Fiscal Systems of New Hampshire and Vermont, 1940–1974*. Monograph from Hampton, NH: Wheelabrator Foundation, Inc.

Campbell, Donald and Donald W. Fiske. 1959 "Convergent and Discriminant Validation by the Multi-Trait-Multimethod Matrix." *Psychological Bulletin* 56(2): 81–105.

Campbell, Donald and Julian C. Stanley. 1963. *Experimental and Quasi-Experimental Designs for Research*. Chicago, IL: Rand-McNally.

Carsey, Thomas M. 2000. *Campaign Dynamics: The Race for Governor*. Ann Arbor: University of Michigan Press.

Carsey, Thomas M. and Barry Rundquist. 1999. "Party and Committee in Distributive Politics: Evidence from Defense Spending." *Journal of Politics* 61(4): 1156–1169.

Carsey, Thomas M. and George C. Wright. 1998b. "State & National Factors in Gubernatorial & Senatorial Elections: A Rejoinder." *American Journal of Political Science* 42(3): 1008–1011.

Case, Anne. 1994. "Taxes and the Electoral Cycle: How Sensitive Are Governors to Coming Elections." *Business Review*. Federal Reserve Bank of Philadelphia, pp. 17–26.

Cash, Kevin. 1975. *Who the Hell Is William Loeb*? Hooksett, NH: Amoskeag Press.

Caughey, Devin and Christopher Warshaw. 2018. "Policy Preferences and Policy Change." *The American Political Science Review*. 112(2): 249–266.

Caughey, Devin, Christopher Warshaw and Yiqing Xu. 2017. "Incremental Democracy: The Policy Effects of Partisan Control of State Government." *Journal of Politics* 79(4): 1342–1358.

Chubb, John. 1985. "The Political Economy of Federalism." *American Political Science Review* 79(4): 994–1015.

Chubb, John E. 1988. "Institutions, The Economy, and The Dynamics of State Elections." *American Political Science Review* 82(1): 133–154.

Clynch, Edward J. and Thomas P. Lauth, eds. 1991. *Governors, Legislatures, and Budgets: Diversity across the American States*. Westport, CT: Greenwood Press.

Cnudde, Charles and Donald McCrone. 1969. "Party Competition and Welfare Policies in the American States." *American Political Science Review* 63(3): 858–866.

Cohen, Jeffrey. 2006. *Public Opinion in State Politics*. New York: Oxford University Press.

Compendium of State Government Finances. 1964, 1974. Washington, DC: Department of Commerce.

Cook, Thomas D. and Donald T. Campbell. 1979. *Quasi-Experimentation: Design and Analysis Issues for Field Settings*. Chicago, IL: Rand McNally College Publishing Co.

Cowart, Andrew T. 1973. "Electoral Choice in the American States: Incumbency Effects, Partisan Forces, and Divergent Partisan Majorities." *American Political Science Review* 67(3): 835-

David B. Truman. 1951. *The Governmental Process: Political Interests and Public Opinion*. New York: Knopf.

Davies, David G. 1986. *United States Taxes and Tax Policy*. New York: Cambridge University Press.

Dawson, Richard E. and James A. Robinson. 1963. "Inter-Party Competition, Economic Variables, and Welfare Policies in the American States." *Journal of Politics* 25(2): 265–289.

Delano, Sophia and Richard F. Winters. 2002. *Men/Women Voting for/against Men/Women Candidates for Elective Office*. Chicago, IL: Midwest Political Science Association.

DeLeon, Richard E. 1973. "Politics, Economic Surplus and Redistribution in the American States: A Test of a Theory." *American Journal of Political Science* 17(4): 781–796.

Dennis, Christopher, William S. Moore and Tracey Somerville. 2007. "The Impact of Political Parties on the Distribution of State and Local Tax Burdens." *Social Science Journal* 44(2): 339–347.

Derthick, Martha. 1970. *The Influence of Federal Grants*. Cambridge, MA: Harvard University Press.

Derthick, Martha. 1975. *Uncontrollable Spending for Social Services Grants*. Washington, DC: Brookings Institution.

Dilger, Robert Jay. 1998. "Does Politics Matter? Partisanship's Impact on State Spending and Taxes, 1985–95." *State & Local Government Review* 30(2): 139–144.

Dincer, Oguzhan and Michael Johnson. 2016. "Political Culture and Corruption Issues in State Politics: A New Measure and a Test of Relationships to Political Culture." Publius: The Journal of Federalism 47(1): 131–148.

Dixon, Robert. 1968. *Democratic Representation*. New York: Oxford University Press.

Dominguez, Nicholas and Richard Winters. 2001. "Revisiting, ... One More Time, the Effects of a Divisive Primary on General Election Outcomes," a paper prepared for the Midwestern Political Science Association, April 15–17, 2001, Chicago, IL.

Dominguez, Nicholas, Tyler E. Frisbee and Richard F. Winters. 2009. "...Divided, We Fail: The Impact of Primary Divisiveness on Gubernatorial Elections," a paper presented at the 2009 Conference on State Politics and Policy at Temple University.

Dougherty, Keith. 2001. *Collective Action under the Articles of Confederation*. Cambridge: Cambridge University Press.

Downs, Anthony. 1957. *An Economic Theory of Democracy*. New York: Harper and Row.

Downs, Anthony. 1960. "Why the Government Budget Is Too Small in a Democracy." *World Politics* 12(4): 541–563.

Dye, Thomas R. 1966. *Politics, Economics, and the Public: Political Outcomes in the American States*. Chicago, IL: Rand McNally.

Economic Report of the President (various issues). United States, Council of Economic Advisers (U.S.). Washington, DC. U.S. G.P.O., 2024.

Eismeier, Theodore J. 1979. "Budgets and Ballots: The Political Consequences of Fiscal Choice." in D. Rae and T. Eismeier, eds., *Public Policy and Public Choice*, Beverly Hills: Sage Publications.

Eismeier, Theodore J. 1983. "Votes & Taxes: The Political Economy of the American Governorship." *Polity* 15(3): 368–379.

Epstein, Leon. 1958. *Politics in Wisconsin*. Madison: University of Wisconsin Press.

Erikson, Robert S. 1971. "The Relationship between Party Control and Civil Rights Legislation in the American States." *Western Political Quarterly* 24(1): 178–182.

Erikson, Robert S., Gerald C. Wright and John P. McIver. 1989. "Political Parties, Public Opinion and State Policy in the United States." *American Political Science Review* 83(3): 729–750.

Erikson, Robert S., Gerald C. Wright, Jr. and John P. McIver. 1993. *Statehouse Democracy*. New York: Cambridge University Press.

Fair, Ray C. 1978. "The Effects of Economic Effects on Votes for President." *The Review of Economics and Statistics* 60(2): 159–173.

Fehr, Ernst and Urs Fischbacher. 2003. "The Nature of Human Altruism." *Nature* 425: 785–791.

Fellowes, Matthew and Gretchen Rowe. 2004. "Politics and the New American Welfare States." *American Journal of Political Science* 48(2): 362–373.

Fenno, Richard. 1966. *The Power of the Purse*. Boston, MA: Little Brown and Co.

Fenno, Richard. 1973. *Congressmen in Committees*. Boston, MA: Little Brown & Co.

Fenton, John. 1966. *Midwest Politics*. New York: Holt Rinehart and Winston.

Ferejohn, John. 1974. *Pork Barrel Politics*. Stanford, CA: Stanford University Press.

Ferejohn, John and Barry Weingast, eds., 1997. *The New Federalism: Can the States Be Trusted?* Stanford, CA: Hoover Institution Press.

Field, Alexander. 2001. *Altruistically Inclined*. Ann Arbor: University of Michigan Press.

Fiorina, Morris P. 1977 and 1989. *Retrospective Voting in American National Elections*. New Haven, CT: Yale University Press.

Fisher, Louis. 1997. "Biennial Budgeting in the Federal Government." *Public Budgeting & Finance* 17(3): 87–97.

Flavin, Patrick. 2012. "Income Inequality and Policy Representation in the American States." *American Politics Research* 40(1): 29–59.

Fong, Christina M. and Erzo F. P. Luttmer. 2009. "Do Race and Fairness Matter in Generosity? Evidence from a Nationally Representative Charity Experiment." National Bureau of Economic Research, Cambridge, MA, working paper # 15064.

Frank, Robert H. 1996. "Motivation, Cognition, and Charitable Giving." in Jerome B. Schneewind, ed., pp. 130–152. *Giving*, Bloomington: Indiana University Press.

Franzese, Robert. 2008. "Political-Economic Cycles." in Barry R. Weingast and Donald Wittman, eds., *The Oxford Handbook of Political Economy*, Oxford: Oxford University Press. pp. 545–560.

Fredriksson, Per G., Le Wang and Patrick L. Warren. 2013. "Party Politics, Governors, and Economic Policy." *Southern Economic Journal* 80(1): 106–126.

Frey, Bruno S. and Friedrich Schneider. 1978. "An Empirical Study of Political-economic Interactions in the United States." *Review of Economics and Statistics* 60(2): 174–183.

Frisbee, Tyler and Richard F. Winters. 2008. "The Divisive Primary Hypothesis Redux: The Effects of Candidates' Ideological Distances in Party Primary Contests on General Election Outcomes," a paper presented at the State Politics and Policy Conference, May 31, 2008 at Temple University, Philadelphia, PA.

Frohlich, Norman and Joe Oppenheimer. 2000. "How People Reason about Ethics." in Arthur Lupia McCubbins, Mathew D. and Popkin, Samuel L. eds., *Elements of Reason*, New York: Cambridge University press.

Fry, Brian and Richard F. Winters. 1969. "The Politics of Redistribution," a paper presented before the 1969 annual meeting of the American Political Science Association.

Fry, Brian and Richard F. Winters. 1970. "The Politics of Redistribution." *American Political Science Review* 64(2): 508–522.

Gamm, Gerald and Thad Kousser. 2021. "Life, Literacy, and the Pursuit of Prosperity: Party Competition and Policy Outcomes in 50 States." *American Political Science Review* 115(4): 1442–1463.

Gilens, Martin. 2009. "Preference Gaps and Inequality in Representation." *PS: Political Science and Politics* 42(2): 335–341.

Gillies, Paul. 1977. "History of the Vermont Income Tax," at: https://vermonthistory.org/journal/misc/EvolutionTaxSystem.pdf.

Gilligan, Thomas W. and John G. Matsusaka. 1995. "Deviations from Constituent Interests: The Role of Legislative Structure and Political Parties in the States." *Economy Inquiry* 33(3): 383–401.

Ginsberg, Leon. 1992. *Social Work Almanac*. Washington, DC: NASW Press.

Giving USA. 2008. New York: American Association of Fund-Raising Counsel.

Glaeser, Edward L. and Raven Saks. 2004. "Corruption in America," Harvard Institute of Economic Research, discussion paper 2043.

Goetz, Charles, J. 1977. "Fiscal Illusion in State and Local Finance." in Thomas Borcherding, ed., *Budgets and Bureaucrats: The Sources of Government Growth*, Durham, NC: Duke University Press; as quoted in Mikesell, p. 99.

Goodin, Robert E. 1988. *Reasons for Welfare: The Political Theory of the Welfare State*. Princeton, NJ: Princeton University Press.

Gordon, Sanford. 2009. "Assessing Partisan Bias in Federal Public Corruption Investigations." *American Political Science Review* 103(4): 534–554.

Gouldner, Alvin. 1957. "Cosmopolitans and Locals." *Administrative Science Quarterly* 2(3): 281–306.

Graetz, Michael and Ian Shapiro. 2005. *Death by a Thousand Cuts: The Fight Over Taxing Inherited Wealth*. Princeton, NJ: Princeton University Press.

Gray, Virginia. 1973. "Innovation in the States: A Diffusion Study." *American Political Science Review* 67(4): 1174–85.

Gray, Virginia and David Lowery. 1996. *The Population Ecology of Interest Representation: Lobbying Communities in the American States*. Ann Arbor: University of Michigan Press.

Gray, Virginia and David Lowery. 2001. "The Institutionalization of State Communities of Organized Interests." *Political Research Quarterly* 54(2): 265–284.

Gray, Virginia, David Lowery, Matthew Fellowes and Andrea McAtee. 2004. "Public Opinion, Public Policy, and Organized Interests in the American States." *Political Research Quarterly* 57(3): 411–420.

Grossman, Matt, Marty P. Jordan and Joshua McCrain. 2021. "The Correlates of State Policy and the Structure of State Panel Data." *State Politics and Policy Quarterly* 21(4): 430–450.

Hansen, Susan B. 1983. *The Politics of Taxation: Revenue without Representation.* New York: Praeger.

Hansen, Susan B. 1999. "'Life Is Not Fair': Governors' Job Performance Ratings and State Economies." *Political Research Quarterly* 52(1): 167–188.

Harris, Louis. 1959. "Why the Odds Are Against a Governor's Becoming President." *Public Opinion Quarterly* 23(3): 361–370.

Hartley, Robert E. 1999. *Paul Powell of Illinois: A Lifelong Democrat.* Carbondale: Southern Illinois University Press.

Hauk, William R. and Roman Wacziarg. 2007. "Small States, Big Pork." *Quarterly Journal of Political Science* 2: 95–106.

Henning, Peter J. and Lee J. Radek. 2011. *The Prosecution and Defense of Public Corruption.* New York: Oxford University Press.

Hero, Rodney and Caroline Tolbert. 1996. "A Racial/Ethnic Diversity Interpretation of Politics and Policy in the States of the U.S." *American Journal of Political Science* 40(3): 851–871.

Hettich, Walter and Stanley L. Winer. 1988. "Economic and Political Foundations of Tax Structure." *The American Economic Review* 78(4): 701–712.

Hibbing, John R. 1991. *Congressional Careers: Contours of Life in the U.S. House of Representatives.* Chapel Hill: University of North Carolina Press.

Hibbing, John R. and Elizabeth Theiss-Morse. 1995. *Congress as Public Enemy: Public Attitudes Toward American Political Institutions.* Cambridge; New York: Cambridge University Press.

Hibbing, John R. and Elizabeth Theiss-Morse. 2002. *Stealth Democracy: Americans' Beliefs about How Government Should Work.* Cambridge; New York: Cambridge University Press.

Hibbing, John R. and John R. Alford. 1981. "The Electoral Impact of Economic Conditions: Who is Held Responsible?" *American Journal of Political Science* 25(3): 423¬439.

Hill, Kim Quaile. 2003. "Democratization and Corruption: Systematic Evidence from the American States." *American Politics Research* 31(6): 613–631.

Hirschman, Albert. 1970. *Exit, Voice, and Loyalty: Responses to Decline in Firms, Organizations, and States.* Cambridge, MA: Harvard University Press.

Hofferbert, Richard A. 1966. "Ecological Development and Policy Change in the American States." *Midwest Journal of Political Science* 10(4): 464–483.

Hofferbert, Richard. 1966. "The Relation between Public Policy and Some Structural and Environmental Variables in the American States." *American Political Science Review* 60(1): 73–82.

Hofferbert, Richard. 1972. "State and Community Policy Studies: A Review of Comparative Input-Output Analysis." in James Robinson, ed., *Political Science Annual*, Indianapolis: Bobbs-Merrill, pp. 3–72.

Holbrook, Thomas. 1987. "National Factors in Gubernatorial Elections." *American Politics Quarterly* 15(4): 471–483.

Hothorn, Torsten, Kurt Hornik and Achim Zeileis. 2006. "Unbiased Recursive Partitioning: A Conditional Inference Framework." *Journal of Computational and Graphical Statistics* 15(3): 651–674.

Howell, Susan E. and James Vanderleeuw. 1990. "Economic Effects on State Governors." *American Politics Quarterly* 18(2): 154–162.
Jacob, Herbert and Michael Lipsky. 1968. "Outputs, Structure and Power: An Assessment of Changes in the Study of State and Local Politics." *Journal of Politics* 30(2): 510–538.
Jacobson, Gary C. 1983. *The Politics of Congressional Elections*. Boston, MA: Little Brown and Co.
Jacobson, Gary C. 1990. *The Electoral Origins of Divided Government: Competition in U.S. House Elections 1946–1988*. San Francisco, CA: Westview Press.
Jacobson, Gary C. and Samuel Kernell. 1981. *Strategy and Choice in Congressional Elections*. 2nd ed. New Haven, CT: Yale University Press.
Jacoby, William and Sandra Schneider. 2009. "A New Measure of Policy Spending Priorities in the American States." *Political Analysis* 17(1): 1–24.
Jay, Robert. 2012. *Oxford Dictionary of Political Quotations*. New York: Oxford University Press.
Jewell, Malcolm. 1982. "The Neglected World of State Politics." *Journal of Politics* 44(3): 638–657.
Jewell, Malcolm E. and Sarah M. Morehouse. 2000. *Political Parties and Elections in American States*, 4th Edition. Washington, DC: CQ Press.
Johnson, Martin. 2001. "The Impact of Social Diversity and Racial Attitudes on Social Welfare Policy." *State Politics & Policy Quarterly* 1(1): 27–49.
Jones, Zachary M. and Fridolin Linder. 2015. "Exploratory Data Analysis Using Random Forests," Working Paper, and available at https://zmjones.com/static/papers/rfss_manuscript.pdf.
Kahneman, Daniel. 1982. *Judgement under Uncertainty: Heuristics and Biases*. Cambridge: Cambridge University Press.
Keech, William R. 1995. *Economic Politics: The Costs of Democracy*. Cambridge: Cambridge University Press.
Keefe, William and Morris Ogul. 1964. *The American Legislative Process: Congress and the States*. Englewood Cliffs, NJ: Prentice Hall Inc.
Kenney, Patrick J. 1983. "The Effect of State Economic Conditions on the Vote for Governor." *Social Science Quarterly* 64(1): 154–162.
Kenney, Patrick J. and Tom W. Rice. 1984. "The Effect of Primary Divisiveness in Gubernatorial and Senatorial Elections." *Journal of Politics* 46(3): 904–915.
Key, Valdimir O. 1949. *Southern Politics in State and Nation*. New York: A.A. Knopf.
Key, Valdimir O. 1956. *American State Politics: An Introduction*. New York: A.A. Knopf.
Key, Valdimir O. Jr. 1966. *The Responsible Electorate: Rationality in Presidential Voting, 1936–1960* with the assistance of Milton C. Cummings, Jr. Cambridge: Belknap Press of Harvard University Press.
Kiplinger Magazine. "38 States that Don't Tax Social Security Benefits." at https://www.kiplinger.com/slideshow/retirement/t037-s001-states-that-don-t-tax-social-security-benefits/index.html#:~:text=Income%20Tax%20Range%3A%20New%20Hampshire,%24100%2C000%20of%20assessed%20home%20value. Accessed 10/24/2020.
Klarner, Carl. 2013a. "Governors Dataset." https://hdl.handle.net/1902.1/20408 IQSS Dataverse Network [Distributor] V1 [Version].

Klarner, Carl. 2013b. "State Partisan Balance Data, 1937–2011." https://hdl.handle.net/1902.1/20403. Harvard Dataverse. V1.

Klarner, Carl E., Justin Phillips and Mathew Muckler. 2012. "Overcoming Fiscal Gridlock: Institutions and Budget Bargaining." *Journal of Politics* 74(4): 992–1022.

Knack, Stephen. 2002. "Social Capital and the Quality of Government: Evidence from the American States." *American Journal of Political Science* 46(4): 772–785.

Kone, Susan L. and Richard F. Winters. 1993. "Taxes and Voting: Electoral Retribution in the American States." *Journal of Politics* 55(1): 22–40.

Kostroski, Warren Lee. 1973. "Party and Incumbency in Postwar·Senate Elections." *American Political Science Review* 67(4): 1213–1234.

Kousser, Thad. 2002. "Politics, Economics, and State Policy: Discretionary Medicaid Spending, 1980–1993." *Journal of Health Politics, Policy and Law* 27(4): 639–671.

Kousser, Thad and Justin H. Phillips. 2012. *The Power of American Governors*. New York Cambridge University Press.

Kovenock, David and James Prothro. 1973. *Explaining the Vote*. Chapel Hill, NC: Institute for Research in the Social Science.

Kramer, Gerald. 1983. "The Ecological Fallacy Revisited: Aggregate- Versus Individual-Level Findings on Economics and Elections and Socio-Tropic Voting." *American Political Science Review* 77(1): 92–111.

Krutz, Glenn S. 2001. "Tactical Maneuvering on Omnibus Bills in Congress." *American Journal of Political Science* 45(1): 210–223.

Kuklinski, James H. and Darrell M. West. 1981. "Economic Expectations and Voting Behavior in U.S. House and Senate Elections." *American Political Science Review* 75(2): 436–448.

Lacy, Dean. 2002. "A Paradox of the Red States and Blue States: Federal Spending and Electoral Votes in the 2000 U.S. Presidential Election," ms. Dartmouth College accessible at https://cpb-us-e1.wpmucdn.com/sites.dartmouth.edu/dist/9/280/files/2016/10/Paradox-of-Red-and-Blue-2002.pdf.

Lane, Robert. 1962. *Political Ideology: Why the American Common Man Believes What He Does*. New York: Free Press of Glencoe.

LaPorta, Rafael, Florencio Lopez-de-Silanes, Andrei Shleifer and Robert Vishney. 1999. "The Quality of Government." *The Journal of Law, Economics, and Organization* 15(1): 222–279.

Lassen, David Dreyer. 2003. "Ethnic Divisions and the Size of the Informal Sector," EPRU Working Paper Series 03–01, Economic Policy Research Unit (EPRU), University of Copenhagen. Department of Economics.

Lasswell, Harold. 1936. *Politics: Who Gets What, When, and How. New York, McGraw Hill.*

Lasswell, Harold and Abraham Kaplan. 1950. *Power and Society: A Framework for Political Inquiry*. New Haven, CT: Yale University Press.

Lathem, Edward Connery, ed. 1969. *The Poetry of Robert Frost*. New York: Holt, Rinehart and Winston.

Lazarsfeld, Paul F., Bernard Berelson and Hazel Gaudet. 1944. *The People's Choice: How the Voter Makes Up His Mind in a Presidential Campaign*. New York: Duell, Sloan and Pearce.

Leigh, Andrew. 2008. "Do Redistributive Taxes Reduce Inequality?" *National Tax Journal* 61(1): 81–104.

Lile, Stephen. 1976. "Family Tax Burden Differences Among the States." Lexington, Ky: Council of State Governments, Chicago, IL: Council of State Governments, pp. 9–17.

Litt, Edgar. 1965. *The Political Culture of Massachusetts*. Cambridge: M.I.T. Press.

Lockard, Duane. 1959. *New England State Politics*. Princeton, NJ: Princeton University Press.

Loomis, Burdett. 1994. *Time, Politics, and Policies: A Legislative Year*. Lawrence: University of Kansas Press.

Lowery, David, Ronald Weber and Richard Winters. 2008. "State Politics and Policy for the Next Term." *State Politics & Policy Quarterly* 8(1): 1–6.

Lowry, Robert. 2003. "Organized Interests, the Capacity for Influence, and the Size of Government: Evidence for Nonprofit Social Services Organizations and State Public Welfare Spending," Unpublished ms. Iowa State University.

Lowry, Robert and Michael Potoski. 2004. "Organized Interests and the Politics of Federal Discretionary Grants." The Journal of Politics 66(2): 513–533

Lowry, Robert C., et al. 1998. "Fiscal Policy Outcomes and Electoral Accountability in American States." *American Political Science Review* 92(4): 759–774.

Lupsha, Peter. 1975. "Social Position and Public-Regardingness...." *Western Political Quarterly* 28(4): 618–634.

MacDonald, Jason A. and Lee Sigelman. 1999. "Public Assessments of Gubernatorial Performance: A Comparative State Analysis." *American Politics Quarterly* 27(2): 201–215.

MacKuen, Michael B., Robert S. Erikson and James A. Stimson. 1992. "Peasants or Bankers? The American Electorate and the U.S. Economy." *American Political Science Review* 86(3): 597–611.

MacManus, Susan A. 1995. "Taxing and Spending Politics: A Generational Perspective." *Journal of Politics* 57(3): 607–629.

Maimonides, Moses. 1979. (translated from the Hebrew by Isaac Klein). *The Code of Maimonides, Book Seven: The Book of Agriculture, Treatise Two, Chapter Ten*. New Haven, CT: Yale University Press, p. 91.

Manley, John. 1970. *The Politics of Finance: The House Committee on Ways and Means*. Boston, MA: Little, Brown.

Markus, Gregory B. 1988. "The Impact of Personal and National Economic Conditions on the Presidential Vote...." *American Journal of Political Science* 32(1): 137–154.

Mauro, Paolo. 1995. "Corruption and Growth." *Quarterly Journal of Economics* 110(3): 681–712.

Maxwell, Amanda E. and Richard F. Winters. 2003. "A Quarter-Century of (data on) Corruption in the American States," a paper presented at the 2003 Midwestern Political Science Association, and available from the author at rfw@dartmouth.edu.

Maxwell, Amanda E. and Richard F. Winters. 2005 and 2006. "Political Corruption in the American States," a paper presented at the 2005 and 2006 American and Southern Political Science Associations, and available at: https://www.dartmouth.edu/~rwinters/workingpapers.html.

Mayhew, David R. 1974. *Congress: The Electoral Connection*. New Haven, CT: Yale University Press.

McConnell, Grant. 1966. *Private Power & American Democracy*. New York: A.A. Knopf.

McDowell, James L. 1967. *The Politics of Reapportionment in Illinois*. Carbondale: Public Affairs Research Bureau, Southern Illinois University.

Meier, Kenneth and Thomas Schlesinger. 2002. "Variations in Corruption among the American States." in Arnold Heidenheimer and Michael Johnson, eds., *Political Corruption: concepts and contexts*, 627–644. New Brunswick, NJ: Transaction Publishers.

Meier, Kenneth J. and Thomas M. Holbrook. 1992. "'I Seen My Opportunities and I Took'em:' Political Corruption in the American States." *Journal of Politics* 54(1): 135–155.

Merton, Robert Merton. 1957. *Social Theory and Social Structure*. Glencoe: Free Press, pp. 387–420.

Michael Gratz and Ian Shapiro. 2006. *Death by a Thousand Cuts: The Fight Over Taxing Inherited Wealth*. Princeton NJ: Princeton University Press.

Mikesell, John L. 1978. "Election Periods and State Tax Policy Cycles." *Public Choice* 33(3): 99–105.

Mikesell, John L. 1998. "The Future of American Sales and Use Taxation." in David Brunori, ed., *The Future of State Taxation*, Washington, DC: The Urban Institute Press.

Milliken, John J. and Mark Rozell. 2024. *The New Dominion: The Twentieth-Century Elections That Shaped Modern Virginia*. Charlottesville: University of Virginia Press.

Moffitt, Robert. 1983. "An Economic Model of Welfare Stigma." *American Economic Review* 73(5): 1023–1035.

Moffitt, Robert. 1990. "Has State Redistribution Policy Grown More Conservative?" *National Tax Journal* 43(2): 123–142.

Mondak, Jeff and Carl McCurley. 1994. "Cognitive Efficiency and the Congressional Vote: The Psychology of Coattail Voting." *Political Research Quarterly* 47(1): 151–175.

Monroe, Kristen R. 1996. *The Heart of Altruism: Perceptions of a Common Humanity*. Princeton, NJ: Princeton University Press.

Mooney, Christopher. 2001. "State Politics and Policy Quarterly and the Study of State Politics: The Editor's Introduction." *State Politics and Policy Quarterly* 1(1): 1–4.

Mooney, Christopher. 2020. *The Study of US State Policy Diffusion: What Hath Walker Wrought?* New York: Cambridge University Press.

Morehouse, Sarah McCally. 1997. *The Governor as Party Leader: Campaigning and Governing*. Ann Arbor: The University of Michigan Press.

Mueller, Dennis C. 1979. *Public Choice*. New York: Cambridge University Press.

Murray, Charles A. 1984. *Losing Ground–American Social Policy, 1950–1980*. New York: Basic Books.

Myrdal, Gunnar. 1968. *Asian Drama: An Inquiry into the Poverty of Nations*. New York: Pantheon Books.

National Association of State Budget Officers. 1977, 1987, 1989, 1992, 1995, 1997 1999, 2002. *Budget Processes in the States*. 444 North Capitol Street, NW, Suite 642, Washington, DC, 20001-1511.

National Association of State Budget Officers. 1987–2012. *The Fiscal Survey of the States*, spring and fall issues, multiple years, National Governors Association, National Association of State Budget Officers, Washington, DC.

National Conference of State Legislators. 1988. *Legislative Budget Procedures in the 50 States: A Guide to Appropriations and Budget Processes*. Denver Colorado.

Nelson, Michael. 2000. "Electoral Cycles and the Politics of State Tax Policy." *Public Finance Review* 28(6): 540–560.

Nice, David. 1983. "Political Corruption in the American States." *American Politics Quarterly* 11(4): 507–511.

Niemi, Richard G., Harold W. Stanley and Ronald J. Vogel. 1995. "State Economies and State Taxes: Do Voters Hold Governors Accountable." *American Political Science Review* 39(4): 936–957.

Nordhaus, William. 1975. "The Political Business Cycle." *Review of Economic Studies* 42(2): 169–190.

Norrander, Barbara. 2000. "The Multi-Layered Impact of Public Opinion on Capital Punishment Implementation in the American States." *Political Research Quarterly* 53(4): 771–793.

Norrander, Barbara. 2001. "Measuring State Public Opinion with the Senate National Election Study." *State Politics & Policy Quarterly* 1(1): 111–125.

Nye, Joseph. 1967. "Corruption and Political Development: A Cost-Benefit Analysis." *American Political Science Review* 61(2): 417–427.

O'Connor, Edwin. 1956. *The Last Hurrah*. Boston, MA: Little, Brown.

Olasky, Marvin. 1992. *The Tragedy of American Compassion*. Washington, DC: Regnery and Co.

Olson, Mancur. 1965. *The Logic of Collective Action: Public Goods and the Theory of Groups*. 355–384. Cambridge, MA: Harvard University Press.

Olson, Mancur. 1973. "Evaluating Performance in the Public Sector." in Milton Moss, ed., *The Measurement of Economic and Social Performance,* New York, National Bureau of Economic Research; distributed by Columbia University Press.

Peirce, Neal. 1976, *The New England States of America*. New York: Norton.

Peltzman, Sam. 1987. "Economic Conditions and Gubernatorial Elections." *American Economic Review* 77(2): 293–297.

Penniman, Clara. 1976. "The Politics of Taxation." in Herbert Jacob and Kenneth N. Vines, eds., *Politics in the American States*, Boston, MA: Little, Brown.

Perry, James M. "This Rockefeller Campaign is..." *National Observer*, October 26, 1970 as quoted in Peirce, The Mega-states, p. 49.

Peters, Guy. 1979. "Determinants of Tax Policy." *Policy Studies Journal* 3(7): 787–793.

Peterson, Paul. 1981. *City Limits*. Chicago, IL: University of Chicago Press.

Peterson, Paul. and M. Rom. 1989. *The Case for a National Welfare Standard.* Washington, DC: Brookings Institution.

Phares, Donald. 1980. *Who Pays State and Local Taxes*? Cambridge, MA: Oelgeschlager, Gunn & Hain.

Phillips, Justin and Jeffrey Lax. 2009. "Public Opinion and Policy Responsiveness: Gay Rights in the States." *American Political Science Review* 103(3): 367–385.

Piereson, James. 1977. "Sources of Candidate Success in Gubernatorial Elections 1910–1970." *Journal of Politics* 39(4): 939–958.

Plotnick, Robert D. and Richard F. Winters. 1985. "A Politico-Economic Theory of Income Redistribution." *American Political Science Review* 78(2): 458–473.

Plotnick, Robert D. and Richard F. Winters. 1990. "Party, Political Liberalism and Redistribution." *American Politics Research* 18(4): 430–458.

Pomper, Gerald et al. 1976. The Election of 1976. Englewood Cliffs, N.J.: Prentice Hall.

Pomper, Gerald. 1968, 1976. *Elections in America*. New York: Dodd, Mead.

Poterba, James M. 1994a. "Capital Budgets, Borrowing Rules, and State Capital Spending." *Journal of Public Economics* 56(2): 165–187.

Poterba, James M. 1994b. "State Responses to Fiscal Crises: The Effects of Budgetary Institutions and Politics." *Journal of Political Economy* 102(4): 799–821.

Poterba, James M. 1995. "Balanced Budget Rules and Fiscal Policy: Evidence from the States." *National Tax Journal* 48(3): 329–337.

Poterba, James M. 1996. "Budget Institutions and Fiscal Policy in the U.S. States." *American Economic Review* 86(2): 395–400.

Primo, David. 2007. *Rules and Restraint*. Chicago, IL: University of Chicago Press.

Putnam, Robert D. 2000. *Bowling Alone: The Collapse and Revival of American Community*. New York: Simon & Schuster.

Rainey, Carlisle, Kevin Stout and Richard Winters. 2014. "The Effects of Party Control, Electoral Cycles & Institutional Design on Tax Policy Changes," a paper presented at 2015 conference of the Midwest Political Science Association, Chicago, IL.

Ranney, Austin. 1965, 1976. "Parties in State Politics." in Herbert Jacob and Kenneth Vines, eds., *Politics in the American States*, Boston, MA: Little Brown.

Ravo, Nick. 1989. "Bridgeport's Novice Mayor Jolts City." *The New York Times*, November 15, 1989, p. B9.

Rhodebeck, Laurie A. 1993. "The Politics of Greed? Political Preferences Among the Elderly." *Journal of Politics* 55(2): 342–364.

Richardson, Jr. Jesse J., Meghan Zimmerman Gough and Robert Puentes. 2003. *Is Home Rule the Answer? Clarifying the Influence of Dillon's Rule on Growth Management*. Washington, DC: The Brookings Institution.

Ridley, Matt. 1996. *The Origins of Virtue*. New York: Viking.

Rigby, Elizabeth and Gerald Wright. 2013. "Political Parties and Representation of the Poor in the American States." *American Journal of Political Science* 57(3): 552–565.

Riker, William H. 1964. *Federalism: Origin, Operation, Significance*. Boston, MA: Little Brown.

Riker, William H. 1986. *The Art of Political Manipulation*. New Haven, CT: Yale University Press.

Riordan, William L. 1948. *Plunkitt of Tammany Hall*. New York: Knopf.

Roberts, Russell D. 1984. "A Positive Model of Private Charity and Public Transfers." *Journal of Political Economy* 92(1): 136–148.

Roemer, John E. 1999. "The Democratic Political Economy of Progressive Income Tax." *Econometrica* 67(1): 1–19.

Romer, Cristina D. and David H. Romer. 2007. "Do Tax Cuts Starve the Beast? The Effect of Tax Changes on Government Spending," NBER Working Paper 13548, Cambridge, MA.

Romero, David and Francine Sanders. 1994. "Loosened Partisan Attachments and Receptivity to Incumbent Behaviors: A Panel Analysis, 1972–1976." *Political Research Quarterly* 47(1): 177–192.

Rose-Ackerman, Rose. 1975. "The Economics of Corruption." *Journal of Public Economics* 4(2): 187–203.

Rose-Ackerman, Susan. 1986. "Do Government Grants to Charity Reduce Private Donations?" in Susan Rose-Ackerman, ed., *The Economics of Nonprofit Institutions: Studies in Structure and Policy*, New York: Oxford University Press.

Rose-Ackerman, Susan. 1996. "Altruism, Nonprofits, and Economic Theory." *Journal of Economic Literature* 34(2): 701–728.

Rose, Shanna. 2008. "The Political Manipulation of U.S. State Rainy Day Funds under Rules versus Discretion." *State Politics and Policy Quarterly* 8(2): 150–176.

Rundquist, Barry. 1980. *Political Benefits: Empirical Studies of American Public Programs*. Lexington, MA: Lexington Books.

Sabato, Larry. 1978. *Goodbye to Good-Time Charlie...* Lexington, MA: Lexington Books.

Salamon, Julie. 2003. *Rambam's Ladder*. New York: Workman Publishing Company.

Sanders, Arthur. 1988. "Rationality, Self-Interest, and Public Attitudes on Public Spending." *Social Science Quarterly* 69(2): 311–324.

Sayr, Lois W. 1989. *Pooled Time Series Analysis*. Newbury Park, CA: Sage Publications.

Scammon, Richard, et al. *American Votes*, various biennial volumes. Congressional Quarterly Press, Washington, D.C

Schelling, Thomas. 1960. *The Strategy of Conflict*. Cambridge, MA: Harvard University Press.

Schelling, Thomas. 2006. *Strategies of Commitment and Other Essays*. Cambridge, MA: Harvard University Press.

Schiff, Jerald. 1985. "Does Government Spending Crowd Out Charitable Contributions." *National Tax Journal* 38(4): 535–546.

Schleicher, David. 2019. "Vermont is a Constitutional Problem." *Arizona Law Review* 61(2), pp. 253–289.

Schlesinger, Joseph. 1957. *How They Became Governor*. East Lansing: Governmental Research Bureau, Michigan State University.

Schlesinger, Joseph A. 1966. *Ambition and Politics*. Chicago, IL: Rand McNally.

Schlesinger, Thomas and Kenneth Meier. 2002. "Variations in Corruption among the American States." in A. Heidenheimer and M. Johnston, eds., *Political Corruption*, New Brunswick: Transaction Publishers.

Schram, Sanford, Richard C. Fording and Joe Soss. 2003. *Race and the Politics of Welfare Reform*. Ann Arbor: University of Michigan Press.

Sharkansky, Ira. 1967a. "Economic and Political Correlates of State Government Expenditures." *Midwest Journal of Political Science* 11(2): 173–192.

Sharkansky, Ira. 1967b. "Government Expenditures and Public Services in the American States." *American Political Science Review* 16(4): 1066–1067.

Sharkansky, Ira. 1971. "Economic Theories of Public Policy: Resource Policy and Need-Policy Linkages between Income and Welfare Benefits." *Midwest Journal of Political Science* 15(4): 722–740.

Scheve, Kenneth and David Stasavage. 2016. Taxing the Rich: A History of Fiscal Fairness in the United States and Europe. Princeton, NJ: Princeton University Press.

Shleifer, Andrei and Robert Vishney. 1993. "Corruption." *Quarterly Journal of Economics* 108(3): 599–617.

Simon, Dennis. 1989. "Presidents, Governors, and Electoral Accountability." *Journal of Politics* 51(2): 286–304.

Simon, Dennis M., Charles W. Ostrom Jr. and Robin F. Marra. 1991. "The President, Referendum Voting, and Subnational Elections in the United States." *American Political Science Review* 85(4): 1177–1192.

Smallwood, Frank. 1976. *Free and Independent*. Brattleboro, VT: S. Greene Press.

Sobel, Joel. 2005. "Interdependent Preferences and Reciprocity." *Journal of Economic Literature* 43(2): 392–436.

Sperlich, Peter W. 1975."Bargaining and Overload." in Aaron Wildavsky, ed., *Perspectives on the Presidency*, Boston, MA: Little Brown, pp. 406–430.

Squire, Peverill. 1992. "Challenger Profile and Gubernatorial Elections." *Western Political Quarterly* 45(1): 125–142.

Squire, Peverill and Christina Fastnow. 1994. "Comparing Gubernatorial and Senatorial Elections." *Political Research Quarterly* 47(3): 705–720.

Stanley, Harold, William T. Bianco and Richard G. Niemi. 1986. "Partisanship and Group Support Over Time." *American Political Science Review* 80(3): 969–976.

Stanton, Mike. 2003. *The Prince of Providence: The Life and Times of Buddy Cianci, America's Most Notorious Mayor, Some Wise-Guys and the Feds*. New York: Random House.

Stein, Robert M. 1990. "Economic Voting for Governor and U.S. Senator: The Electoral Consequences of Federalism." *Journal of Politics* 52(1): 29–53.

Steinberg, Richard. 1993. "Does Government Spending Crowd Out Donations?" in Avner ben-Ner and Benedetto Gui, eds., *The Nonprofit Sector in the Mixed Economy*, Ann Arbor: University of Michigan Press.

Steiner, Gilbert and Samuel Gove. 1960. *Legislative Politics in Illinois*. Urbana: University of Illinois Press.

Steinmo, Sven. 1993. *Taxation and Democracy*. New Haven, CT: Yale University Press.

Stephen Ansolabehere, Jonathan Rodden and James M. Snyder Jr. 2006. "Purple America." *Journal of Economic Perspectives* 20(2): 97–118.

Stigler, George J. 1971. "The Theory of Economic Regulation." *The Bell Journal Economics and Management Science* 2(1): 3–21.

Stimson, James. 1985. "Regression in Space and Time: A Statistical Essay." *American Journal of Political* Science 29(4): 914–947.

Stonecash, Jeffrey M. 1996. "The State Politics Literature...." *Polity* 28(4): 559–579.

Strobl, Carolin, Anne-Laure Boulesteix, Achim Zeileis and Torsten Hothorn. 2007. Bias in random forest variable importance measures: Illustrations, sources and a solution. *BMC Bioinformatics* 8, 25 (2007). https://doi.org/10.1186/1471-2105-8-25.

Stults, Brian and Richard F. Winters. 2005. "The Political Economy of Taxes and the Vote." *Manuscript*, Dartmouth College. Manuscript available from the author at rfw@dartmouth.edu

Sullivan, Denis G., Robert Nakamura and Richard Winters. 1980. *How America Is Ruled*. New York: Wiley.

Sullivan, John L. 1972. A Note on Redistributive Politics. *American Political Science Review* 66(4): 1301–1305.

Svoboda, Craig J. 1995. "Retrospective Voting in Gubernatorial Elections: 1982 and 1986." *Political Research Quarterly* 48(1): 135–150.

Tax Administrators News. 2001. *Various Monthly Issues by the Federation of Tax Administrators*. 444 North Capitol Street, NW, Washington, DC. Federation of Tax Administrators, 444 North Capitol Street.

Tax Foundation, Inc. 1967. *Tax Burdens and Benefits of Government Expenditures by Income Classes*, 1961 and 1965. New York: Tax Foundation, Inc.

Tiebout, Charles. 1956. "A Pure Theory of Local Expenditures." *Journal of Political Economy* 64(5): 416–424.

Tompkins, Mark. 1984. "The Electoral Fortunes of Gubernatorial Incumbents: 1947–1981." *Journal of Politics* 46(2): 520–543.

Tompkins, Mark. 1988. "Have Gubernatorial Elections Become More Distinctive Contests?" *Journal of Politics* 50(1): 192–205.

Treisman, Daniel. 2000. "The Causes of Corruption: A Cross-National Study." *Journal of Public Economics* 76(3): 399–457.

Turett, J. Stephen. 1971. "The Vulnerability of American Governors, 1900–1969." *Midwest Journal of Political Science* 15(1): 108–132.

U.S. Bureau of the Census. *State Government Finances*. Washington, DC: U.S. Govt. Print. Various years.

U.S. Census Bureau. 1950–2006. *Statistical Abstract of the United States*. Washington, DC: U.S. Government Printing Office.

U.S. Department of Commerce. May 1989. Bureau of the Census, ICPSR Study #9472. Current Population Survey, Multiple Job Holdings, Flextime and Volunteer Work. See p. 8–17.

U.S. Economic Council. 1950–2003. *Economic Report of the President*. Washington, DC: U.S. Government Printing Office.

U.S. House of Representatives, Committee on Rules, 99th Congress, 2nd Session. 1986. *Item Veto: State Experience and Its Application to the Federal Situation*. Washington, DC: U.S. Government Printing Office.

Uslaner, Eric M. 2002. *The Moral Foundations of Trust*. Cambridge; New York: Cambridge University Press.

Uslaner, Eric M. and Ronald E. Weber. 1975. "The 'Politics' of Redistribution: Toward a Model of the Policy-Making Process in the American States." *American Politics Quarterly* 3(2): 130–170.

Veblen, Eric P. 1975. *The Manchester Union Leader in New Hampshire Elections*. Hanover: University Press of New England.

Volden, Craig. 2004. "Origin, Operation, and Significance: The Federalism of William H. Riker." *Publius: The Journal of Federalism* 34(4): 89–107.

Von Hagen, Jürgen. 1991. "A Note on the Empirical Effectiveness of Formal Fiscal Restraints." *Journal of Public Economics* 44(2): 199–210.

Walker, Jack. 1969. "The Diffusion of Innovations Among the American States." *American Political Science Review* 63(3): 880–99.
Warr, Peter G. 1982. "Pareto Optimal Redistribution and Private Charity." *Journal of Public Economics* 19(1): 131–138.
Warren, Robert Penn. 1946. *All the King's Men*. Harcourt: Brace and Company.
Weber, Max. 1919. "Politics as a Vocation." in Hans Gerth and C. Wright Mills. 1946. *From Max Weber: Essays in Sociology*, pp. 77–128. New York: Oxford University Press.
Weber, Ronald E., Anne Hopkins, Michael Mezey and Frank Munger. 1971–1972. "A Computer Simulation of Methodology for Estimating State Policy Preferences." *Public Opinion Quarterly* 36(4): 549–565.
Welch, Susan and John Peters. 1978a. "Political Corruption in America: A Search for Definitions and a Theory, ..." *American Political Science Review* 72(3): 974–984.
Welch, Susan and John Peters. 1978b. "Politics, Corruption, and Political Culture: A View from the State Legislature." *American Politics Quarterly* 6(3): 345–356.
Westlye, Mark C. 1983. "Competitiveness of Senate Seats and Voting Behavior in Senate Elections." *American Journal of Political Science* 27(2): 253–283.
Wildavsky (a), Aaron B. 1964, 1974. *The Politics of the Budgetary Process*. Boston, MA: Little, Brown.
Wildavsky (b), Aaron B. 1988, 1992, 2001. *The New Politics of the Budgetary Process*. Glenview, IL: Scott Foresman.
Wildavsky, Aaron. 1961. "Political Implications of Budgetary Reform." *Public Administration Review* 21(4): 183–190.
Wildavsky, Aaron. 1975a. *Budgeting*. Boston, MA: Little Brown &Co.
Wildavsky, Aaron. 1975b. *The Deficit and the Public Interest*. Berkeley: University of California Press.
Wilson, James Q. 1966. "Corruption: The Shame of the States." *Public Interest* 2: 28–38.
Wilson, Woodrow. 1885. *Congressional Government*. Boston, MA: Houghton Mifflin Company.
Winters, Richard. 1976a. "Legislators' Budgetary Attitudes and the State Spending Process." Dartmouth College, mimeo. Available from the author.
Winters, Richard. 1976b. "Party Control and Policy Change." *American Journal of Political Science* 20(4): 597–636.
Winters, Richard. 1980. "Political Choice and Expenditure Change." *Polity* 12(4): 598–622.
Winters, Richard and Daniel Rygorski. 2011. Giving to the Poor: Private/Public, Religious/Secular, and Spatial/Temporal Charitability in the American States," unpublished manuscript, available from the corresponding author at rfw@dartmouth.edu.
Winters, Richard F. 1999. "The Politics of Taxing and Spending." Virginia Gray and Russell Hanson, eds. *Politics in the American States*, Washington, DC: CQ Press, pp. 304–348.
Winters, Richard F., Ralph Carlton and Timothy Russell. 1981. "Distributive Benefits, Congressional Support and Agency Growth." in Barry Rundquist ed., *Political Benefits*, Lexington, pp. 93–116. MA: Lexington Press.

Wolfinger, Raymond. 1971. "Nondecisions and the Study of Local Politics." *American Political Science Review* 65(4): 1063–1080.
Wright, Gerald and Bryan Schaffner. 2002. "The Influence of Party: Evidence from the State Legislatures." *American Political Science Review* 96(2): 367–379.
Wright, Gerald C., Robert S. Erikson and John P. McIver. 1985. "Measuring State Partisanship and Ideology with Survey Data." *Journal of Politics* 47(2): 469–489.
Wright, Gerald C., Robert S. Erikson and John P. McIver. 1993. *Statehouse Democracy: Public Opinion and Democracy in the American States*. New York: Cambridge University Press.

INDEX

Note: **Bold** page numbers refer to tables; *italic* page numbers refer to figures and page numbers followed by "n" denote endnotes.

For Product Safety Concerns and Information please contact our EU representative GPSR@taylorandfrancis.com
Taylor & Francis Verlag GmbH, Kaufingerstraße 24, 80331 München, Germany

www.ingramcontent.com/pod-product-compliance
Ingram Content Group UK Ltd.
Pitfield, Milton Keynes, MK11 3LW, UK
UKHW022347190926
475702UK00015B/2144

* 9 7 8 1 0 3 2 9 4 0 4 4 1 *